Islamic Financial Economy and Islamic Banking

Islamic Financial Economy and Islamic Bankingis a thorough, deeply conceptual, analytical and applied work in the epistemological foundation of the Islamic world-system.

The book provides an original contribution to the generalized-system model of shari'ah. The model, derived from the Qur'an and Sunnah (Prophetic guidance) incorporates wide, analytical coverage of the purpose and objective of the Islamic worldview (maqasid as-shari'ah) in Islamic economics and finance in particular.

The author covers issues that contrast with the existing understanding of Islamic economics and finance, including some specific goals defining the field and how they compare in today's unstable world of financial volatility. A new heterodox thinking in economic theory is outlined.

Its presentation and analysis, methods and approach, overarch the fields of philosophy of science, rigorous analysis, mathematical and other presentations of the understanding given, and all taken up in the light of the exegesis of the Qur'an and coverage of the Sunnah. The result is substantive in the field of scholarship and application; and in analytically proving the universality and uniqueness of the epistemic worldview for the academic and practitioner world at large. The totality of the multiverse diversity of issues and problems reviewed comprise the study of the world-system by the Tawhidi methodological approach. Yet this methodology and its empirical configuration are universally applicable to all users without any need for unnecessary religious overtones.

Dr Masudul Alam Choudhury is Professor and International Chair of the Postgraduate Program in Islamic Economics and Finance, Faculty of Economics, Trisakti University, Jakarta, Indonesia. He is a Visiting Professor at the Social Economy Center, Ontario Institute for Studies in Education, University of Toronto.

Professor Choudhury is the pioneer in the field of the epistemological treatment of Islamic Economics and Finance over the past 35 years by way of his original works in this area.

He is the Editor-in-Chief of the SCOPUS-listed and Australian ABDC JEL-catalogued journal *HIJSE* (*Humanomics: International Journal of Systems & Ethics*) currently in its 33rd year of publication. His works have been reviewed by the *Times Higher Education Supplement, Economic Journal, Southern Economic Journal, Middle East Review* and *Journal of Economic Literature*.

Islamic Business and Finance Series

Series Editor:
M. Ishaq Bhatti, La Trobe University, Australia

There is an increasing need for western politicians, financiers, bankers, and indeed the western business community in general, to have access to high quality and authoritative texts on Islamic financial and business practices. Drawing on expertise from across the Islamic world, this new series will provide carefully chosen and focused monographs and collections, each authored/edited by an expert in their respective field, from all over the world.

The series will be pitched at a level to appeal to middle and senior management in both the western and Islamic business communities. For managers with a western or Islamic background, the series will provide detailed and up-to-date briefings on important topics; for academics, postgraduates and business communities, the series will provide a guide to best practice in business in Islamic communities around the world, including Muslim minorities in the west and majorities in the rest of the world.

1. God-Conscious Organization and the Islamic Social Economy
Masudul Alam Choudhury

Islamic Financial Economy and Islamic Banking

Masudul Alam Choudhury

Routledge
Taylor & Francis Group

LONDON AND NEW YORK

First published 2016 by Routledge

2 Park Square, Milton Park, Abingdon, Oxfordshire OX14 4RN
52 Vanderbilt Avenue, New York, NY 10017

Routledge is an imprint of the Taylor & Francis Group, an informa business

First issued in paperback 2019

British Library Cataloguing in Publication Data
A catalogue record for this book is available from the British Library

Library of Congress Cataloguing in Publication Data
A catalog record for this book has been requested

ISBN: 978-1-4724-3877-5 (hbk)
ISBN: 978-0-367-87946-4 (pbk)

Typeset in Sabon
by Out of House Publishing

Contents

List of Figures

List of Tables

Preface

My thanks are to those who have contributed to this rare title in the field of scholarly and analytical exposition of Islamic financial economics – an area that has not been attended by Islamic economic and finance writers. My thanks to Gower for the early contract that enabled me to start and complete this work on time. My time as visiting professor in the Social Economy Center in the Ontario Institute for Studies in Education, University of Toronto between August and December 2014 has been instrumental in completing this work. The epistemological content and its applications were presented in 23 lectures delivered university-wide at the Institute of Islamic Banking and Finance while I was Professorial Chair in Islamic Banking and Finance, International Islamic University Malaysia between February and August 2014.

The subject of a critique of financial engineering in view of Islamic financial economics was opened up by my paper, "Islamic Critique and Alternative to Financial Engineering Issues", *King Abdulaziz University Journal – Islamic Economics*, 22:2, 2009. In the present volume, an approach that is substantially Islamic in its epistemological foundation was carried further into the field of financial economics. Such an approach has not been undertaken by many others, including the so-called 'gurus' of Islamic economics and finance, who wandered in the axioms and theories of rationalism. The result of such meaningless pursuits was a complete misrepresentation of the *Tawhidi* (oneness of God = unity of knowledge) methodological worldview, specific to the epistemological approach and its application to Islamic financial economics. The result has been a complete misrepresentation of Islamic economics, banking. The starkest outcome is the rampant legitimation of secondary financing instruments and a misunderstanding of primary Islamic financing instruments in terms of *shari'ah*-compliance while abandoning the sublime field of *maqasid as-shari'ah* (purpose and objective of the *shari'ah*). Paradoxically, this situation is true even in respect of a comparative study of Islamic financial economics and banking with contemporaneous theories and applications. Our work here challenges and criticizes this kind of an approach as being without any methodological substance. This work presents the epistemological approach of *Tawhid* and its application to various issues of Islamic financial economics, banking, and finance. It is also a thoroughly critical comparative study.

A greater challenge to the reader is the evaluation of the ethico-economic and ethico-financial comparative understanding of the endogenous processes that underlie the methodology and applications presented in this work.

Masudul Alam Choudhury[1]

---

[1] This work was initiated during the editor's term as Professorial Chair of Islamic Finance in the Institute of Islamic Banking and Finance, International Islamic University Malaysia, Kuala Lumpur, Malaysia. It was completed while he was Visiting Professor in the Social Economy Center, Ontario Institute for Studies in Education, University of Toronto. The author is Professor of Islamic Economics and Finance, and International Chair of the Post-Graduate Program in Islamic Economics and Finance, Faculty of Economics, Trisakti University, Jakarta, Indonesia.

Prologue

The crowning foundation of knowledge in Islam for everything of mind, matter, and the sublime applications rests on *Tawhid*. *Tawhid* means 'Oneness of God'. It is understood both in thought and experience by the structure of the divine law as laid down in the *Qur'an*. The *Qur'an* is further complemented by the *sunnah* (Prophetic teaching). These primal premises are conjoint with the guidance of the widest participation of the learned ones on the *Tawhidi* worldview. The result of learning arising from the divine episteme of knowledge comprehends the holistic totality interconnecting 'everything'. Such a transcending totality embraces the boundary of unification between the specialized disciplines. The holistic boundary of organic relationships embraces the specializations of economics, finance, political economy, science, society, self and other. The understanding and application of the holistic worldview is conceptualized and carried through into applications by the incessant search for the unique and universal methodological nature of the *Tawhidi* worldview. Thus, the law of *Tawhid* embraces the sure reality presented by the *Qur'an*.

On the systemic unity of being and becoming by the universal epistemic language for everyone, the *Qur'an* (26:192–195) declares: "Verily this is a Revelation from the Lord of the Worlds: With it came down the Spirit of Faith and Truth – to thy heart and mind, that thou may admonish in the perspicuous Arabia language."

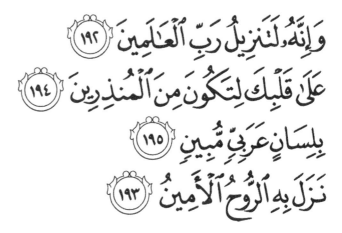

On the primordial law of unity (divine Oneness) as Knowledge to all the worlds, the *Qur'an* (96:1–5) declares: "Proclaim! (or Read!) in the name of thy Lord and Cherisher, who created – created man, out of a (mere) clot of congealed blood: Proclaim! And thy Lord is Most Bountiful, – He Who taught (the use of) the Pen, – taught man that which he knew not."

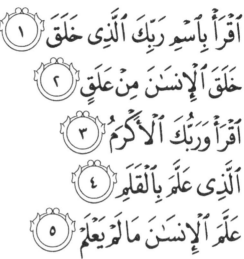

On the permanence of the divine law across the design of everything, the *Qur'an* (48:23) declares: "(Such has been) the practice (approved) of God already in the past: no change wilt thou find in the practice (approved) of God".

سُنَّةَ ٱللَّهِ ٱلَّتِي قَدْ خَلَتْ مِن قَبْلُ وَلَن تَجِدَ لِسُنَّةِ ٱللَّهِ تَبْدِيلًا ﴿٢٣﴾

On the holistic universal evidence revealed by the conscious reflection on the Signs of God, the *Qur'an* (51:53) declares: "Soon will We show them Our Signs in the (furthest) regions (of the earth), and in their own souls, until it becomes manifest to them that this is the Truth. Is it not enough that thy Lord doth witness all things?"

سَنُرِيهِمْ ءَايَـٰتِنَا فِي ٱلْأَفَاقِ وَفِىٓ أَنفُسِهِمْ حَتَّىٰ يَتَبَيَّنَ لَهُمْ أَنَّهُ

ٱلْحَقُّ أَوَلَمْ يَكْفِ بِرَبِّكَ أَنَّهُۥ عَلَىٰ كُلِّ شَىْءٍ شَهِيدٌ ﴿٥٣﴾

On the universality of the message of divine Oneness as of the unity of knowledge of the divine law, the *Qur'an* (49:13) declares: "O mankind! We created you from a single (pair) of a male and a female, and made you into nations and tribes, that you may know each other (not that ye may despise each other). Verily the most honoured of you in the sight of God is (he who is) the most righteous of you. And God has full knowledge and is well acquainted (with all things)".

يَـٰٓأَيُّهَا ٱلنَّاسُ إِنَّا خَلَقۡنَـٰكُم مِّن ذَكَرٖ وَأُنثَىٰ وَجَعَلۡنَـٰكُمۡ شُعُوبٗا وَقَبَآئِلَ لِتَعَارَفُوٓاْۚ إِنَّ أَكۡرَمَكُمۡ عِندَ ٱللَّهِ أَتۡقَىٰكُمۡۚ إِنَّ ٱللَّهَ عَلِيمٌ خَبِيرٌ ۝١٣

This prologue leads the reader into the nature of this scholarly work as one beyond the world of crass capitalism and the unconscionable formal imitation of Occidentalism by present-day Muslims.

Introduction

The Nature of Islamic Financial Economics in the *Tawhidi* Methodological Framework

Introducing the *Tawhidi* epistemology in developing the theory of financial economics

Initially defined, financial economics, in mainstream terms, means the study of the interplay of conceptual and applied relationships between economic and financial theories. In such a definition, no academic demand is made on the study of the interactive, integrative, and creative multidisciplinary and multi-dimensional phenomenon of systemic relationships caused by inter-causality between the representative variables (e.g. the study of social justice is considered as an exogenous (external) factor of social consideration). Such an ethical factor is at best influenced by government actions, institutions, and policies and by sheer human choice in society at large. There is no scope in such exogenous treatment of the theme of social justice and ethics to invoke in society-at-large a response towards consciousness caused by the interaction between self, collective human preferences, and conscious experience that can automatically generate inter-causality between ethical character, actions and responses.

The embedding of knowledge with the generality and specifics of the world system, as in the case of financial economics, also conveys the idea of phenomenology. Phenomenology is the study of consciousness through the organic inter-relationship between deontological characteristics of self with its dynamic preferences and the creative actions and responses generated by relational experiences. The resulting attribute of ethics thus formed is explained as an endogenous actualization as opposed to ethics as exogenous behaviour in mainstream financial economics.

An example of the meaning of ethics is based on the formation of preferences regarding ecological consciousness on matters needing ethical preferences as natural reaction. Such an attitude is contrary to being enforced by institutional policies. There is no conflicting enforcement in the relationship between action and response in a conscious framework of endogenous ethics. The conscious self in concert with the world-system generates and sustains integrity between self, dynamic preferences, and the sustainable ecological experience in our example. The result of endogenous ethical behaviour is the generation of a system of interaction, integration, and evolutionary learning in the domain of unity of knowledge as episteme and its induction of the issues under study. In our study, such issues belong to the field of financial economics.

The epistemological nature of Islamic financial economics

We can now introduce the nature of Islamic financial economics, which we will discuss in this book. The epistemological core of this work will steer our attention to Islamic foundational issues and their theory and application. However, much that has gone on under the umbrella of Islamic economics and finance, being bereft of epistemological foundations, has failed to establish a genuine methodological worldview of Islamic financial economics.

This book will focus on the genuinely epistemological foundation of Islamic financial economics on a comparative framework with mainstream financial economy, and test the new analytical formalism that is derived in this context both mathematically and empirically. It will also keep in touch with the comparative approach in these areas of investigation.

What is Islamic financial economy?

We look now at the distinctive nature and perspective of Islamic financial economy, including Islamic banking, in today's world of financial and institutional innovation. According to the epistemology of unity of knowledge, this is referred to in the Qur'an by Tawhid. It stands for monotheistic law and its function and practice in the order of reality. The extensive interpretation of the worldly interpretation of the monotheistic law by its function of organic unity of knowledge and the induced diversity of things can be read in many verses of the Qur'an.[1]

The central embedded role of the divine law of monotheism pervades the socio-scientific domain of 'everything'. The important meaning here is of the universal and unique nature of the imminent methodology that arises from the *Tawhidi* epistemology for every issue and problem. This is despite variations in the diversity of issues, problems, theories, and applications in various disciplinary areas.

The *Tawhidi* episteme, nonetheless, is not a theory and application derived from any kind of interdisciplinary germination. On the contrary, it arises from its independent and substantive origin that is distinctive in the three core contexts.

These are first, the law of monotheism established irrevocably in the Qur'an. Second, there is the guidance of the Prophet Muhammad by his actions and sayings called the *sunnah*. The third essential component of *Tawhidi* epistemology is the guidance of the learned ones based on both the Qur'an and the *sunnah*. These three components must be understood at the outset of the epistemological inquiry. Such inquiry grounds the true nature of Islamic methodology and the desired methods of analytical and applied formalism. The foundational methodological worldview of monotheism as the explained evidence of the organic unity of knowledge in 'everything' is unavoidable in Islamic socio-scientific inquiry. There cannot be any thought, conception, inquiry, and application without the conscious understanding of the *Tawhidi* methodological worldview. Such are the instructions of the Qur'an on the search for the deeper meaning of truth and reality.[2,3]

Thus in the *Tawhidi* methodological worldview as the primal and foundational Islamic epistemology of 'everything', three key perspectives stand out as irrevocable. First, the episteme represents the organic unity of knowledge of the 'paired' universe. Second, the singular precept of unity of knowledge constructs the world of unity of being and becoming. Third, such things belong to life-fulfilment needs. The universe of such three attributes of things exists perpetually and evolves continuously in the dimensions of knowledge, space, and time.

The truly epistemological study of Islamic financial economics, like all other worldly fields of study, is embedded in the *Tawhidi* nature and design of its universe within the dimensions of knowledge, space, and time. The market is sensitized by the endogenous or interrelated nature of ethics across systems. The institution is the body framework for the study and implementation of ethics and the financial economy. Human economy and financial activity is entrenched in both moral and ethical consciousness. The objectivity of purpose and objectivity conceptualized and quantified by the wellbeing criterion of maslaha is in everything and is everywhere.

Understanding the knowledge, space, and time dimensions in universal evanescent *Tawhidi* law

These three attributes of reality cannot be known in knowledge, space, and time by manifestation. The Qur'an (3:190–191) declares regarding such limitation of knowledge to know the unseen: 'Behold! In the creation of the heavens and the earth, and the alternation of Night and Day, – there are indeed Signs for men of understanding, – men who celebrate the praises of God, standing, sitting, and lying down on their sides, and contemplate the (wonders of) creation in the heavens and the earth (with the thought): "Our Lord! Not for naught have You created (all) this! Glory be to You! Give us salvation from the Penalty of the Fire".'

An exegesis of these verses is the following: The *Tawhidi* law in its manifestation and explication of the universe comprehends 'everything' ('Creation of the heavens and the earth'). This enables us to see and understand that these are not impossible divine attributes. Rather they are the cognitive and material unravelling of these attributes in things that are manifesting ('Behold!').

The extensive meaning of 'Night and Day' embodies in it the meaning of differentiation, the discernment of falsehood as 'darkness' and truth as 'day'. In such a situation between truth and darkness advances the human comprehension of total reality. Such realization exists in a seamless and continuous way, across continuums of 'everything'. The evidences form the 'Signs of God'. They manifest the 'ontic' proofs arising from the ontology and epistemology of the *Tawhidi* law and its deep explications.

Men of understanding see and reflect; they make the Signs of God the premise for knowing the organic unity of our worldly designs and experience ('men of understanding'). An example here is the uninitiated way of knowing mathematics, as a tool to be used in the study of finance. Contrary to such a mundane practice, there is the use of mathematics as a logical basis for understanding the epistemological vastness of the meaning of relational oneness by the *Tawhidi* law *vis-à-vis* the generality and specifics of the world-system, as of financial economy, that we study. The nature of such contemplative inquiry and its domain of investigation are marked by the dynamic knowledge implications of the *Tawhidi* law.

The interactive, integrative, and evolutionary learning experience of *Tawhid* and the world-system forms the need to understand the inner construct of reality. Thus, by the ontology, epistemology, and the ontic proofs based on the understanding and extensions of the *Tawhidi* law and the universe, we invoke the organic multidimensional

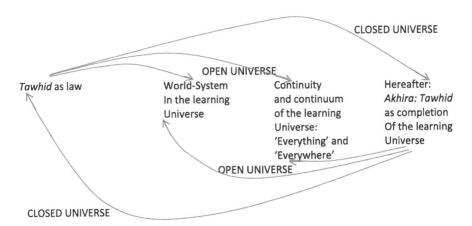

Figure I.I Closure of the complete universe of Signs of God in the order of 'everything', 'everywhere'

The *Qur'an* (55:26–27) declares: "All that is on earth will perish: But will abide (for ever) the Face of your Lord full of Majesty, Bounty, and Honour. Then which of the favours of your Lord will you deny? Of Him seeks (its need) every creature in the heavens and on earth: Every day in (new) Splendour does He (shine)!"

investigation of the systemic model connecting self, family, community, society, institutions, global relationships and strategic policies.

The result, then, is an evanescent and unravelling framework of reality as we perceive it. This is to discover meaning, purpose, and the search and discovery both at the core and the precincts of the universe in its generality and details – 'wonders of creation'. Yet such observation and analytical comprehension and design of the complex, ordered, universe of generality and details form the dynamics of totality of knowledge in space and time dimensions – 'praises of Allah'. The total overarching universe in knowledge, space, and time comprises 'the heavens and the earth'.

In such a structure of creation, the *Tawhidi* law is reflected by its purpose and meaning – 'Our Lord! Not for naught have You created (all this)'. Such an encompassing universe, as far as human comprehension can understand, is defined by the 'Closure' enclosing the open evolutionary learning universe. We present this idea in Figure I.1.

The nature of evolutionary equilibriums to be studied in Islamic financial economy à la Tawhid

Closure: $(\Omega,S) \leftrightarrow$ World-System$(\theta, X(\theta), t(\theta)) \leftrightarrow$ Tawhid: Akhira

Open Universe (learning universe): World-System$(\theta, X(\theta), t(\theta))$

(Ω,S) denotes the primal ontology of Tawhïd (Ω: symbolically to represent the super-cardinal topology of the Qur'an) mapped in degrees by the *sunnah* of Prophet Muhammad (S).

θ denotes worldly knowledge derived from the epistemology of (Ω,S).

$X(\theta)$ denotes the mathematical ensemble of knowledge-induced variables.

$E(\theta),X(\theta),t(\theta))$ denotes an event $(E(.))$ represented by the multi-systemic coordinate in knowledge (θ), space $(X(\theta))$, time $(t(\theta))$.

Time, $t(\theta)$ is induced by knowledge because, knowledge, not time, causes an event to occur. Time reads the event and its systemic relationships.[4]

The Closure encompassing the Open Universe is a necessary and sufficient condition for the existence of meaningful evolutionary equilibriums. The existence of equilibrium is established by the Fixed Point Theorem (Brouwer, 1910; Kakutani, 1941; Nikaido, 1987). The evolutionary nature of such equilibrium is established by neighbourhoods around equilibrium points within the Fixed Point Closure (Choudhury, Zaman and Sofyan, 2007). In the *Tawhidi* epistemological formulation of Islamic financial economy, all equilibriums are evolutionary equilibriums within the purposeful Closure. Steady-state equilibriums are denied relevance. They can be explained by the degenerate case of neoclassical economics and full-information assumption.

The event $E(\theta),X(\theta),t(\theta))$ of our worldly category are very many in diversity across systems of experiences. In regard to the study of Islamic financial economy, the Qur'an points out very many specifics from which human beings can learn extensive lessons for worldly functions. We discuss here three specific areas on which the study of economics and finance rests. These cases comprise the events $E(.)$. The vector (or higher order of mathematical transforms) $X(\theta)$ comprise consumption along with consumer behaviour; production along with production function and production, distribution, and ownership relationships; wealth, money, and spending, and many more. Over all such categories is the defining place of conscious purpose, objectivity, and meaning (Masud on Shatibi's theory of meaning, 1994).

On the matter of consciousness (θ) induced in consumption and production, the Qur'an instructs (these verses are just some of many) moderation and balance for a happy self, family, community, and society.[5] On the theme of ownership and distribution, the Qur'an has declared fairness and equity.[6] The Qur'an has, nonetheless, left the equality not in terms of measure but in terms of justice. The theme of justice and spending is connected with abundance and sharing.[7] Money is connected with resource mobilization.[8] All these activities of sustainability and the social economy are treated in an interconnected way of organic pairing and inter-causality. The extent of such interconnectivity is widely inter-systemic.[9]

The interconnectedness of the conscious attributes is exemplified by the sustainability of life-fulfilment regimes of development. Along such a trajectory of development we note the complementarities, and thereby participative functions, over the dimensions of knowledge, space, and time of the organic inter-causal relationships between consumption and production and the underlying agential behaviour in the reality of the ethically induced market process and market system. Preferences in such a market system are dynamic in nature by the impact of θ-values and are aggregated by the functions of interaction, integration, and creative evolution under innovation occurring along with the evolutionary learning attributes of θ-values in unity of knowledge via their diverse complexity and non-linearity of form. Every point of continuity is sustained by the equitable, just and fair distribution of wealth, property, and ownership that a life-fulfilment regime of development ensues. That is because of the nature of needs and the stable prices and wages and returns on spending that are engendered along with the stable form of the price–output relationship, the nature of appropriate technology, and returns on these activities to profit-sharing, wages, and rates of return. At the end, the resource mobilization without diminishing returns is regenerated by the fullest channelling of money capital into spending. This is logically possible when monetary expansion along the life-fulfilment regimes of development replaces interest rates with trade. The result is abundant rewards in the life-fulfilment regime of development. The social wellbeing function (*maslaha*) is elevated to higher levels by the force of resource regeneration and equitable ownership by all. Thus, by the impact of evolutionary learning in unity of knowledge as episteme, the nature of life-fulfilment regime of advancement becomes dynamic. We refer to such a regime of change as the dynamic life-fulfilment regime of development, or the dynamic basic-needs regime of development.

The meaning of consciousness

Those who have seen the movie Transcendence will recall how the element of transcendence is shown to regenerate immortality. Yet, when man chooses to relinquish this spirit of being immortal in consciousness, after transcendence was over him, then death and extinction of spirit overtakes immortality. The idea of consciousness, like transcendence, is derived equally from the *Tawhidi* primal origin of monotheistic truth.[10]

According to the immortality premise of the primal origin of *Tawhid* (transcendence), and premised on it of consciousness, there is the following cast of realism:

True reality		Worldly causation	Continuity	True reality
$[(\Omega \rightarrow_s) \equiv (\Omega, S)] \quad \rightarrow \quad \{\theta^*\} \rightarrow \{\theta\} \quad \rightarrow$		$W(E(\theta, \mathbf{X}(\theta), t(\theta))) \rightarrow dW/d\theta > 0 \ldots \rightarrow (\Omega, S)$		
The primal origin of God and His Divine Law (*Sunnat Allah*) Transmitted by the functional ontology of the Prophet Muhammad's teaching, guidance (*sunnah*):[11] Unitary Epistemology	Consciousness as indestructible Transcendental realism in God-Man-Creation Circular Relations:[12] Unity of knowledge	Conscious world-system endowed by unity of knowledge	Sustainability: Continuity across systemic continuums: Unity of knowledge	Consciousness: Transcendental realism in God-Man-Creation: Circular Relationships: Unity of Knowledge

An overview of the book

This book studies many contemporary theories in the light of *Tawhidi* methodology as this is reflected in the principle of complementarity between the good things in life mandated by the Qur'an, the *sunnah*, and the guidance of the learned in Islam. Such choices find their way into the purpose and objective of the *shari'ah*, termed as *maqasid as-shari'ah*. In spite of this, the logical and analytical derivation of ideas in the area as commonly understood as Islamic economics and finance is critically examined in the light of the implications of the *Tawhidi* methodology. Consequently, many subtle differences arise between the epistemological approach and the today's cursory study of Islamic economics and finance from the mainstream perspective. This latter field of study makes no reference to the foundational episteme of *Tawhid*, unity of knowledge and its induction of the generality and specifics of the evolutionary learning world-system.

The study of *maqasid as-shari'ah* in this book leads into its vastly extended scope of the interactive, integrative, and evolutionary study of worldly affairs together with the wider scale of universal inquiry. The topics of finance and development, ethical issues, and co-determination of these by an organic relational system of formal relationships are examined in the light of *Tawhidi* methodology.

Consequently, new methodical formalism arises that is foreign to today's approach in Islamic financial economy, and thereby to the functioning and objectives of Islamic banks. The Islamic financing portfolio is thereby formalized by developing interactive pooled funds of participatory instruments. This kind of a participatory (complementary) construction of the Islamic financial portfolio in the light of the organically paired and unified principle of the Qur'an is contrary to the segmented treatment of the instruments separately.

The organically unified financing instruments, present some new functional ideas of Islamic financing. These instruments include foreign trade financing certificates, and a *Tawhidi* methodological outlook on an interactive model of Islamic bonds (*sukuk*), and Islamic mark-up (*murabaha*). By the same kind of methodological and methodical approach the imminent Islamic generalized system model is formalized in contrast with the mainstream Islamic approach. Other issues of moral relevance in the theory of financial economics studied in the light of *Tawhidi* methodology are asset valuation *contra* mainstream valuation methods. Thereby, the sensitivity of such a valuation method to the discursive process of making choices and developing institutional endogenous preferences to interactively integrate and learn continuously across continuums over knowledge, space, and time dimensions, are formalized by requisite models.

Even when the field of Islamic financial economics is treated within the emergence of the project of Islamicization of knowledge, this field is shown to be distinct in its purpose and methodology from the *Tawhidi* methodological worldview used in this book. Thereby, social goals such as poverty alleviation and sustainability are studied differently from an exogenous financing of microenterprises and the rural sector by government spending policy. Instead, the endogenous theory emanating from the *Tawhidi* methodological worldview of organic participation and systemic complementarities between inter-causal variables is adopted.

The language of the text is a combination between narrative, analytical, formal, empirical, and mathematical. A good deal of philosophy of science in comparative perspective and as arising from the *Tawhidi* epistemological worldview is used to establish the morally embedded theory across diverse systems governed by unity of knowledge. Professor Robert D. Crane of Qatar Faculty of Islamic Studies comments on such a nature of erudition regarding one of my published articles: 'I have read this excellent article and would highly recommend that it be published for the small group of scholars who can appreciate it, especially since holistic education is becoming a new frontier in the interconnection of ontological truth, epistemological process, and axiological application through compassionate justice.'

Such an erudite manuscript has not been published in mainstream Islamic economics and finance, except those contributed by this author (Choudhury, 2014a, 2014b, 2012; Choudhury and Hoque, 2012, Choudhury and Zaman, 2006, etc.). It is noted by a positive development of the *Tawhidi* methodological worldview of Islamic financial economy and a critical examination of the existing studies in mainstream Islamic financial economics that, as a result no real contribution has come about to academia and practicality except by way of establishing Islamic banks only within a mainstream garb. The mainstream axioms of financial economics, the usual models and objective criteria of the mainstream field of study have remained intact without any epistemological questions and thus paradigmatic principle in Islamic economics and finance, affecting also the conduct of Islamic banking. The fact discussed in this work is that, interest-free banking alone is neither a necessary nor a sufficient basis for Islamic banking operations. At the same time, with the goal of interest-free banking, the economic, financial, social, and scientific interrelationship between trade in the good things in life and monetary and financial resource mobilization with holistic integration must be understood. Such an inter-causal organic circularity of relationships needs to be formalized. The conventional study of Islamic economics, finance, and banking has failed to approach the study of Islamic financial economy from such an interactive, integrative, and evolutionary dynamic. Our present work combines the three perspective of Islamic financial economy in the *Tawhidi* methodological formal worldview.

We hope that this work in its *Tawhidi* methodological perspective will be a contribution to the world of learning. The erudition in it is global and trans-cultural in nature. Its findings and critical approach are not limited to the captioned 'Islamic' economics and finance. The book is a contribution to the realm of ideas where the monotheistic law functions in the formal, analytical, and applied ways of the epistemological unity of knowledge and unity of the knowledge-induced world system.

Notes

1 *Qur'an* (10:22): "He it is who enables you to traverse through land and sea; so that ye even board ships; – they sail with them with a favourable wind, and they rejoice thereat; then comes a stormy wind and the waves come to them from all sides, and they think they are being overwhelmed: They cry unto God, sincerely offering (their) duty unto Him, saying, "If Thou do deliver us from this, we shall truly show our gratitude!"

2 *Qur'an* (41:53): "Soon will We show them Our Signs in the (furthest) regions (of the earth), and in their ouwn souls, until it becomes manifest to them that this is the Truth. Is it not enough that your Lord does witness all things?"

3 *Qur'an* (96:3–5): "Proclaim! And your Lord is Most Bountiful, – He Who taught (the use of) the Pen, – Taught man that which he knew not."

4 *Qur'an* (76:1): "Has there not been over man a long period of Time, when he was nothing – (not even) spoken?" Thus 'time' was dysfunctional until functional knowledge dawned with the creation of man.

5 *Qur'an* (6:141–142): *On production*: "It is He who produces gardens, with trellishes and without, and dates, and tilth with produce of all kinds, and olives and pomegranates, similar (in kind) and different (in variety): Eat of their fruit in their season, but render the dues that are proper on the day that the harvest is gathered. But waste not by excess: for God loves not the wasters." (141)*On consumption and good things of life*: "Of the cattle are some for burden and some for meat: Eat what God has provided for you, and follow not the footsteps of Satan: For he is to you and avowed enemy." (142)

6 *Qur'an* (4:161): "That they took usury, though they were forbidden; and that they devoured men's substance wrongfully; – We have prepared for those among them who reject Faith a grievously penalty."

7 *Qur'an* (2:261): "The parable of those who spend their substance in the way of God is that of a grain of corn: it grows seven ears, and each ear has a hundred grains. God gives manifold increase to whom He pleases: and God cares for all and He knows all things."

8 *Qur'an* (18:19): "Now send ye then one of you with the money of yours to the town: let him find out which is the best food (to be had) and bring some to you, that (you may) that (you may) satisfy your hunger therewith: and let him behave with care and courtesy, and let him not inform any one about you."

9 *Qur'an* (13:3): "And fruit of every kind he made in pairs, two and two: He draws the Night as a veil Over the Day. Behold verily in these things there are Signs for those who consider!"

10 *Qur'an* (2:117): "To Him is due the primal origin of the heavens and the earth: When He decrees a matter, He says to it: 'Be', and it is."

11 *Qur'an* (3:109): "To God belongs all that is in the heavens and on earth: To Him do all questions go back (for decision)."

12 *Qur'an* (42:52): "And thus have We by Our command, sent inspiratiuon to thee: Thou knewest not (before) what was Revelation, and what was Faith; but We have made the (*Qur'an*) a Light, wherewith We guide such of Our servants as We will; and verily thou dost guide (men) to the Straight Way."

References

Brouwer, L.E.J. (1910). "Uber un eindeutige, stetige Transformationen von Flachen in sich", *Mathematische Annalen*, 69:2, 176–80.

Choudhury, M.A. (2012). *Islamic Economics and Finance: An Epistemological Inquiry*, Emerald Publications, Derby, UK in its series, *Contributions to Economic Analysis* 291.

Choudhury, M.A. (2014a). *Tawhidi Epistemology and its Applications (Economics, Finance, Science, and Society)*, Cambridge Scholars' Publishing, Cambridge, UK.

Choudhury, M.A. (2014b). *The Socio-Cybernetic Study of God and the World-System*, Ideas Group Inc. Global, Philadelphia, USA.

Choudhury, M.A. and Hoque, M.Z. (2004). *An Advanced Exposition of Islamic Economics and Finance*, Edwin Mellen Press, O. Lewiston, NY.

Choudhury, M.A. and Zaman, S.I. (2006). "Learning sets and topologies", *Kybernetes: International Journal of Systems and Cybernetics*, 35:7.

Choudhury, M.A. Zaman, S.I. and Sofyan S. Harahap (2007). "An evolutionary topological theory of participatory socio-economic development", *World Futures: Journal of General Evolutionary Systems*, 63:8, 176–80.

Kakutani, S. (1941). "A generalization of bouwer's fixed point theorem", *Duke Mathematical Journal*, 8:3, 457–59.

Masud, M.K. (1994). *Shatibi's Theory of Meaning*, Islamic Research Institute, International Islamic University, Islamabad, Pakistan.

Nikaido, H. (1987). "Fixed point theorems", in J. Eatwell, M. Milgate and P. Newman (eds), *The New Palgrave: General Equilibrium*, pp. 139–44, W.W. Norton, New York, NY.

Chapter 1

The *Tawhidi* Methodology

Abstract

The methodology of the *Tawhidi* worldview, the primordial and monotheistic law of Oneness of God in an Islamic epistemological context concerning socio-scientific reasoning, formalism, and application is distinctly contrary to mainstream economics in general and Islamic mainstream economics in particular. There is a fundamental flaw in all of this latter kind of reasoning. This is due to the ignorance of the *Tawhidi* epistemological moorings by those who profess Islamic mainstream economic reasoning. In the field of participatory financing, the consequences of such intellectual ambivalence have seen the complete misunderstanding of the extensively relational epistemological methodology of participation derived from the *Qur'an* and the *sunnah* in the development of the purpose and objective of the *shari'ah*, namely *maqasid as-shari'ah*. The result has been a demeaning position of Islamic economics and finance in new ideas that emerge from new epistemological and ontological foundations. The latter kind of challenging erudition can be enabled by the new and irreducible epistemic reasoning premised on the *Tawhidi* methodology and its functioning in the generality and particulars (e.g. Islamic participative financing) of the world-system of unity of knowledge. This chapter bridges this methodological gap and applies that analytical *Tawhidi* methodology to general and participatory financing instruments in light of the *Tawhidi* precept of inter-causal relational 'pairing' occurring in diversity as the sure worldly meaning and evidence of the *Tawhidi* epistemic oneness.

Allah sent down the *Qur'an* with the embodiment of *Tawhid* contained within it in its ontological and evident form to unravel the fact that, indeed, Truth is manifest. Yet complete knowledge of Truth remains with *Allah* to be unveiled in the Hereafter (*Akhira*). Thus learning from aye to eternity and through the Prophet's *sunnah* (guidance) is the command of *Allah*; it also comprises the thought and practice of the learning world-system. Syed Qutb (Mousalli, 1990) talked about such a functional ontology of learning as the divine attribute to humankind and the world system. The *Qur'an* speaks of integration in the discursive experience emanating from the learning process of the *shura* (*Qur'anic* consultation and discourse) thereby, extracting the cognitive worshiping state of the world-system in 'everything'. There is, thus, the complex embedded wrapping of everything in this world-system by the relational epistemology of learning in unity of knowledge and its construction of unity of the induced world-system.

Economics is a sub-system of such an embedded, complex, interrelated, and unified organic world-system. 'Everything' shares the solely universal and unique law of oneness without differentiation. The *Qur'an* revealed the same law to all the prophets of antiquity. The *Qur'an* says in its allegorical language that the worldview of monotheism and its explanatory law has been bestowed on all the prophets (*Qur'an*, 87:18–19). Thus *Tawhid* is true of all the divine revelations and the world-system comprising soul, mind, matter; human and jinn (abstraction).

Meaning of *Tawhid* as monotheistic functional ontology

What, then, is the extended meaning of *Tawhid*? *Tawhid* is the primordial reality of the Oneness of *Allah*. It is expressed in its epistemological sense by the law of monotheism. The order and scheme of all things comprise the signs of *Allah* (*ayath Allah*) and their unravelling in the resulting world-system called *a'lameen*.

The *Tawhidi* epistemology is the learning process forming a methodological order of reasoning, thought, formal construction, and action (application), followed by inferences and continuity. This whole system of recursive learning is continuously regenerated in the knowledge, space, and time dimensions. Such a domain of 'everything' is premised on unity of knowledge and its unifying deductive–inductive circularity of reasoning as the very meaning of continuity *res extensa* across continuums (*Qur'an* 2: 115; Bakar, 1991).

Islamic political economy (economics) shares in the same *Tawhidi* methodology as an embedded sub-system wrapped up in the organic interaction, integration, and evolutionary (IIE) relational world-system, made possible by the episteme of unity of knowledge. The resulting intellection is universal and unique in respect of all the diversity of being. Yet the analytical *methods*, but not the substantive *Tawhidi methodology* of investigation, can be pertinently diverse.

Here is an example: The mathematical method of calculus can be used to explain progressive learning via simulation of relational functions by the process of knowledge creation. Yet, the same method of calculus, when used for an optimization problem or to explain a resource scarcity problem in economic functions, is not pertinent to the *Tawhidi methodology*. The optimization character and the scarcity axiom of economics cannot logically exist in the pervasively learning knowledge, space, and time dimensions of relational functions caused and regenerated by the episteme of unity of knowledge premised on *Tawhid*.

This last situation is simply not possible; except for two distinct and special cases. First, a possibility for optimization can exist in the infinitesimally small, instantaneous sub-universe. Such a state manifests the atomism of classical and neoclassical economics and the scientific emanation from the monadology of Leibniz (Saville, 2000). Such a state forms a case of no importance in the learning universe of endogenously related events happening *res extensa* in the knowledge, space, and time dimensions. The second singular possibility of optimization is at the event of the Hereafter (*Akhira*), which the *Qur'an* (Chapter 78, *Naba*) declares as the Great Event. At this eventual case, knowledge is complete; truth is fully manifest; the supreme felicity is bestowed; and falsehood has vanished, drowned in its own illogical entropy (*Qur'an*, 16: 36).

To formalize, define the *Tawhidi* episteme as the super-cardinal topology: (Ω,S); Ω: *Qur'anic* super-space; S: *sunnah* as mapping of the *Qur'an* to living experience. Knowledge flows from (Ω,S). This is denoted by $\{\theta\}\in(\Omega,S)$. $x(\theta)$ denotes the knowledge-induced vector, matrices, tensor, all pertaining to the problems under investigation.

Consequently, $\{\theta,x(\theta),t\}$ denotes the multidimensional triplet spanning the knowledge $\{\theta\}$, space $\{x(\theta)\}$, and time (t) dimensions. That is, the *Tawhidi* methodology spans the following extensive and rich system of interrelationships:

Tawhidi rich and complex world-system

Tawhid $\rightarrow_{(s)unnah}$ World-System $\rightarrow_{(s)unnah}$ *Tawhid* : The large-scale closure

$(\Omega,S) \quad \rightarrow \quad \{\theta,X(\theta),t\} \quad \rightarrow \quad (\Omega,S)$ through the passage of finitely open World-System

$\downarrow$

Islamic Embedded Economy as complex relational socio-scientific (1.1)
sub-system is characterized as,

$\downarrow$

$E\{\cup_i \cap_j (R,Y,p;Pref)[\theta]^s_{ij}$; R: resource — financial, natural, labor; Y: output;

p: price level; i = interaction = $1,2,..,n_1$; j = integration = $1,2,..,n_2$;

s = systems = $1,2,..,n_3$. This symbolism is an extension of Debreu (1959)
Furthermore, $dE/d\theta > 0$, denoting evolutionary epistemology; $dE'/d\theta' > 0$ by evolutionary 'de-knowledge' (i.e. rationalism).

Thus, the process of knowledge derivation from the *Tawhidi* epistemic core is represented by the inter-causal, inter-variables, intra-systemic, and inter-systemic Interaction (I), Integration (I), and Evolutionary (E), assuming the IIE evolutionary learning processes. This forms the permanent property of the *Tawhidi* epistemological construction of pairing by evolutionary learning in 'everything' (Barrow, 1991). The *Qur'an* explains all of this in the framework of reorigination (*khalq in-jadid*).

No quick, short and complete description can be given of such a comprehensive *Tawhidi* epistemological methodological worldview. The imminent project is a vastly detailed methodological investigation. It carries analytical, applied, inferential, and policy implications (Choudhury, 2006). We have pointed out examples of these implications below.

Configuring the steps of the *Tawhidi* methodology: problem-solving in the *Tawhidi* methodological worldview contra neoclassical economics

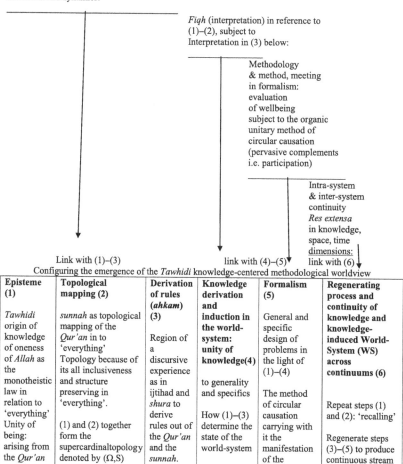

The study of the structure of reasoning in *Tawhidi* unity of knowledge: leading to the formation of the *maqasid as-shari'ah* through its formative structure, function, derivation and dynamics:

Fiqh (interpretation) in reference to (1)–(2), subject to Interpretation in (3) below:

Methodology & method, meeting in formalism: evaluation of wellbeing subject to the organic unitary method of circular causation (pervasive complements i.e. participation)

Intra-system & inter-system continuity *Res extensa* in knowledge, space, time dimensions:

Link with (1)–(3)   link with (4)–(5)   link with (6)

Configuring the emergence of the *Tawhidi* knowledge-centered methodological worldview

Episteme (1)	Topological mapping (2)	Derivation of rules (*ahkam*) (3)	Knowledge derivation and induction in the world-system: unity of knowledge(4)	Formalism (5)	Regenerating process and continuity of knowledge and knowledge-induced World-System (WS) across continuums (6)
Tawhidi origin of knowledge of oneness of *Allah* as the monotheistic law in relation to 'everything' Unity of being: arising from the *Qur'an*	*sunnah* as topological mapping of the *Qur'an* in to 'everything' Topology because of its all inclusiveness and structure preserving in 'everything'. (1) and (2) together form the supercardinaltopology denoted by (Ω,S)	Region of a discursive experience as in ijtihad and *shura* to derive rules out of the *Qur'an* and the *sunnah*.	to generality and specifics How (1)–(3) determine the state of the world-system	General and specific design of problems in the light of (1)–(4) The method of circular causation carrying with it the manifestation of the	knowledge-induced World-System (WS) across continuums (6) Repeat steps (1) and (2): 'recalling' Regenerate steps (3)–(5) to produce continuous stream

Figure 1.1 Methodological steps in configuring the *Tawhidi* methodology

		This practice carries the practice of *Figh* to the *Qur'an* and the *sunnah* to examine 'every' issue and problems of multiverse. Thus steps (1)–(3) comprise the purpose and objective of the *shari'ah* (*maqasid as-shari'ah*) leaving aside details for subsequent steps in conjunction with steps (1)–(3)	firstly, as is in generality and specifics, and then (ii) reconstructs the generality and specifics according to the steps (1)–(3) Thus (θ,x(θ))- *Tawhidi* coordinates of the world-system leading to the evaluation of W(x(θ)) Evaluation meaning (estimation of the problem as is; followed by simulation of that problems into the state as it ought to be according to (1)–(3).	monotheistic law and *Tawhidi* episteme An example: Theory of justice as balance in the relationships of production, distribution, and systemic participation (complements) Evaluate W = W(x(θ)) Subject to the circular causation relations: $x_i=f_i(x_j(\theta))$, $\theta=W(x(\theta))$ $i \neq j = 1,2,..,n$ End of Process comprising (3)–(5) and start of a new one	of knowledge-flows and the continuity of the knowledge-induced world-system on the basis of the *Tawhidi* episteme. Until the completion of knowledge and the knowledge-induced world-system in the End, the Akhira. Thus the total *Tawhidi* process is denoted by" $(\Omega,S) \to WS \to (\Omega,S)$

Super-cardinality is defined here as large cardinalities (Rucker, 1982). We define this as follows: (Ω,S) is the open, non-measurable topological super-space of the *Qur'an*. See Dewitt (1992) for the mathematical idea of supermanifolds. It is mapped and explained in the midst of the *Sunnah* and the principal learned authorities (*ululumriminum*) (*Qur'an*, 4:59) of all times. Thus the function of (Ω,S) is to establish the monotheistic law in the form of evolutionary learning relations of the world-system. The cardinal relations defined on $\{\theta,x(\theta)\}$ are indefinitely many in diversity. These are contained in the supercardinal knowledge-space and its relations on describing the supreme felicity as is the description of Heaven in the *Qur'an* (25:46-77). The relational completeness within the precincts of the *Tawhidi* law is confirmed by the verse (Qur'an, 55: 31). According to these confirmations we write, $(d/d\theta)(T\{\theta,\mathbf{x}(\theta)\}) = T[\cup_{interaction}\cap_{integration}\{(d/d\theta)_{evolution}(\theta,\mathbf{x}(\theta)\} \subset (\Omega,S))$, by the topological preserving property of monotonic positive mappings well-defined in (Ω,S). Besides, the expression (1) establishes, $(\Omega,S) \leftrightarrow (\Omega,S)$ through the openness of the world-system. Thus by the Fixed Point Theorem (Nikaido, 1989) in open topological space, evolutionary learning equilibriums exist; and this correspondence is relationally measurable in the open space. It is completed in the closure of *Tawhid* in equivalence with *Akhira* as events. Universal ontological reality. Thus,

$$(d/d\theta)(T\{\theta,\mathbf{x}(\theta)\}) = T[\cup_{interaction}\cap_{integration}\{(d/d\theta)_{evolution}(\theta,\mathbf{x}(\theta)\} \subset (\Omega,S)) \qquad (1.2)$$
$$(\Omega,S) \leftrightarrow (\Omega,S)$$

These together define the meaning of supercardinality in respect of the ontological topological mappings generated as open-ended mappings completing in the universal space of $(\Omega,S) \leftrightarrow (\Omega,S)$.

Figure 1.1 (Cont.)

We take three examples here to understand the nature of political economy (economic and financial) in contrasting understanding between mainstream, Islamic neoclassical, and *Tawhidi* epistemological worldviews in theory and practice.

Example 1: The generalized worldview of causality intra-system and inter-system: trade versus interest[1]

(1)–(3)	(4)–(5)	(6)
Axiomatic foundation in the generalized worldview problem of trade in the light of *Qur'an*, *sunnah* and learned discourse versus *riba* – as *maqasid as-shari'ah* (*Qur'an*, 4:59) process in the light the *Qur'an*, states that knowledge of *Tawhidi* unity of knowledge is intrinsic in the world-system of everything but is gained by contemplation and effort, which is the concept of evolutionary learning processes of knowledge formation according to the *Tawhidi* episteme of unity of knowledge (*Qur'an*, 29:19–20). On *sunnah* as epistemic explication of *Qur'an*, and thus the topological preservation of the *Qur'an*, the *Qur'an* statesin (42:52–53). These verses establish the endogenous nature of *sunnah* as the functional mapping of the *Qur'an* into itself and Reality.	Of evaluating wellbeing W($\mathbf{T}$rade, (1/$\mathbf{R}$iba),θ) Subject to circular Causation continuum in the light of the *Tawhidi* premise res *extensa*. The formulation of the problem in this respect is to evaluate by processes of evolutionary learning, the objective functional system: W=W($\mathbf{x}(\theta)$) subject to, T(θ) = f1((1/R),θ) (1/R)(θ) = f2(T(θ),θ) θ = W(T,1/R)[θ].	Continuity of the process in relational evolutionary epistemology: sustainability of methodology carried across learning processes (relational evolutionary epistemology) $\theta \rightarrow \theta_{new}$ now repeat the problem-solving in the link (4)–(5) alternatively, θ-values generated by evolutionary learning processes as in links (5) and (6) can be used to estimate new predictor values and measured wellbeing functions. It is to be noted that the plethora of new simulated θ-values form simulacra of learning possibilities.

Example 2: Dynamic preferences in evolutionary learning space

(1)–(3)	(4)–(5)	(6)
Same as above.	Interactive and integrative preference formation under knowledge induction: dynamic preferences under evolutionary relational	Simulating Wellbeing Functions
Epistemology leading to the formalism of evolutionary learning surfaces in terms of unity of knowledge in complex interactions. Hence complex surfaces are caused by, $\{\cup_i\cap_j \textbf{Pref}erences(\theta)\}^s$. See definitions of i,j,s given above.	with dynamic interactive and integrative evolutionary learning preferences in sustainable evolutionary	
	The problem in trade, *riba*, and θ: Evaluate $W=W(x(\theta);\cup_i\cap_j Pref(\theta))$, subject to, $T(\theta) = f1((1/R),\theta)$ $(1/R)(\theta) = f_2(T(\theta),\theta)$. $\theta = W(T,1/R;\cup_i\cap_j Pref(\theta))[\theta]$, implying polity-market interaction.	Learning processes

Analytical implications in the *Tawhidi* methodology contra neoclassicism

Examples (1) and (2) together establish a critical theorem arising from the *Tawhidi* methodological worldview and rendering the central neoclassical axioms null and void. The result proves the permanent rejection of the neoclassical methodology and method in the face of the *Tawhidi* methodological worldview. The proof for this is provided later on in this chapter.

Theorem: To obtain the consensual evolutionary learning path from the simulacra of evolutionary learning processes, *Tawhidi* methodology requires that the results of such processes are subjected to polity-market interaction and integration (consensus).

Proof

The experience of choice of a simulated trajectory is determined throughout links (1)–(6) give above in the light of continuity and continuums of intra-systemic and inter-systemic unifying experience of diverse possibilities by the action of the *shura* as an analytical discourse on diverse issues with consciousness of the *Tawhidi* world-view (*tasbih*). Thus the evolutionary learning term, *shura-tasbih* is used to explain the objectivity-centred analytical discourse on the diversity of issues and problems under study (Choudhury, 2007–8). In this way, the knowledge-flows of θ-values derived from $[(\Omega,S) \rightarrow \{\theta^*\}]$form the simulacra. From these simulacra, relational epistemology is derived, and consensual results of choice obtained.

Consequently, θ (knowledge-flow belonging to a process) = $\cup_i\cap_j\lim \{\theta_{ij}\}^p$, corresponding to a given process (p) generated by the above-mentioned links (1)–(6). We note that there are say j=1,2,..,n_j number of consensus associated with i = 1,2,..$n_{i(j)}$

finite number of interactions in jth finite consensus formation. Therefore, there are $(n_j * j)$ number of interactions in forming jth consensus. Therefore, $\cup_i \cap_j \lim\{\theta_{ij}\} \neq \phi$. Hence, in finitude, $\lim[\cup_i \cap_j \lim \{\theta_{ij}\}^p]$ exists, for all processes 'p'. This result is true for every discrete and continuously continuum values of $(i, j, p, \{\theta_{ij}\})$ in the light of link (1)–(3). Thus, the limiting function is over $(n_{ij} *)$ points of this vector.

Polity-market interactions remain essential in determining the evolutionary learning path intra-system (i.e. within processes defined in links (4)–(5)) and inter-systems, that is across processes defined by links (5)–(6) and by the continuous repetition of links (1)–(6) over continuums).

The result of the polity-market interactions, integration, and evolutionary learning is to generate simulacra of possibilities that cannot otherwise be reduced to singular probabilistic paths by methods such as Bayesian probability distributions, Data Envelopment Analysis (DEA) and stochastic frontier methods. Better methods, are Spatial Domain Analysis of the Geographical Information System applied to socio-scientific analysis. Also see Kupka and Peixoto (1993) for the multilinear foliation method applied to open manifold. In our case, such a manifold is the knowledge-space of $[(\Omega,S)\rightarrow\{\theta^*\}]$ and diverse evolutionary relations defined on them in reference to (Ω,S), which remains the primal ontology of super-cardinality defining links (1)–(6) shown above and by their co-evolutions.

Consequently, in neither the deterministic nor the probabilistic version of neoclassical methods can the optimal surfaces of various maximization (minimization) problems be defined. The entire resource allocation problem under the axiom of scarcity of resources, the consequential economic rationality assumptions, and the consequences of these axioms in optimization and steady-state states are logically annulled in *Tawhidi* methodology. This destructive result for neoclassical methodology implies the annulment of price relatives as determined by the first- and second-best conditions of optimization of utility, welfare, and production functions (Quirk and Saposnik, 1968).

All this is tantamount to asserting that notions of competition, or 'co-operation with competition', or the neoclassical ways of explaining co-operation (Phelps, 1985) cannot be tenable. This point will be proved in the third detailed example in this chapter. The neoclassical study of co-operation is based on the steady-state efficient ways of combining goods and services to stay in equilibrium by an invisible contract based on self-interest for gains. This self-interest and its equilibrium consequences are explained by the marginalist conditions comprising production and consumption; production and factor costs; welfare and utilities; and social choice involving the Walrasian general equilibrium model.

Furthermore, there is the Prisoners' Dilemma problem on co-operation for mutual gains. Yet the contract which leads to such a co-operative arrangement remains unknown. If such a contract was revealed as a discursive medium in the prisoners' independently constituted individual evaluation of the expected payoffs, then the pay-off matrix would be null by its determinant and non-invertibility (Choudhury, 2000). Thereby, no ethical, moral, and social contract is evident in game-theory trying to study co-operation with a non-interactive meaning. The possibility of recognizing perturbations caused by the endogenous moral, ethical, social and band-wagon and snob effects (Pindyck and Rubinfeld, 2001) is ignored. The emergent disequilibrium dynamics or evolutionary equilibrium dynamics in the context of punctuated learning equilibriums are incapable of studying by neoclassical economic theory despite its analytical innovation by utilizing probabilistic methods (Bertuglia andVaio, 2005; Choudhury, 2013). Since the steady-state equilibrium and optimality cannot exist in the *Tawhidi* simulacra, therefore, marginalist formulas and opportunity cost cannot exist.

Next we note what can happen if, ridiculously, the neoclassical economic methodology was applied to the 'evaluation' problem of the wellbeing model, subject to circular causation relationshipsas shown in links (4)–(5).[2] These results will be re-visited and expanded during the course of this chapter.

Example 3: *Tawhidi* methodology on the participatoriness of Islamic financing instruments *contra* mainstream Islamic economics with neoclassical roots

Questions addressed

How is the idea of participatoriness, meaning the nature of organic linkages according to the *Qur'an* and the *sunnah*, explained by the precept of 'pairing' in creation (*Qur'an*, 36:36) and by the discursive nature of *maqasid as-shari'ah*?

How does the epistemological meaning of participatoriness affect the participatory nature of Islamic financing instruments?

Can a similar derivation be obtained from any other epistemological outlook, for example from mainstream and neoclassical economic theory?

These questions are examined in this part by a detailed explanation of the polarity between *Tawhidi* methodological and mainstream economics, especially adopted by those who practice the neoclassical economic genre. This topic is vast as it is out to destroy the neoclassical agenda of marginalist economic thought. Consequently, some of the arguments are provided *ad hoc* and require some 'reading between the lines' of the arguments presented.

The *Qur'an* (1:2) declares that *Allah* is the Lord of all world systems (*a'lameen*). The *a'lameen* is the learning world system of 'everything' in conscious cognition of *Tawhid* in the form of the intrinsic learning and organic unity of relations between diversity of things and events. The evolutionary learning processes of unifying linkages between self and the world system taken in its generality and specifics is established by the *Qur'an* according to the principle of reorigination (*khalq in-jadid*). Such a message of *Tawhid* manifested through the *sunnah* in terms of the interconnection between soul, mind, and matter together spanning the knowledge, space, and time dimensions was completed in the last sermon of the Prophet Muhammad. On this issue, the *Qur'an* emphasizes submission to the complete message of the *Qur'an*, which is *Tawhid* (*Qur'an*, 5:4).

In the *Sura* (Chapter), *Ra'd* (13:1–4), *Sura Hashr* (59:24), and *Sura Fussilat* (41:53) we read about monotheistic governance over different systems of experience. Such experience is gained through the conscious action of the soul, mind, and matter; as the abstract and reflective consciousness based on *Tawhid* meaning 'oneness of *Allah*' and the monotheistic law at work in the unification of the world system of the good things of life. *Tawhid* is thus perceptually and functionally central in the study of the multiverses. *Tawhid* is unveiled by the joint actualization of *Allah's* oneness as metaphysical ontological reality *together with* the intrinsically expressed and explained unity in the order of 'everything'. This unravelling is enabled by the *Tawhidi* methodological worldview (42:49–53).

The evolutionary learning experience of soul, mind, and matter in the multiverse of unified interrelations in being and becoming is the sure approach for understanding *Tawhid* as ontology and law. Such an integrated worldview of *Tawhid* comprises the *Tawhidi* epistemology of total organic, relational, pervasive oneness by unity of knowledge (*Allah* as Creator = *Tawhid al-Rububiyya*) and its construction of the unified world system as cognitive worship (*Tawhid al-Uluhiyya*). We will invoke this holism between the two as phenomenology to explain the concept of participation as pairing in the *Qur'an*. The principle of organic pairing as evolutionary learning on the episteme of unity of knowledge explains the principle of *Tawhidi* participatoriness.

This epistemic meaning of *Tawhidi* participatoriness in terms of the *Qur'anic* precept of the paired universe is brought out in the form of its complete phenomenological model in Figure 1.2.

Formalizing the string model of *Tawhidi* phenomenology

We now formalize and symbolize the methodological steps of *Tawhidi* worldview in continuity with Figure 1.1. The emergent model is of an extensive nature; though it can be always subject to inquiry and criticism, to which every aspect of our worldly life is subjected. A vast domain of human intellection in theoretical, conceptual, and applied perspectives has been studied in reference to this imminent phenomenological model of *Tawhidi* methodology. Besides the emergent phenomenological model being focused on in *Tawhidi*, episteme of unity of knowledge is of a universal nature. That is, it can comprehend all areas of human intellection without differentiation by religion, faith, and culture. This universality and uniqueness is due to the mathematical nature of the *Tawhidi* phenomenological model, which also leads this model into its polity-market (socio-scientific) application and inferences for all problems in the light of the episteme of unity of knowledge (e.g. Vienna Circle investigated on the unity of science; see Neurath, Carnap and Morris, 1970). We are now utilizing the same phenomenological model to study participatoriness by organic unifying interrelations between the pairing nature of Islamic financial instruments.

Brief review of the literature

The evolutionary epistemological field to which the *Tawhidi* approach to Islamic economics, finance, and socio-scientific reasoning complies is nonetheless different from the similar process-oriented economic reasoning that has been launched in the literature by Boulding (1967, 1971) in his conception of evolutionary equilibriums in the face of the moral economy. There is no convergent ending to the evolutionary process, even with moral and social implications. Consequently, no long-term equilibrium conclusion can be drawn to formulate predictable near futures. Likewise, the *Tawhidi* evolutionary epistemological approach is different from the disequilibrium, entropy-based process model of Georgescu-Roegen (1981) and Schumpeter's non-convergent model of creative destruction to any temporal point. Similar differences based on disequilibrium and the non-convergence of evolutionary economic and

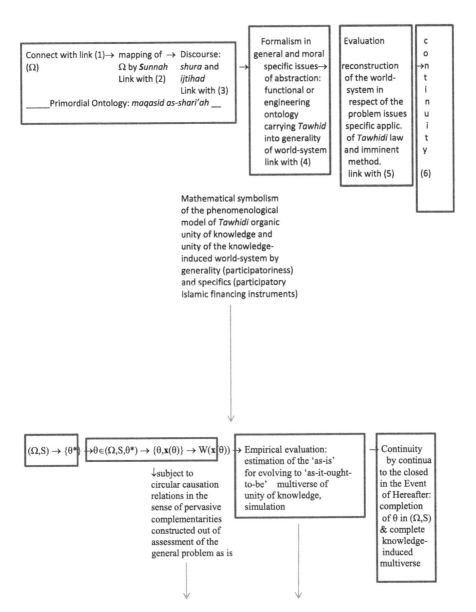

Figure 1.2 The *Tawhidi* phenomenological model of being and becoming by unity of knowledge: participatoriness

social models can be found in Myrdal's recognition of the importance of the wider field of valuation (see Toner, 1999). Marx also fell victim to the over-determination problem of too many competing epistemologies, from which only power and conflict can make a dominant epistemology emerge (Resnick and Wolff, 1987). Nelson and

general theory of
participation as
In Islamic financial instruments

Problem of participatoriness

Tawhidi unity of knowledge
& its induction of the
unified multiverse

Participatoriness is thus defined by a logical derivation from the *Tawhidi* epistemic origin of knowledge and the knowledge-induced world-system:
It describes the state of the world-systemic relations between *maqasid as-shari'ah* determined variables that construct pervasive reconstructioninto a learning world-systemaway from the differentiated world-system

mudarabah, musharakah murabaha as primary financing instruments along with the secondary instruments as of participatory bonds are misnomer in the absence of the specific application of the general theory of *Tawhidi* financing mode in pervasive relational complementarities. This brings about the evolutionary learning world-system asopposed to an optimal and stead-state equilibrium model as of mainstream economics (neoclassicism). Optimality does not exist; but Evolutionary learning equilibriums With pervasive inter-variable causal *Tawhidi* episteme exist.

simulacra in general system of wellbeing defined as the simulated degree of relational unity of The system of financing modes in *Tawhidi* unity of knowledge

The evolutionary learning *Tawhidi* world-system logically annuls all the postulates of rational choice that grounds economic theory, especially neoclassicism and its prototypes in microeconomics and macroeconomics. Economic rationality arising from the rationalist dichotomy of God (*a priori*) differentiated from the world-system(*a posteriori*) [dualism] is denied.

Figure 1.2 (Cont.)

Winter (1982) have treated evolutionary economics from the neoclassical economic viewpoint; this carries all the trappings of the relational evolutionary epistemology that we formalize in this chapter.

Yet, the *Tawhidi* evolutionary methodology with its concept of human potentiality is nearer to Sen's (1988, 1990, 1999) social economic conception of human freedom and potential. There is also a similarity to Sen's deontological model of moral and ethical preferences replacing the static datum character of utilitarian individual and social preferences such as that of Arrow's. The difference, though, is the absence of the final epistemological foundation in Sen's deontological theory that must relent to rationalism once again; God is absent in his model of reality. Monotheism and rationalism are polar to each other in all of epistemological literature (Overman, 1988).

What causes continuous learning and complementarities *a la maqasid as-shari'ah* in the functional ontology of the *Tawhidi* ontological law to form the *Tawhidi* epistemology of the participatory model?

Resources are critical. They must be *continuously regenerated and mobilized* across multiverse continuums. Resource generation and mobilization needs the development of endogenous contracts with moral, ethical, and social embedding to adjust to the free flow of financial resources between all trade-related instruments in the specific study of Islamic financing instruments. This would comprise the diversity of primary and secondary instruments developed by discourse (*shura*) and authoritative epistemic research (*ijtihad*). Both of these functions are instilled by the learning processes to progressively fathom the worship (*tasbih*) of the world system (pairing, pervasively relational complementarities, and participatoriness).

To formalize, let R denote resource, $R = R(\theta, \mathbf{x}(\theta))$. It remains to be proved that R is continuously reproductive across knowledge (θ), space ($\mathbf{x}(\theta)$), and time to read knowledge and the event of knowledge-induced space dimension ($t(\theta)$) dimension. That is,

$$dR/d\theta = (\partial R/\partial\theta) + (\partial R/\partial \mathbf{x}).(d\mathbf{x}/d\theta), \tag{1.3}$$

implies that, each of the terms on the right-hand side of expression (1.3) is positive due to the evolutionary learning effect of θ in its continuity in the $(\theta, \mathbf{x}(\theta), t)$-dimensions. Thus, $dR/d\theta > 0$ strictly, for all values of $\theta \in (\Omega, S, \theta^*)$ and for every $E(\theta, \mathbf{x}(\theta), t)$.[3]

Along with expression (1.3) and its meaning, we define the wellbeing function $W(\mathbf{x}(\theta))$ with circular causation (see below). Together in a simulation model, these mark quantitatively the degree of unity attained by the functional ontology of *maqasid as-shari'ah*, as is defined in Figure 1.1.

The evaluation problem comprises firstly 'estimation' of the world system 'as is' for the problem under investigation. 'Estimation' is followed by 'simulation' in respect of the world as it 'ought to be' in light of the *Tawhidi* unitary worldview. Evaluation means the total of 'estimation' followed by 'simulation' and the moral reconstruction inferred therefrom.

We write this comprehensive problem as,[4]

Evaluate, $W = W(\mathbf{x}(\theta))$ $\qquad$ (1.4)
s.t. $x_i = f_i(\mathbf{x}_j(\theta))$, for all values of $i \neq j = 1, 2, .., n$

Finally, the estimated and simulated values in the quantitative forms of the conceptual $W(.)$-function is obtained. Note that there are many intermediate econometric steps in the 'estimation-to-simulation' process involving the simulation of coefficients, thus regarding predictors of variables, for developing complementarities out of underlying polity-market (socio-scientific) discourse, interaction, integration (consensus), and creative evolution resulting thereby in configured reality. Such a sequence of experience is gained by the medium of the *shura*, *tasbih* (consciousness of worship), and *ijtihad* on the selection of values of the simulated coefficients following their empirical determination.

Thus in the measured form of an index as W(.)-function – the wellbeing functional – is evaluated as,

$$\text{Evaluate,} \theta = W(\mathbf{x}(\theta)) = A(\theta) \cdot [\textstyle\prod_i x_i^{\alpha i}](\theta), \tag{1.5}$$

W(.) denotes the conceptual formalism of wellbeing function by epistemic reference to *Tawhidi* unity of knowledge

s.t. $x_i = f_i(\mathbf{x}_j(\theta))$, circular causation system of equations
$i \neq j = 1,2,..,n$
$dW/d\theta > 0$

The 'estimated' followed by 'simulated' predictors are obtained by econometric evaluation of (1.5).

By combining expressions (1.3)–(1.5) we obtain, $x_i = R(\theta, \mathbf{x}_j(\theta))$. Now, say, $x_1 = $ *mudarabah*; $x_2 = $ *musharakah*; $x_3 = $ *murabaha*; $x_4 = $ secondary; $x_5 = $ money; $x_6 = $ real output by *maqasid as-shari'ah* sectors of goods and services denoted by k; $x_7 = $ employment; $x_8 = $ inverse of *riba*; $x_9 = $ HRD; $x_{10} = $ technology; etc. as the selection of variables increases with the available data.

Now the complete formalism follows the implications of expression (1.3) for all the variables. That is, in order to attain continuous regeneration of resources, all other interactive, integrative, and evolutionary (IIE) complementary variables must follow suit. Furthermore, link (6) (given above) implies that, such a complementary evolutionary-learning phenomenology must span diverse world systems and inter-linked issues in the light of *maqasid as-shari'ah*. Thus, the resource reproduction and mobilization along with that of all complementing variables is realized over the dimensions of knowledge, space, and time – *continuously across continuums*.

Result – Rejection of mainstream and neoclassical postulates by the *Tawhidi* methodological worldview

Mainstream economic assumptions are annulled in the *Tawhidi* epistemological knowledge, space and time multiverse study of complementarities. A few of such postulates are: scarcity of resources, rational choice, the suggestion of economic rationality, optimization criterion, efficiency and marginalist trade-off, opportunity cost, steady-state equilibrium, competition, perfect information; the flawed notion of imperfect competition, utility, welfare, and preferences and technology as exogenously given datum. Even in the case of endogenous growth theory (Romer, 1986) the neoclassical postulates prevail (Turnovsky, 1995).

Can mainstream economic theory offer a *Tawhidi* methodological worldview out of its episteme?

This is impossible; even in the best scenario of endogenous growth theory, and all such economic theories that use ideas depending on utility and welfare postulates.

All of these functions are based fundamentally on the epistemology of rationalism. Rationalism deconstructs into economic rationality via the application of Kantian problems of heteronomy that separate a priori reasoning (God) from a posterior (the world). The *Qur'an* has denied this dichotomy in the light of the unitary reasoning worldview of *Tawhid* and the world system. Ibn Al-Arabi (trans. Chittick, 1989) wrote on this point: 'Two ways lead to the knowledge of God... The first way is the way of unveiling... The second way is the way of reflection and reasoning (*istidlal*) through rational demonstration (*burhanaqli*). This way is lower than the first way, since he who bases his consideration upon proof can be visited by obfuscations which detract from his proof, and only with difficulty can he remove them'. On a similar note, Imam Ghazali wrote (Marmura, 1997).[5]

In the light of endogenous nature of knowledge, morality, ethics, and inter-variable causality in *Tawhidi* methodology, note the following contrary model for mainstream economics (details of the optimization results not given here). Such a model would be used to 'estimate' the 'as is' state of the specific problem under study. See for a similar formulation of technological change in growth model Mankiw (2003, p. 74).

$$R = R(T, x_1(T), x_2(T)), \text{ T denotes technological change;}$$
$$\text{and, } T = T(R(T), x_1(T), x_2(T))$$
$$x_1 = x_1(R(T), x_2(T), T)$$
$$x_2 = x_2(R(T), x_1(T), T)$$
(1.6)

By the postulate of rational choice based on the postulate of scarcity of resource allocation of mainstream economics, $(x_1, x_2)[T]$ are substitutes on the technologically induced production possibility (tradeoff) surfaces between $(x_1, x_2)[T]$ for all states of T.

In the special case, if T is variable like θ is, then one must determine the epistemology underlying this derivation. In neoclassical economics the epistemology of rational choice denies pervasively complementary effects. Only local complementarities are possible by the Slutzky equation (Henderson and Quandt, 1971). Such complementarities are non-sustainable due to the coalition effect between technology and specific variables on the basis of the rationality postulate of optimal choice.

Now since $x_1(T)$ and $x_2(T)$ remain substitutes of all kinds, then T generates coalition effect with one or the other of these variables. The result is an extension of the marginal rate of substitution to everything in (x_1, x_2, T). Endogenous growth theory causes an endogenous inter-variable relationship, but does not attain the pervasively complementary processes between these variables and their monotonic functional transforms.

Mainstream economists may argue that endogenous continuity of resource allocation via the route of technological change is maintained by way of first allocating the resource to factors of production including technology. Then, in the roundabout way of regeneration and re-circulation of resources, the generated technology re-augments resources, and circularity goes on. While the circulation of resources is understandable, the critical facts remain. That is, according to the rational choice theory of mainstream economics, the regenerated resources are allocated to variables (factors) that remain as marginal substitutes. Consequently, technological effects advance in complementarity between the postulates of marginalism. This permanent characteristic of mainstream resource allocation with or without any kind of technological effect, and with only instantaneous and local complementarities, can be referred to as the *evolutionary complementarism of rationality postulates*.

The mainstream and neoclassical application of economic and finance theory to Islamic financing causes just these problems. The confined nature of legal contracts denies *shari'ah* its essential general-system perspective of overarching reality. Instead, our knowledge of the *shari'ah* deconstructs to '*uqud*' (contracts) pertaining to specific financing modes as isolated entities. There is no automatic pooling of funds into a complementary relational portfolio and its treatment as a paired participatory organism in this case.

An example here is of *murabaha*, cost-plus pricing in procuring real assets by the financial intermediary on behalf of the buyer. *Murabaha* delinks cost-plus financing from market pricing by the mark-up. Thereby, the fair profit and the risk cannot be measured, as these are not market determined. Hence mark-up pricing is like *riba* (interest); it functions as such in generating *murabaha* returns for the financier up front. Another example is the almost complete disappearance of *mudarabah*, which is a primary Islamic financing instrument in the global Islamic portfolio. *Mudarabah* has been almost perfectly substituted by *musharakah* and *murabaha*. There is no sense of participatoriness left in the Islamic portfolio, except in calling an instrument 'Islamic' by fashion. Profitable instruments, but they have no participatory effect of the type adhering to the *Tawhidi* epistemic worldview of unity of knowledge and its induction of the unified financial, economic, social, and wellbeing system by inter-causal relations between the instruments *res extensa*.

The result of the mainstream perspective of so-called 'participatory' Islamic financing instruments is a linear aggregation of independently constituted instruments without inter-causality by way of organic unifying interrelations. Such a financing state is thoroughly defeating conceptually and theoretically in the light of the *Tawhidi* meaning of participatoriness derived from the *Qur'anic* meaning of 'pairing' across systems. Let us examine this matter further.

Methodological impossibility of the neoclassical Islamic economic approach

Take M1 and M2 as two so-called financing instruments. In the mainstream sense, they are competing substitutes with a given amount of resources to be allocated between them, but they have no *Tawhidi* implications of pervasively complementary evolutionary learning in unity of knowledge with the *maqasid as-shari'ah* variables. This is the usual perception of the world of Islamic thought and action today, moving towards the *taqlid* (unquestioned submission to authority) of desuetude thought. *Taqlid* (blind submission to authority) takes the mind away from the *tajdeed* (revival) of the study of the *Qur'an* and *sunnah* within the *generalized* worldview of *maqasid as-shari'ah*.

In a neoclassical economic approach to the study of Islamic financing instruments as practised today, the utility function, $U_i(M1, M2)$ is maximized in the two domains, namely of (M1, M2), subject to the resource allocation between M1 and M2; i=1,2 (say) two financial contracts. This is a well-known classical optimization problem. The dual results are represented in Figure 1.3.

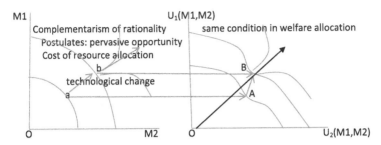

Figure 1.3 Permanent and pervasive substitution by competition between M1 and M2 with scarcity of resources according to the neoclassical postulate of rationality

The inference from the arrowed consequences (aA, bB) in Figure 1.3 points out that the welfare function (W) is of the utilitarian type. Such a formulation of the utilitarian form of welfare function signifies the independence of the inter-variable and inter-utility type of methodological individualism between the financing instruments in the Islamic portfolio. This consequence of independence and individualism is further extended to the property of entities and institutions. In this respect, we find today a weakest form of networking between Islamic banks globally and nationally in Islamic countries (Haq, 3 Nov. 2012).

The utilitarian form of the wellbeing function (Harsanyi, 1955; Hammond, 1987) is given by,

$$W(U1,U2) = U1(M1,M2) + U2(M1,M2) = \alpha M1' + \beta M2' \tag{1.7}$$

An example of further deconstruction of utility function in terms of the components M1 and M2 is the present value of discounted cash-flows (M1', M2'; W(.)) from investment in M1 and M2. In expression (1.7), $\alpha = 1/(1+i_1)$; $\beta = 1/(1+i_2)$, i_1 and i_2 are discount factors of the one-period discounted cash-flows from M1 and M2, that is M1' and M2', respectively.

The discounted cash-flows method carries two serious problems: i_1 and i_2 are shadow interest rates in the form of discount rates. M1 and M2 are then seen as debt financing due to their deferment of returns over time and holding back of liabilities. Both of these consequences stand against the *Tawhidi* precept of participatoriness by pairing unifying relations and debt overhang.

The debt-free financing in the latter case stands even for the evaluation of probabilistic cash-flows 'nearest' to an event point (Choudhury, 2011 op cit; Gauthier, 1986). Such 'nearest' points of valuation are identified in the evolutionary learning regions of unity of knowledge in Figures 1.4 and 1.5, shown by system intersections signifying overlapping generations or inter-relating and unifying the portfolio instruments. This signifies the precept of organic pairing by unity of knowledge and its induction into objects, as the Sign of Oneness of *Allah* conveyed by the *Qur'an*.

By the application of *Tawhidi* methodology in valuation of cash-flows 'nearest' to probabilistic events, the problem of inter-temporal debt vanishes. In this case, at every given terminal valuation point of participatory financial returns occurring

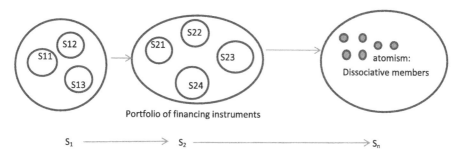

Figure 1.4 A topological representation

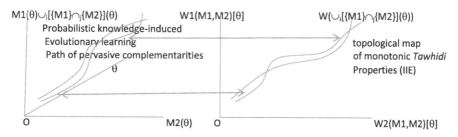

Figure 1.5 Tawhidi participatory financing instrumentation; i: interactions; j: integration

continuously, liabilities equal assets. This cancellation of debts happens continuously and across diversified participatory domains of financing instruments. Consequently, no debt can exist. Indeed, the *sunnah* of Prophet Muhammad decries the holding of debt.

The neoclassical form of Figure 1.3 is further represented in the set theoretic case of dissociated systems with many financing instruments in Figure 1.4.

Monotonic topological mappings generate mappings of the same kind of dissociative members leading to atomism

In Figure 1.3, S_i, i=1,2,3 represent portfolio of financial instruments that continuously diversify into independent instruments as indicated by $\cap_{ij} S_{ij} = \phi$, i,j=1,2,3,.... The ultimate scenario is that of a large number of secondary instruments become atomistic between them. This presents the extreme kind of legalistic contractual scenario of independent and individualized financing instruments. Along with them, the methodological individualism and independence between the agents and relations of the financing instruments, such as banks and mind-sets (today's neoclassical Islamic economists), become dissociated entities.

Indeed, such a consequence bears the signs of many declining primary Islamic financing instruments and a weak level of networking between Islamic banks.[6] An increasing number of isolated Islamic financing instruments demonstrate a complete lack of the *Tawhidi* precept of participatoriness. The relevance of participatory financing instruments, both between themselves and in the context of an evolutionary system of interaction, integration, and creative evolutionary, is lost.

The methodological orientation of resource mobilization and valuation according to *Tawhidi* methodology: inter-financing instrument participation

In Figure 1.4, no price relative, even in the probabilistic sense, can exist on methodological grounds along permanently evolutionary learning points of organic relationships between variables. This implies a pervasive complementarity between the variables and the wellbeing functional, U(.)'s and W(.)'s. To determine prices now in their absolute and relative forms, the circular causation relationshipsin prices are 'estimated' and 'simulated' consecutively using the corresponding equations of expression (1.4) or (1.5).

The portfolio of participatory financing instruments according to Tawhidi methodology

Using the topological property of continuity across continuums shown in the set-theoretic representation of Figure 1.5 in Figure 1.6, we can write:

The evolutionary property in pervasive complementarities,

$$
(d/d\theta)[\cup_i[\{M1\}\cap_j\{M2\}](\theta)] > 0 \text{ is copied}
$$
$$
\text{in } \cup_i\cap_j(d/d\theta)W(\cup_i[\{M1\}\cap_j\{M2\}](\theta)) > 0, \tag{1.8}
$$

and to all monotonic positive transformations of these.[7]

Annulment of mainstream postulates of Islamic economics and finance in the light of *Tawhidi* methodology

In the end, the question is now answered. Mainstream economics does not have the capability to derive the *Tawhidi* worldview by its mainstream and neoclassical postulates and theory. Thereby, the application of mainstream economic theory cannot map itself into the practice of the *Tawhidi* worldview. Therefore, no Islamic intellection can arise from the mainstream economic and finance side, including emphatically neoclassical economic postulation.

The universal and unique methodology of Tawhidi worldview

Yet in spite of the failure of mainstream reasoning to comprehend the *Tawhidi* methodological worldview, contrarily, it is capable of abstracting the mainstream theory and postulates as degenerate cases by setting $\theta = 0$. For this to happen, the *Tawhidi* epistemological foundation is not needed. Thereby, $\{(\Omega,S),\theta^*\} = 0$ as the degenerate case of reality in forming unity of knowledge and its induction of the world system.

Thus, the *Tawhidi* methodological worldview of unity of knowledge in the light of *maqasid as-shari'ah* is universal. It also uniquely explains the entire 'belief space' of

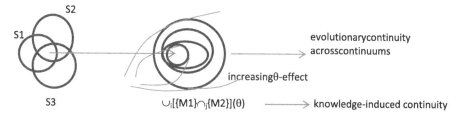

S2

S1

evolutionarycontinuity
acrosscontinuums

increasingθ-effect

S3

$\cup_i[\{M1\}\cap_j\{M2\}](\theta)$ knowledge-induced continuity

Figure 1.6 Topological representation of the *Tawhidi* evolutionary learning processes

diverse belief systems including rationalism and mainstream economics, emphatically neoclassical economics.

Now when such facts are not understood by Islamic mainstream and neoclassical economics and finance protagonists, the resulting intellectual poverty and academic imperialism are equivalent to abandoning the *Tawhidi* roots of unity of knowledge of the *Qur'an* and the *sunnah*. Such scholarship has ignored and replaced the *Qur'an* and the *sunnah* by rationalism and its mainstream genre. The *shari'ah* has been flouted away from its true participatory worldview of unity of knowledge and unity of the world system, as explained by the functional ontology of wellbeing (*maslaha*). The participatoriness by organic unity of *Qur'anic* principle of 'pairing' applied to participatory Islamic financing has not been understood.

Conclusion

To conclude, here is a quote from Sayuti Hasibuan (2008) an Indonesian professor of economics: "… the failure of Muslims to reach their potential is because the Muslim countries, basing their planning on neoclassical economic concepts, have employed the paradigms of individualism and materialism in managing their development."

Beyond simply a polemical disqualification of mainstream and neoclassical economic approaches, to embed the economic reasoning and problems of man in the moral, ethical, and social complex by using the *Tawhidi* methodology of unity of knowledge and its induction of the relationally unified world system and the neoclassical and mainstream annulment is a methodological issue. This rigorous analytical project is the methodological worldview of *Tawhid* and the world-system in respect of the episteme of unity of knowledge. It negates the postulates and approaches of mainstream and neoclassical economics and their prototypes.

The rejection of neoclassical economic theory in the moral and ethical embedding of economic problems and issues invokes the challenge of an altogether new reasoning and vision of reality. This *Tawhidi* awakening in the general socio-scientific thought, and particularly in Islamic economics and finance, belongs to the genre of evolutionary social system and cybernetic approach that is deeply epistemological in its core. Without such an epistemological mooring of socio-scientific thought, no true science can emerge (Bohr on Einstein's construction of science, 1951).
Islamic economics and finance, as other Islamic socio-scientific themes of scholarship, have become flawed by missing out the epistemological investigation of *Tawhid* in the first place. Instead, this kind of investigation has adopted impossible reasoning and corresponding models that do not fit. Nicety decays in the face of reality.

Notes

1 *Qur'an* (2:274–276) is all inclusive in respect of the choice of θ to represent value of charity and divine blessing of trade against interest *(riba)*. The wellbeing function is thereby in terms of trade and θ in the good things of life and is complementary with the inverse of *riba*. The expectation of the Islamic political economy in the midst of the learning variable θ to represent the learning and progress around charity and blessing is that *riba* will have an inverse relationship to trade. When such a relationship is not noted, the moral and material value of that system is low in the 'as-is' state of reality. Now a moral and ethical transformation is necessary. This calls for simulation of the coefficients and of the predictor variables.

2 By neoclassical maximization of Lagrangian, $L = W(\mathbf{x}(\theta)) + \Sigma\lambda_i(x_i - f_i(\theta, \mathbf{x}_j(\theta)))$, i,j = 1,2,…, i≠j. Also, $W(\mathbf{x}(\theta))$ is a monotonic positive transformation of θ, say $W = F(\theta)$; and $\theta = G(\mathbf{x}(\theta))$ in the measured form of wellbeing function.

Obviously, by Lagrangian maximization in the neoclassical frame, $d[W = F(\theta)]/d\theta > 0$. This is a contradiction to the first-order maximization condition of maximization.

Therefore, neither steady-state equilibrium nor optimization can exist in the *Tawhidi* evolutionary learning world system as otherwise axiomatically assumed and worked out by the neoclassical postulates.

3 Because all variables are θ-induced and are driven by moral, ethical, and belief preferences, which are dynamic in nature, non-material values must be considered in the signs of the simulated coefficients. For example, a person may be satisfied with his meagre resources but place a high value of submission to God *(ibadah)*. In this case, although R as material artefact can be meagre, if the θ-value is high, it will cause the non-monetary induction of such value in $R(\theta)$ to be high. Consequently, $dR(\theta)/d\theta > 0$ always.

4 The assignment and estimation of θ-values in reference to the endogenous variables is a separate topic not covered in this chapter. With my *Tawhidi* colleagues, I have simulated such θ-values using SPSS, cointegration, and Spatial Domain Analysis of GIS-method applied to socio-economic problems noting participatoriness between Islamic financial instruments in Indonesia (Choudhury, 2011), and a dynamic intersectoral development model for Oman (Choudhury & Hossain, 2006).

5 Imam Ghazali (trans. Marmura, 1997) wrote: "Thus every knowledge is knowledge of itself and of its object. The object of knowledge becomes multiple, while knowledge remains one. What also shows this is that you [theologians] perceive that objects of God's knowledge are infinite, while His knowledge is one, and [you] attribute to Him cognitions that are infinite in number. If the multiplicity of what is known necessitates the multiplicity of the essence of knowledge, then let there be in the divine essence cognitions that are numerically infinite, which would be impossible."

6 The recent state of networking, and thereby financial diversification in the Islamic banking system towards serving the synergistic goal of complementing economic targets between the corporate sector and development at the grassroots, can be seen in the following comment on Al-Baraka Bank in Pakistan (Haq, 3 Nov. 2012). The point of concern here is that if a major Islamic bank cannot even expand in itself, how can it establish networking with the Islamic banking system and the greater development goals beyond corporatism?

Haq wrote: "The current year, however, appears to be a reversion to its loss-making ways, since the bank earned a net loss of Rs213 million for the first six months of 2012, compared to a net profit of Rs324 million for the same period in the previous year. The loss happened largely on the back of rising non-performing loans in the bank's portfolio.

Meanwhile, after strong growth in 2011, deposit growth appears to have stalled, with deposits having stayed virtually stagnant during the first half of 2012.

Ahmad did not specify that the bank would expand its presence in Punjab, but his visit to Lahore appears to be part of what is now becoming a trend among Karachi-centric banks to seek expansion in the industrial triangle between Lahore, Faisalabad and Islamabad. The visit to the Lahore Chamber of Commerce appears to be part of a bid by the bank to attract corporate customers in that belt. The Al Baraka CEO seemed keen only to burnish the bank's Islamic credentials."

7 The $\mathbf{x}(\theta)$ can be a vector, a matrix, and a tensor with knowledge-induced probabilistic coefficients, such as dynamic (evolutionary learning) input-output coefficients connected with $\mathbf{x}(\theta)$ as matrix; and the study of the properties of *maqasid as-shari'ah* in the supercardinal *Tawhidi* topological space of knowledge. See Choudhury (2012).

References

Bakar, O. (1991). *Tawhid and Science*, Penang, Malaysia: Secretariat for Islamic Philosophy and Science, The Science University of Malaysia and Nurin Enterprise.

Barrow, J.D. (1991). "Laws", in his *Theories of Everything, the Quest for Ultimate Explanation*, pp. 12–30, Oxford University Press, Oxford, UK.

Bertuglia, C.S. and Vaio, F. (2005). "Dynamical systems and the phase space", in *Nonlinearity, Chaos and Complexity, the Dynamics of Natural and Social Systems*, pp. 49–70, Oxford University Press, Oxford, UK.

Bohr, N. (1951). "Discussions with Einstein on Epistemological Problems in AtomicPhysics", in *Albert Einstein: Philosopher-Scientists*, P.A. Shilpp (ed.), Tudor Publishing Co, New York, NY.

Boulding, K.E. (1971). "Economics as a moral science", in F.R. Glabe (ed.), *Boulding Collected Papers 3*, Association of University Press, Boulder, CO.

Boulding, K.E. (1967). "Evolution and revolution in the developmental process", in *Social Change and Economic Growth*, Development Centre of the Organization for Economic Co-operation and Development, Paris, France.

Chittick, W.C. (1989). *Sufi Path of Knowledge*, State University of New York Press, Albany, NY.

Choudhury, M.A. (2000). "A social contractarian theory of markets: neoclassicism, Rawls, Gauthier and the alternative", *International Journal of Social Economics*, 27:3, 194–213.

Choudhury (2006). *Science and Epistemology in the Qur'an*, 5 volumes. The Edwin Mellen Press, Lewiston, NY.

Choudhury, M.A. (2007–8). "Islam versus liberalism: contrasting epistemological inquiries", *International Journal of Social Economics*, 35:1, 239–68.

Choudhury, M.A. (2011). *Islamic Economics and Finance, an Epistemological Inquiry*, Emerald Publishers, Derby, UK.

Choudhury, M.A. (2012). "The *Qur'anic* universe in knowledge, time and space with a reference to matrix game in Islamic behavioral financial decision-making", *Philosophical Papers and Reviews*, 4:2, 17–24.

Choudhury, M.A. (2013). "Complexity and endogeneity in economic methodology", *Kybernetes: International Journal of Cybernetics, Systems, and Management Sciences*, 42:2, 226–40.

Choudhury, M.A. and Hossain, M.S. (2006). *Development Planning in the Sultanate of Oman*, The Edwin Mellen Press, Lewiston, NY.

Debreu, G. (1959). *Theory of Value, an Axiomatic Analysis of Economic Equilibrium*, John Wiley, New York, NY.

Dewitt, B. (1992). *Supermanifolds*, Cambridge University Press, Cambridge, UK.

Gauthier, D. (1986). *Morals by Agreement*, Oxford University Press, Oxford, UK.

Georgescu-Roegen, N. (1981). *The Entropy Law and the Economic Process*, Harvard University Press, Cambridge, MA.

Hammond, P.J. (1987). "On reconciling Arrow's theory of social choice with Harsanyi's fundamental utilitarianism", in G.R. Feiwel (ed.), *Arrow and the Foundations of the Theory of Economic Policy*, pp. 179–221, Macmillan, London, UK.

Haq, S. (2012). "Seeking growth: Al-Baraka Islamic Bank seeks major expansion of its branch network", *The Express Tribune*, 3 November.

Harsanyi, J.C. (1955). "Cardinal welfare, individualistic ethics, and interpersonal comparisons of utility", *Journal of Political Economy*, 63, 309–21.

Hasibuan, S. (2008). "Muslim-managed organizations: a case study of the Indonesian development agenda", *Review of Islamic Economics*, 12:2, 137–56.

Henderson, J.M. and Quandt, R.E. (1971), *Microeconomic Theory*, McGraw-Hill, New York, NY.

Imam Ghazali trans. M.E. Marmura. (1997), *The Incoherence of the Philosophers*, Brigham Young University Press, Provo, Utah:

Mankiw, G.N. (2003). *Macroeconomics*, p. 74. World Publishers, New York, NY.

Mousalli, A. (1990). "Sayyid Qutb's view of knowledge", *American Journal of Islamic Social Sciences*, 7:3, 315–35.

Nelson, R.R. and Winter, S.G. (1982). *An Evolutionary Theory of Economic Change*, Harvard University Press, Cambridge, MA.

Neurath, O., Carnap, R. and Morris, C. (eds) (1970). *Foundations of the Unity of Science*, University of Chicago Press, Chicago, IL.

Nikaido, H. (1989). "Fixed point theorems", in Eatwell, J. Milgate, M. and Newman, P. (eds), *The New Palgrave: General Equilibrium*, pp. 139–44, W.W. Norton, New York, NY.

Overman, S. (1988). "Introduction", in his *Methodology and Epistemology for Social Science, Selected Papers of Donald T. Campbell*, pp. vii–xix, University of Chicago Press, Chicago, IL.

Phelps, E.S. (1985). *Political Economy*, Chapters 4, 5, 6, W.W. Norton, New York, NY.

Pindyck, R.S. and Rubinfeld, D.L. (2001)."Network externalities", in their *Microeconomics*, pp. 127–30, Prentice Hall, NJ.

Quirk, J. and Saposnick, R. (1968). "Pareto optimality and competitive equilibrium", in *Introduction to General Equilibrium Theory and Welfare Economics*, pp. 124–48, McGraw-Hill, New York, NY.

Resnick, S.A. and Wolff, R.D. (1987).*Knowledge and Class, A Marxian Critique of Political Economy*, The University of Chicago Press, Chicago, IL.

Romer, P.M. (1986)."Increasing returns and long-run growth", *Journal of Political Economy*, 94, 1002–37.

Rucker, R. (1982). "Large cardinals", in his *Infinity and the Mind*, pp. 273–86, Bantam Books, New York, NY.

Saville, A. (2000). "Monadic nature", in *Leibniz and the Monadology*, Chapter 4, Routledge, London, UK.

Saposnik, R. (1968). "Fixed-point theorems and related mathematical tools", in their *Introduction to General Equilibrium Theory and Welfare Economics*, pp. 70–5, McGraw-Hill, New York NY.

Sen, A. (1988). "Conduct, ethics and economics", in his *On Ethics and Economics*, pp. 88–9. Basil Blackwell, Oxford, UK.

Sen, A. (1990). "Economic judgements and moral philosophy", in *On Ethics and Economics*, pp. 29–34, Basil Blackwell, Oxford, UK.

Sen, A. (1999). "Functioning and well-being", in his *Commodities and Capabilities*, pp. 17–21, Oxford University Press, New Delhi, India.

Toner, P. (1999). "Gunnar Myrdal (1898–1987): circular and cumulative causation as the methodology of the social sciences", in *Main Currents in Cumulative Causation, the Dynamics of Growth and Development*, Chapter 5, Macmillan Press Ltd, Houndmills, Hampshire.

Turnovsky, S.J. (1995). "An introduction to endogenous growth", pp. 391–425 in his *Methods of Macroeconomic Dynamics*, The MIT Press, Cambridge, MA.

Chapter 2

The Philosophy of Knowledge in Islam

Abstract

The first cardinal value of the Islamic worldview is the integration of God's oneness in knowledge and the world-system, even in the minutest details, through monotheistic oneness (*Tawhid*). We refer to this primordial axiom as 'the episteme' in this chapter. The *Qur'an* says in this regard (96:1–5): "Read: In the name of your Lord Who created, created man from a clot. Read: And your Lord is the Most Bounteous, Who taught by the pen, taught man that which he knew not." The early thinkers on the *Qur'anic* worldview delved deeply into the *Qur'an* and the meaning of its verses using the practices and sayings of the Prophet Muhammad, referred to as the *sunnah*. This is followed in the Islamic epistemological practice by the discourse in reference to the episteme (*shura* by *ijtihad*) of the learned Islamic community to derive and establish meaning out of the *Qur'anic* verses. Such an exercise on the functional relationship between the *Qur'an* incorporating the *sunnah* and learned discourse on the diversities of the world-system cannot be completed in temporal experience. The *Qur'an* establishes this openness of the immanent search, discovery and evolution of knowledge without end. The *Qur'an* thus builds and explains the openness of evolutionary learning within and across the diversity of everything in terms of knowledge and its induction of the world-system in general and in specifics.

Objective

This chapter is an original contribution to the theme of the *Tawhidi* (monotheistic) Scientific Research Program conceptually formalized in terms of the evolutionary theory of the Islamicization of knowledge. Such an evolutionary learning theory that interactively integrates the epistemology of monotheism (*Tawhid*) in the *Qur'an* to general and specific issues and problems of the world-system is an original field of intellection. It has not been taken up fully by most leading studies of the theme of the Islamicization of knowledge. This is true of classical and modern literature on the theme.

The objective of this chapter is to formalize the *Tawhidi* meaning of knowledge and explain how it is transmitted to the world system in formalizing relations that explain organic unification and related applications. The chapter presents a methodological worldview as the phenomenology of integrative mind and matter relations in evolutionary epistemology. Hence, while the derivation of the methodology is purely

Qur'anic in essence, along with the presence of the Prophetic guidance (*sunnah*), it is also formal in its expression. Hence the epistemological and formal precepts establish the explanation and application of the resulting formal model of monotheistic unity of knowledge that can be applied to the general and specific issues of various unified and socially embedded world systems.

Nature of knowledge in the *Qur'an*

To understand the nature of knowledge endowed by the *Qur'an* to the world system, the meaning of knowledge as an ontological essence must be first understood. This initial quest for knowledge in the epistemological sphere of the *Qur'an* is from and of the law of the oneness of God. Following the many peripatetic Islamic philosophers including significantly Abu Hamid Muhammad Ibn Muhammad Al-Ghazali (1058 CE–1111CE), the functional meaning of the oneness of God is taken as the manifestation of the organic pairing of the universe and its details by the medium of the monotheistic law, referred to as *Tawhid*. This refers to the *Qur'anic* monotheistic belief relating to the oneness of God and the Divine *Law*.

In this chapter, *Tawhid* in its functional category is represented *not* in terms of the *being* of God, who is incommensurate in every shape, form, attribute and functionality. Rather, the meaning of oneness as the completion of absolute and perfect knowledge without partnership (duality and multiplicity) while remaining incommensurate in any dimension, is manifested in its organic form of unity. This has long been studied on the topic of be-ing and becoming (Heidegger, trans. Hofstadter, 1988). The organic becoming as being invokes the relational and evidential (ontic) states of learning in the experiential world system by its generality and specifics of issues and problems.

Thus, the cardinal principle of Islamic belief – namely the consciousness, meaning, understanding, and the embracing of the oneness of God – is manifested in the organic becoming of beings in experience. *Tawhid* manifests through, and is learnt by, the universe in the consciousness of understanding, by the learning process in unity of knowledge. The *Qur'an* refers to this learning process in terms of the interminable capacity to comprehend the organic unity of knowledge of *Tawhid* as the Monotheistic *Law* in the order and scheme of creation. Such attributes of knowledge and knowing are conveyed by the expanded meaning of *Qur'anic* terms such as *khalq in-jadeed* – re-originated creations taken over a continua of experiences (*Qur'an* 17:49). The re-originative positivism which alerts consciousness is pointed out in verse (*Qur'an* 29:19–22). The created universe's state of continuous worship, which man endeavors to know by searching, is indicated in verse (*Qur'an* 17:44). The *Qur'an* introduces the idea of a learning universe in terms of its paired ontology of being and becoming 'everything' in a verse (*Qur'an* 36:36).

The phenomenological model of knowledge and its induction of the world system according to the *Qur'an*

The *Qur'an* classifies the elements of the knowledge concept and its relationship with the world system. This comprises the *Qur'anic* phenomenological model of knowledge and the world system. Figure 2.1 presents this model.

The sequences (1–5) in expression (2.1) comprise the undivided progress of the learning process across 'everything' in a world system made up of unified sub-systems.

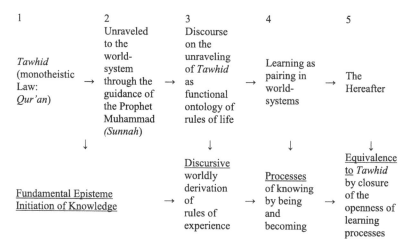

Figure 2.1 Structure of the *Qur'anic* phenomenological model of the learning world-system premised in the episteme of unity of knowledge

Each of these has the common episteme of learning within the episteme of unity of knowledge. Yet, even as the embodiment of knowledge is achieved through unity, the experiential facts may reveal differences between the representative variables and entities of the specific world-system under study. Therefore, learning processes axiomatically unravel the knowledge and world system of epistemic unity. At the same time, they also lead to the correction of the differentiated world systems, bringing them to better states of unification. Such a transformational correction of differentiated world systems by specifics and totality characterizes the moral–social reconstruction. It then characterizes the basis of two integral functions that lead to consciousness in the *Qur'an*.

First, there is the discursive medium that extracts rules in the light of *Qur'anic* law through the *sunnah*. This is the stage of deriving rules from the monotheistic law of *Tawhid*. The institution engaging in such a derivation of rules from the *Tawhidi* law is called the *shura*. Its discursive pursuit is called *ijtihad*, meaning the deriving of rules from fundamental epistemic sources.

The second fundamental element of knowledge derivation through the discursive process in the *shura* discourse exercising *ijtihad* is called *tasbih* (60:24). *Tasbih* represents the worshipping nature of unification of knowledge and the functional ontological forms in the *Qur'anic* principle of 'pairing' (uniting by organic complementarities and agency participation) between variables, their relations and entities representing the issues and problems under investigation.

In this chapter we will combine this paired knowledge-forming process of the *Qur'an* and refer to it as *tasbih-shura* (*TS*). It marks the intrinsic experience of learning in unity of knowledge and the unified world system out of embedded consciousness in the order of things.

The Islamic phenomenology of unity of knowledge and its impact on the moral-social reconstruction of the unified world system is thus cast in the framework of a logical, consistent and *functionally* ontological (Gruber, 1993) model of being and becoming in reference to the axiomatic episteme of unity of knowledge (*Tawhid*).

All properties of the emergent learning process general system model built upon the phenomenological worldview form dynamics of synergistic relations, but not axioms. There is this minimal axiom to hold onto in the description of the unified mind-matter world system and its specifics as in the grand design of unification.

Meaning of knowledge in the context of *Tawhidi* phenomenology

We therefore inquire: What is the substantive meaning of knowledge in the context of such a phenomenological worldview? The meaning can be best unraveled by way of the *Tawhidi* functionalism in the *Qur'anic* phenomenological model. This is now explained by Figure 2.2. Throughout this chapter the bold symbols, such as **x**(.) denote vectors.

A review of the literature on the Islamic characterization of knowledge: the Islamicization of knowledge project

In the above schematic explanation of the idea of knowledge, I have left out the deeply mathematical details that embody the entire phenomenological model of unity of knowledge and the emergent unified world system and its specifics that arise in the study of mind-matter complementarities (unification). However, the learning processes depicted in Figures 2.1 and 2.2 present the author's formal characterization of the 'Islamicization of knowledge' project. To the author (1993), Islamicization means an evolutionary epistemological explanation of junctures of moral–social change wherein mind and matter (i.e. thoughts and events) interact to establish new epistemological socio-scientific realities in reference to the *Tawhidi* worldview. Islamicization is characterized by such immanent processes of learning in unity of knowledge. These are multiversal in nature (cybernetic systems), existing in knowledge, time and space dimensions. They sustain the emergent Islamicization of knowledge and education, knowledge and life, by the substantive *Tawhidi* evolutionary dynamics (Choudhury, 2011a).

The Islamicization of knowledge and education is an idea to which many have subscribed in the light of Islamic epistemology and human resource transformation. Such efforts have been less than effective in bequeathing any significant ideas of advancement to scholarship as it presently stands. The main failure of the Islamicization project has been the inability to understand the logical formalism and functioning of the *Tawhidi* worldview of *tasbih-shura (TS)* in the scheme and order of the worldly issues (specifics) and in the cosmological all (generality). This totality comprises the multiverse concept.

Instead, Islamicization has remained a nominally Islamic appendix rather than epistemologically original Islamic thought. Likewise, the Islamicization of education, which is a subset of the phenomenological knowledge domain in the entire socio-scientific thought, has produced non-substantive add-ons to mainstream books and the paraphernalia of education using an ostensibly Islamic garb.

However, those who aimed at an epistemological reconstruction of Islamic thought have dwelt only on the metaphysical aspects. This has yielded no fresh insight to the formalism of knowledge, thought, and designs of the world system in which the

--- Phenomenology of the learning world-system and specifics in unity of knowledge ----

The completeness→ ontological→ ontological→ functional→ Inductive→continuity
of knowledge as mapping of formulation: ontological evaluation
episteme of unity formal law (Ω) discursively formalism of deductive
of being and becoming into rules derived rules in deductive formalism
Tawhid as axiom S θ* reasoning for moral-social
treated mathematically leading to reconstruction
as super-cardinal abstraction $W(x(θ))$
topology (Rucker, 1983a) of reality in reference to
having relational property $\{θ,x(θ)\}$ inter-relations
but not measurability between$\{θ,x(θ)\}$
    Ω

-----(Ω,S): Fundamental ---- --- relativism---------- post-evaluation and
or Absolute Epistemology: Axiom in *functional* ontological of functional formal
    Formalism of rules and ideas ontological rules and
    relations: moral-social
    reconstruction of
    specific issues in the
    light of (Ω,S)

------------------------- Epistemic Knowledge ---------------- --- Evaluation and -----
    based on deductive continuity in learning
    reasoning leading to processes integrating
    formal ontological deductive and
    construction as inductive reasoning:
    abstraction of reality moral and social
    reconstruction

    evolutionary
    epistemology:
    knowledge,
    time, space
    intra-and inter-
    systemic
    continuum

----- axiomatic derivation and continuity of *Tasbih-Shura* ---- construction of the
    TS experience Islamic discursive society knowledge-induced
    world-system and its
    specifics -------------

Figure 2.2 The meaning of knowledge in the framework of *Tawhidi* phenomenology

fundamental episteme of unity of knowledge functions. In the end, the Islamic universities, Islamic institutions such as the Islamic Development Bank, the Islamic Research and Training Institute, and the many Islamic banks, together with scholarly pursuits in recent times, have simply impelled Muslims to return to the scientific crux of modernity. This is not equivalent to returning to the *Qur'an*.

One may refer here to the following glimpses in regard to the criticism: In his defense of the thoughts of Al-Attas, Daud establishes an utterly metaphysical learning concept (Daud, 1998a). There is a total absence of the formal and analytical dynamics of the epistemological worldview of *Tawhid* in the construction and working of the world system in light of the *Tawhidi* phenomenological methodology and worldview (Daud, 1998b). The same implications are found in Al-Attas's views on the contemporary education field with particular reference to Malaysia (Daud, 1998c).

Faruqi (1982a) failed in the same sort of project; his book *Tawhid* contained speculation rather than a substantive analysis of fundamental issues. Faruqi also promoted the Islamicization of mainstream textbooks in university educational programs (1982b).

Choudhury (2006) has pointed out that in the entire area of economic and social thought, contemporary Islamic scholars have failed to incorporate a substantive study of the *Tawhidi* methodological worldview in the form and functioning of epistemological analytics. In like mind, both Sardar (1984) and Rahman (1988) raise intellectual criticism against the idea of the Islamicization of knowledge and education. This has resulted in chatter in academic circles, but without making any significant contribution to the world of learning and academia on the new epistemological birth of knowledge in a socio-scientific scope. Without epistemology there can be no science. Science without epistemology is no more than a muddled form of thinking. This message was conveyed by Einstein to his colleague Neils Bohr (1985).

Imam Ghazali's phenomenology of knowledge

Figure 2.3 presents Imam Ghazali's phenomenology in regards to knowledge and education in Islam. Ghazali sheds importance on the micro-level moral, social and ethical values of individuals to form a good society, market, economic system, and institutional order, all through the application of Islamic law (*shari'ah*) as the best moral law. Still, the *methodology and dynamics* of the *Tawhidi* epistemological worldview were absent at this level. Ghazali's contribution, despite pointing out the importance of *Tawhid* and the *shari'ah* in human experiences, remained focused on *Tawhid* at the metaphysical levels.

We have argued in this chapter that the ontological argument dealing with the existence of being and becoming cannot be attributed to God *per se* in terms of a process model. God as *being* can at best be an axiom of assumed existence without the possibility of commensurateness in any shape, form, and representation. Hence it is impossible to assign process-driven attributes to God as being. In other words, there is no meaningful relationship between, say, the attribute of 'seeing' by God and the human act of seeing. Likewise, there is no such relationship between God as the Merciful and human beings as merciful. There is no relationship between the Absolute and Perfect knowledge of God and the created knowledge of the world and its human experience.

In the process model of *Tawhidi* dynamics, God enters the scene of action and responses in models of circular causation of unity of knowledge and worldly beings only by way of the divine law. It becomes concretized by the *sunnah* of the Prophet Muhammad and the discourses of the learned society. Consequently, the order of (Ω, S) (Figure 2.2) in the fundamental epistemology of the being of God is translated into the completeness and absoluteness of the divine law of monotheism that is relationally extracted by 'bits' through the medium of the *sunnah* and the discourse based on *TS* dynamics across continuums of evolutionary epistemology. This is the phenomenology of knowledge explained in Figures 2.1 and 2.2. Consequential models and inferences are thereby enabled in the process model of learning.

The same is not possible in the metaphysical construction of God's Purity as being in relation to the world system. Even the following two cases are impossible to interpret and use in the phenomenological process model of learning: (1) God is One. There cannot be any tenable interpretation of the invincible principle of monotheism by equating God to the number 'one'. God is One in terms of the absence of partnership with God in creation. This assumes the embodiment of the divine law in 'everything'. (2) 'Neither slumber nor sleep overtakes God.' This *Qur'anic* statement, too, is impossible to interpret in any *being*-state of God, except to invoke the being and becoming of creation as it unfolds by the embodiment of the divine law in it.

The same ontological problem is cast in the following argument: If we hold God as metaphysical ontology and take parts of this ontological God, then inevitably metaphysics drowns in the 'Trinity' or 'One-Many' question (Rucker, 1983b). The entire *Qur'anic* meaning of God is then negated.

Thus, only the divine law can be understood in 'bits', not God as a metaphysical being. God cannot be taken in 'bits'. The divine law of monotheism, when so enabled by its transmission into 'bits', becomes useable in the learning process, and the moral–social reconstruction of the world system and its specifics through the *functional* ontology of the *sunnah* and the discursive intervention of the learned society as pointed out in Figure 2.2.

The epistemological dynamics of *Tawhid* is now alive and creative in the learning world system, which is washed by the law of organic oneness (*Tawhid* = monotheism as unraveled and explained). The *Qur'an* establishes such an understanding of God and the world system explained by the monotheistic law of unity of knowledge, instead of submerging the mind in the impossibility of knowing the metaphysical ontology of God as One.

Therefore, when Imam Ghazali classifies knowledge into stages of its realization, he ascends from the heart and soul to the heights of unraveling the heart and mind to know the world. Ghazali's classification of knowledge is now explained in Figure 2.3. His phenomenological model is premised on a perfect nature of the knowledge model towards which the heart, soul, and self rise to attain certainty. Ghazali envisions unraveling seventy veils of knowledge while coming closest to God, the Certain One. The last of such stages is '*fana*'. This means 'self-annihilation in the presence of God as One'.

Ghazali explains the gaining of knowledge of *Tawhid* by unraveling the heart, soul and mind to the kernel of a coconut (Karim, n.d.). A man who simply hails God as the One (*Tawhid* in its initial expression) is a believer, yet one on the lowest rungs of the ladder of true belief. This represents the outer kernel of a coconut. In the second stage, the believer sees the inside of the coconut. This represents a growing consciousness towards comprehending *Tawhid*. The believer then continues on, seeing the oil of the coconut. This represents the movement towards purity. The journey continues across the seventy stages of evolutionary *Tawhid* knowledge.

In the delineation of knowledge formation, our *Tawhidi* epistemological model resembles that of Ghazali's. The substantive difference is that the origination and continuity of our *Tawhidi* worldview, through the passage of human imperfection

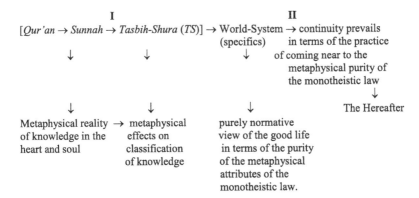

Similar, yet contrasting Tawhid knowledge-induced worldview (phenomenology) in the learning model:

Process 1	Evolutionary Processes

$[(\Omega,S) \rightarrow \theta^*] \rightarrow (\theta,x(\theta)) \rightarrow$ Simulate $W(x(\theta)) \rightarrow$ [Recall] $\rightarrow$ continue $\rightarrow$ The Hereafter
Subject to, interrelations   across $\equiv (\Omega,S)$
between the $(\theta,x(\theta))$-variables   systemic
with the estimated θ-variable   continuums
being a representation of wellbeing   (multiverse)
(see Figure 2.2)

Figure 2.3 Imam Ghazali's classification of knowledge
Legend to Figure 2.3: Ω denotes the completeness and absoluteness of the monotheistic law (*Tawhid*) as super-cardinal (non-commensurate, only relational) topology (Maddox, 1970). S denotes *sunnah* as *functional* ontological mapping carrying 'bits' of the monotheistic law as knowledge from Ω into learned discourse generating rule out of the law. This stage is denoted by θ^*. The total *Qur'anic* epistemology combines the fundamental part (Ω,S) and the discursive part θ^*. θ denotes 'bits' of knowledge-flows epistemologically derived from the part within [.]. The tuple $(\theta,x(\theta))$ denotes the knowledge-induced 'paired' variables, relations and entities of the world-systems (specific issues). The vector of variables $\{x(\theta)\}$ is brought into simulation by their 'paired' (complementary, symbiotic) interrelations in the wellbeing criterion, $W(.)$, in order to estimate the degree of unity of knowledge established by complementary interrelations between the variables and knowledge-flows in all. The moral-social reconstruction towards the *Tawhidi* worldview follows.

and incompleteness, does not allow for knowing the divine law of monotheism in its perfect form. Human knowledge in the learning-process phenomenology will simply simulate an idea of the embodiment of reality in *Tawhid*. The emergent mind-matter unification in the *Tawhidi* phenomenological model would then proceed to worldly application, and the empirical and inferential evolutionary designs of the moral–social reconstruction of the world system. Our *Tawhidi* epistemological model both explains and formalizes the two opposite phenomenological models: knowledge and 'de-knowledge'. In the end, a process model of simulated learning replaces the metaphysical conception of the perfect state. The latter is characterized by the *primus optimum* of Ghazali's idea of *fana*. Yet this sublimity is impossible in the worldly state due to human limitation.

Contrasting Ghazali's phenomenology and the *Tawhidi* evolutionary learning model of Islamicization of knowledge

Despite the striking epistemological similarities between Ghazali and our model, the two phenomenological perspectives lead to different mechanisms to explain the process of knowing existents. For Ghazali, this process is based on the five stages of knowing (Ismail, 2002, p. 21): "namely, the sensory, imaginative, intelligential, cogitative (or ratiocinative) and prophetic faculties." These are attributes of knowledge formation embodied in stage I within the bracketed term [.] in Figure 2.3. Yet the progress of knowledge from stage I to its impact on the design of stage II in Figure 2.3 is not within the domain of Ghazali's phenomenology. For instance, the interaction between the world system and its specific issues do not explain how new rounds of knowledge flows are regenerated once the fundamental epistemology impacts upon the continuity of the learning processes between knowledge derivation and the specifics of the world system.

Ghazali's phenomenological worldview explains the creation of knowledge in its original stages by the divine will. The divine will as law continues to be present in the world system. Our model shows that, knowledge flows and their impact on the states of the world system are always primordially created by recalling the fundamental epistemology of *Tawhid*. Yet, in the initiation of learning processes, the world system constantly produces fresh rounds of knowledge.

While Ghazali's phenomenology relies on deductive reasoning *per se*, our model has a unifying continuity between deductive and inductive reasoning, inasmuch as each learning process evolves from the previous one by recalling the fundamental epistemology of *Tawhid*. This, then, originates the next learning process between newly generated knowledge flows and the emergent states of the world system in specific issues and problems, in the continua of knowledge, space and time dimensions.

This difference between the two phenomenological models of knowledge-induced reality also results in another consequence. Ghazali's knowledge-world only relates to the human cogitation of knowing and its sensory attributes. Our knowledge model extends learning to *all* worlds – 'everything' (Barrow, 1992). Hence in our model, knowledge and its impact on the plethora of world systems are intra- and inter-systemic across interrelated multiverses. Consequently, the knowledge of *Tawhid* is embodied in 'everything'. It is of human pursuit to know and benefit from knowledge flows in epistemic unity to unravel the nature of unity (organic 'pairing') of details and generality in the world system. In our model, the *Tawhidi* worldview is axiomatically premised on organic relational unity between all good things of life, be these animate or inanimate. In our model, the fallen world that is not so unified due to its departure from knowledge induction is reconstructed towards unity of being and becoming.

Ghazali's model rising towards *fana* is an optimal model of knowledge-induced worldly impact. Our model, being a continuous-learning model, denies optimality. It replaces the impossibility of an optimal state by the objectivity of simulation across simulacra of possibilities resulting in moral–social reconstructions towards attaining *Tawhidi* unity of knowledge and life. Such is the perspective inherent in *tasbih-shura (TS)* evolutionary learning in unity of knowledge.

An interpretation of other classical and modern views on Islamicization of knowledge in the *Tawhidi* context of evolutionary learning worldview

The focus of this chapter is on understanding the concept of Islamicization of knowledge in terms of the dynamics of evolutionary learning premised on the epistemology of *Tawhid* and its unifying consequences in the world system. Thus, we will maintain this relevance when considering some salient features of Ibn Khaldun and Mawdudi and others' understanding of the Islamicization of knowledge.

Ibn Khaldun's *magnum opus*, the *Muqaddimah* (Mahdi, 1964) attempted to describe the rise and fall of civilization in terms of its rise from the rudimentary stages of *assabiyya* (community) to the evolution of *umran* (city state) and onwards to *hadara* (civilization). Yet the solidarity with community and religion fades along the path of this social transformation as politico-economic pressure to maintain an increasingly complex social order introduces conflicts between the urban and village organizations of the state – *assabiyya* and *umran*, respectively. In the end, the increasing politico-economic pressure of complexity spells out the decadence of the state, leading to the distressed state of civilization dynamics?

Ibn Khaldun limited his study of the historical process of social evolution to an observation of North Africa, so he did not provide a universal theory of social evolution and of historical change in his *Muqaddimah*. The consequence of this limited outlook resulted in the inability of *Muqaddimah* to explain the fall and the rise of a social order along the advancing path of its creative evolution. A revolutionary contribution made to this path of creative evolution is knowledge. Knowledge remains undiminished. In the evolutionary learning path of social change, its path is marked by incessant progress towards increasing levels of socio-scientific wellbeing. Thus, under the concrescent theory of knowledge, a decadent social order is capable of rising to its moral–social reconstruction. This cyclical nature of evolutionary learning was not explained either in *Muqaddimah* or in Ibn Khaldun's philosophy of history. Consequently, he could not explain the theme of Islamicization of knowledge in terms of its evolutionary dynamics.

Turning to recent times, Maulana Mawdudi's Islamic ideas contributed to the field of Islamicization of Knowledge. Yet, in line with the political and social outlook of the Jamaat i-Islamic, a political movement in Pakistan established by Maulana Mawdudi and his colleagues, the idea of originality in knowledge development based purely on the *Qur'an* remained paramount. Consequently, the nature and philosophy of knowledge and education in Occidentalism could not be the basis of Islamicization of knowledge. In its pure state, this idea this was an honest manifestation of the philosophy underlying the political movement. However, the problem with such an outlook lies in its inability to establish a universal theory of the Islamicization dynamics out of the *Qur'an* for the whole socio-scientific intellection process that would be equally acceptable to Muslims and others. Yet the *Qur'an* bestows such a worldview that remains universal, just as it is possible to unite the rationalist classical Islamic school (*mutakallimun*) and the epistemologists (*kalam*) in the unique *Tawhidi* mold of thought (Choudhury, 2006).

Sir Muhammad Iqbal (1934) was one such pioneer who molded the universal *Qur'anic* worldview into western thought and also invoked in it *Qur'anic* thought.

In his cosmopolitan thought, Iqbal upheld the potential of integrating some of the dialectical nature of historical change between the *Qur'an* and the western idea of historicism that became central in the explanation of social transformation in Hegel's philosophy of history. An important precept that Iqbal extracted from the *Qur'an* was creative re-origination (*khalq in-jadid*). He used it to integrate with the dialectical theory of social and historical change. This precept is a key note for deriving and establishing the *Qur'anic* precepts of pairing (organic unification) and creative re-origination in the evolutionary learning process that is causally related to the dynamics of Islamicization of knowledge.

Some knowledge-induced socio-scientific examples

1. Social justice in the wellbeing function (maslaha)

An example here of the social order examined in the light of our phenomenological model of unity of knowledge is the theory of justice and freedom that must govern social preference formation in an Islamic social contract. Imam Shatibi looked at this important topic in his theory of maslaha wal-istihsan (preference formation for the public purpose) (Shatibi trans. Draz, undated *Maslaha* revealed that the single most important function of the Islamic state was transforming and realizing social preference in accordance with the *maqasid as-shari'ah* (purpose and objective of the Islamic Law) pertaining to choices in economy, institutions, and society, and in the extensive domain socio-scientific study. The domain of socio-scientific study comprises the interplay of social and scientific issues and problems. All of these are analytically studied by the same theory. In our case, this is the theory of *Tawhidi* unity of knowledge as episteme and its organic unity of inter-variable relations in the world-system.

Social contractarianism in human ecology is an example of social justice in its wider context. It encompasses the extensive domain of interaction between human communities and ethics, environment and the global order (Hawley, 1986). Since such interactive preferences are the result of the formation of knowledge out of participation between institutions, markets, individuals, households, businesses, communities and the environment, the overarching epistemology of monotheism governs this kind of knowledge formation and its induced variables, entities, and relations. This creatively dynamic feature of the learning process methodology makes the resulting preferences dynamic. Such preferences form the extensive basis of Islamic social choice, and thus of the participatory worldview of *shura* institutions and *tasbih-shura* mind-matter praxis.

Such is the initiating premise of Islamic social contract in the theory of *maslaha* of Imam Shatibi (Choudhury, 1993; Masud, 1984). To Imam Shatibi, *ijtihad* and *ijma* were premised on the uniqueness of (Ω, S), but they evolved dynamically through (θ^*, θ) (see Figure 2.3). The learning process $(\Omega$ to $(\theta, x(\theta)))$ and onwards in sequences of evolutionary epistemology could not, therefore, have been static.

Syed Qutb's understanding of embodied knowledge in the cosmic order (Mousalli, 1990) is similar to our *tasbih-shura* dynamics of integrating the essence of knowledge between mind (*res cogitans*) and matter (*res extensa*). In other words, Syed Qutb explained that the systemic world of matter has knowledge in it as do human beings. But such knowledge appears as causation by interrelations in the presence of mind. Otherwise, knowledge remains innate and inactive in the world of matter. This chapter has explained that the irrevocable premise of knowledge derivation being the *Qur'an* and the *sunnah*, its universality stretches across the dimensions of knowledge, time and space. Hence, by the relational causality between *mind* and *matter* (i.e. *shura* and *tasbih*) knowledge is activated for the universal explanation of the scheme and order of things. Thereby, Islamicization of knowledge in its dynamic concept cannot be independently realized outside the bounds of the dynamic evolutionary learning episteme.

2. Understanding economic fundamentals in Tawhidi evolutionary epistemology

The economy as an *independent* domain of human needs, actions and responses in mainstream theory is replaced in the learning world system by the study of economic problems that can only be understood by interaction between a multitude of forces in the economy which is embedded in society, science, morality and ethics. Behavior is still the starting point of such an embedded economy as a social organism. Yet such behavior is manifest in the formation and aggregation of individual preferences interacting with institutional, government and social domains. Such aggregations, at any level, cannot be linear. On the contrary, complex preferences are formed by the impact of dynamic forces that enter the learning processes at every stage of social embedding.

Markets as ethical venues for realizing preferences that form consumer and market demand and production menus that form supply, are not *wertfrei* systems of exchange of goods at revealed prices. Thereby, demand and supply are concepts that exist in mainstream economics only in the absence of the nexus of interactive dynamics causing embedding to occur and continuously change in the embedded social magna. These dynamic elements are essential in the knowledge-induced conception of market exchange, preference formations, and their aggregation.

3. The socio-scientific multiverse design in the knowledge-induced entirety

Interesting similarities also arise (albeit with substantively different meanings and interpretations) from specific socio-scientific phenomena. One of these is the nature of scientific inquiry. The outwardly but not with substantive similarity in this area is Hawking's characterization of scientific theory. Hawking (1988, pp. 10–11) writes: "The eventual goal of science is to provide a single theory that describes the whole universe. However, the approach most scientists actually follow is to separate the problem into two parts. First, there are the laws that will tell us how the universe changes with time … Second, there is the question of the initial state of the universe. Some people feel that science should be concerned with only the first part; they regard the question of the initial situation as a matter for metaphysics or religion. They would say that God, being omnipotent, could have started the universe off any way he wanted. That may be so, but in that case he also could have made it develop in a completely arbitrary way. Yet it appears that he chose to make it evolve in a very regular way according to certain laws. It therefore seems equally reasonable to suppose that there are also laws governing the initial state."

Socio-scientific reasoning in the *Tawhidi* worldview starts by the sole axiom of the oneness of the divine law and its purposeful, explainable, and applicative consequences in the world-system taken up in both specifics and generality. Thus the substantive meaning of organic unity of the world system explained by the initial state of fundamental unity is by the oneness of the divine law and its functional ontology across multiverses of relational world-systems. Hawking's initial condition and law are essentially and infallibly premised on the oneness of the divine law and its organic moral–social reconstruction of science and society combined interactively. Thus, the emanating knowledge-flow is primal in the *Tawhidi* characterization of all phenomena – 'everything' (Barrow, 1992).

The universe of (Ω,S) is thereby premised on the knowledge (θ)-time $(t(\theta))$-space $(x(\theta))$ dimensions, $\theta \in (\Omega,S)$ (see Figure 2.3). Thus $(\theta,x(\theta),t(\theta))$ denotes an 'event' in such a learning through complex multiverse. Such a characterization is unlike Hawking's and the entire scientific view that projects the universe as being premised in space–time structure. The moral and ethical social construction of the socio-scientific order in the learning multiverse comprises a vast interacting, integrating and evolving world-system spanning science and society.

We would then answer the question: 'How did we get here at a stately point of time in our existence?' *Tawhidi* worldview answers this question by fundamental reference to its epistemic axiom first. It then analyzes, proves and explains the geometrical coordinate of existence in reference to a plethora of learning processes. Some of these have passed through learning possibilities experiencing inter-systemic oneness inter-generationally. We have, thereby, learning histories that brought us here. The mind is invoked to comprehend, observe and reflect on *Tawhid* in such 'paired' universes.

Hawking and Mlodinow (2010, p. 80) write about similar learning (probabilistic general system) histories: "…for a general system, the probability of any observation is constructed from all the possible histories that could have led to that observation. Because of that (t)his method is called the 'sum over histories' or alternative histories' formulation of quantum physics." Yet for this profound assertion of Feynman's description of the probabilistic learning universe (Choudhury, 2011b), there cannot be linear aggregation of histories in the learning multiverse. Instead, there are complex, interrelating and evolving learning geodesics (Kupka and Peixoto, 1993). These exist as subspaces of the multiverse manifold and share the same universal and unique law of organic unity of being and becoming.[1]

How could the *Tawhidi* worldview in knowledge and education be a universal paradigm?

The model of the *Tawhidi* worldview presented in the chapter and explained by Figures 2.1 and 2.2 offers a universal approach to address the theory of 'everything' (Barrow, 1992). The proof of this claim lies in a mathematical way of applying the *Qur'anic* verse: "To Him belongs the End and the Beginning" (*Qur'an*, 92:13). The proof is summarized here, but its detailed coverage lies beyond the scope of this chapter. One may refer to Choudhury (2014) for a detailed discussion on the basis of the universal theory of historicism in the *Qur'an*.

The conceptualization of the *Tawhidi* evolutionary learning methodology in this chapter translates to the following string relation:

$(\Omega,S) \rightarrow$ World-System spanned by the multiverse complexity,$\{f(\theta,\mathbf{x}(\theta))\} \rightarrow (\Omega,S)$
(Ω,S) denotes the *Qur'an* and the transmitter, *sunnah* denoted by S. That is $\Omega\rightarrow_S$

This mapping, being epistemological in nature, is claimed to be the fullness of knowledge. Hence $\Omega\rightarrow_S$ is characterized by the properties of super-cardinality (Rucker, 1983a) by its ultimate exogenous influence on the world-system.

Let $L \in (\Omega,S)$ as a derived *law* of unity from the epistemic origin belong to (Ω,S). Thereby $F(L) \rightarrow$ a complex relational form, $f(\theta,\mathbf{x}(\theta))$.

Furthermore, the existence and definition of $f(\theta,\mathbf{x}(\theta))$ is established by the compactness of the very large-scale continuous multiverse across continuums of $f(\theta,\mathbf{x}(\theta))$ both intra- and inter-systems. This is the consequence of the open-ended mapping of an open topology into itself in evolutionary neighborhoods (Choudhury, 2011) and is an extension of Brouwer and Kakutani's Fixed Point Theorem (Kakutani, 1941).

Hence, the generality of spanning world systems by the extension of the law $\{L\}\in(\Omega,S)$, establishes the proof of the universality of the *Tawhidi* law in 'everything' as represented by $(\Omega,S) \rightarrow$ World System spanned by the multiverse complexity,$\{f(\theta,\mathbf{x}(\theta))\}$ $\rightarrow (\Omega,S)$. Footnote 1 further expands the nature of this spanning *Tawhidi* multiverse in the language of tensors. However, the treatment can be applied to many issues and problems of socio-scientific experience. The universal domain is thus mathematically characterized by the evolutionary concept of Islamicization of knowledge in terms of its permanent dynamics, rather than in terms of narrowly defined territories.

Conclusion

This chapter has presented knowledge as an epistemological category wherein 'everything' self-actualizes in *Tawhid*, the monotheistic law of unity of knowledge in relation to the world system and its end-event, the Great Event of the Hereafter (*Qur'an*, 78:1–5). This is the perpetual evolutionary learning history of the relationship between mind and matter: the *tasbih-shura* process. The chapter has interconnected the arch between knowledge, education, and the world system (with its specifics and generality of issues) by using the premise of the epistemology of oneness. The emergent episteme and phenomenological model of unity of knowledge and of the unified world system is found to have its holism in the *Qur'an* according to the Islamic worldview of monotheistic oneness. We called this phenomenological model of unity of knowledge and its induction of the unified world system as comprising the socio-scientific consciousness of the *Tawhidi* worldview.

The chapter has formalized this *Tawhidi* phenomenological model without mathematical details. It discussed the *Tawhidi* worldview, its selected application in the real world, and compared and contrasted it with several other scholarships in Islamic epistemology. The most important of these cases were the phenomenology of Imam Ghazali and of Islamicization of knowledge in contemporary times. The salient features of the *Tawhidi* Scientific Research Program have been introduced to reflect and build upon.

Note

1 Such a general system of multilinear relationships of evolutionary nonlinear functionals can be represented as a tensor functional (Gel'fand & Shenitzer, 1961). The following is the way to write tensor functionals: $(\mathbf{x(\theta)}, \mathbf{f(x(\theta))}; \mathbf{(Fof)(x(\theta))}) = a_{ij}{}^k.\xi^i\eta^j\zeta_k$, where, $\mathbf{x(\theta)} = \xi^i.e_i$; $\mathbf{f(x(\theta))} = \eta^j.e_j$; $\mathbf{(Fof)(x(\theta))} = \zeta_k.e^k$. $(e_i; e_j)$ are the contravariant basis vectors of region R. e^k are the covariant basis vectors of $\mathbf{(Fof)(x(\theta))}$ in region R^, which is the dual of covariant vector space of region R, meaning the functionals that are linearly additive of nonlinear functionals in R.

References

Abu Hamid M. (Imam) Ghazali (1966). *The Book of Knowledge*, trans. by N.A. Faris, Shah Muhammad Ashraf, Lahore, Pakistan.

Al-Faruqi, I.R. (1982a). *Tawhid: Its Implications for Thought and Life*, International Institute of Islamic Thought, Herndon, VA.

Al-Faruqi, I.R. (1982b). *Islamicization of Knowledge: General Principles and Workplan*, The International Institute of Islamic Thought, Herndon, VA.

Barrow, J.D. (1992). *Theories of Everything, the Quest for Ultimate Explanation*, Oxford University Press, Oxford, UK.

Bohr, N. (1985). "Discussions with Einstein on epistemological issues", in H. Folse, *The Philosophy of Niels Bohr: The Framework of Complementarity*, North Holland Physics Publishing, Amsterdam, the Netherlands.

Choudhury, M.A. (1993). *The Unicity Precept and the Socio-Scientific Order*, University Press of America, Lanham, MD.

Choudhury, M.A. (2006). "Development of Islamic Economic and Social Thought", in M. Kabir Hassan and Mervin Lewis (eds), *Handbook of Islamic Banking*, Edward Elgar Publishing, London, UK.

Choudhury, M.A. (2011a). "Knowledge and life: comparative Islamic development perspectives", *International Journal of Education, Education and Development*, 2:1, 1–17.

Choudhury, M.A. (2011b). "A probabilistic model of learning fields", *The Journal of Muamalat and Islamic Finance Research*, 7:1.

Choudhury, M.A. (2014). *Tawhidi Epistemology and Its Applications (Economics, Finance, Science, and Society)*, Cambridge Scholars' Publishing, Cambridge, UK.

Daud, W.M.N.W (1998a). "Metaphysical worldview", in his *The Educational Philosophy and Practice of Syed Muhammad Naquib Al-Attas, an Exposition of the Original Concept of Islamicization*, International Institute of Islamic Thought and Civilization, pp. 33–68, Kuala Lumpur, Malaysia.

Daud, W.M.N.W (1998b). "On knowledge and knowing", in his *The Educational Philosophy and Practice of Syed Muhammad Naquib Al-Attas, an Exposition of the Original Concept of Islamicization*, International Institute of Islamic Thought and Civilization, pp. 69–120, Kuala Lumpur, Malaysia.

Daud, W.M.N.W (1998c). "Islamicization of contemporary knowledge: theoretical dimensions and practical contributions", in his *The Educational Philosophy and Practice of Syed Muhammad Naquib Al-Attas, an Exposition of the Original Concept of Islamicization*, International Institute of Islamic Thought and Civilization, pp. 291–370, Kuala Lumpur, Malaysia.

Foucault, M. trans. A.M. Sheridan (1972). *The Archeology of Knowledge and the Discourse on Language*, New York, Harper Torchbooks.

Gel'fand, I.M. and Shenitzer, A. (1961). "Introduction to tensors", in their *Lectures on Linear Algebra*, Interscience Publishers, Inc. pp. 164–85, New York, NY.

Gruber, T.R. (1993). "A translation approach to portable ontologies", *Knowledge Acquisition*, 5:2, 199–200.

Hawking, S.W. (1988). *A Brief History of Time, From the Big Bang to Black Holes*, Bantam Books, Inc., New York.

Hawking, S.W. and Mlodinow, L. (2010). *The Grand Design*, Transworld Publishers, London, UK.

Hawley, A.H. (1986). *Human Ecology*, The University of Chicago Press, Chicago, IL.

Heidegger, M. trans. Hofstadter, A. (1988). "The thesis of modern ontology: the basic ways of being are the being of nature (res extensa) and the being of mind (res cogitans)", in *The Basic Problems of Phenomenology*, Indiana University Press, pp. 122–224, Bloomington and Indianapolis, IN.

Iqbal, M. (1934). *The Reconstruction of Religious Thought in Islam*, Oxford University Press, Oxford, UK.

Kakutani, S. (1941). "A generalization of Bouwer's fixed point theorem", *Duke Mathematical Journal*, 8:3, 457–59.

Karim, F. (n.d.). *Imam Ghazali's Ihya Ulum-Id-Din*, Shah Muhammad Ashraf, Lahore, Pakistan.

Khaldun, Ibn. trans. F. Rozenthal (1958). *Muqaddimah, an Introduction to History*, in 3 volumes, Routledge and Kegan Paul, London, UK.

Kupka, I.A.K. and Peixoto, M.M. (1993). "On the enumerative geometry of geodesics", in Hirsch, M.W. Marsden, J.E. Shub, M. (eds.), *From Topology to Computation: Proceedings of the Smalefest*, Springer-Verlag, pp. 243–53, New York, NY.

Maddox, I.J. (1970), *Elements of Functional Analysis*, Cambridge University Press, Cambridge, UK.

Mahdi, M. (1964). *Ibn Khaldun's Philosophy of History*, University of Chicago Press, Chicago, IL.

Masud, M.K. (1994). *Shatibi's Theory of Meaning*, Islamic Research Institute, International Islamic University, Islamabad, Pakistan.

Mousalli, A. (1990). "Sayyid Qutb's view of knowledge", *American Journal of Islamic Social Sciences*, 7:3, 315–35.

Rahman, R. (1988). "Islamicization of knowledge: a response", *American Journal of Islamic Social Sciences*, 5:1, 3–11.

Rucker, R. (1983a). "Large cardinalities", *Infinity and the Mind, the Science and Philosophy of the Infinite*, Bantam Books, New York, NY.

Rucker, R. (1983b). "The one and the many", in his *Infinity and the Mind, the Science and Philosophy of the Infinite*, Chapter 5, Bantam Books, New York, NY.

Sardar, Z. (1984). "Islamisation of knowledge, or the westernisation of Islam?" *Inquiry*, 1:7.

[Imam] Shatibi, trans. Abdallah Draz. (n.d.), *Al-Muwafaqat Fi-Usul Al-Shari'ah*, Al-Maktabah Al-Tijariyah Al-Kubra, Cairo, Egypt.

Chapter 3

Religion and Social Economics[1]

Abstract

A methodological study of religion including moral, ethical, social values, and economics takes us into the search, discovery, and establishment of a formal epistemological premise. Social economics is now studied as a methodological investigation of evolutionary and embedded systems integrating the moral, social, and economic systems. Thus, an integrated theory of religion representing the realm of moral and social values and economics is formalized. We write on the conjoint methodological perspective of the integrated domain of religion and economics. A formal ontology of the unified field of religion and economics is established in such an inter-causal and organically unified realm of moral, social, and economic values. A phenomenological model of the unified worldview that applies to a systemic concept of 'everything' emerges. This methodology and the immanent phenomenological model relating to it convey the principle of inter-systemic organic symbiosis by a unique and universal worldview. The systemic integration between religion and economics is formally studied within the immanent system-methodology that formalizes multidisciplinary symbiosis.

Introduction

For some time now, papers published in social economics have enriched a spectrum of intellectual diversity in heterodox economic thought. The history of economic thought including in it the social and moral elements of eminent contributions is a candidate in this intellectual diversity (ex. Doeringer, 1985). Other fields comprised social areas of economics, such as education, health, and philanthropy. There were also significant contributions on the development of catholicity in human wellbeing (McKee, 1992; especial issues of RSE, 1991). Other papers have examined methodological questions on new horizons of thought in economic theorizing, which have spanned the model of the embedding of economic and social disciplines (Etzioni, 1987). The field of inquiry in social economics has not ceased to expand in such diversity of scope.

Emulating the nature of this diverse spectrum of social economics, the present chapter aims to set up an intellectual discourse in the methodology of economic and social embedding with moral overtones. The argument is made that in the development of the social economic worldview and its meaning, none of these fields, and the wider diversity, remain independent of each other. One discipline without the other does not serve the holistic concept of wellbeing of individuals and communities; nations; and the global order. Therefore, a fresh methodology is needed to lay down a universal conception of wellbeing that can be embedded in complementary relations between critical inter-disciplinary domains. This chapter explores the novelty. A few examples of such socio-scientific thought are provided with a critical view.

Social economics defined

In general, therefore, the methodological orientation leading to a methodical derivation of formalism in the above-mentioned conception of social economics is examined. The emergent general theory of social economy as established by the moral, ethical, and social embedding of economics and vice versa in such an inter-disciplinary approach leads to particular examples. Thus, generality of methodology yields particulars of methodical treatment. Such a focus being our goal of study, the meaning of social economics and its intellection is examined in terms of the organic unity of knowledge that epistemologically establishes the unified field of economic and social embedding with the overarching moral worldview. The emergent theory and formalism then enables the organic study of such embedded complementarities between the variables and characteristics of the embedded domains.

In this introductory section, the learned words of Professor A.N. Whitehead (1979, p. 48) on the concepts of the general as universal and the particular as the partially derived case are recalled: "The notion of a universal is of that which can enter into the description of many particulars; whereas the notion of a particular is that it is described by universals, and does not itself enter into the description of any other particular."

The research question

We have the tripartite domains to study in their interactive, integrative, and evolutionary dynamics: economics, society, and the moral function within these. Epistemologically speaking, therefore, this chapter will develop the basis of unity of knowledge that can organically serve the embedding function of economics, society, and moral values as an interrelated complex. While the concept of moral values can be a rationalistic derivation (Kant, trans. Friedrich, 1949), it can also be derived from the origin of Religion (moral, ethical, and social values). The contrast between these two variants is brought out by the possibility of organic unity between diversity.

So, if we claim that social economics is characterized by the complementary functioning between social values (e.g. a just society), and economic growth (e.g. economic goals), then rationalism, which reflects on economic rationality, cannot answer the complementarity between the moral, social, and economic goals comprising an embedded holism. Such is the perennial property of all kinds of rational choices and human behavior, utilitarianism, preference preordering, and tradeoff as assumed by neoclassical economics. Indeed, the property of rational choice underlies all of mainstream economics (Dasgupta, 1987). The theory of social economics in its quest for the methodology of pervasive complementarities between choices, rather than remaining locked in marginal rates of substitution between competing ends, is disabled in mainstream economics. The result has thus been a differentiated and incomplete total wellbeing. Wellbeing here means the degree of organically unified complementary relations between economics, society, and moral values in respect of their symbiotic embedding. This is an inter-causal relational idea. It is foreign to all mainstream economic theory and social Darwinism.

In our definition of methodological social economics, the emergent field of holistic scholarly understanding leads to the formalism of an embedded field of inquiry. The resulting formalism assumes an epistemological meaning of its derivation from the generalized methodology of unity of knowledge. As a generalized methodology conveying unity of knowledge, holistic embedding, and inter-causal relations, it invokes the concept of universality (Barrow, 1991) emulating the idea conveyed by Whitehead.

Over time, the parting knell of moral values from its functional embedding between society and economics can thus be expressed in the quote: "Give unto Caesar what is Caesar's (materiality); and unto God what is God's (spirituality)" (Lewis, 2010). The existing *wertfrei* methodology in the study of moral values, society, and economics fails to establish an integrated worldview that otherwise is central in the methodological understanding of unity between embedded diversity (Holton, 1992).

We, therefore, note that the definition of social economics, which we have adopted, achieves several interrelated tasks. First, there is first the episteme of organic unity of knowledge as the basis for explaining the holistic inter-causal relational embedding between economy, society, and moral values for the objective of attaining wellbeing as a global participatory functioning of pervasively complementary inter-causal variables. Second, there is then the deeper question of formalizing a methodology and its derived methodical formalism to explain the relational inter-causality between diverse domains and their representative variables. These are all creatively complemented by the epistemic foundation of unity of knowledge functioning in systemic totality. Third, there is the application and social economic restructuring that arises from the methodology and methodical formalism. These are deeply analytical issues that will be discussed in this chapter.

Objective

The objective of this chapter is to break out of the exclusiveness between economic, social, and moral domains and formalize a methodology that unifies the disciplines into a social economy as we have defined it. Emulating Foucault, we refer to this totality of the overarching methodology as episteme.[2] Ours is the search for the episteme of unity of knowledge between inter-disciplinary socio-economic systems. The methodology that we will formalize will be based on the organic complementarities between the emergent knowledge-induced inter-disciplinary fields.[3]

The research problem of this chapter is that socio-scientific reality as the domain of total human experience is not a collection of its dissociated parts. Thus, taken separately, the social, economic, and moral domains cannot answer the total objective of wellbeing as the measure of the degree of organic unity between the inter-disciplinary domains. The intent of this chapter is to build up an appropriate integrative methodology.

Definition of wellbeing

In the development of the social economic methodology we will use the oft-repeated term, 'wellbeing'. This conveys the meaning of the relational organism of unity of knowledge in the system of inter-variable causality. The methodological concept of social wellbeing is quite different from that of social welfare, either in neoclassical economics or the welfare state (Anderson, 1984). The methodical formal model that emerges from the general methodology is shown to be rigorously analytical and applied in nature. An organic relational approach as the expression of the episteme of unity of knowledge is thereby possible between the embedded domains (Choudhury, 2011).

Review of the literature

Our review of the literature will cover those intellectual aspects that might address our search for integration between the disciplines towards explaining a holistic formal methodology. See Appendix for a non-parametric representation of methodological unity between the disciplines as interactive, integrative, and creatively evolutionary systems.

Looking at the classical axiomatic nature of economics, Nelson (2001) uses the economic postulates of rationality, efficiency, investment and growth under certainty as the conditions for attaining a well-functioning, perfectly competitive, economy which reduces transaction cost. The argument made is that, if individuals were religiously (morally) honest in their behaviour, the result would be minimum transaction cost. This would lead to the attainment of the postulates of a perfectly competitive market economy. Consequently, the objectives of both utility and profit maximization yielding normal profits with efficient production at the minimum levels of average cost of production would all be morally conscious behavior in economic dealings by the perfectly rational individual.

Based on such implications, the new institutionalists inferred (Nelson, 2001, pp. 208–09) "an awkward compromise rejecting neoclassical assumptions but employing the same analytical formalism long favored by the neoclassicals". In reference to the neoclassical economic methods, the argument is further made that, if religious (moral) values induce a lower average cost of producing cultural, social and ethical capital than physical capital, at least of some sort, then the economic choice for moral values (e.g. represented by social capital) would result in efficient capital investment and growth. By using traditional neoclassical economic assumptions operating on the moral sphere of utilitarian behavior and production and costs, the economists subsume the study of moral values as social capital within a classical and neoclassical economic explanation. The end result is the study of moral values as social capital *by* economic theory.

In this kind of model there is no such moral and social theory that would simultaneously apply to economic reasoning. An embedding is thus not possible by a unique methodology that commonly belongs to economic, social, and moral reasoning. A *wertfrei* treatment of socio-scientific reasoning has caused the widest possible difference between moral, social, and economic values in terms of methodology, analytical methods, perspectives, objectives, and applications. On the contrary, if moral and social values could transcend into a holistic endeavor with economic ends, and not be limited to individual wellbeing, then the resulting inter-system embedding methodology would extend the individual to the social totality with a subtle socio-economic aggregation.

Zweig (1991) attributes such a task of social aggregation of the individual preferences within the social whole to theology. He thus considers the social premise as the extension of religious values to society at large. Zweig writes (pp. 3–49): "It is theology that seeks to address and change social institutions, not just individuals. It is therefore theology that extends the bounds of traditional religious discourse to dialogue with social science, to better understand society and the role of religion in it."

Using the theological approach, religion introduces the theme of aggregation and extension of individual preferences, beliefs, behaviors, and choices to the social level. However, economics of social choice has not finalized the theory of social aggregation of this kind. The lateral aggregation of individual preferences to form social preference is a utilitarian mistake (Hammond, 1989). Social preference is greater in valuation measure than the lateral aggregation of its individual preferences.

Even in the case of Arrow's (1951) postulation of social choice theory, aggregation is not possible without the presence of a dictator to announce the end of the choice game (Wolff, 1977). The presence of a dictator is realized by introducing the postulate of irrelevant preferences. The presence of a dictator to announce the end of a social choice game, and the postulate of irrelevant preferences, are conjointly needed to affect the formulation and maximization of the social welfare function.

Now, between economics and the social order there is no socially acceptable method to realize perfect participation among all decision-makers, as individuals, to solve the aggregation problem as an equitable participatory social game. Consensus in the social choice game is enforced, not self-governed, by consciousness, to which moral and social values emanating from religion would otherwise aspire.

The fact of the matter is that neither the postulates of economic theory works by its utilitarian methodology of aggregation nor can the social order adhere to the traditional economic postulates. The postulates of economic rationality, efficiency, optimization of resource allocation and maximization of objective functions – as in the case of welfare maximization, utility maximization, profit-maximization, and minimization of transaction costs – are irrelevant methods for endogenously embedding moral, social and economic values in a holistic totality.

Thus, an altogether new ontological approach is now needed to fuse the formal domains of economics and moral and social values. Nelson (2001, p. 229) writes on this issue: "In short, economists would not have much to lose in turning back in their methods of inquiry to the approaches of the old historical and institutional school. They may think they would be losing their scientific value, but it would be more correct to say that they would be abandoning their scientific hypocrisy."

The erecting of a new, but heterodox, approach to ontological economic reasoning is today gaining ground. Such an approach will likely frame the next theory of social economics as we have defined it. Lawson (1977, pp. 238–46) writes in regard to the ontological perspective of heterodox economics towards embedding society and economics by this imminently new emergent methodology: "A commitment to (ontological) realism combined with epistemological relativism sustains a judgmental rationality, and from this perspective the practice of contemporary economic modeling are found to be wanting."

The methodology and methodical formalism to study the endogenous inter-relational between economics and moral and social values

The discovery of the hitherto-evaded methodology of the ontological economic and social problem of organic inter-relationship requires the identification of the universal core that uniquely establishes unity of knowledge between interacting, integrating, and creatively evolutionary (IIE) learning systems. Economic, moral and social values are particular examples of such IIE-systems. The epistemic core of unity of knowledge that induces all complementing systems by evolutionary learning in their embedding experience can come either from the roots of rationalism or religion (as monotheism), but with opposite consequences.

The question is this: Which of these two premises yields the unique methodology of unity of knowledge that the other one cannot offer?

First, it must be recognized that a new ontological social and economic premise of reasoning for the sake of actualizing inter-systemic embedding is required. Second, there is a need to identify the *most* irreducible premise from where the unity of knowledge as the ontological methodology arises. Does rationalism or religion define the moral foundation that integrates the economy, and the moral and social domains as an inseparable causal whole?[4]

Once again, the words of Lawson (1997, pp. 62–65) as a pioneer on ontological economics in the University of Cambridge Ontological Economic Project resounds on this theme: "… The conception which we must embrace is of a world that is completely structured, open, intrinsically dynamic, characterized by emergence and so novelty, and inclusive of totalities and causally efficacious absences, amongst other things. And we can immediately see just how shallow in compromise is the ontology presupposed by the scientific ideal which informs the project of economic ontology."

The method of circular causation

To meet the ends of the methodology of the ontological economic school in heterodox economic reasoning of social economics, as we have defined this field, the derived method of circular causation proves to be a powerful formalism. By this method it becomes possible to test, assert or correct for the presence or lack of complementarities between the variables. Such inter-variable complementarities reflect their organic unity of knowledge.

In economics, the circular causation method was used by Myrdal (1958). However, the method has not become popular in economics overall (Toner, 1999). Economics does not treat pervasively endogenous relations (i.e. continuously evolutionary learning *processes*) between the selected variables of the wellbeing function as the objective criterion. In mainstream economic and social theory, there are always externally induced and exogenous policy variables in economic models. In the religious, sociological, philosophical, and scientific literature we also find the circular causation method. It exists in the concept of simulacra – continuous simulation over simulation (Fitzpatrick, 2003; Hawking and Mlodinow, 2010).

The idea of circular causation has also been used in theological thought. Thomas Aquinas placed the whole universal design on God from the beginning to the end. He then construed the working of the universe in 'everything' according to this feature of ontology and being. The entire *Summa Theologia* expounds this divine design of creation. While God lies in a process of creation, He exists as the sole and exogenous creator of 'everything'. The divine law is thereby a super-space; denote it by Ω. Yet there is no functional ontology, which we denote by 'S', to carry the primal knowledge of unity (metaphysical ontology) onto the functioning world system. The divine law then remains dysfunctional in the affairs of the world system.

Thomas Aquinas' idea of circular causation in *Summa* is explained by Torrell (2005, pp. 27–36): "The work (*Summa*) is in fact constructed according to a circular plan that draws the reader into the 'going-out-from-returning-to' (*exitus-reditus*) movement, which is that of the entire universe coming from God to creation and returning to him as its final end."

Rationalism or religion (the moral domain) in the social economics of moral integration?

Reasoning by rationalism

The phenomenology of Rationalism (R) is defined by the correspondence, $\theta(R) \rightarrow \theta(R)$. $\theta(R)$ is reasoning derived from the rationalist roots in continuity across continuums. Rationalism thus continues on its speculative process *ad infinitum*. Consequently, the constructed world system remains premised on R permanently. Yet the nature of rationalism is randomly differentiated by concepts and meanings.[5]

Such a perception of continuity in rationalist correspondence is found in the writing of Lonergan (see Hosinski, 1987, pp. 63–78): "Lonergan draws his notion of 'finality' in the dynamic structure of becoming from the correspondences to the notion of being as the unifying drive in knowing. Just as the notion of being drives and unifies the process of knowing, so does finality drive and unify becoming." One can note the similarity of the circular causation relationship in the phenomenological process with the mechanism construed by Lonergan (eds Byrne and Heflong, 2001) though in terms of rationalism.

Yet despite the similarity indicated above, Lonergan placed the study of God *within a process* (Vertin, 1987). In doing so, rationalism once again supplants the divine origin of knowledge and law affecting the world-system in the phenomenological model. Kant's heteronomy is brought back into the picture of phenomenology. Thereby, a rationalist conception of truth and goodness replaces the divine text (Lonergan ed. McShane, 1908).

Instead, in the case of the ontological origin of unity of knowledge by the divine text, the moral law is mapped onto the world system through the *functional* ontological mapping 'S' along with the participation of a discursive community.

Lonergan's kind of reversion of thought is always into rationalism in every case that we have noted. These are, namely, an economic approach to religion; or rationalist speculation of the ontological problem of religion in embracing the economic problem. The gap in integration between religion (moral and social values) and economics is caused by the absence of the worldly element of the religious law in deriving rules in cogent ways and by structured methodology and a moral and social approach, yet not leaving the essential province of the epistemological root of unity of knowledge.

Reasoning by the religious law (monotheism)

Contrary to rationalism, the monotheistic law is not a sheer statement of random values. It is not premised on unity of knowledge as episteme. Instead, this episteme carries with it precise *rules* for enacting the general *law*. In a sense, the need for rules derived from the general law enters the generalized phenomenological model. The resulting unity between deductive and inductive reasoning prevails in continuous, mutually reinforcing rounds of inter-causality. On such an idea of critical realism Lawson (2003, p. 177) writes: "In critical realism arguments are made, for example, for supposing that social reality is an emergent realm that is structured, open, differentiated, dynamic and constituted to a significant degree by internally related totalities."

The phenomenological model premised on religion (moral and social values) (RL) is now written as, $\Omega \to_{RL} \theta(RL)$. In this case, Ω acts as the ultimate reducible premise of the episteme of unity of knowledge. Consequently, between rationalism (R) and religion (RL) we write,

$$\Omega \to_{RL} \theta(RL) \} \text{ or } \begin{array}{l} \to_{RL} \theta(RL) \text{ (continuity)} \\ \\ \to_{R} \theta(R) \text{ (degenerate)} \end{array} \qquad (3.1)$$

Expression (3.1) implies that the assumption of the ultimate, irreducible creative power of Ω is pervasively determinate over both religion (monotheism) and rationalism.

However, it is not possible to have correspondences like the following: $\theta(R) \to \theta(RL) \to \Omega$; $\theta(RL) \to \theta(R) \to \Omega$. This impossibility explains the fact that, there is no uniqueness of any kind of reasoning from the domain of rationalism into the uniqueness of the monotheistic law. Consequently, emanating from the episteme of rationalism there is always the possibility of falsification and refutation of all kinds of reasoning (Popper, 1998, 2004). Thus, there is no exact meaning of moral and social values that otherwise can embed with economics, and likewise with all other systems. The self-referencing theorem does not exist in the case of the rationalist mappings (Godel, 1965). However, it does so in the case of the religious (moral) law mapping into itself after it has mapped across sequences of the religious law (monotheism).

Morality, ethics, society, and economics

Recently, the search for a theory of an endogenous relationship between ethics and economics has drawn much interest in the economic literature (Sen, 1992). Endogeneity here means the organic inter-relationships by inter-causality that enables inter-disciplinary embedding to be realized in argumentative, analytical, and inferential ways. From our study of the Kantian type of heteronomy, according to the rationalist foundation of the moral law, it becomes evident that the endogenous integration of the moral law, and thereby, of integrating the moral, social and economic domains, *vis-à-vis* religion (moral law and social values) and economics, becomes impossible. Consequently, ethics derived from the rationalist domain of humanism does not have a universal principle of permanence. Rationalist moral and ethical understanding remains forever random and unsettled. This different from moral and ethical laws that are derived from the exact foundational premise of religious ontology (monotheism). We have examined this issue in the previous section.

Smart (2000, pp. 114–16) writes on the Kantian understanding of autonomy or independence of morals that transcend direct religious vision. Kantian categorical imperative "implies that we can by reason establish what is right and wrong; morality does not have any external source, not even God. It derives, as [I have] said, from each person as his or her own moral legislator."

This implication of Kant's categorical imperative drifting to the domain of practical reason (a posteriori) solely, apart from the functionalism of God (a priori reason), brings into economic reasoning what Marx treated as the problem of over-determination (Resnick and Wolff, 1987). Every different reasoning, culture, people and economy will then derive its own independent meaning of morality and ethics from the differentiated understanding that the rationalist mind bestows on individual and group choices. The possibility for universality by consensus of a discoursed moral law is disabled.

Contrarily, the pre-assignment of the meaning and nature of morals by the source of the religious (moral) law must be of the universal and naturally acceptable type, nothing cumbersome. Such a most reduced premise of functional power in scientific reasoning is monotheism. Consequently, moral, ethical and social values derived from the monotheistic law of unity of knowledge would be the only way of proposing the methodology of pervasively endogenous inter-causal relationships (i.e. of embedding between morality, ethics, society and economics). This is the method of forming deontological preferences in social choice formation. Sen (1992) writes about this kind of deontological social economic phenomenon.

Ethics, as derived from the moral law of monotheism, is different in meaning and application than the rationalist meaning. The precept of monotheism precedes that of morality. Its text then gives meaning to morality. Ethics thereafter flows out of the monotheistic moral law. This point was explained in the previous section.

By our explanation of the contrasting episteme of rationalism and religion (monotheism), rationalism cannot attain such a unique and universal premise of inter-systemic unification, upon which the world system theory, structure, inferences and applications can be constructed. We must, then, turn to the phenomenology generated strictly by the monotheistic law. This kind of contrasting reasoning between unity of knowledge and rationalism that differently induces social embedding of economics by opposite forms of inter-causal relational epistemology is depicted in Figure 3.1.[6]

The epistemic embedding of the social economy by unity of knowledge and its applications

Examples can be found that show that if moral, ethical and social and economic values are to be endogenously integrated into a holistic theory of the social economy

M: moral domain
S: social domain
E: economic domain
θ = θ(R) or θ(RL)

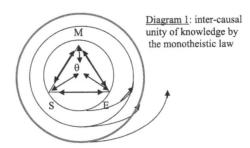

Diagram 1: inter-causal
unity of knowledge by
the monotheistic law

The two-directional arrows of Diagram 1 indicate the evolutionary learning of the embedding system of {M,S,E}[θ(RL)]. [θ(RL)] means overarching influence of each and all of the components of the vector, {M,S,E} by the episteme of θ(RL), etc. Such inter-causal mappings constitute reinforcing endogenous inter-relations as the derived and continuing dynamics of unity of knowledge inducing the world-system of {M,S,E}[θ(RL)]. The substantive field of inter-systemic embedding as our definition of the social economy explains the endogenous nature of the moral, social, and economic domains interactively integrated and evolved by the episteme of θ(RL).

Next consider Diagram 2. Because of the exogenous nature of (M,S) in the presence of θ(R), the shape of the diagram turns into the following type:

Diagram 2

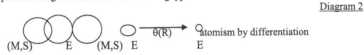

Figure 3.1 Contrasting methodologies on embedding in the social economy: unity of knowledge versus rationalism

followed by application, then the partitioned worldview emanating from rationalism can be replaced. A subtle heterodox theory of social economics emerges by the processes of inter-causal embedding between diversity of interactive, integrative, and evolutionary (IIE) learning systems. Such embedding has been variously characterized in this chapter. We referred to the central methodology enabling such organic inter-causal relationships to actualize pervasive complementarities between variables and entities. We now refer to the same kind of interdependent and unifying phenomenon of the wellbeing function with its methodical system of inter-variable circular causation relationships as the sign of participation. Participation *qua* complementarity, therefore, presents synonymously the sure sign of existing or reconstructed inter-disciplinary embedding by the impact of unity of knowledge as episteme. We provide a few examples in respect of the above-mentioned ethical rule derived from the moral law of monotheism contrary to a rationalist epistemological approach.

Example 1: the role of interest rate in the social economy

Abolition of the rate of interest to attain resource mobilization, distribution of wealth, generating ownership, equity, empowerment and entitlement among the rich and poor, is an enabling approach of the moral law. Yet a rationalistic basis of religious values may not ratify this matter of interest rate abolition.

Note the following two are contradictory paths of economic relations in monotheistic and rationalist approaches:

(1) Based on rationalism:

$$\text{Nominal } i\uparrow \Rightarrow P\uparrow \Rightarrow Y_R\downarrow \Rightarrow I\downarrow \Rightarrow r\downarrow \Rightarrow L\downarrow \Rightarrow D\downarrow \qquad (3.2)$$

$\Rightarrow$ economic and social linkages (complementarities)$\downarrow$
$\Rightarrow$ marginalist condition of resource allocation, hence methodological Individualism$\uparrow$.

(2) Based on the monotheistic law of unity of knowledge in relation to the unified world-system:

$$i \rightarrow 0 \Rightarrow I\uparrow \Rightarrow r\uparrow \Rightarrow Y_R\uparrow \Rightarrow P\downarrow \Rightarrow L\uparrow \Rightarrow D\uparrow \qquad (3.3)$$

$\Rightarrow$ economic and social linkages (complementarities)$\uparrow$
$\Rightarrow$ marginalist condition disappears; methodological individualism disappears; hence pure participation as the economic signature of unity of knowledge between inputs and goods$\uparrow$
i denotes nominal interest rate;
I denotes gross investment;
r denotes rate of return on spending (I);
Y_R denotes real income;
P denotes price level;
L denotes mobilization of labor force (employment; labor force participation rate);
D denotes distribution of income, wealth, and resources (equity, entitlement, ownership, empowerment).

The fullest extent of complementarities between the good possibilities, signified also by extensive inter-variable and inter-agential participation (complementarities), conveys the sure sign of material fusion of unity of knowledge as derived from the attributes and tenets of monotheistic law. The complementary or participatory attribute equally applies to the specifics of the generalized world-system. They are represented by their characteristic variables symbolizing the issues under study. Case (2) (expression 3.3) based on the representation of monotheistic unity of knowledge in the form of pervasive participation and complementarity becomes the apt consequence of moral, social, and economic embedding.

Example 2: The role of Bishops' Pastoral Letters vis-à-vis Centesimus Annus

Another example is of the Bishops' Pastoral Letters on the state of the North American economy during the hyperinflationary period of the 1980s. This example, despite its noble objectives, remained silent on the central effect of the interest rate on economic and social adversities.

I. Problem of the social economy embedding caused by Kantian heteronomy in CA

Centesimus Annus (see also other papal encyclicals noted as companions of CA)[7] placed a great deal of concern on the plight of workers during times of unbridled capitalism that deprives them of their social rights. The same philosophy and its consequences would also prevail for the problems of social inequality within and between nations in today's age of global capitalism and on the plight of the abject poor. The same extension applies to loss of empowerment and entitlement in an age of continued financial uncertainty, instability, and deprivation.

What was the epistemological premise of *Centesimus Annus* in respect of the evolutionary learning model of sustainability of ethical and moral values? Does *CA* present a systemic sense of continuity and pervasiveness of its reconstructive thought across the knowledge, space and time dimensions of learning that monotheism versus rationalism invokes? The problem can be traced back to Kantian heteronomy.

Kant was indeed a moralist of the Western world. His works influenced many, particularly the Catholic Church at the time of the Eighteenth Century Enlightenment (Makkreel, 1990). Thus the Kantian philosophy of 'authentic theodicy' in his heteronomy is deeply reflected in the theme of *Centesimus Annus vis-à-vis* moral, social, economic, financial and institutional contractarianism. This is one area of evidence of the dichotomy between the moral, ethical, social and economic values despite the importance that Catholicity upholds but within the demarcated domain of Kantian a priori reasoning or dissociated a posteriori reasoning.

2. Labor-capital socio-economic conflict in CA

On the issue of labor-capital relationship, *Centesimus Annus* throughout depicts this as a permanent binary conflict during times of oppressive capitalism. On this matter *CA* writes:

> The Pope and the Church with him were confronted, as was the civil community, by a society which was torn by a conflict all the more harsh and inhumane because it knew no rule or regulation. It was *the conflict between capital and labour,* or – as the Encyclical puts it – the worker question. It is precisely about this conflict, in the very pointed terms in which it then appeared that the Pope did not hesitate to speak.

Toward resolving this conflict between labor and capital, and likewise in another instance between capitalism and socialism, the Papal Encyclicals prescribed a return to Christian values. On this matter the *Centesimus Annus* wrote:

> In a certain sense, it was a struggle born of prayer, and it would have been unthinkable without immense trust in God, the Lord of history, who carries the human heart in his hands. It is by uniting his own sufferings for the sake of truth and freedom to the sufferings of Christ on the Cross that man is able to accomplish the miracle of peace and is in a position to discern the often narrow path between the cowardice which gives in to evil and the violence which, under the illusion of fighting evil, only makes it worse.

The missing endogenous learning link between the ontological precept of God and the reality of the world-system marked the Kantian heteronomy. The gap between Kantian a priori and a posteriori (*noumenon* and phenomenon) reasoning could not be filled by tenets of the divine law presented in the cast of worldly laws and functioning instruments, except by applying exogenous laws and instruments acting independently of the epistemic premise. On this matter *Centesimus Annus* writes:

> In this regard, *Rerum Novarum* points the way to just reforms which can restore dignity to work as the free activity of man. These reforms imply that society and the State will both assume responsibility, especially for protecting the worker from the nightmare of unemployment. Historically, this has happened in two converging ways: either through economic policies aimed at ensuring balanced growth and full employment, or through unemployment insurance and retraining programmes capable of ensuring a smooth transfer of workers from crisis sectors to those in expansion.

We note from this extract that moral, ethical, social and economic policies and structures are determined as usual – independently of any endogenous presence of consciousness. Instead, the intervention remained to be by the rationalist artefacts.

3. The economic and financial implications of Kantian heteronomy in CA

Take the case of a problem referred to above, namely, the impossibility of achieving economic stabilization in the presence of interest rates. The argument made here is that interest rates rupture the much-needed unifying function between money, finance, and the real economy to deliver economic and social justice through the endogenous process of systemic inter-relations. In such an endogenous embedding process, markets and governments would learn in co-determination. In the absence of such evolutionary learning, the Kantian heteronomy abides between the a priori and the a posteriori, between *noumena* and phenomena, between God and the world-system, between deductive and inductive reasoning, and between the synthetic and analytic reasoning.

Basing their arguments of dualism between markets and social values, there are those who consider such alienation and competition between these sectors of human experience as inevitable. Consequently, moral, ethical and social values embedded in economy, state and global politics, although voiced in *Centesimus Annus*, remains a purely rationalistic project. It is independently treated as being humanistic. On this matter *Centesimus Annus* writes:

> The State must contribute to the achievement of these goals both directly and indirectly. Indirectly, and according to the *principle of subsidiarity*, by creating favorable conditions for the free exercise of economic activity, which will lead to abundant opportunities for employment and sources of wealth. Directly, and according to the *principle of solidarity*, by defending the weakest, by placing certain limits on the autonomy of the parties who determine working conditions, and by ensuring in every case the necessary minimum support for the unemployed worker.

4. The rationalist element in CA over all

Centesimus Annus was incorrect in yet another area of its arguments concerning the issue of rationalism entrenched in Kantian heteronomy. That is, if rationalism has been humanly engineered, and God has a different ontological premise of argumentation for the world-system, then God must be a law-giver with well-defined laws brought into the world-system to unite the ontological with the ontic (evidential). Yet, in the social characterization explained in this chapter, there is no such characterization of the social economy. Thus, God and the monotheistic law remain insulated ontological precepts, disconnected from the world-system. God the creator has left the world to evolve by itself, except for murmurs of humanistic feelings in the hearts of good men.

Conclusion

Increasingly now, the rise of heterodox thought in economic theory and the project of social economy, has been struggling to find a cogent methodology that would establish the integrated worldview of moral, ethical, social and economic values embedded in the world-system. The methodology remains in abeyance because of the prevailing academic ineptness to get out of rationalism and move into ontological unity of knowledge as the epistemic methodology.

In conclusion, we point out that inter-causality establishes the foundation of monotheistic faith in the form of its organic inter-relationship with the details of the world-system. Such an epistemological approach must integrate the a priori with the a posteriori reasoning (deductive and inductive; noumena and phenomena, etc.) by an evolutionary learning process across continuums. The emergent formalisms, then, comprise the *functional* ontological domains of actions and responses. Such evolutionary emergences are necessary to explain total reality by way of critical realism. Methodology and its derived methodical formalism cannot either be limited to specifics or be separable between them (Maxwell, 1962; Lawson, 2003). It must be universal and generalized, from which specifics are cogently derived.

This quest for the overarching epistemology, which we have launched in this chapter, when applied to the state of the world economy today, brings out certain structural problems of economic theory. According to the epistemology of unity of knowledge that we have propounded, the endogenous moral, ethical, social and economic embedding suggests that the dichotomies between these inter-disciplines is a flawed concept.

Differentiation between deductive and inductive reasoning, and between the a priori and a posteriori reasoning has invaded pure scientific theories as well. The kind of conjectures and scientific refutations, the silence on unity of knowledge between forms, entities, and their relations, has caused loss of directions in the purpose of science. Husserl (1970) lamented on such a state of moral emptiness in the pure natural sciences. Finally, even Godel's (1965) rejection of self-referencing according to his theorem of incompleteness of the arithmetical system, which was a rejection of the claim of the finality of mathematical machinery given by Russell and Whitehead (1910–13) in their *Principia Mathematica* is great, but it is subject to question. Godel's denial of self-referencing leaves out the theme of unity of knowledge in explaining the possibilities of the socio-scientific 'everything' (Choudhury and Zaman, 2009).

Conclusively, therefore, the rationalist socio-scientific epistemology is bereft of the overarching epistemology of unity of knowledge and the world-system. Prevalent theories and their empirical and institutional pursuits cannot, therefore, succeed in analyzing and reconstructing the economic, financial, and social worlds into a cohesively relational unity for the sustainable common human future. This is social wellbeing.

The intrinsic nature of creative experience in the learning universe calls forth the inexorable embedding of concepts and experiences. Without such an intellectual enterprise, neither can there be a meaning of critical realism, continuous and complete, nor is there a meaning of goodness as knowledge, the sublime creative endowment.

Appendix: Non-parametric representation of what integration between economics and religions means in the evolutionary learning methodological worldview

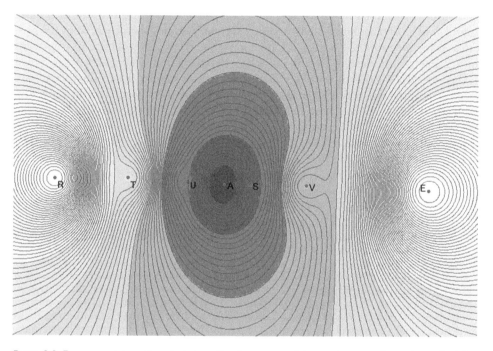

Figure 3.2 From non-integration to integration between religion and economics as inter-disciplines when embedded by the epistemology of unity of systemic knowledge[8]

Explanation:

SDA is a specialized sub-project of the Geographical Information System. It is here applied to socio-scientific topography involving economics and religion (moral, ethical, and social values), being governed by the epistemology of unity of knowledge. In actual practice, the SDA forms a pervasive field of numbers that arise as all possible estimated and simulated values of coefficients representing inter-causal relations between selected variables as of the inter-systemic wellbeing function. The wellbeing function relates to the study of integration between economics and religion (moral, ethical, social values) as two inter-causal embedded systems. The pervasive field of numbers next represents simulated choices of improved and revised numerical values of the estimated coefficients in order to build on the principle of complementarities between the inter-causal variables of the wellbeing function. The underlying method in such integration out of interaction, thereby growing outwards into evolutionary learning processes, is circular causation. Although numbers are invoked in actual estimation and simulation by the SDA method, in our case the representation remains non-parametric and hence illustrative.

The origins of Economics and Religion ($\{M,S,E\}[\theta(RL)]$) denote those of initially disjoint systems. The improvising of the epistemology of unity of knowledge causes the disjoint systems to become knowledge-induced ($\theta(RL)$). Now the circular causation method works towards simulating greater embedding by the interactive, integrative, and evolutionary (IIE) learning processes across systems. The regions extensively denoted by TU and VS move toward their complementary integration in the region around A. The evolutionary SDA-waves as shown, signifies the progressing IIE processes wherein estimated values of inter-variable relational coefficients represent non-parametric simulations to gain on unity of systemic knowledge.

The emergent theory of ontological economics as a field of heterodox economics within social economics is now enabled by its cogent methodology, its critical realism, and methodical formalism. This is explained by the method of circular causation causally inter-relating variables and entities by their complementarities in degrees of creative evolutionary change. These attributes comprise the building blocks of the theory, explanation, analytics, and application of the emergent field of ontological economics, heterodox economics, and the specific field of social economics as defined in this chapter.

Notes

1 Extracted from M.A. Choudhury's, "Religion and Social Economics", *International Journal of Social Economics*, forthcoming, 2016.
2 Foucault (see Sheridan, 1972, p. 191) defines the word *episteme* as follows: "By *episteme* we mean ... the total set of relations that unite, at a given period, the discursive practices that give rise to epistemological figures, sciences, and possibly formalized systems ... The episteme is not a form of knowledge (*connaissance*) or type of rationality which, crossing the boundaries of the most varied sciences, manifests the sovereign unity of a subject, a spirit, or a period; it is the totality of relations that can be discovered, for a given period, between the sciences when one analyses them at the level of discursive regularities."
3 The world-system comprises the totality of all unraveling universes that embed in each other by relational dynamics. It is governed by an ontological formalism, giving it meaning, shape, form, explanation, and application. In the religio-scientific conception of the socio-scientific entirety the causality is like this: World-System, $WS = \{(X,Y)_s[\theta \in \Omega]\}$, together with all possible monotonic positive functional transformations of the knowledge-induced tuple of variables, $\{X,Y\}_s$. This is true intra- and inter- systems denoted by 's'. $\{X\}$ denotes the space of variables. $\{Y\}$ denotes the totality of functional transformations of $\{X\}$ intra- and inter- systems denoted by 's'. $(X,Y)_s$ are induced by knowledge-flows $\{\theta\}$ in a unique way that explains the general picture and its specifics in what we refer to as the universal way. $\{\theta\}$-knowledge values are derived by consciousness, discourse (interaction), and consensus (integration). These attributes are derived from the super-space of the governing ontology, which is denoted by Ω. The super-topology as open mapping defined on the super-space of Ω (Rucker, 1982) includes all possible functional transforms in the world-system (WS). That is, truth and falsehood are both understood in light of the moral law. This comprises all kinds of related variables, their interdependencies and functional transformations. The usual topological properties of union and intersection, nullity and universality of topological sub-spaces apply (Maddox, 1970).

4 Knowledge, K = f(I,X), where f is a function of impressions {I} and sensate materiality {X}. Since I is defined by X, therefore I = F(X). The speculative nature of such relations is conveyed by the randomness of {I,X,F}. The values of this sequence are caused by the primacy of R (reason as perception caused by rationalism). The compound functional (f·F) generating knowledge K(R): K(R) = (f·F)(X)[R] therefore exists.

    Such a functional can be disaggregated at the individual (i.e. micro-)level, and formed at the macro-level. At the micro-level, we can associate I with individual preferences; X with goods and services; K with information flow; and (f·F) as processes that transform economic materiality into 'objective criteria'. The microeconomic example of K(R) is the ordinal nature of utility function in consumption (or cardinal expected utility in risk and return of investment). The underlying preferences in expected utility function appear as datum.

    At the macroeconomic (aggregate) level there is no method of aggregation from the microeconomic level except by the utilitarian postulates of irrelevant preferences and the existence of a dictator. Such postulates defy the integrated world system by way of participation (unity by pairing). Hume's rationalist basis of reasoning, like Kant's by heteronomy, thus leads to speculation of knowledge formation by R. The result is individualism by methodical independence between systems, categories, agents, and goods.

5 Such a random differentiated property of rationalism can be read from the problem of Kant's heteronomy between the a priori and the a posteriori domains of reasoning. Carnap (1966) refers to this problem as that of lack of synthesis between the moral imperative (a priori) and the world system (a posteriori). The consequences are far-reaching. Heteronomy also spells out the demarcation problem between deductive and inductive reasoning; between *noumenon* and phenomenon, synthetic and analytical truths in the philosophy of science; the moral law and materiality, and between moral, social, and economic values.

6 In the endogenous inter-causal relations of {M,S,E}[θ(RL)], the following property abides: (i) (Diagram 1): (M∩S∩E)[θ(RL)]≠φ; (ii) (Diagram 2): (M∩S∩E)[θ(RL)]=φ, 'almost everywhere' in the language of mathematical measure theory.

7 Leo XIII, Encyclical Letter *Rerum Novarum* (May 15, 1891): *Leonis XIII P.M. Acta*, XI, Romae 1892, 97–144. Pius XI, Encyclical Letter *Quadragesimo Anno* (May 15, 1931): *AAS* 23 (1931), 177–228; Pius XII, Radio Message of June 1, 1941: *AAS* 33 (1941), 195–205; John XXIII, Encyclical Letter *Mater et Magistra* (May 15, 1961): *AAS* 53 (1961), 401–64; Paul VI, Apostolic Epistle *Octogesima Adveniens* (May 14, 1971): *AAS* 63 (1971), 401–41.

8 My thanks are to Professor M. Shahadat Hossain of the Department of Computer Science, Chittagong University for improvising Figure A1 in the SDA form.

References

Anderson, B.R. (1984). "Rationality and Irrationality of the Nordic Welfare State", *Daedalus*, Winter.

Arrow, K.J. (1951). *Social Choice and Individual Values*, New York, NY, John Wiley and Sons.

Barrow, J.D. (1991). "Laws", in his *Theories of Everything, the Quest for Ultimate Explanation*, Oxford, UK, Oxford University Press, pp. 12–30.

Carnap, R. (1966). "Kant's synthetic *a priori*", in his *Philosophical Foundations of Physics* (ed.), M. Gardner, New York, Basic Books, Inc.

Centesimus Annus (see http://faculty.cua.edu/pennington/Law111/PapalSocialEncyclicals.htm).

Choudhury, M.A. (2011). "A meta-epistemological general-system model of Islamic economics", *Social Epistemology*, 25:4, 423–46.

Choudhury, M.A. and Zaman, S.I. (2009). "Self-referencing as socio-scientific methodology in contrasting paradigms", *Kybernetes, The International Journal of Systems and Cybernetics*, 38:6, pp. 994–1008.

Dasgupta, A.K. (1987). "Marginalist challenge", in his *Epochs of Economic Theory*, pp. 74–98, Oxford, UK: Blackwell.

Doeringer, B. (1985). "The economics of Jacques Maritain", *Review of Social Economy*, 43:1, April.

Etzioni, A. (1987). "Towards a Kantian socio-economics", *Review of Social Economy*, XLV:1, April.

Fitzpatrick, T. (2003). "Postmodernism and new directions", in Alcock, P., Erskine, A. and May, M. (eds),. *Social Policy*, pp. 125–33, Oxford, UK, Blackwell.

Foucault, M. trans. A.M. Sheridan (1972). *The Archeology of Knowledge and the Discourse on Language*, New York, Harper Torchbooks.

Godel, K. (1965). "On formally undecidable propositions of Principia Mathematica and related systems", in M. Davies (ed.), *The Undecidable*, New York, NY Raven Books.

Hammond, P.J. (1989). "On reconciling Arrow's theory of social choice with Harsanyi's Fundamental Utilitarianism", in G.R. Feiwel (ed.), *Arrow and the Foundation of the Theory of Economic Policy*, pp. 179–221, London, UK, Macmillan.

Hawking, S.W. and Mlodinow, L. (2010). *The Grand Design*, London, UK, Transworld Publishers.

Holton, R.L. (1992). *Economy and Society*, London, UK, Routledge.

Hosinski, T. (1987). "Lonergan and a process understanding of God", in Fallon, T.P. and Riley, P.B. (eds), *Religion and Culture: Essays in Honor of Bernard Lonergan* pp. 63–78, Albany, NY, State University of New York Press.

Hume, D. (1960). "Principles of morals", in his *An Enquiry Concerning the Principles of Morals*, La Salle, IL, The Open Court Publishing Co.

Husserl trans. Q. Lauer (1970). *Phenomenology and the Crisis of Philosophy*, p. 155, New York, NY, Harper & Row Publishers, particularly note his comment on the perceived absence of ethical roots in Occidental scientific inquiry.

Kant, I. trans. Friedrich, C.J. (1949). "Religion within the limits of reason alone", in C.J. Friedrich (ed.), *The Philosophy of Kant*, pp. 365–411, New York, NY, Modern Library.

Lawson, T. (2003). "An evolutionary economics?" in his *Reorienting Economics*, pp. 110–40, London, UK, Routledge.

Lewis, B. (2010). "Religion and politics in Islam and Judaism", in his *Faith and Power, Religion and Politics in the Middle East*, Oxford, UK, Oxford University Press, pp. 39–54

Lonergan, B. (1908). "The pure process" (pp. 11–41) and "Equilibria of the mechanical structure", in

Lonergan, B. (1999). "An essay in circular analysis" in Lawrence, F.G. Byrne, P.H. and Heflong Jr. C.C. (eds), *Collected Works of B. Lonergan, Macroeconomic Dynamics*, Toronto, ON, University of Toronto Press.

McShane, P.J. (ed.), *Collected Works of Bernard Lonergan, for a New Political Economy*, Toronto, ON, University of Toronto Press.

Maddox, I.J. (1970), *Elements of Functional Analysis*, Cambridge, UK, Cambridge University Press.

Mater et Magistra (http://faculty.cua.edu/pennington/Law111/PapalSocialEncyclicals.htm)

Makkreel, R.A. (1990). Teleological ideas and the authentic interpretation of history", in his *Imagination and Interpretation in Kant*, pp. 130–53, Chicago, IL, The University of Chicago Press.

Maxwell, G. (1962). "The ontological status of theoretical entities", in H. Feigl and G. Maxwell (eds), *Minnesota Studies in the Philosophy of Science, II: Scientific Explanation, Space and Time*, pp. 3–27, Minneapolis, MN, University of Minnesota Press.

McKee, A. (1992). "On justice and charity: a comment", *Review of Social Economy*, L:3, Fall.

Myrdal, G. (1958). "The principle of cumulation", in Streeten, P. (ed.), *Value in Social Theory, a Selection of Essays on Methodology by Gunnar Myrdal*, pp. 198–205, New York, NY, Harper and Brothers Publishers.

Nelson, R.H. (2001). "Efficient religion", in *Economics as Religion (from Samuelson to Chicago and Beyond)*, Philadelphia, PA, Penn State University Press, pp. 230–60.

Nelson, R.H. (2001) "A new economic world", in *Economics as Religion (from Samuelson to Chicago and Beyond)*, Philadelphia, PA, Penn State University Press, pp. 208–29.

Octogesima Adveniens (http://faculty.cua.edu/pennington/Law111/PapalSocialEncyclicals.htm).

Penrose, R. (1989). *The Emperor's New Mind*, Oxford, UK, Oxford University Press.

Popper, K. (1998). *Conjectures and Refutations: The Growth of Scientific Knowledge*, London, UK, Routledge and Kegan Paul.

Popper, K. (2004). *The Logic of Scientific Discovery*, London, UK, Routledge.

Quadragesimo Anno (http://faculty.cua.edu/pennington/Law111/PapalSocialEncyclicals.htm).

Rerum Novarum (http://faculty.cua.edu/pennington/Law111/PapalSocialEncyclicals.htm).

Resnick, S.A. and Wolff, R.D. (1987). *Knowledge and Class, A Marxian Critique of Political Economy*, Chicago, IL, The University of Chicago Press.

Rucker, R. (1982). "Large cardinals", in his *Infinity and the Mind*, pp. 273–86, New York, NY, Bantam Books.

Russell, B. and Whitehead, A.N. (1910–13). *Principia Mathematica*, New York, NY, Cambridge University Press.

Sen, A. (1992). "Conduct, ethics and economics", in his *On Ethics and Economics*, pp. 88–9, Oxford, UK, Basil Blackwell.

Smart, N. (2000). "The nature of morality", in his *Worldviews*, pp. 114–16, Upper Saddle River, NJ, Prentice Hall.

South Commission (1990). *The Challenge to the South*, Oxford, UK, Oxford University Press.

Toner, P. (1999). "Gunnar Myrdal (1898–1987): circular and cumulative causation as the methodology of the social sciences", in *Main Currents in Cumulative Causation, the Dynamics of Growth and Development*, Chapter 5, Houndmills, UK, Macmillan Press Ltd.

Torrell, J.P. trans. Gueven, B.M. (2005). "A circular plan", in *Aquinas' SUMMA, Background, Structure, and Reception*, pp. 27–36, Washington, DC, The Catholic University of America Press.

Vertin, M. (1987). "Is God in Process?" in Fallon, T. P. and Riley, P.B. (eds), *Religion and Culture: Essays in Honor of Bernard Lonergan*, pp. 45–63, Albany, NY, State University of New York Press.

Whitehead, A.N. (eds), Griffin, D.R. and Sherburne, D.W. (1979). "Fact and form", in his *Process and Reality*, pp. 39–60, New York, NY, The Free Press.

Wolff, R.P. (1977). *A Reconstruction of a Critique of a Theory of Justice: Understanding Rawls*, Princeton, NJ, Princeton University Press.

Zweig, M. (1991). "Economics and liberation theology", in his edited *Religion and Economic Justice*, pp. 3–99, Philadelphia, PA, Temple University Press.

Chapter 4

A Generalized View of *Maqasid As-Shari'ah*[1]

Abstract

A critical evaluation of the purpose and objective of Islamic Law, namely *maqasid as-shari'ah* as it has evolved in Islamic scholastic experience is undertaken. The deeper philosophy and potential of *maqasid as-shari'ah* within the great design of the monotheistic law, *Sunnat Allah*, is explained. Such explanation is carried out in the light of the core of Islamic epistemology that directly induces Islamic Law. This critical evaluation is pursued in the light of the epistemological worldview and its methodical formalism of unity of knowledge *contra* a differentiated and conflicting view of human experience in rationalism. The episteme of unity of knowledge is *Tawhid* as the law of everything in the precept of unity as understood by the monotheistic law, *Sunnat Allah*. In the light of the extendibility of *maqasid as-shari'ah* across the relationally unifying domain of *Sunnat Allah* we discuss the potentiality of *shari'ah* in terms of *res extensa* (epistemic extension) and *res cogitans* (cognitive capacity).

Various occidental thoughts in this quest for extendibility of the epistemic totality are critically examined by the *Tawhidi* monotheistic law. The universality of the *Tawhidi* law of monotheism in respect of its characteristics of *res extensa* and *res cogitans* is studied to bring out the potentiality of *maqasid as-shari'ah*. Thereby, the new vision of inter-systemic extensions across diverse domains of intellection interactively unified together is formalized. This formalism goes beyond the existing limits of *maqasid as-shari'ah,* confined as it is to *muamalat*.

The critical discussion launched in reference to the wider meaning, objective, and purpose of *maqasid as-shari'ah* under the epistemology of the *Tawhidi* methodological worldview results in the substantive understanding of *maslaha*, well-being. This forms the ultimate index of socio-scientific valuation under *maqasid as-shari'ah* in the light of the *Tawhidi* epistemological worldview. Thereby, the perspective of socio-economic development; and more extensively socio-scientific intellection, is brought out as extensively participatory evolutionary process under the principle of unity of knowledge (*Tawhidi* episteme). Brief examples are invoked to establish this fact. An example of measured multidimensional well-being (*maslaha*) as the final index of participatory organic relations that *maqasid as-shari'ah* ought to project in reference to *Tawhidi* methodological worldview is represented.

Background

Meanings of res extensa *and* res cogitans *between Islam and the Occident*

Imam Ghazali on res extensa *and* res cogitans

Imam Ghazali yearned for intellectual liberation from doubt in the search for deepest belief in the certain One. For attaining such heights of certainty in belief and reason Imam Ghazali wrote of the magnificent Pen that *Allah* has commanded to write from the Beginning to the End of the universe of 'everything'. This extant of evolution of knowledge in and through the universal details comprises the divine monotheistic law (*Tawhid*). The monotheistic law by its integrative nature establishes the *res extensa* of reality that Imam Ghazali dwelt on for comprehending truth. The reflection of *res extensa* in the order and scheme of all world-systems is diversely represented in both corporeal and abstract realities by the signs of *Allah*. Such a domain of comprehension of the *res extensa* of corporeal being comprises the *res cogitans* (cognition) regarding 'everything'.

The domains of *res extensa* and *res cogitans* are intrinsically and pervasively inter-related to present the meaning of total reality. Any one of these ought not to, and, in fact, cannot exist without the other in the total meaning of reality. Such delineation is derived from the *Qur'an*.[2] The inter-causality between the domains of *res extensa* and *res cogitans* in Imam Ghazali's thinking explains the unity of knowledge and being regarding everything. It is this kind of a definition of the comprehensive meaning of reality that enters the *maslaha* wellbeing function. The *maslaha* function thus expresses the principle of pervasive unity as complementarities. Complementarities also convey the meaning of the participatory pairing of organic relations between the good things of life (*halal at-tayyabah* or *hayath at-tayyabah*).

An order of pairing also exists in the forbidden things (falsehood). But the nature of pairing is then shown by the property of conflict, competition, and differentiation between all things in the eventual shape and form of the domain of such forbidden things, between them, and the good things of life, in growing depths of opposition. The objective criterion of *maslaha* as the wellbeing function of pervasive unity and organic interrelations between the good things of life and its negation by the forbidden things (falsehood) is the measurable goal of the divine law – *Sunnat Allah*.

The technical objective function of conflict, competition, differentiation, and marginalist substitution between all things – good and bad – is the economic utility function and its aggregation into the economic welfare function. Complementarities and participation equivalently of the *res extensa* (soul, mind, matter, and time continuum) combined relationally with *res cogitans* (evident and abstract entities by reason) form the being and becoming of *maslaha*. Contrarily, the pervasive nature of differentiation between everything by the postulate of marginalist substitution in economics and Darwinian opposites forms the nature of the economic welfare criterion. Welfare is contrary to the *maslaha* concept and the objective of unity.

Rene Descartes on res extensa *and* res cogitans

Rene Descartes, like Imam Ghazali, yearned for freedom from uncertainty in his quest for the certain truth and belief by reason. Thus Descartes used the term *res extensa* to mean the continuum space of events that happen and can be understood and explained by reason. He used the term *res cogitans* to mean the domain of being and becoming of reason. Liberation from uncertainty in reasoning and consciousness meant to Descartes the integration of these two domains to establish an integrated way of understanding the process of being and becoming.

There was thus a procedural similarity between Ghazali and Descartes in the humanly limited understanding of the divine law within the conscious and complete ordering of total reality. Yet there was a substantive difference despite procedural similarity. Ghazali argued that God, and hence the monotheistic law, could not be understood by reason alone. Belief transcends reason and forms the core of knowledge. Descartes was concerned with the reasoned and corporeal world despite deep abstraction in it, to attain knowledge. Thereby, truth was limited to Cartesian rationalist thought and was instrumental in the human understanding of God and the universal law. Reasoning and consciousness were thus confined in Descartes to the domain of *res extensa* and *res cogitans* spanning the limits of the human world and its reasoned abstraction. Yet materiality is a subspace of the monotheistic worldview in the divine signs and reasoned abstraction. The rest of the total reality without the corporeal world was incapable of, and unnecessary for use in, understanding the Cartesian world of rationalism – "I think; so I am."

The contrasting, yet comparative, experiences to attain certainty of belief, knowledge, and reasoning, all that must profoundly underlie understanding of the *res extensa* integrated with *res cogitans*, are manifest in the words of the great thinkers – Ghazali and Kant, yet another profound rationalist.

The human realm of cognition and experience moves into bliss through the subtle combination of knowledge, belief, and action (the world) in Ghazali (Ghazali trans. by Karim, n.d., p. 237, edited):

> What is *Tauhid* (monotheism)? Know O readers, that God–reliance is a door out of the doors of faith. All the doors of faith are not kept in order except with knowledge, condition, and action. Out of these three elements, God-reliance is born. Knowledge is the basis, action is its fruit.

On a similar note of unity of knowledge across diversity of the material world, contemplated Kant (1949) in the following words:

> Two things fill the mind with ever new and increasing awe and admiration the more frequently and continuously reflection is occupied with them; the starred heaven above me and the moral law within me. I ought not to seek either outside my field of vision, as though they were either shrouded in obscurity or were visionary. I see them confronting me and link them immediately with the consciousness of my existence.

The centrally contrasting problem between Ghazali on the one side; and Kant and Descartes on the other in respect of the functioning of the universal law, rests on Kantian heteronomy and Cartesian duality between God and world (Choudhury, 2014c). To Ghazali, this was a seamless *res extensa* integrated with *res cogitans*. With Ghazali, *maqasid as-shari'ah*, meaning the philosophy underlying the purpose and objective of the *shari'ah*, ought to be embedded in the same properties of *res extensa* and *res cogitans* of *Sunnat Allah*. We will discuss this significant problem of heteronomy in a critical evaluation of *maqasid as-shari'ah* and its potentiality.

The permanent problem of science in occidental reasoning: the duality of rationalism

Descartes, like Kant, froze science in the constrained crucible of the worldly domains of *res extensa* and *res cogitans* in order to understand reality that is argued to be present in materiality and abstraction. However, the approach failed to have the potentiality for knowledge of reality existing in and objective continuity across systemic continuums of learning systems. The very objective that Descartes and Kant aimed for – attaining certainty in belief and consciousness – failed to look beyond the limited material horizon of science.

In Kant (Carnap, 1966; Choudhury, 2009) the problem of such impossibility for knowledge of reality framed his problem of heteronomy. This is the problem of differentiation and unattainability of unity between the a priori world of pure reason and the a posteriori world of practical reason. It is the same as understanding reality in a disjointed way between *noumena* and phenomena; between deductive and inductive reasoning. The organic integration between these separated parts of reasoning could not be unified into an organic causality by the cogent episteme of an otherwise integrated abstraction between *res extensa* and *res cogitans* across all domains of ultimate possibility; this is explained by the monotheistic law. In brief, heteronomy presents the separation of the divine law (moral imperative) from rationalist reasoning (the world). The divine law thus becomes unnecessary and dysfunctional in the Kantian concept of heteronomy.

Maqasid as-shari'ah and maslaha

Maqasid as-shari'ah, meaning the philosophy underlying the purpose and objective of the *shari'ah*, has an established beginning with the concept of *maslaha* as the all-inclusive social wellbeing criterion complementing *istihsan* (public preferences) in determining the good choices of life-fulfillment needs. The imminent complementary relations between *maqasid* choices become codetermined events in the unified domains of *res extensa* and *res cogitans* of *shari'ah* embedded within *Sunnat Allah*.

The question, then, is this: Why is it that the *maqasid as-shari'ah*, despite its overarching meaning and dynamics within the *res extensa* and *res cogitans* domains of the monotheistic law governing 'everything' (*Sunnat Allah*), remained a dissociated subspace of this limitation devoted to matters of *muamalat* alone; then, too, without the dynamics of relational evolutionary epistemology that can engage the theory and application of the *maqasid as-shari'ah* in the ever-widening domains of inter-causality and unity of knowledge in diversity and purpose of 'everything'. This perspective is the meaning that *maqasid as-shari'ah* acquires in relation to the generalized system design of the universe. Such is also the principle of overarching pairing by unity explained by the *Qur'an*.[3] Without such a grand design of *maqasid as-shari'ah*, the science of *maqasid* in relation to *Sunnat Allah* has remained non-dynamic, limited, and dimmed; even though the science of nature and society have been advancing along the great threshold of their inter-connectivity (Human Brain Project, 2013). The domain of inter-connectivity between everything as the intensifying learning in unity of knowledge expands.

Such holism must be the project of *maqasid as-shari'ah*. Without such a project, the *res extensa* and *res cogitans* domains that ought to be overarching within the entirety of *Sunnat Allah,* remain incomplete. Consequently, the full relevance of *Tawhid* as signified by the monotheistic law and its manifest in the universal pairing between the good things of life, differentiated from the forbidden and false things of life, cannot be found.

A brief example showing the incompleteness in understanding *maqasid as-shari'ah* and its universal potentiality otherwise

A brief example of this critical reflection can be mentioned here for a further elaboration later on: First, we relate Ghazali's invoking the *hadith al-qudsi* (the divinely inspired saying of the Prophet Muhammad, which though is not a *Qur'anic* revelation). It states: "At the beginning of creation *Allah* commanded the mystic Pen to write from the Beginning to the End. The Pen followed *Allah's* command. Indeed, it is writing the praises of *Allah* all the time, everywhere, and in everything. Its encompassing dimensions comprise the knowledge, space, and time structure of the universe." That is the universe of *Sunnat Allah* in respect of the monotheistic law presenting the unity of being and becoming.

The *Qur'an* declares: "*Allah* is the Light of the Heavens and the Earth." Such is the *Tawhidi* domain of evolutionary learning in everything. The *Qur'an* further declares: "*Allah* is the End and the Beginning" of the Great Design. All matters return back to *Allah* for the final determination. All things learn to rise from and move towards *Allah* by evolutionary epistemological learning regarding the Great Event (*Naba ul-Azim*). Such actualization in everything takes place through the entire learning processes of the universe. The *Qur'an* refers to this experience as the precept of *khalq in-jadid* (re-originated reality) within the entirety of the pairing universe in the good and false things taken in their differentiated pairs; but unified within them in distinct ways of convergence to unity, and contrary nature of conflicting opposites, respectively. The accumulation of such evolutionary unity of knowledge is towards the Great Event as the complete universe of the *khalq in-jadid* (evolutionary learning). Within this framework of the great design of *Sunnat Allah* must rest the evolutionary episteme of *maqasid as-shari'ah* towards embracing the universal totality.[4]

An example of the cosmic relationship of energy interrelating maqasid as-shari'ah with Sunnat Allah

As an example, consider the relationship of energy with the *maqasid as-shari'ah* as understood and as proposed in this chapter in respect of the domains of *res extensa* and *res-cogitans*. As usually stated, the precepts of *maqasid as-shari'ah* are: (1) protection of the religion of Islam (*Tawhid*); (2) protection of reason (*aql*); (3) protection of family and progeny (*nasb*); (4) protection of property rights (*maal*); and (5) life (*nafs*), which is sustainable over the inter-temporal continuity. All these elements are comprised within the Imam Shatibi-recommended basket of the good things of life (*hayat at-tayyabah*), namely, *dururiyath* (necessaries), *hajiyath* (comforts), *tahsaniyy-ath* (refinements).

In the context of these five-fold precepts, energy is an input in the *maqasid* to attain wellbeing (*maslaha*). By the fifth pillar of *maqasid*, the input of energy on sustaining life must be continued over the dimensions of knowledge, space, and time. The question then lies in the possible extendibility of *maqasid as-shari'ah*.

Yet there is no specific mention of, or a development by latter-day Muslims of how such an extendible sustainability concept can be explained by means of intercausal evolutionary learning relations between energy sources in abstractions (science) and the energy input into the Shatibi-*maqasid* basket (social order). In the absence of this critical issue, the *res extensa* and *res cogitans* of the sustainability theme has not been understood in terms of the underlying dynamics of interrelational continuity across continuums of the knowledge, space, and time domains.

In other words, latter-day Muslims have not inquired about the great question of the extendibility of *maqasid as-shari'ah* into the following kind of interrelationship that carries forward sustainability by means of unity of knowledge (*Tawhid*):

[energy $\rightarrow$ *maqasid as-shari'ah* $\rightarrow$ energy] as the regenerative circular causal relationship.

We extend this argument:

Let, $T(\{\theta\} \in (\Omega, S, \theta^*)$
$= [\{energy\}(science) \leftrightarrow_{\{\theta\}} \{maqasid\ as\text{-}shari'ah\}(society)]$
    (spanning knowledge, space, time)

The following is a property: $dT/d\theta > 0$ for values of $\{\theta, T(\theta)\}$ determined by $\{\theta\} \in (\Omega, S, \theta^*)$.

$\{\theta^*\}$ is the advisory guidance (not as details on particular issues) by the learned participants in the exercise of *fiqh al-Qur'an* and *sunnah* on generality, but not particulars. The latter is left to investigation and interpretation through the medium of $\{\theta\}$. This knowledge flow is launched here in the particular study of $\{energy\} \leftrightarrow_{\{\theta\}} \{society\}$.

The universality of this precept of inter-systemic (energy $\leftrightarrow$ society) continuity for attaining sustainability by the relational epistemology of $\{\theta\} \in (\Omega, S, \theta^*)$ acting on $\{energy\} \leftrightarrow_{\{\theta\}} \{society\}$, is established by its application to the space of good things (truth, θ); but also to the false things (rationalism of the forbidden things $\{\theta'\}$). The concept of intercausal sustainability by unity of knowledge is contrary to the rationalist (Descartes and Kant etc.) paradigm of duality and dichotomy.

In *Sunnat-law*, $(\Omega, S) \supset (\theta, \theta')$, where, $\{\theta\}$: domain of unity of knowledge (monotheism). $\{\theta'\}$: domain of rationalism. Thereby, the following properties are preserved but in $\{\theta\}$ and $\{\theta'\}$ oppositely: $\{\theta\} \cap \{\{\theta'\} = \phi$; $\{\theta\} \cup \{\theta'\} \subset (\Omega, S, \theta^*)$:

Using this formal explanation we note,

$(d/d\theta)$(Rationalism) < 0 in the energy-*maqasid* topic.
$(d/d\theta')$(Rationalism) > 0 in negation of energy-*maqasid* topic;

First, in relation to *maqasid as-shariah*, the science and society interrelationship implies a choice of such intercausal relationships and the development of energy source in view of the life-fulfillment needs of a sustainable society. All this comprises scientific models of energy in science with the inducement of the ethical factor as of the IIE-model and the consequences of such analytical investigation on the intertemporal sustainability question, such as production property of energy in the sustainability model. The sustainable society, in turn, further responds to the appropriate supply and diversification of energy source. Such a sustainable intercausal relation of unity of knowledge between the two domains establishes the circular causal relationship:

$$\{energy\ (science)\} \leftrightarrow_{\{\theta\}} \{maqasid\ as\text{-}shari'ah\ (society)\}.$$

Second, in relation to the rationalist domain of reasoning, the codetermination between energy and society is overlooked for an exploitation of the energy and ecological sources to meet not life-fulfillment needs, but 'wants' of an acquisitive society. Sustainability is broken and inter-systemic participation is decapitated (Korten, 1995).

Next, we note what results from the ineffectiveness of the existing theory of *maqasid as-shari'ah* on the debate between rationalism and unity of knowledge and evolutionary learning. In the existing understanding of *maqasid as-shari'ah* and the absence of a generalized relational system worldview, causality cannot be explained by scientific methodical formalism between society and science (e.g. *maqasid* and energy circular causation). Only the relationship from the side of energy to *maqasid* (society) is explained. The result is dysfunction of the *maqasid as-shari'ah* as the philosophy of Islamic law (Muslehuddin, n.d., Kamali, 1991) in relation to its *res extensa* and *res cogitans* inter-causal dynamics of pairing within *Sunnat Allah*.

There are two implications of the above argument: First, there exists a formal scientific episteme and a formalism of the *Tawhidi* (monotheistic) methodological worldview that extends the bounds of scientific thought and analysis from the sheer a posteriori world-system to the holism of a priori and a posteriori conjoint in the total world-system. Such a methodology in the causally unified *res extensa* and *res cogitans* domains of total reality is not possible either in rationalism or in the present state of intellection in *maqasid as-shari'ah*. Second, the extension of the existing narrow domain of *maqasid as-shari'ah* to *muamalat* by the expanding evolutionary learning in *Sunnat Allah* is both real and functionally possible by the *Tawhidi* methodology and its application (Choudhury, 2014a; Choudhury, 2014b). Thus the sectarian (*madzhab*) conflicts on details of the *maqasid as-shari'ah* are avoided by the universal and unique methodological worldview of *Tawhidi* epistemology. A harmonization in everything entailing the *maqasid as-shari'ah* embedded and learning within the *Sunnat Allah* is made possible.

Objective

The above implications of our discussion bring forth the principal objective of this chapter: to lay down the positive methodology of the *Tawhidi* worldview. Within this rests the existing philosophy of *maqasid as-shari'ah*. However, in its existing state, the narrow philosophy of *maqasid as-shari'ah* fails to address the socio-scientific *problematique*. This attains the realm of generality and a generalized system model within the great design of *Sunnat Allah*. This chapter will establish if the extend-ibility of *maqasid as-shari'ah* within the domain of *Sunnat Allah* is indeed possible, both by its episteme and by the methodical formalism applying to real issues. Several socio-scientific issues will be discussed and critically reformulated in light of *Tawhidi* methodology and its methodical formalism. This will bring out the potential of a newer precept of *maqasid as-shari'ah* which must be addressed in the complexity and richness of evolutionary learning with the diversity of being and becoming of our new age, and in the light of the *Qur'an* and the *sunnah*.[5]

Finally, this chapter will examine some practical topics of science–society synergy as a principal example of socio-economic development within the *Tawhidi* methodo-logical worldview, even as the potentiality of studying such issues cannot be gained from the existing understanding of *maqasid as-shari'ah* within *muamalat* alone. In pursuit of the imminent critical realism, the philosophy of *maqasid as-shari'ah* is developed within the relational unified inter-causal learning universe of *Sunnat Allah*.

Development of science within the monotheistic domain: a critic

Tawhid means oneness as the primal attribute of God. Every Muslim and non-Muslim believes in the oneness of God as the cardinal attribute of their religion. Yet the understanding of *Tawhid* in its ontological, epistemological, and phenomenological relationship in the articles of faith and its relationship with the world-system is not easily understood. This is equally true of Muslims and non-Muslims. Consequently, the substantive meaning of monotheism in relationship to God, self, the world, and the ultimate closure of knowledge and temporal order in the hereafter (*akhira*) is not understood. Only a casual reference is made to this otherwise substantive know-ledge premise for all socio-economic development and beyond. The gradual decline of interest and pursuit in the intellectual world of a substantive understanding of monotheism as the unity of organic relationship explained by invoking the structure and functionalism of scientific knowledge has caused the gradual abandonment of the study of the monotheistic law in hardcore scientific inquiry.

Such an abandonment of the monotheistic essence from the core of scientific and worldly inquiry has caused a fading away on several fronts of intellection. In the age of scholasticism, the departure occurred first due to the inability of the church to explain the growing challenge of understanding both the abstraction and the material reality that arose during the eighteenth-century Enlightenment. This paucity of know-ledge in the (then) apprehended meaning of the monotheistic essence and the analyt-ical world-system, caused the dichotomy between church and science (Schumpeter, 1966). This dichotomy expanded to every quarter of human activity, including socio-scientific relations. It entered the domain of knowledge and education; of cul-ture and politics; and of science, morality, ethics, economics and society; altogether forming the differentiating pillars of the mental construct and its application in the realms of practice and enforcement of the monotheistic law.

Such growing division between religion and the social and scientific orders has now permanently marked the whole of human thought, practice, and application. Even the scientific application of religion has been disabled due to the fundamental failure on the part of the church to explain scientific phenomena by the edicts of monotheism. However, it was equally necessary to explain monotheism by the edicts of science and analytics. Such a circular causality between monotheism and science does not mean the acceptance of a final and unchangeable epistemology of science, which once unbarred, remains the unquestionable finality for all times. This belief is itself questionable, even after age-old reliance on scientific facts, as the supreme knowledge in rationalism.

Scientific theories have been changing by the force of abstraction and experimentation for a long time now. Yet certain facts have never been questioned despite the dynamic nature of scientific inquiry. Examples are legion. Of special note is the failure to establish a sound methodology that will integrate ethics endogenously into scientific theory. This was a broader dream of Einstein (Bohr in Folse, 1985). No methodology has been established to integrate the micro-and macro-universe phenomena, in spite of the grandiose works of Penrose (1989) on quantum gravity. The essential program of systemic unification between relativity and quantum physics has stalled in the absence of a viable methodology to explain, formalize, and yield some unity of social and scientific knowledge.

The Vienna Circle (Neurath, Carnap and Morris, 1970) tried but failed to do this. This was essentially due to two factors: First, a generalized formalism to integrate ethics with scientific theory could not be conceptualized, let alone the failure of application of ethics in a troubled world, except for giving theoretical context to the study of the field (Edel, 1970). Second, specialization not only narrowed down the scope of science and economic study to logical positivism, but also to invoke God and the divine law in scientific study was considered scientific blasphemy (Pheby, 1988).

In economics, the dynamic preference formation in rational choice theory, and the resulting effects on social choice theory, could not be explained outside the paradigm of economic rationality and transitivity of preferences. Heterodox economics has seriously questioned these static conditions of the growth of economic thought as sheer scientific thought. Lawson (2003) has revived the quest for new and functional ontological beginnings of economic reasoning. In the name of specialization, scientific and social inquiry has receded into a narrow domain that excludes a systemic, and therefore, complex and endogenous, inter-related study of morality, ethics, culture, and values from social and scientific calculus.

Consequently, the treatment of technology and choices by interactive dynamic preference formation, with the exception of the distant linear aggregation of utilitarian social choice, has remained ethically benign in the study of economics, science, and society. Now, for example, no positive circular causation is possible between distributive justice and economic efficiency to link these up in the presence of the prevailing core axiom of economic science, namely scarcity of resource and competition for scarce resources, to maximize certain so-called 'objective functions' under rational choice at any given point in time.

However, economics suffered from the contesting schools of Keynes and the Keynesians (Hunt, 1979) on the one side, and Friedman and the monetarists on the other. Keynes, though a rationalist, believed in economic rationality to solve the ethical problem signified via government expenditure in goods and services, deficit financing, and the spending problem versus the saving problem (Ventelou, 2005). Yet he was a normative thinker. He was swayed by the ethical thought of G.E. Moore (1903) concerning the extraneous elements of a theory of probability concerning economic events. Friedman (1989) was a champion of the role of money in the economy. His prescription for economic stabilization with stable prices and economic growth was the private market solution. Here, the quantity of money played the central role; it measured the quantity in accord with the exchange demand of the economy. Ethics, to Friedman, descended to market competition and economic efficiency. Only ethical positivism in this sense mattered against the normative view towards ethical reconstruction.

On the issue of economic epistemology, the contested views of Keynes and Friedman, with a whimper of this debate in many others, could not expand the horizons of economics as science into the cybernetic synergy of religion and related values. Among these are other works by Hayek (1976), von Mises (1976) as the Austrian economic epistemologists; Sen (1988), and the evolutionary economists like Myrdal (1958), Schumpeter (1961), Georgescu-Roegen (1981) in economic process, and North (1981) on economic institutions.

Lucas' economic aggregation and behavioral theory subjected macroeconomics to the neoclassical form of rational choice and static preferences towards framing up the rational expectations hypothesis. Nordhaus delineated aggregate behavior in relation to economics and politics also by reference to rational choice theory. Arrow's social choice theory is a replica of utilitarianism arising from the transitivity assumption of rational choice. He allows dictatorial termination of a discursive game, but leaves the terminating agent undefined. Hayek and von Mises, from the Austrian School of Economics, stand out as economic epistemologists based on the axiom of economic rationality as was Keynes as an economic philosopher (O'Donnell, 1989). Consequently, justice and institutions, being important elements in their thinking, took on a solely economic meaning. Economics was attempting to be a handmaiden of ethics. Yet the idea of social justice was seen as mirage in the market system.

The works of Myrdal, Schumpeter, and Georgescu-Roegen were a combination of the Austrian form of evolutionary economics and an evolutionary epistemology affecting economic theory. For example, Myrdal's concept of 'the wider field of valuation' introduced the importance of cultural values in the form of a dual economic reasoning. Yet it could not formulate an abiding general theory of economics based on the ethical idea. The evolutionary economic thought of Boulding (1971) tried to incorporate ethics and values as part of a general theory of economic science. Yet the endogenous nature of resource formation, ownership, and distribution remained subject to the postulate of scarcity of resources. Such an approach annulled the understanding of the endogenous nature of creative evolution.

Schumpeter and North's evolutionary institutions do not point out any definite normative goal towards which the political economy of transformation and technological future ought to be directed. Thereby, a narrative study of economic history overshadows the theory of normative change and social transformation.

Sen's theory of ethics and economics is a new development. It incorporates deontological preferences in developing a phenomenological perspective of dynamic preferences and economic behavior away from rational choice theory. Sen's theory, like Arrow's, is not a time-and-preference dynamic. Consequently, a theory of change cannot be empirically viable to study a normative future of change with ethics endogenously embedded in economics. The most important theory of endogenous ethics in economic, social, and scientific worldview is yet to materialize. One wonders why the project has not been realized thus far.

In the light of the monotheistic inclusion in a theory of 'everything' that would expand the scope and deepen the explanatory power of science, economics, finance and society, we must break down the wall of impermeability that divides monotheistic methodological worldview from that of science and the social entirety. We refer to this totality as the field of human intellection – *res extensa* and *res cogitans*. It imbibes of a general, unique, and universal theory for everything in the form of an evolutionary learning process system.

We refer to such a methodological unified totality as the socio-scientific order of *Sunnat Allah*. Its methodology is premised on the epistemology of unity of knowledge. The realm of this socio-scientific unification is governed by textual laws and their applications out of the good things of life, while also studying the consequences of the falsehood approach. The good things of life unify abstraction and materiality with the life-sustaining regime of moral actualization. The moral foundation of the immanent methodological worldview thereby, generates ethical endogeneity. Its approach is the organic unification of the interrelationship of being and becoming. It is signified by evolutionary learning processes across systems.

The real scientific *problematique*: Kantian heteronomy

The divisive wall of intellection in systemic discontinuity between micro and macro aspects of socio-scientific inquiry, most critically, the difficulties of integrating monotheistic law into mainstream socio-scientific thought, is due to the permanence of what is termed as heteronomy of the Kantian type. The problem of heteronomy is not simply of a philosophical nature. Its identical effects of divisiveness between disparate types of socio-scientific reasoning are found in economics, finance, and social order (Choudhury, 2010).

The meaning of heteronomy can be derived from the words of Kant (reprinted 1949, p. 25): "This, then, is a question which at least calls for closer examination, and does not permit any off-hand answer: whether there is any knowledge that is thus independent of experience and even of all impressions of the senses. Such knowledge is entitled a priori, and is distinguished from the empirical, which has its sources *a posteriori*, that is, in experience."

Kant continues, detailing the problem of dichotomy in reasoning (reprinted 1949, p. 25): "In what follows, therefore, we shall understand by *a priori* knowledge, no knowledge independent of this or that experience, but knowledge absolutely independent of all experience. Opposed to it is empirical knowledge, which is knowledge possible only a posteriori, that is, through experience."

Heteronomy is thus the epistemological problem of the dichotomy between a priori and a posteriori reasoning; likewise between deductive and inductive reasoning; and thereby also between normative analysis and logical positivism, *noumena* and phenomena. Kant's problem of heteronomy is explained by Carnap as the divided understanding between the moral imperative and the material world-system. This also attracts attention to the meaning of intellectual rationalism. The epistemological dichotomy in reasoning can be explained as follows: A synthetic gap exists between the metaphysical order of pure reason that is contained in the a priori domain, and the material world of concrescence that is embodied in a posteriori domain.

Consequently, even though much desired in Kant's critical moral imperative, and arising from the a priori domain, such imperative cannot be mapped *onto* the a posteriori domain and vice-versa. Inter-causality becomes impossible. All this is due to there not being a well-defined correspondence between the enactment of an overarching law and rules governing uniquely the domains of a priori and the a posteriori reasoning. To resolve this problem, morality becomes embodied in human rationalism as the sole determiner. The divine law of a priori reasoning cannot create positive action in its metaphysical form. It becomes dysfunctional in the material world and is replaced by a rationalist interpretation of moral and ethical imperatives (Kant, trans. Friedrich, 1949). In the end, monotheistic law failed to be integrated in mainstream socio-scientific intellection. The endogeneity of the moral and ethical law had to be discarded.

Endogeneity in socio-scientific reasoning between a priori and a posteriori domains formalizes, by way of a functional ontological approach, a seamless circular continuity between them. For example, a policy variable is taken to be exogenous, and hence normative. Thus, an ethical perspective is carried forward by policy variables to affect socio-economic change that is endogenous in nature. However, policy variables, being exogenous, are not affected by a set of endogenous variables. Heteronomy exists between the policy and socio-economic variables of the dichotomy between positivistic reasoning (endogenous socio-economic variables) and the normative variable (exogenous policy variable). To create continuous endogeneity, the policy variables must be turned into endogenous variables. This can happen by changing the structure of decision making between government-as-institution and the socio-economic system. Such a decision making becomes participative. Therefore, the imminent conditions that affect socio-economic variables also affect policy variables and institutions.

In respect of society and economics we can refer to Sztompka's (1991) model of endogenous continuity as a historical processes evolving over time and regenerating social structures, agencies, and agents through the intervening mediums of operation, praxis, and action. This is also true of a continuous function between these elements over time, say structure (y_{1t}), agencies (y_{2t}), agents (y_{3t}) through the regenerated inputs of operation (x_{1t}), praxis (x_{2t}), and action (x_{3t}). The continuous function involving these variables is written as, $F(y_{1t}, y_{2t}, y_{3t}, x_{1t}, x_{2t}, x_{3t})$ = knowledge-induced parameter. The properties of continuity and differentiability of this function in terms of the stated variables establishes the well-known implicit functions theorem of differential calculus (Baldani, Bradfield and Turner, 2005). Every variable can now be written by inter-causality in terms of the other variables. Thus, all the variables become endogenously inter-related. The participatory policy variables would be in the list of variables. Now, no variable remains exogenous in nature.

The result of a Kantian-type dichotomy and the problem of lack of synthesis (i.e. the ineluctable problem of heteronomy by Kantian reasoning applied in economics and finance) is caused by the mainstream economic postulate of resource scarcity. Kantian rationalism is now seen to enhance this constriction in the augmenting of resources which causes widening systemic differentiation. 'Learning' cannot now be extensively realized, as it should be by the endogenous sustainable nature of inter-causal relations between ethical choices everywhere.

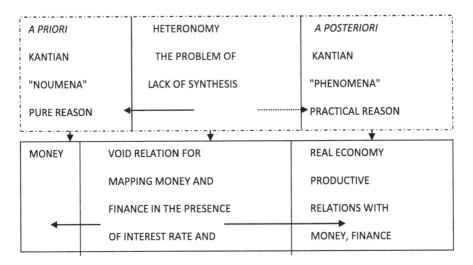

Figure 4.1 Socio-economic effect of the problem of Kantian heteronomy

Thus, there remains a pressing epistemological need to examine, study, and implement a new perspective based on the endogenous nature of unity of knowledge and of its induction into the world-system (Hubner, 1985). In this context, the monotheistic law becomes applicable to the question of money, finance, and the real economy. This gives an example of a primal way of cancelling the debilitating problem of heteronomy caused by the presence of interest rates as the price that drives financial resources away from the real economy and into bank savings. Annuling the problem of heteronomy in both the monotheistic issue of unity of knowledge across systems, and the cancelling of its debilitating effect on establishing the endogenous relationship between a priori and a posteriori reasoning, are essential for the effective working of monotheistic law in its conceptual and evidential results. This is argued, presently, in respect of the particular problem of economics, finance and the real economy. Figure 4.1 summarizes the Kantian heteronomy effect in respect of money, finance, and real economy.

Figure 4.2 summarizes the kinds of reasoning in the three different epistemological viewpoints towards understanding reality, namely, Kant, Ghazali, and *Tawhidi* circular causation dynamics.

1. *Kantian heteronomy*: Functional mappings $f_1(\Omega), f_2(\Omega), f_4 \bullet f_3$ and $f_3 \bullet f_4$ are undefined. Consequently, $f_3 \bullet f_1$ is undefined; $f_4 \bullet f_2$ is undefined. The result is that, the mappings f_1, f_2, f_3, f_4 are independent of each other and separable functional maps.
2. *Ghazali's causality*: f_1 is well-defined; f_4 is well-defined. Therefore, $f_4 \bullet f_1$ is well-defined. Besides, $f_3 \bullet f_4$ and $f_4 \bullet f_3$ of the material world of inter-causality are well-defined. Yet the reverse mappings $f_3^{-1} \bullet f_2^{-1}$ and $f_4^{-1} \bullet f_1^{-1}$ are not well-defined.
3. *Tawhidi circular causation dynamics*: All the functions as shown are well-defined. Consequently, $f_3^{-1} \bullet f_2^{-1}$ and $f_4^{-1} \bullet f_1^{-1}$ are well-defined. Yet because of the permanent incompleteness of evolutionary knowledge, circular causality will leave gaps

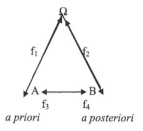

Figure 4.2 Comparative and contrasting epistemologies between Kantian heteronomy and Ghazali's peripatetic thoughts and the *Tawhidi* explanation

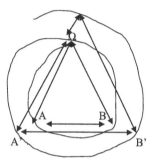

Figure 4.3 Evolutionary learning processes under circular causation caused by the monotheistic law

in our consciousness and applications, and therefore, in the moral construct of the world-system. Therefore, $(f_2 \bullet f_3) \bullet (f_3^{-1} \bullet f_2^{-1}) = f_2(f_3 \bullet f_3^{-1}) \bullet f_2^{-1} = f_2(a.I)f_2^{-1} = a.I \bullet (f_2 \bullet f_2^{-1}) = a.I \bullet b.I = a.b.I \neq I$. Because of this, parallax effects of incompleteness of knowledge on knowledge regeneration and the consequential development of the unified world-system, happen either on the positive or negative scale of evolutionary learning (conversely 'de-learning'). For this reason, the dynamics of the evolutionary learning processes, the coefficients 'a' and 'b', are functions of knowledge flows arising from the monotheistic epistemology of unity of knowledge and unity of the knowledge-induced world-system.

Figure 4.3 depicts this last case of evolutionary learning, and thus the *Tawhidi* circular causation dynamics, on the phenomenological plane of unity of knowledge and the unified world-system.

Critical inquiry the extendibility of *maqasid as-shari'ah* in monotheistic epistemology and in the total world-system *res extensa* and *res cogitans*

We now build on the substantive research issues underling the analysis of Figures 4.2 and 4.3. The scientific research program that emanates from the underlying inquiry first negates the Kantian heteronomy that has spread in contemporary perspectives of science and society. Second, the research program completes the causality underlying Ghazali's one-directional correspondence between the monotheistic law and its concrescence. Third, the completeness by the *Tawhidi* methodological worldview of Ghazali's *problematique* of causality, and the logical annulment of Kantian heteronomy, enable the monotheistic law to attain unity of knowledge and unification of details in the world-system. Such a dynamic is true in both the general and particular issues of the world-systems relating to 'everything' (*res extensa* and *res cogitans*). Accordingly, such an integrated unity of knowledge is cast in the reality of the super-arching law, *Sunnat Allah*.

The establishing of the scientific research program of *Tawhidi* epistemology requires a detailed explanation and scientific delineation of each of the following steps in the light of the *Qur'an*. The *Qur'an* is explicated by the guidance of the Prophet Muhammad.

First, the functional ontology (Gruber, 1993; Maxwell, 1962) of the *Qur'an* and the Prophetic guidance, the *sunnah*, will be established as a super-cardinal topology. Corresponding to this, the topological mappings defined on the super-cardinal topology attain mathematical conception.

Second, the primal derivation of knowledge addressing the general system pertaining to the problems and issues under study is to be explained. The meaning of the purpose and objective of the Islamic law, the *maqasid as-shari'ah*, is to be established in reference to the primal *functional* ontology of (Ω,S).

Third, the knowledge-flows as rules derived from the *maqasid as-shari'ah*, which is, in turn, derived from the *Tawhidi* ontological origin in respect of a particular set of problems under study, will be explained.

Fourth, the functional ontology of the derived knowledge-flows representing the epistemology of unity of knowledge as derived from the *Tawhidi* premise through the medium of the *maqasid as-shari'ah*, is induced in the organization of the specific problem and issue of the world-system under study. Such an investigation enables the attainment of the normative moral transformation in the light of *Tawhid*.

Fifth, the *Tawhidi* knowledge-induction of the variables of the specific problem under study is formalized as a generalized model for evaluating the wellbeing criterion (*maslaha*). This conveys the measure of the degree of unity of relations by participation between the variables in the problem under study. The emergent simulation of the wellbeing criterion under the episteme of unity of knowledge is carried out by the circular causation relationshipbetween the variables of the wellbeing objective function.

Sixth, the final process of evaluation of the wellbeing criterion by empirically measuring the degree of complementarities or substitutions as required in the light of the *maqasid as-shari'ah* between the selected variables, is carried into the next process of evolutionary learning. The foundational *Tawhidi* episteme is recalled to restart the next and subsequent co-evolutionary learning processes in continuity and across continuums of knowledge, space, and time.

Seventh, the continuity of the learning processes through their variegated experience between truth and error is shown to end in the Hereafter (*akhira*). The Hereafter is thus equated with the Great Event of the fully unraveled *Tawhid* at the end as it was in the beginning.

Figure 4.4 shows that, *Tawhid* as episteme[6] is the totality of the three cells shown:

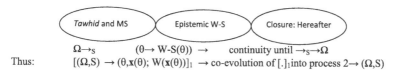

Thus:

MS: *maqasid as-shari'ah*; W-S: specifics issues of world-system in the light of *Tawhid*.

Figure 4.4 The continuous loops of inter-relations along the *Tawhidi* unified worldview

Establishing the primal functional ontology of *Tawhid* and *maqasid as-shari'ah*

(Ω,S) is the super-cardinal space of all relational mappings across 'everything'. This totality comprises both the truth domain and the falsehood domain over which the *Qur'anic* law prevails as the criterion between truth and falsehood. In this regard, the *Qur'an* (8:29) declares, "O ye who believe! If ye fear God, He will grant you a Criterion (to judge between right and wrong) ..."

Furthermore, in respect of the fullness of both knowledge $\{\theta\}$, and the oppositeness of de-knowledge (falsehood) $\{\theta'\}$, both being determined in the primal ontology of the monotheistic law (the *Qur'an*), the *Qur'an* (25:1–2) states: "Blessed is He Who sent down the Criterion to His Servant, that it may be an admonition to all creatures – He to Whom belongs the dominion of the heavens and the earth: ... no son has He begotten, nor has He a partner in His dominion: It is He Who has created all things, and ordered them in due proportion." These verses establish the conjoint functions of the *Tawhidi* worldview in the absolute oneness of being and the relational becoming of the world of mind and matter *res extensa* and *res cogitans* on the basis of the *Tawhidi* relational praxis governing both good *and* bad – the total reality.

The universal role that the ontological mapping 'S' plays irrevocably in mapping the *Qur'anic* monotheistic law onto the world-system can be read from the following *Qur'anic* (25:6) verse: "The (*Qur'an*) was sent down by Him Who knows the mystery (that is) in the heavens and the earth: verily He is oft-forgiving, Most-Merciful."

Yet for all, 'de-knowledge' has its determination in and by the *Qur'an*, it has no independent power of existence. In this regard, the *Qur'an* (7:16–18) affirms: "He (*iblis*) said: 'Because thou hast thrown me out of the Way, lo! I will lie in wait for them on Thy Straight Way: Then will I assault them from before them and behind them, from their right and their left: Nor wilt Thou find in most of them, gratitude (for Thy mercies).' (God) said: 'Get out from this (paradise), disgraced and expelled. If any of them follow thee, – Hell will I fill with you all.' "

The primal ontology of the monotheistic law in (Ω,S) bears the essence of universality and uniqueness by virtue of its capacity to explain *both* truth and falsehood as contrasting domains of reality. Anything in between these two opposites are aberrations that soon disappear in temporal experience as knowledge advances, thereby, well-defining truth while it identifies falsehood opposite to truth.[7] These verses establish knowledge as mercy; and 'de-knowledge' as darkness of the heart, mind, and the world. Thereby, monotheism annuls rationalism as the ground for knowledge by its self-created vision of reality that does not understand the purpose and order that is ingrained in creation as unity of being and becoming. This is manifest in 'everything' as a system and cybernetic grand design of the multiuniverses (Choudhury, 2014b). The result, then, is the annulment of heteronomy in human understanding of unified reality. The domain of knowledge, comprehension, and consciousness is then extended beyond the space-time limitation of reality to the knowledge-space-time structure encompassing 'everything' by the monotheistic law.

Importantly, in this final overarching universality of the monotheistic law that annuls the rationalist postulate of heteronomy is the mapping of super-cardinality of Ω by the transmission medium of the *sunnah* (S). The problem of dichotomy of synthesis, as in Kant's heteronomy, is now resolved by this bridging of the relational mappings. They form the topology of all monotheistic rules that emanate from Ω and are carried through by the well-defined mapping S. Thus $S(\Omega) \subset \Omega$, with the closure property of the large-scale multiuniverse of the seen and unseen; abstract and revealed. Yet all these are causally interrelated by the organism of the monotheistic episteme. The property of systemic closure is thus given by the *Qur'an* as, $\Omega \rightarrow S(\Omega) \rightarrow \Omega$.

This mathematical 'complete' but not terminally 'compact' topological mapping in the sense of the unbounded domain of Ω establishes universality of law, relations, form, and explanation of the multiuniverse by the interentity causality of the unity of knowledge. Such a mapping has the power to explain both knowledge and 'de-knowledge' (i.e. truth and falsehood or monotheism and rationalism, respectively) explains the nature of the rationalistic folds of thought, function, and structure. On the contrary, rationalist mappings, governed as it is by rationalism everywhere, cannot explain the kind of *Tawhidi* mapping given above. Rationalism, therefore, cannot access the completeness realm of monotheism *res extensa* and *res cogitans*.

A further extension can be made of the meanings of the monotheistic continuity by the evolutionary epistemology arising from circle 1 of Figure 4.4. The small-scale universes are embedded in the large-scale universe. As these sub-universes (world-systems) are members of the total multidimensional universe of creation, and because the latter is a super-cardinal topology, every member of this topological super-space is, therefore, a topological subset. Consequently, the dynamics of evolutionary learning in the large-scale universe, namely the string depiction, $\Omega \rightarrow S(\Omega) \rightarrow \Omega$, is repeated in the small-scale and the infinitesimal inter-event cases. The *Tawhidi* phenomenology thus transcends from (Ω, S) in respect of any event to (Ω, S) along the evolutionary learning processes as they emerge and continue across continuums of the (knowledge, space, and time) structure. Such a topological continuity of evolutionary learning character in monotheistic unity of knowledge is asserted by the *Qur'an* (1:1–2): "In the name of God, Most Gracious, Most Merciful, Praises be to God, the Cherisher and Sustainer of the Worlds" (*Alameen*). We will now explain this important second circle of Figure 4.4 in itself and in relation to the (Ω, S)-circle.

Maqasid as-shari'ah in relation to the *Tawhidi* primal ontological box

The purpose and objective of Islamic law (*shari'ah*) is the functional derivation of rules out of the monotheistic law aimed at the wellbeing (*maslaha*) of all. Wellbeing (*maslaha*) measures the degree of complementary relations between human beings and the world-system. Such unified relations convey the service to *Allah* by way of the monotheistic law as denoted and explained in (Ω, S). The notation for such epistemic relationship of *maqasid as-shari'ah* with the primal *Tawhidi* premise is denoted by $(\Omega, S) \rightarrow \{\theta^*\}$. Here (Ω, S) stands for the completion of the overarching mapping of the super-cardinal topological super-space[8] by the mapping S, such that the following mapping applies: The property $S(\Omega) \subset \Omega$ is true for both the small-scale events and the large-scale multidimensional universe. $\{\theta^*\}$. It forms the general derivation of rules out of the primal sources, the *Qur'an* and the *sunnah*, to understand the grand generalized perspective of the *Qur'anic* meaning of unity of knowledge in studying the issues at hand. The medium in such a derivation of the generalized *Qur'anic* worldview is the *sunnah*. The result, then, is to understand, decipher, and interpret the generalized meaning of the issues under consideration in light of both the *Qur'an* and the *sunnah*.

A conclusion that naturally arises from the understanding of the *maqasid as-shari'ah* in its direct link with the *Qur'an* and the *sunnah* towards developing the interpretive capacity of the general perspective, surrounds the topic of *fiqh*, jurisprudential interpretation. *Fiqh*, despite its critical importance in understanding the general and specific issues at hand in the light of the *Qur'an* and the *sunnah*, must return every new investigation on such matters to continuous reference to the primal ontological sources of Islamic knowledge. All human interpretations developed over time can at best serve as assistance and reference, rather than episteme. *Fiqh*, therefore, needs to be continuously renewed in the epistemological light of *Tawhid* in reference to both the *Qur'an* and the *sunnah*.

The problem that has arisen from using the traditional conception and practice of *fiqh* as the benchmark for an old and legalist aspect of interpretations have reduced the scope of both *fiqh* and its influence on the development of the *shari'ah*. Today, instead of focussing on the epistemological wealth of knowledge and generalization of the *maqasid as-shari'ah*, and *fiqh*, the *shari'ah* has become a set of edicts on legal contracts. The field of *fiqh* and *shari'ah* has narrowed down to just personal law and public affairs (*muamalat*) (Asad, 1987). In the midst of their deepening in these areas alone, the *shari'ah* has not been able to encompass the greater scope of the monotheistic law that generalizes the expanding relations between God, the individual, the mind and the world-system, and creates the multidimensional abstraction, discourse, application, and analysis.

Examples of particulars within the generalized system domain of *Sunnat Allah* for extendibility of *maqasid as-shari'ah*

What ought to be the nature of maqasid as-shari'ah in the embedded totality of Sunnat Allah?

The legal contractual nature as opposed to the generalized system nature of the *shari'ah* is pointed out by Hassan (2002) in relation to business and social ethics. Hassan points out the clear absence of a holistic approach to social ethics involving business. Such imperfection of the humanly developed theories of *shari'ah* contracts in different and segmented contracts (*'aqd*) is due to the failure of Islamic scholarship to formulate a generalized universal theory of contracts in the *shari'ah*, be this in personal law or in the law of contracts pertaining to commercial dealings. Instead of a universal and holistic understanding and formalism of a theory of integrated social contracts, scholars have instead evolved a segmented idea of contracts. The result has been a series of contradictions, inefficiencies, and impossibilities in the development and application of business social ethics by a theory of business ethics ethics that results from the interactive engagement of economy, finance, science, and society A better picture of social business ethics, one that would flow from a universal and unified theory of contracts in Islam could have some of the inner contradictions and conflicts between Islamic financing instruments. For example, the law of avoidance of financial interest (*riba*) is not well integrated with the financing mode of cost-plus pricing in real assets (*murabaha*). The idea of fair profit-sharing ratios between partners in a profit-sharing contract (*mudarabah*) and equity participation (*musharakah*) remains a difficult concept. The idea of a Diversified Pooled Fund to meet the goals of the *maqasid as-shari'ah* is replaced by a plethora of secondary financing instruments characterized as *shari'ah*-compliant. Yet these segmented instruments miss the epistemic foundation of *maqasid as-shari'ah* in the general-system sense of social ethics and morality. This concern has also been expressed by Coulson (1984) and Schacht (1964) in respect of their understanding of the Islamic law of contracts, contrary to a unique and universal generalized law of contracts that can be rendered by the substantive broadness of *maqasid as-shari'ah*.

The legal and contractual nature of the *shari'ah* being limited to personal, commercial, and public affairs, has prevented the Islamic community from developing *Tawhidi*-type relational links between the world and the cosmic generality. For instance, there has not arisen a treatise in modern times on the theme of justice as balance (*mizan*) except from the learned scholars of the Islamic scholasticism. (Bayrakli, 1992) writes on Farabi's theory of justice spanning horizontally in *muamalat*; and vertically in relation to the balance of the cosmic order. From a *Tawhidi* perspective, we consider the domain of *shari'ah* both horizontally and vertically by evolutionary circular causation between these dimensions in the entirety of the world-systems across (knowledge, space, and time) structure. This last part is the scientific research program interfacing with the social order.

The general-system perspective of the *shari'ah* also leaves another important note. That is, since diversity in unity is a hallmark of the *Tawhidi* episteme, simply limiting the *maqasid as-shari'ah* to its five traditional precepts is not enough. From the perspective of the world-system embedded in *Sunnat Allah*, the emergent learning universe presents the potential for a further extension of the traditional five elements into countless diversity within these given parts of the *maqasid as-shari'ah*. The *Qur'an* unravels such countless *many* diversities as the signs of God (*ayath-Allah*) (59:24)[9] that are embedded in *Sunnat Allah*.

Imam Ghazali can be understood as conveying the same idea of emanation of meanings according to the emergence of knowledge in its continuous form enabling ever-higher flights towards truth (*Tawhid*). He wrote (trans. Karim, n.d., p. 245):

> When knowledge was puffed up in his heart, his oil was enkindled. Then light upon light came to him. Then knowledge said to him: Value this moment greatly. Open your eyes, so that you may find the path. When he opened his eyes, he found the pen of God as described. It is not made of reed, it has got no head. It is incessantly writing in the mind or soul of men. He said being surprised at it: What a good thing is knowledge.

Formalizing *maqasid as-shari'ah* in the midst of the monotheistic law: the generalized world-system in unity of knowledge

The *Qur'an*, by its explanation of the monotheism-centered completion of knowledge as the result of circularly causal interaction, integration, and evolutionary phenomenology, annuls heteronomy understood as the separated a priori and a posteriori domains of reasoning. The result is a holistic, seamless, and continuous inter-relationship by unity of knowledge inducing the unified world-system in its generality and particulars. Such a phenomenology with its epistemological basis and constructive description of the world-system is summarized in the *Qur'an* by the precept of *a'lameen*. Centered in the *a'lameen* is the evanescence of the monotheistic law: "Praise be to God, the Lord of the universes" (*Qur'an*, 1:2).

The emergent world-system forms a unified combination of diverse sub-systems that are paired together in the light of complementarities and participation as the observed signs of unity in the order of reality. The combination of interactive, integrative, and evolutionary systems (IIE) is explained by the *Qur'anic* verses (*Qur'an*, 13: 1–5).[10] Here we can categorize the following sub-systems. Together, these unify the organic interrelations to form a unified world-system with diversity in unity between them. The result is the attainment of wellbeing for all (*al malslaha wal-istihsan*) using the dynamics of the monotheistic law of oneness in action.

Consider the sub-systems:

Sub-system S_1 denotes the heavens and cosmology endowed by knowledge in the (knowledge, space, and time) structure *res extensa* and *res cogitans*.

Sub-system S_2 denotes earthly topography, again defined by the knowledge-centricity of the monotheistic law.

Sub-system S_3 denotes the ecological and sustainable environmental dimensions of the richness of God's favor on mankind.

Sub-system S_4 denotes the extended diversity of divine favors on mankind and the world-system.

Each of these sub-systems is shown to overarch the paired multiuniverses for the sole purpose of gaining wellbeing (*maslaha*). Wellbeing is maximized in the conscious realization of the moral values only at the final moment of the Great Event of the Hereafter and the divine Beginning.

The crowning principle over all such paired (i.e. participatory and complementary) diversities in explaining the unity of the world-system by the dynamics of consciousness as knowledge is declared as the Throne (*Istawa*) of God in sole authority. This concludes the principle of *Tawhid*. It governs the generality and details of both unity of knowledge and unity of the knowledge-induced (conscious) world-system.

The evolutionary function of unity of knowledge as the epistemology of *Tawhid* is explained by the principle of unraveling reality for human comprehension. Revelations of the *Qur'an* commenced with the first four verses of the chapter named *Iqra*, meaning Read – in the Name of your Lord. The fourth verse declares the evolutionary dynamics of knowledge from the source of *Tawhid* in the *Qur'an*: "Proclaim! (or Read!) in the name of thy Lord and Cherisher, Who created .... He Who taught (the use of the Pen, – taught man that which he knew not." Knowledge and learning are thereby evolutionary processes of the highest order of moral construction comprising the conscious understanding of the monotheistic law, *Tawhid*, by its functions in the multi-dimensional universe.

Heteronomy in the world of economics and finance globally emulated by the existing *maqasid as-shari'ah* approach

Another example from economics and finance in the global economic situation is the relationship between money and the real economy. Kantian heteronomy with its differentiation between a priori and a posteriori analysis, *noumena* and phenomena, pure and practical reason, deductive and inductive reasoning, reflects the separation of the monetary sector from the real economy. This is manifest in all features of capitalism and capitalist globalization. In the midst of this dichotomy, the financial instruments lose their participatory function due to the holding back of resource mobilization by the rate of financial interest in bank savings.

Figure 4.1 explains the above problem of Kantian differentiation both in respect of the epistemological questions of science and religion, and for the broken links between money, finance, and real economy. This subject matter is then capable of studying within monotheism and its relationship with the economic and financial world-system. Kant's theoretical construct, failing to apply to the organic need for methodological synthesis between the moral law and materiality, denies that the immanent causality will prevail.

This kind of formal consequence is utterly destructive for modern socio-scientific reasoning and its application to the facts. The entire domain of the sciences has always claimed an isolated existence of its own, separated from any endogenous theory of morality, ethics, and sociality within it. Even when social Darwinism is invoked to explain process in scientific theory (Hull, 1988), then, competition, conflict, methodological individualism and biological differentiation are found to fully color the organic relational domains. Symbiosis in socio-scientific processes is instead meant to explain the continuum of endogenously embedded forces of competition, conflict, methodological individualism and differentiation (Holton, 1992).

We note here that, in accordance with the implications of Kantian heteronomy regarding the ruptured relationship between money, finance, and real economy, there is no mechanism that can make the system of production diversification and risk diversification 'learn' adaptively to recursively establish unity of knowledge. Such feedback-type recursive relations establish unity of knowledge in the form of circular causation. Thereby, the state of heteronomy is annulled. The implication of Kantian heteronomy in this case is that, although the a priori knowledge has its moral imperative, it remains causally disjointed from a posteriori reason and the moral law. Hence, the moral law as intellectual formalism, and the instruments and social arrangements as functional ontological artifacts to bring about complementary links between the a priori and the *a posteriori* domains, remains absent. As long as there is no substantive theory for the avoidance of interest and its replacement by participatory financing instruments, the endogenous relationship between money, finance, and the real economy cannot be formalized by a cogent methodology followed by its application.

In the absence of a theory of endogenous causal relations enabled by the relational epistemology of *Tawhid* applying to money and real economy, the invoking of *maqasid as-shari'ah*, like Kantian heteronomy, has failed to offer a circular causation between money, finance, and real economy. Thereby, a credible methodical formalism

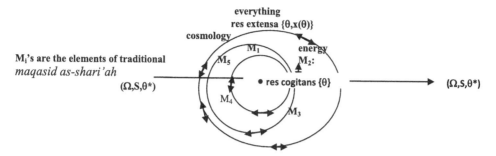

Figure 4.5 The inter-systemic conception of *maqasid as-shari'ah* within *Sunnat-Allah*

has not evolved as a scientific rendering of *maqasid as-shari'ah* to endogenously interrelate science and society. Utterances and mechanisms are floated to recognize the fact of inter-causality, but these have no credible methodology. It is in such areas of rising intellection that *maqasid as-shari'ah* ought to advance to establish not only the mechanism of *maslaha* as wellbeing, but also the epistemology underlying unity of knowledge in intellection and applying it under the multiuniverse domain of *Sunnat Allah*.

Figure 4.5 brings out the overarching unity and intercausal embedding of the dynamic concept of *maqasid as-shari'ah* within *Sunnat Allah*. Notice how an evolutionary epistemology of *Tawhidi* unity of knowledge and the world-system is established in increasing domains of newness and novelty.

Double-arrows denote the inter-systemic and inter-variable causality of organic unity of knowledge.

Formalism of the measured index (wellbeing = *maslaha*) of *maqasid as-shari'ah* within *Sunnat Allah* in socio-scientific comprehension

By combining the above-mentioned verses explained here, the study of the conscious multiuniverse (multidimensional) induced by knowledge, and thereby, with divine mercy and balance, can be signified by,

$$S(\theta) = \cup_j \cap_i S_{ij}(\theta). \qquad (4.1)$$

This expression next yields the wellbeing criterion (*maslaha*) of unity of knowledge and its induction of the unified world-system (particularity = multidimensional participatory socio-economic domain) comprising the interaction ($\cup_j$) and integration ($\cap_i$)of the sub-systems $\{S_{ij}(\theta)\}$. The *maslaha* wellbeing function is expressed as,

$$W(\theta) = W(\cup_j \cap_i S_{ij}(\theta)) = W(\mathbf{x}(\theta)). \qquad (4.2)$$

W(θ) as the index of the extensively participatory socio-scientific (particular = multidimensional socio-economic) process premised on Tawhidi epistemology of unity of knowledge is evaluated by the circular causation method in terms of the variables of the vector-x(θ). That is, $\mathbf{x}_s = f_s(\mathbf{x}_s'(\theta))$; $s = 1,2,\ldots$ n number of intercausal variables. $\mathbf{x}'(\theta)$ denotes the intrasystem and intersystem variables of the vector- $\mathbf{x}(\theta)$. Finally, the wellbeing function can be expressed in its empirical form as the knowledge function, $\theta = F(\mathbf{x}(\theta))$. The evolutionary property is signified by the condition, $dF(\mathbf{x}(\theta))/d\theta > 0$ in its simulated form of positive relationship between knowledge flows, $\{\theta\}$, while correcting for the variation of signs in the 'estimated' coefficients of the circular causation relationshipto attain inter-variable balance by complementarities, and thus participation.

With regard to the big picture of social evolution, including the socio-scientific evolutionary theory premised on unity of knowledge, the verses of *Iqra* (Read!) establish the evolutionary socio-scientific worldview of *Tawhid* in action. Such a *Qur'anic* exegesis goes beyond the limited, though profound, understanding of the divine description of the human reproductive process, as a global example. The exegesis of the verses can now be organized as follows to bring out the socio-scientific *Tawhid*-centered worldview in the multidimensional formalism of the *maslaha* as the measured index of wellbeing to evaluate the pervasively complementary impact of *maqasid as-shari'ah* according to the *Tawhidi* methodological worldview

Verses 1–5 explain the fundamental power of *Tawhid* in all of creation, specific to the human reproductive process but extended to the advent of human society.

Verses 6–17 denote the description of the events of the world-system that are variegated between truth and falsehood in the choices by free human will.

Verses 18–19 denote returning back to God, with the stock of knowledge opposing 'de-knowledge'. This is the ultimate determination of total reality. It marks the episteme of our total existence comprising the integrated *res extensa* and *res cogitans* domains. This seals the sure reality of truth overwhelming all of falsehood: "Nay, heed him not: But bow down in adoration, and bring thyself the closer (to God)" (*Qur'an*, 96, 19). Abdullah Yusuf Ali (1946, p. 1763) comments on this concluding verse of the chapter *Iqra* (edited): ".... For God is always close to him – closer to him than his jugular veins[11]. Man's humility and adoration remove him from being an insolent rebel on the one hand, and on the other, prepare his will to realize his nearness to God."

Conclusion

In the end, in reference to Figure 4.4, the *Tawhidi* phenomenological worldview is completed by the above-mentioned *Qur'anic* exegesis. The stages of the small- and large-scale universes embedded in 'everything' are now organized as follows: (1) *Tawhid* is engrained in the monotheistic law. (2) The monotheistic law is the criterion of the world-system between truth (knowledge) and falsehood (de-knowledge). (3) The closure of the multidimensional universes returns the large-scale (knowledge, space, and time)-dimensions to *Tawhid* in the End as in the Beginning. Within this complete universe, governed by *Sunnat Allah*, must evolve the potential domain of *maqasid as-shari'ah* in order to attain its true extension and potential in intellectual, examined, and observed reality.

Notes

1 Extracted from M.A. Choudhury's paper by this title to appear in *International Journal of Law and Management*, forthcoming 2016.

2 *Qur'an* (29:22): "Not on earth nor in heaven will ye be (fleeing) to frustrate (His Plan), nor have ye, besides God, any protector or helper." The *res extensa* and *res cogitans* are manifest by the overarching domains under the authority of Allah. That is under explanation by the monotheistic law in *Sunnat Allah*.

3 *Qur'an* (36:36) on pairing: "Glory to God, Who created in pairs all things that the earth produces, as well as their own (human) kind and (other) things of which they have no knowledge."

4 On a similar idea, but without invoking the monotheistic entirety, wrote Foucault. See fn 6.

5 *R'ad* (13:1–5) presents the inter-systemic abeyance to the monotheistic law.

6 Foucault on episteme: Foucault (see Sheridan, 1972, p. 191) defines the word *episteme* as follows: "By *episteme* we mean ... the total set of relations that unite, at a given period, the discursive practices that give rise to epistemological figures, sciences, and possibly formalized systems ... The episteme is not a form of knowledge (*connaissance*) or type of rationality which, crossing the boundaries of the most varied sciences, manifests the sovereign unity of a subject, a spirit, or a period; it is the totality of relations that can be discovered, for a given period, between the sciences when one analyses them at the level of discursive regularities."

7 *Qur'an* (3:7): "He it is Who has sent down to thee the Book: In it are verses basic or fundamental (of established meaning); they are the foundation of the Book; others are allegorical. ... and those who are firmly grounded in knowledge say: 'We believe in the Book; the whole of it is from our Lord' and none will grasp the Message except men of understanding."

8 The mathematical version of this theory was presented in the lecture series in the Institute of Islamic Banking and Finance, International Islamic University Malaysia, Feb. 20, 2014. The lecture was entitled, "The supercardinality property of the primal ontology of *Tawhid* as *sunnat Allah*", under the series title, "The epistemic understanding of Tawhidi methodology and its applications".

9 *Qur'an* (59:24): "He is God, the Creator, the Evolver, the Bestower of Forms (or Colors). To Him belong the Most Beautiful Names..."

10 *Qur'an* (13:1–4): "A.L.M.R. These are the Signs of the Book: that which has been revealed unto thee from the Lord is the Truth; but most men believe not. God is He who raised the heavens without any pillars that ye can see; is firmly established on the Throne (of Authority); He has subjected the sun and the moon (to His Law)! Each one runs (its course) for a term appointed. He does regulate all affairs, explaining the Signs in detail that you may believe with certainty in the meeting with your Lord. And it is He Who spread out the earth, and set thereon mountains standing firm, and (flowing) rivers; and fruit of every kind He made in pairs, two and two: He draws the Night as a veil over the Day. Behold, verily in these things are Signs for those who consider! And in the earth and tracts (diverse though) neighbouring. And gardens and vines and fields sown with corn and palm trees – growing out of single roots or otherwise watered with the same water, yet some of them We make more excellent than others to eat. Behold, verily in these things there are Signs for those who understand! "

11 *Qur'an* (50:16): "It was We Who created man, and We know what dark suggestions his soul makes to him: for We are nearer to him than (his) jugular vein." Thus *Tawhid* is evanescent everywhere and in 'everything.'

References

Asad, M. (1987). *The Law of Ours*, Dar Al-Andalus, Gibraltar.

Baldani, J., Bradfield, J. and Turner, R.W. (2005). *Mathematical Economics*, 129–31, Thomson, Canada.

Bayrakli, B. (1992). "The concept of justice (*Adl*) in the philosophy of Al-Farabi", *Hamdard Islamicus* (V3).

Bohr, N. (1985). "Discussion with Einstein on epistemological issues", in H. Folse (ed.), *The Philosophy of Neils Bohr: The Framework of Complementarity*, North Holland Physics Publications, Amsterdam, the Netherlands.

Boulding, K.E. (1971). "Economics as a moral science", in Glass J.F. and Staude J.R. (eds), *Humanistic Society*, Goodyear Publishing Co. Inc., Pacific Palisades, CA.

Buchman, D. (1998). *Al-Ghazali The Niche of Lights*, Brigham Young University Press, Provo, Utah.

Cantor, G. ed. by Jourdain, P. (1955). *Contributions to the Founding of the Theory of Transfinite Numbers*, Dover, New York, NY.

Carnap, R. (1966). "Kant's synthetic *a priori*", in his *Philosophical Foundations of Physics* (ed.) M. Gardner, Basic Books, Inc., New York, NY.

Choudhury, M.A. (1997). The epistemologies of Ghazali, Kant and the alternative, formalism in unification of knowledge applied to the concepts of markets and sustainability", *International Journal of Social Economics*, 24:7/8/9, 918–40.

Choudhury, M.A. (2009). "Which of the two? – knowledge or time", *Philosophical Papers and Review* (1):1.

Choudhury, M.A. (2010). "Unity of knowledge versus Kant's heteronomy with reference to the problem of money, finance, and real economy relations in a new global architecture", *International Journal of Social Economics*, 37:10, 764–78.

Choudhury, M.A. (2014a). *The Socio-Cybernetic Study of God and the World-System*, IGI-Global Inc., Philadelphia, PA, USA.

Choudhury, M.A. (2014b). *Tawhidi Epistemology and Its Applications*, Cambridge Scholarly Publications, Cambridge, UK.

Choudhury, M.A. (2014c). "Kantian heteronomy and contrasting economic epistemology: a mathematical approach", PsySoc Conference, Brussels (Nov. 2013).

Coulson, N.J. (1984). *Commercial Law in the Gulf States: The Islamic Legal Tradition*, Graham and Trotman, London, UK.

Edel, A. (1970). "Science and the structure of ethics", in Neurath, O., Carnap, R. and Morris, C. (eds), *Foundations of the Unity of Science*, University of Chicago Press, Chicago, IL.

Foucault, M. trans. A.M. Sheridan (1972). *The Archeology of Knowledge and the Discourse on Language*, Harper Torchbooks, New York, NY.

Friedman, M. (1989). "The quantity theory of money", in Eatwell, J., Milgate, M. and Newman, P. (eds), *New Palgrave: Money*, pp. 1–40, W.W. Norton, New York, NY.

Georgescu-Roegen, N. (1981). *The Entropy Law and the Economic Process* Harvard University Press, Cambridge, MA.

Godel, K. (1965). "On formally undecidable propositions of *Principia Mathematica* and related systems", in Davis, M (ed.), *The Undecidable*, Raven Press, Hewlett, NY.

Gruber, T.R. (1993). "A translation approach to portable ontologies", *Knowledge Acquisition*, 5:2, 199–200.

Hassan, H. (2002). "Contracts in Islamc law: The principles of commutative justice and liberality", *Journal of Islamic Studies*, 13:3, 257–97.

Hayek, F.A. (1976). *Law, Legislation and Liberty, the Mirage of Social Justice*, 2, The University of Chicago Press, Chicago, IL.

Holton, R.L. (1992). *Economy and Society*, Routledge. London, UK

Hubner, K. (trans.) by Dixon, P.R. Jr. and Dixon, H.M. (1985). "Foundations of a universal historistic theory of the empirical sciences", in his *Critique of Scientific Reason*, pp. 105–22, The University of Chicago Press, Chicago, IL.

Hull, D.L. (1988). *Science as a Process, an Evolutionary Account of the Social and Conceptual Development of Science*, The University of Chicago Press, Chicago, IL.

Human Brain Project (2013). (www.kcl.ac.uk/newsevents/news/newsrecords/2013/01Jan/Human-Brain-Project-Funded.aspx).

Humaine (16 Dec. 2003). (http://emotion-research.net/Members/KCL).

Hunt, W.H. (1979). *The Keynesian Episode, a Reassessment*, Liberty Fund Inc., Indianapolis, Indiana, USA.

Kamali, M.H. (1991). *Principles of Islamic Jurisprudence*, Islamic Texts Society, Cambridge, UK.

Kant, I. trans. by Friedrich, C.J. (1949). "Religion within the limits of reason alone", in Friedrich, C.J. (ed.), *The Philosophy of Kant*, pp. 365–411, Modern Library, New York, NY.

Kant, I. trans. by Infeld, L. (1963). "The general principle of morality"; also see "Natural religion", "Prayer", in *Kant's Lectures on Ethics*, Hackett Publishing Co., Indianapolis, IN.

Karim, F. (n.d.). *Imam Ghazali'sIhyaUlum-Id-Din*, Shah Muhammad Ashraf, Lahore, Pakistan.

Korten, D.C. (1995). *When Corporations Rule the World*, Earthscan, London, UK.

Lawson, T. (2003). "An evolutionary economics?", in his, *Reorienting Economics*, pp. 110–40, Routledge, London, UK.

Lucas, R.E. Jr (1975). "An equilibrium model of the business cycle", *Journal of Political Economy*, 83:10, 1113–44.

Macdonald, D.B. (1987). *"Tawhid"*, in E.J. Brill, *First Encyclopaedia of Islam*, E.J. Brill, New York.

Maddox, I.J. (1970). *Elements of Functional Analysis*, Cambridge University Press, Cambridge, UK.

Maxwell, G. (1962). "The ontological status of theoretical entities", in Feigl, H. and G. Maxwell, G. (eds.) *Minnesota Studies in the Philosophy of Science, II: Scientific Explanation, Space and Time*, pp. 3–27, University of Minnesota Press, Minneapolis, Minnesota.

Moore, G.E. (1903). *Principia Ethica*, Cambridge University Press, Cambridge, UK.

Muslehuddin, M. (n.d.) *Philosophy of Shari'ah and the Orientalists*, Islamic Publications, Lahore, Pakistan.

Myrdal, G. (1958). "The principle of cumulation", in Streeten, P. (ed.), *Value in Social Theory, a Selection of Essays on Methodology by Gunnar Myrdal*, pp. 198–205, Harper & Brothers Publishers, New York, NY.

Neurath, O. Carnap, R. and Morris, C. (eds) (1970). *Foundations of the Unity of Science*, University of Chicago Press, Chicago, IL. This is the work of the Vienna Circle.

North, D.C. (1981). "A theory of institutional change and the economic history of the Western World", in his, *Structure and Change in Economic History*, Chapter 15, W.W. Norton, New York, NY.

O'Donnell, R.M. (1989). "Some philosophical background", in his, *Keynes: Philosophy, Economics & Politics*, pp. 11–28, Macmillan, London, UK.

Penrose, R. (1989). *The Emperor's New Mind*, Oxford University Press, Oxford, UK.

Pheby, J. (1988). *Methodology and Economics, A Critical Introduction*, Macmillan, London, UK.

Rucker, R. (1983). "Transfinite Cardinals", in *Infinity and the Mind*, Bantam New Books, New York, NY.

Schacht, J. (1964). *Introduction to Islamic Law*, Clarendon Press, Oxford, UK.

Schumpeter, J.A. (1961). *The Theory of Economic Development*, Harvard University Press, Cambridge, MA.

Schumpeter, J.S. (1966). "The scholastic doctors and the philosophers of natural law", in his, *History of Economic Analysis*, Oxford University Press, New York, NY.

Sen, A. (1988). "Conduct, ethics and economics", in his, *On Ethics and Economics*, pp. 88–9, Basil Blackwell, Oxford, UK.

Sztompka, P. (1991). *Society in Action, the Theory of Social Becoming*, The University of Chicago Press, Chicago, IL

Ventelou, B. (2005). "Economic thought on the eve of the General Theory", in *Millennial Keynes, Chapter 2*, M.E. Sharpe, Armonk, New York.

Von Mises, L. (1976). *The Ultimate Foundation of Economic Science*, Sheed, Andrews and McMeel, Kansas City, Kansas.

Wehr, H. (1976). *A Dictionary of Modern Written Arabic*, Cowan, J.M. (ed.), Spoken Language Services, Ithaca, New York.

Chapter 5

The Performance Measurement of Islamic Banking Based on the *Maqasid* Framework[1]

Mustafa Omar Mohammed[2] *and Fauziah Mohammad Taib*[3]

Abstract

It has been taken for granted that Islamic banking (IB) is only about avoiding interest, *riba*. The objectives of Islamic banking have not been formally addressed. As such, the present conventional performance yardsticks being used by IB have focused largely on financial measures. Hence there is a need to develop other performance measurements that would complement the financial objectives of IB. This chapter, therefore, proposes the objectives of IB from the theory of *maqasid as-shari'ah* and derives a model of IB performance measurement based on these objectives. A behavioral approach operationalization method (Sekaran, 2000) is used to quantify the *maqasid* into measurable IB performance indicators that are later used for testing on a sample of six Islamic banks. The banks are evaluated and ranked at three levels based on their: (1) performance ratios, (2) performance indicators and (3) the overall *Maqasid* Index.

Introduction

Why has IB come into existence? The obvious answer, apparently, would be that banking as a financial institution has become so vital to almost all modern economies that governments, firms, and individuals cannot afford to do without it. Governments use banks – especially the central banks, among others – to regulate and supervise the health of their economies. Firms and individuals rely on banks for savings, investments, and the purchase of goods and services. Modern banks, through financial intermediaries, are central to the activities of the product and factor markets. The rapid changes in government regulations, technology and financial innovation due to globalization have resulted in more banking facilities. Such facilities include the provision of banking services through electronic channels, namely Automated Teller Machines (ATMs), PC banking, phone banking, banking kiosks, credit cards, debit cards and prepaid cards to mention but a few. These changes have revolutionized the way people raise and use their money.

The first experiment of the modern IB is the Mit Ghamr bank in Egypt, which was established in 1963. The bank lasted for only four years until 1967 as cited by Ariff (1988). Compared to conventional banking, which has been around for over 900 years, modern IB is only 39 years old: the first Islamic bank, the Dubai Islamic Bank was established in 1975. However, the expansion and performance of IB within this period has been remarkable despite the fact that it is operating in a competitive environment alongside its conventional counterpart.

In May 1997, 22 years after the inception of the first Islamic bank, there were already about 150 Islamic banks and financial institutions managing investments estimated at about USD75.5 billion in Asia, Africa, Europe and the US, covering more than 27 countries (Kamel, 1997). Just less than ten years later (i.e. May 2006) there were more than 250 Islamic financial institutions in about 100 countries globally, the majority being in Asia. The IB industry has been growing at 15% to 20% annually over the last two decades, much higher than the conventional banking growth rate. Total assets managed by Islamic financial institutions in 2002 was close to USD300 billion, while Islamic equity funds and off-balance-sheet investment accounts were conservatively estimated between USD15 billion and USD30 billion. Taken together, that is roughly the equivalent of Russia's gross domestic product.[4] Therefore, IB seems to be expanding rapidly. However, the real question still stands. What are the objectives of IB? Unfortunately, no serious effort has been made to address this question. It has never been discussed formally. What can be seen in much of the literature on the subject are scant, disjointed, discussions about the objectives of IB. It has been taken for granted that IB is only about avoiding *riba* (Siddiqi, 2000). Even the concept of *riba* itself has been confined to interest.

Most Islamic banks shy away from clearly specifying their objectives. This failure to address the objectives of Islamic banks has left some scholars with no choice but to adopt conventional yardsticks to measure the performance of Islamic banks. Whether these are the right criteria is subject to empirical testing. However, evidence from most studies using conventional yardsticks to measure the results of Islamic banks show that they are trailing behind conventional banks.

Research problems

The absence of a careful study of the objectives of IB has resulted in misinformation and misgivings about the primary reasons for the existence of Islamic banks. Accordingly, most Islamic banks have mainly relied on conventional financial yardsticks to measure their results. Hence, many IB stakeholders cannot clearly see the difference between Islamic and conventional banking. Furthermore, by using the same conventional yardstick to measure Islamic banking there is a mismatch between these conventional performance indicators and the wider objectives of IB. Whether the present criteria are sufficient to measure the overall performance of IB is subject to empirical test. Given all these shortcomings, no careful study – to the best knowledge of the authors – has been conducted to review the objectives of IB.

Objectives of the research

(a) To identify the ideal objectives of IB from the theory of *maqasid as-shari'ah*.
(b) To propose an idea of developing a model of IB performance measurement based on the objectives identified in (a) above.
(c) To test the IB performance measurement developed in (b) above on a sample of six Islamic banks.

The introductory section begins with the background to the study. It then provides a problem statement after a thorough review of both the literature and the research objectives. Section two deals with the literature review, which also includes discussion on the theory of *maqasid as-shari'ah*, and relevant literature on IB performance measurement. The third section proposes an idea of developing a model of IB performance measurement based on the broad objectives identified in section two. In section three, the research method is discussed; this is followed by the fourth section which tests the performance measurement developed in section three. The empirical results and discussion are dealt with in section five. The final section concludes the study and makes suggestions for future research.

Literature review

Introduction

Objectives are specific commitment consistent with the mission of the organization over a specified time period. They may be quantified, and may be inappropriate in some circumstances (Lynch, 1997, p. 425). Objectives are measurable, defined, operational, simple steps, and specific. They contribute to the fulfillment of specified goals, complete with a beginning and an end.[5]

Most of the discussions by modern Muslim scholars on the objectives of Islamic banking, however, have not looked in depth at the theoretical framework underlying the objectives of Islamic economics, banking and finance. For example, Kamel (1997) opines that unless the impact of the implementation of IB is reflected in economic development, the creation of value added, increased exports, fewer imports, job creation, rehabilitation of the incapacitated and training of capable elements, the gap between the Islamic and conventional banks would be narrower. He also eludes to the fact that IB would strive for a just, fair and balanced society; it is community oriented and entrepreneur friendly emphasizing productivity and expansion in the real economy; it will promote brotherhood and cooperation (Dusuki, 2005) citing (Chapra, 1985, Siddiqui 2000; and Naqvi 2003). Chapra (1985) has outlined the following distinctive features of Islamic banks, among others: abolition of interest, adherence to public interest, catalyst for development, promotion of economic well-being, establishment of social and economic justice, and equitable distribution of income.

The objectives of IB based on the *maqasid as-shari'ah* framework

The main aim of this chapter is to propose the objectives of Islamic banking based on the *maqasid as-shari'ah* framework, so the theory of *maqasid as-shari'ah* will not be referred to in much detail in this section. For a detailed discussion on the same, the readers can refer to our previous publication and conference chapters (Mustafa, 2006, 2007).

As mentioned earlier in this chapter, the objectives of IB have not been formally reviewed. Hence, the authors have tried to derive the objectives of IB from the theory of the objectives of *al-shari'ah* (*maqasid as-shari'ah*), which Muslim scholars developed as far back as the third century after Hirah, ninth century A.D. (al-Raysuni, 1992).

Almost all the scholars of *maqasid* are unanimous about the general objectives of *al-shari'ah*: to promote welfare (*jalb al-masalih*) and prevent harm (*dar' al-mafasid*) (Ibn 'Ashur, 1998, p.190). However, some differ in their classification of the specific objectives in spite of some similarities. For example, Ibn 'Ashur mentions that the specific objectives of the *shari'ah* should include the preservation of order, promotion of human welfare, prevention of corruption, establishment of justice, and maintaining stability and harmony (al-Risuni, 1992). Meanwhile, 'Ilal al-Fasi's classification objectives include reforming the human mind, developing the earth, managing benefits for all, preserving the order and system of livelihood, establishing justice and, utilizing *Allah's* natural resources (Ibid). A more refined form of the specific objectives of *al-shari'ah* is provided by Abu Zaharah (1997). He classified them into three broad areas:

1. *Tahdhib al-fard* (educating the individual).
2. *Iqamah al-'adl* (establishing justice).
3. *Jalb al-maslaha* (promoting welfare).

This chapter adopts Ibn 'Ashur's definition of the general objectives of *al-shari'ah* and Abu Zaharah's classification of specific objectives (1, 2 and 3 above) as the basis for the objectives of Islamic banking.

Performance of IB

The word performance may itself be subjective as it is rarely clearly defined. Different authors have given various meanings to the word. Nevertheless, performance measurement is regarded as a feedback which an organization receives from the activities that it has undertaken. It is also a process of determining whether an organization has achieved its objectives (Rouse and Puterill, 2003). Thus, performance measurements or indicators are in direct relation to the objectives of the firm; they allow the firm to align its activities to its objectives (Brignall, 1993).

Almost all the current Islamic banks have adopted conventional yardsticks to measure their performance. This is partly due to the absence of formal study on the objectives of Islamic banking. Using the conventional yardsticks, Islamic banks appear to be trailing behind conventional banks in their performance.

Naqvi (2000) citing (IRTI, 1998) related to a survey of expert opinion on 30 major Islamic banks reveals dismal performance levels of Islamic banks. Based on the results of the study, it was found that the rate of return offered by Islamic banks was generally lower than that of the interest-based banks. The study also concluded that cases of loan default had risen dramatically among Islamic banks, which appeared less able to deal with such cases effectively than the interest-based banks. Mokhtar et al. (2006) in their comparative study of fully fledged Islamic banks, Islamic windows and conventional banks in Malaysia for the period 1997–2003 conclude that fully fledged Islamic banks were less efficient than the conventional banks. Abdus Samad (1999) conducted a study comparing the efficiency of Islamic Bank (BIMB) and conventional banks in Malaysia. His result using the ANOVA test showed that conventional banks had a higher managerial efficiency than Islamic Bank of Malaysia. A study by Abd el Rahman et al. (2003) to investigate the X-efficiency of Islamic banks in Sudan reveals that these banks suffered from technical inefficiency.

The dismal performance of Islamic banks may be attributed partly due to the mismatch between their objectives, which is supposed to be multidimensional in nature, and the conventional yardsticks that are unidimensional, focusing on financial measures. This means that the performance of Islamic banking would require other measures besides the financial measures.

A review of literature shows that traditional performance measurement systems (based on financial measures) failed to identify and integrate all those factors that are critical in contributing to business excellence (Valiris et al., 2005).

Hasan (2004) suggests that the performance of Islamic banks should be evaluated with reference to their social responsibilities in an Islamic framework. He said the mainstream techniques of cost-profit considerations in assessing bank performance: ratio analyses and various sorts of input or output frontier models Islamic economists appear to have used are often marred by gaps, errors, and inconsistencies that render their conclusions vulnerable even in their own framework (Islamic banking).

Recently, there have been some considerable attempts to shift from the uni-dimensional measures of IB to the multidimensional measures. Nearly all these attempts, however, have dealt with the subject matter cursorily with reference to *maqasid as-shari'ah*. For example, Martan et al. (1984) used a 'fuzzy-set' approach to measure the performance of Islamic banks *vis-à-vis* traditional banking. The study also touched on some aspects of non-financial measures such as income distribution and social solidarity, economic development, investments and motivation to invest. However, it linked these measures to the objectives of Islamic banks bur spuriously. Similarly, Munawar Iqbal (2001) in his review of 30 years of Islamic banking conducted a survey on the growth, performance, and overall progress of the industry. In the survey, he used a ratio method to measure the efficiency of Islamic banking *vis-à-vis* their conventional counterparts. He used the ratio of 100 top conventional banks as the benchmark for comparison.

Hameed et al. (2005) presented some alternative reporting and performance measurements, which could be used by Islamic banks. The researchers empirically used what they termed as the 'Islamicity Disclosure Index' to measure two Islamic banks and compare their performances. Their index consists of three main indicators: *shari'ah* compliance, corporate governance and social environment. These indicators were represented by seven criteria: profit sharing ratio, *zakah* performance ratio, equitable distribution ratio, director-employee welfare ratio, Islamic investment versus non-Islamic investment, Islamic income versus non-Islamic income, and AAOIFI Index.[6] Although they have taken multidimensional approach to measure IB, they were not rigorous in their analysis relative to *al-maqasid*.

Dusuki (2005), in his doctoral thesis, examined the Islamic perspective of Corporate Social Responsibility (CSR). He investigated whether the stakeholders of Islamic banks in Malaysia subscribe to the idea of CSR. In the third chapter of his thesis, Dusuki also discussed CSR in relation to *maqasid as-shari'ah*. His empirical evidence based on a survey of seven stakeholder groups (customers, depositors, local communities, managers, employees, regulators and *shari'ah* advisors) reveals that the stakeholders of Islamic banks in Malaysia have generally positive views of CSR. This is another interesting study related to *al-maqasid*, but its main focus was on CSR. The present study differs fundamentally from the previous studies in that it has developed the IB performance measurement from the *maqasid as-shari'ah* themselves.

Other forms of performance measurement

The principal other form of performance measurement of Islamic economics, finance, and banking studied in this book is that of the wellbeing function called *maslaha* in Islamic nomenclature of *maqasid as-shari'ah*. The criticism of Islamic financial economic performance by Islamic banks can then be raised in terms of their failure to show effectiveness on financing in the social and ethical front along with the material measure of profitability and stability. The missing gap regarding other forms of financial performance measurement is due to the inability of Islamic financial economics to embrace the episteme of unity of knowledge (*Tawhid*) for understanding the underlying philosophy and methodology.

The above-mentioned performance measure of *maslaha* is formalized as follows: Once the *maslaha* function ($W(\theta)$) is estimated and simulated over θ-values in the complementary variables arising from the *Tawhidi* law of organic relationship between the choices by *maqasid as-shari'ah*, then say simulation of $W = W(\mathbf{x}(\theta))$ is done subject to the circular causation relationship given by, $x_i(\theta) = f_i(\mathbf{x}_j(\theta))$. $\mathbf{x}(\theta)$ denotes the vector of variables denoting *maqasid*-choices; (i,j), $i \neq j = 1,2,\ldots$ number of variables. The alternative performance measure of financial economics is, $dW/d\theta = \Sigma_{s=1}^{n}(\partial W/\partial x_s).(dx_s(\theta))/d\theta$.

There are authors who have been trying to grapple with the topic of performance measurement. Examples here are of recent writings by Rosylin Mohd and Yusof and Mejda Bahlous (2013).[7] These works are merely empirical in nature, without any understanding of what the essential context of performance measurement in Islamic financial economic context means; they ought to be formalized for empirical testing.

Research method

Introduction

As mentioned in the introductory section, the first objective of this study is to identify the ideal objectives of Islamic banking from the theory of *maqasid as-shari'ah*. This has been achieved by going through relevant literature and *shari'ah* sources. Accordingly, three broad objectives were identified: educating individuals, establishing justice and *maslaha*.

Second, this study proposes, besides the financial measures, IB performance measurement from the three objectives identified above. The authors have made use of Sekaran's method (2000, pp.176–95) and content analysis to operationally define these objectives of Islamic banking into measurable items. This is done by looking at the

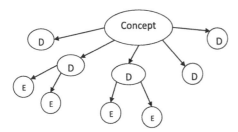

Figure 5.1 Operational definition of the objectives of Islamic banking (IB)

behavioural dimensions denoted by the concept. These are then translated into observable and measurable elements so as to form an index of measurement of the concept.

Overview of Sekaran's concepts of operationalization method

Sekaran's method breaks down abstract notions or concepts (C) into observable characteristic behaviours, termed 'dimensions' (D). The dimensions are then further broken down into measurable behaviours, referred to as elements (E). She cited the example of thirst as a concept. The behavior of thirsty people is to drink a lot of fluid (dimension). The degree of thirst can be measured by the number of glasses drunk by each thirsty individual (element). Sekaran's model can be illustrated as follows: D denotes 'dimensions' and E denotes 'elements'.

Using Sekaran's method, the three broad objectives of IB, namely educating individuals, establishing justice and *maslaha* are operationally defined. Each of these objectives or concepts (C) is then translated into broad characteristics or dimensions (D) and finally into measurable behaviours or elements (E) as follows:

Verification of the performance measurement

The IB performance measurement developed from the *maqasid as-shari'ah* framework (see Table 5.1) were sent to *shari'ah* experts from the Middle East and Malaysia who are well versed in both the Islamic and conventional banks for verification. This was done on two levels. The first level was in the form of interview. Ten experts in the areas of Islamic banking, *fiqh* and Islamic economics were interviewed in order to triangulate the performance measurement developed. Nearly all the experts, through the interview, have verified the appropriateness of the IB performance measurement developed. The profiles of the interviewees are presented in Table 5.2.

The second level of verification was in the form of a questionnaire. Sixteen experts were requested to assign weights to the components to determine whether the performance measurements were acceptable. The profiles of the experts are presented in Table 5.3.

The average weights given by the experts are presented in Table 5.4.

After the newly developed IB performance measurements were verified and the weights were assigned by experts, the author tried to identify the suitable ratios corresponding to the respective elements. This is discussed in section 3.3.

Table 5.1 Operationalizing the objectives of Islamic banking

Concepts (Objectives)	Dimensions	Elements
1. Educating Individual	D1. Advancement of knowledge D2. Instilling new skills and improvements D3. Creating awareness of Islamic banking	E1. Education grant E2. Research E3. Training E4. Publicity
2. Establishing Justice	D4. Fair dealings D5. Affordable products and services D6. Elimination of injustices	E5. Fair returns E6. Affordable price E7. Interest-free product
3. Public Interest	D7. Profitability D8. Redistribution of income and wealth D9. Investment in vital real sector	E8. Profit ratios E9. Personal income E10. Investment ratios in real sector

Table 5.2 Profile of the interviewees (I1–I10)

No.	Interviewee (I)	Academic Qualification	Specialization	Occupation	Institution
1	I1	PhD	Fiqh, Economics and Finance	Professor	King Abdul Aziz University, Jeddah
2	I2	PhD	Shari'ah, Law, Economics and Finance	Professor	Islamic Foundation, U.K
3	I3	PhD	Islamic Economics and Finance	Professor	INCEIF, Malaysia
4	I4	PhD	Islamic Economics and Finance	Professor	Durham University, UK
5	I5	PhD	Islamic Economics and Finance	Professor/ Dean	Department of Economics, University of Brunei
6	I6	PhD	Islamic Economics and Finance	Director	Islamic Research and Training Institute (IRTI), IDB Jeddah
7	I7	Professional Qualification	Economics and Islamic Finance	CEO	Kuwait Finance House, M'sia
8	I8	Professional Qualification	Shari'ah, Fiqh, Usul al-Fiqh and Islamic Finance	Shari'ah Advisor	Over 40 Islamic financial institutions world wide
9	I9	PhD	Islamic Economics and Finance	BNM Shari'ah Advisor/CEO	TAZKIYYAH, Indonesia
10	I10	PhD	Shari'ah, Fiqh, Usul al-Fiqh, Islamic Economics and Finance	Shari'ah Advisor	Al-Rajhi Bank, Saudi Arabia

Table 5.3 Profile of the experts

No.	Expert (E)	Advisory Role	Publications	Conferences	Awards
1	E1	Nil	Below 10	Below 10	Below 2
2	E2	Member of Bank Negara Malaysia (BNM) *Shari'ah* Advisor	10–20	Above 40	2–5
3	E3	EON CAP *Shari'ah* Advisor	Below 10	20–30	Below 2
4	E4	Member of Bank Negara Malaysia (BNM) *Shari'ah* Advisor	Below 10	10–20	Below 2
5	E5	*Shari'ah* Advisor to EON CAP and IBFIM, and member of OIC *Fiqh* Academy	10–20	20–30	n.a
6	E6	EON CAP *Shari'ah* Advisor	Below 10	10–20	Below 2
7	E7	Public Bank *Shari'ah* Advisor	Below 10	Below 10	Below 2
8	E8	*Shari'ah* Advisor to *Ikhlas Retakaful*	Below 10	Below 10	n.a
9	E9	Consultant to Kyrgyzstan government on Islamic finance	n.a.	Above 40	Below 2
10	E10	*Shari'ah* Advisor to HSBC Amanah Malaysia	10–20	Above 40	Below 2
11	E11	*Shari'ah* Advisor to BSN Takaful	Below 10	Below 10	Below 2
12	E12	Nil	Below 10	10–20	Below 2
13	E13	Member of Bank Negara Malaysia (BNM) *Shari'ah* Advisor	10–20	Above 40	Below 2
14	E14	Nil	20–30	30–40	Below 2
15	E15	n.a.	n.a.	Above 40	n.a.
16	E16	Private *Shari'ah* consultant to several Islamic financial intuitions	20–30	Above 40	2–5

Table 5.4 Average weights for the three objectives and ten elements given by *shari'ah* experts

Objectives	Average Weight (Out of 100%)	Elements	Average Weight (Out of 100%)
O1. Education (*Tahdhib al-Fard*)	30	E1. Education grants/donations	24
		E2. Research	27
		E3. Training	26
		E4. Publicity	23
		Total	**100**
O2. Justice (*Al-'Adl*)	41	E5. Fair returns	30
		E6. Fair price	32
		E7. Interest-free product	38
		Total	**100**
O3. Welfare (*Al-Maslaha*)*	29	E8. Bank's profit ratios	33
		E9. Personal income transfers	30
		E10. Investment ratios in real sector	37
Total	**100**	**Total**	**100**

* *Maslaha* includes the bank's interest plus the public interest

The performance ratios (PR)

The ten performance ratios, presented in Table 5.5 below were chosen based on the following criteria:

- Discussion on the objectives of Islamic banking and on the dimensions and elements identified from these objectives.
- Past similar research using the same ratios for measuring performance of Islamic and conventional banks (Mahmood al-Osaymy et al., 2004, Shahul Hameed et al., 2006, Ali Khass, 1996).
- Statistical conveniences in relation to the source of data (Annual reports) and the research method (Multi Attribute Decision Making) – (Hwang and Yoon, 1981).
- Accurate possible representation of the conceptual level of *maqasid as-shari'ah*, though not necessarily exhaustible.

From Table 5.5 above, four ratios, namely (1) educational grant/total income ratio, (2) research expense/total expense ratio, (3) training expense/total expense ratio and (4) publicity expense/total expense ratio are assigned as measures to the first objective of Educating Individual. Hence, the higher the budget that the bank allocates for these

Table 5.5 The performance ratios corresponding to the respective elements

Concepts (Objectives)	Dimensions	Elements	Performance Ratios	Sources of Data
1. Educating individual	D1. Advancement of knowledge	E1. Education grant	R1. Education grant/ total income	Annual report
		E2. Research	R2. Research expense/ total expense	Annual report
	D2. Instilling new skills and improvements	E3. Training	R3. Training Expense/ total expense	Annual report
	D3. Creating awareness of Islamic banking	E4. Publicity	R4. Publicity expense/ total expense	Annual report
2. Establishing Justice	D4. Fair dealings	E5. Fair returns	R5. Profit/ total income	Annual report
	D5. Affordable products and services	E6. Affordable price	R6. Bad debt/ total investment	Annual report
	D6. Elimination of injustices	E7. Interest-free product	R7. Interest-free income/total income	Annual report
3. Public Interest	D7. Profitability	E8. Profit ratios	R8. Net profit/total asset	Annual report
	D8. Redistribution of income and wealth	E9. Personal income	R9. *Zakah*/Net income	Annual report
	D9. Investment in vital real sector	E10. Investment ratios in real sector	R10. Investment deposit/total deposit	Annual report

four indicators, the more it is concerned about educating individuals in its program. This allows the bank to enhance the quality of its human resources, while working towards creating customers who are knowledgeable about its objectives and products.

Three ratios: (1) Profit/total income ratio or interest/total income ratio; (2) Bad debt/total investment ratio; and (3) Interest-free income/total income ratio are identified to measure the second objective: Establishing Justice.

High ratios of bad debt to total investment indicate a widening gap in income distribution. Usually, the banks will end up imposing penalties or repossessing the assets or projects. Likewise, a high ratio of interest-free investment to total investment contributes positively towards minimizing the income and wealth disparity, since interest basically transfers wealth from the poor to the rich.[8] Hence, the bank must ensure that the kind of products they offer do not create high probabilities of default.

Lastly, three PR are selected for the third objective – *maslaha*. They are (1) net profit/total asset; (2) *zakah* paid/net asset; and (3) investment deposit/total deposit. High profitability shows that the bank is enjoying high financial *maslaha*. A high *zakah* net asset ratio shows transfer of income and wealth to the poor and needy, thus helping to bridge the inequality gap. Similarly, investment deposit to total deposit ratio indicates that the bank is directly investing in the real sector of the economy (e.g. agriculture, mining, fisheries, construction, manufacturing and small- and medium-scale businesses, etc.). The importance of these real economic sectors has a direct implication for the wider population, especially those in rural areas, and the long-term capital formation of a country.

Data

In this study, a sample of the following six Islamic banks is considered:

1. Bank Muamalat Malaysia
2. Islami Bank Bangladesh
3. Bank Syariah Mandiri, Indonesia
4. Bahrain Islamic Bank
5. Islamic International Arab Bank, Jordan
6. Sudanese Islamic Bank, Sudan

The aggregate data of the six Islamic banks for six-year period (2000–5) were obtained from Bank Scope Database.

2.0 Testing the performance measurements

The third objective of the study is to test the performance measurement developed and verified by the experts. This has been done by evaluating the performances of the six sample banks at three levels:

• Performance ratios for the six banks.
• Ranking the six banks based on their Performance Indicators (PI) for the first and third *shari'ah* objectives.
• Ranking the six banks based on the overall *Maqasid* Index.

Performance ratios

Out of the ten performance ratios identified, the study has used the following seven ratios to evaluate the individual performance of the sample banks. The first four ratios are related to the first *shari'ah* objective, 'education' while the last three ratios relate to the third objective, *maslaha* (see Table 5.5). The three performance ratios related to the second *shari'ah* objectives (justice) have been omitted from this analysis due to the unavailability of sufficient data for all the six sample banks.

  i. Education grant/total income (R_1^1)
 ii. Research expense/total expense (R_1^2)
iii. Training expense/total expense (R_1^3)
 iv. Publicity expense/total expense (R_1^4)
  v. Net profit/total asset (R_3^1)
 vi. *Zakah*/net income (R_3^2)
vii. Investment deposit/total deposit (R_3^3)

2.1 Ranking the six banks based on their performance indicators (PI)

The Simple Additive Weighting Method (SAW) (Hwang and Yoon, 1981) has been utilized for the weighting, aggregating and ranking processes.[9]

SAW is a Multiple Attribute Decision Making (MADM) method that works as follows:

(a) The Decision Maker (DM) identifies the attributes and intra-attribute values. In our case, the attributes are the three objectives and, the intra-attributes are the ten elements and the ten performance indicators (see Table 5.1).
(b) The DM assigns weights to each attribute and intra-attribute identified in (a) above. Accordingly, the weights for the three objectives and the ten elements have been assigned by the *shari'ah* experts (see Table 5.4).
(c) The evaluations for the ten performance ratios were derived from the annual reports (2000–2005) of the sample banks in the study.
(d) The DM then obtains a total score for each bank by multiplying the scale rating for each attribute by the evaluations obtained for each corresponding intra-attribute and, adding the total score for the products.
(e) Hence mathematically, the evaluation of the individual IB Objectives can be computed as below, where the Performance Indicator for Objective 1 is denoted by PI (O1).

$$PI(O1) = W_1^1 \times E_1^1 \times R_1^1 + W_1^1 \times E_1^2 \times R_1^2 + W_1^1 \times E_1^3 \times R_1^3 + W_1^1 \times E_1^4 \times R_1^4$$

$$OR \quad W_1^1(E_1^1 \times R_1^1 + E_1^2 \times R_1^2 + E_1^3 \times R_1^3 + E_1^4 \times R_1^4) \tag{5.1}$$

Where,

(O1) denotes the 1st *shari'ah* objective, i.e. *tahdhib al-fard* (education)
W_1^1 is the weight assigned to the 1st *shari'ah* objectives (derived from Table 5.4)

E_1^1 denotes the weight assigned to the first element of the 1st objective (see Table 5.4)

E_1^2 denotes the weight assigned to the second element of the 1st objective (see Table 5.4)

E_1^3 denotes the weight assigned to the third element of the 1st objective (see Table 5.4)

E_1^4 denotes the weight assigned to the fourth element of the 1st objective (see Table 5.4)

R_1^1 denotes the evaluations for the performance ratio corresponding to the first element of the 1st objective (see Table 5.5)

R_1^2 denotes the evaluations for the performance ratio corresponding to the second element of the 1st objective (see Table 5.5)

R_1^3 denotes the evaluations for the performance ratio corresponding to the third element of the 1st Objective (see Table 5.5)

R_1^4 denotes the evaluations for the performance ratio corresponding to the fourth element of the 1st objective (see Table 5.5)

Furthermore, PI (O1) = PI11 + PI21 + PI31 + PI41   (5.2)

Where,

$$PI11 = W_1^1 \times E_1^1 \times R_1^1 \tag{5.3}$$

$$PI21 = W_1^1 \times E_1^2 \times R_1^2 \tag{5.4}$$

$$PI31 = W_1^1 \times E_1^3 \times R_1^3 \tag{5.5}$$

$$PI41 = W_1^1 \times E_1^4 \times R_1^4 \tag{5.6}$$

The Performance Indicator for Objective 3 is denoted by PI (O3).

$$PI(O3) = W_3^3 \times E_3^1 \times R_3^1 + W_3^3 \times E_3^2 \times R_3^2 + W_3^3 \times E_3^3 \times R_3^3$$
$$OR\ W_3^3(E_3^1 \times R_3^1 + E_3^2 \times R_3^2 + E_3^3 \times R_3^3) \tag{5.7}$$

Where,

(O3) denotes the 3rd *shari'ah* objective i.e. *al-maslaha* (promoting welfare)

W_3^3 is the weight assigned to the 3rd *shari'ah* objective (derived from Table 5.4)

E_3^1 denotes the weight assigned to the first element of the 3rd objective (see Table 5.4)

E_3^2 denotes the weight assigned to the second element of the 3rd objective (see Table 5.4)

E_3^3 denotes the weight assigned to the third element of the 3rd objective (see Table 5.4)

R_3^1 denotes the evaluations for the performance ratio corresponding to the first element of the 3rd objective (see Table 5.5)

R_3^2 denotes the evaluations for the performance ratio corresponding to the second element of the 3rd objective (see Table 5.5)

R_3^3 denotes the evaluations for the performance ratio corresponding to the third element of the 3rd objective (see Table 5.5)

Furthermore, PI (O3) = PI13 + PI23 + PI33 $\qquad$ (5.8)

Where,

$$PI13 = W_3^3 \times E_3^1 \times R_3^1 \qquad (5.9)$$

$$PI23 = W_3^3 \times E_3^2 \times R_3^2 \qquad (5.10)$$

$$PI33 = W_3^3 \times E_3^3 \times R_3^3 \qquad (5.11)$$

The *Maqasid* index

The total overall Performance Indicators for the three *shari'ah* objectives for each bank constitute its individual *Maqasid* Index (MI). We are using only two *shari'ah* objectives for the analysis in this chapter due to the reasons given in section 4.1, thus

$$MI = PI (O1) + PI (O3) \qquad (5.12)$$

In other words, the *Maqasid* Index (MI) for the individual bank is the sum of its performance indicators in respect to objective 1 and objective 3.

Empirical results

Performance ratios (PR)

Table 5.6 Performance ratios (PR) for 1st and 3rd *shari'ah* objectives

Banks	PRs of the 1st objective Average ratios (2000–2005)				PRs of the 3rd objective Average Ratios (2000–2005)		
	R_1^1	R_1^2	R_1^3	R_1^4	R_3^1	R_3^2	R_3^3
SIB	**0.1021**	0.0033	0.0053	0.0053	0.0139	**0.0631**	0.1447
IIAB	0.0148	**0.0197**	0.0029	0.0207	0.0084	n.a	0.8225
BIB	0.0112	n.a	0.0013	0.0293	**0.0158**	0.0419	0.8603
BSM	n.a	0.0005	0.0234	**0.0916**	0.0136	0.0039	**0.9137**
IBB	0.0053	0.0090	0.0053	0.0075	0.0078	0.0069	0.8768
BMMB	n.a	n.a	**0.0707**	0.0227	0.0023	0.0400	0.6928

Where, SIB = Sudanese Islamic Bank, Sudan, IIAB = Islamic Int'l Arab Bank, Jordan, BIB = Bahrain Islamic Bank, BSM = Bank Syariah Mandiri, Indonesia, IBB = Islami Bank Bangladesh, BMM B = Bank Muamalat Malaysia

Performance ratios for the first objective

(a) Education grant/total income (RI)

From Table 5.3, the Sudanese Islamic Bank (SIB) has performed relatively well in terms of providing education grants or scholarships to the public. Ten per cent of its net income, on average, is allocated for the purpose. On the other hand, IIAB and

BIB have allocated slightly above 1% of their net income for educational purposes. BSM and BMMB did not provie any specific data on educational grants. Recently, however, some Islamic banks such as BMMB have used products such as personal financing or commodity *murabaha* in the form of a student loan for the same purpose. However, this is not covered in the period under investigation. Therefore, the SIB has surpassed the other five Islamic banks in achieving this component of the first *shari'ah* objective.

(b) Research expense/total expense (R2)

In terms of research, the Islamic International Arab Bank of Jordan (IIAB) has shown a relatively good performance compared to the other five banks in the sample. IIAB has earmarked almost 2% of its total expenses for research. IBB has allocated almost 1%. BSM only started its contribution to research activities in 2005. There is no separate data for research allocation in BIB and BMMB's annual reports. The two banks have separate accounting entries for research in their annual reports; this reflects the importance of this activity for their future product development.

(c) Training expense/total expense (R3)

In staff training programmes, Bank Muamalat Malaysia Bhd (BMMB) leads the other five banks in the sample. BMMB has allocated, on average, over 7% of its total budget for training. The high figure for BMMB is due to 'other expenses' being used as a proxy for training expenses. Nevertheless, BMMB has indicated in its annual report that the bank is focused on improving (a) risk management and (b) the core competencies of its staff, by upgrading their skills and knowledge, particularly in financial analysis. Second to BMMB is BSM; it spends over 2% of its total budget on training. The other four banks contribute less than 1% of their total budget to training.

(d) Publicity expense/total expense (R4)

As Table 5.3 shows, Bank Syariah Mandiri, Indonesia (BSM) outperforms the other five banks regarding publicity. Over 9% of its total budget goes on publicity. Three banks, namely BMMB, BIB and IIAB, spend between 2–3% of their total budget on publicity; SIB and IBB spend less than 1%.

Performance ratios of the third objective

Net profit/total asset (R8)

This ratio measures the profitability of the bank. Bahrain Islamic Bank (BIB) has been relatively profitable compared to the other banks in the sample. Its net profit represents almost 1.6% of its total assets. BIB is followed by other two banks, SIB and BSM, whose profit–asset ratios are slightly below 1.5%. Two other banks, IIAB and IBB have profit–asset ratios near to 1%. BMMB's profit–asset ratio is far less than 1%.

Zakah/net income (R9)

Once again, SIB leads the other five banks in terms of its *zakah* contribution, which is slightly above 6% of its net income. BIB and BMMB pay 4% of their net income for *zakah*. IIAB does not pay *zakah*. It leaves that responsibility to depositors and shareholders. IBB and BSM pay less than 1% of their net income towards *zakah*. BSM only started its payment of *zakah* in 2004, so there is just two years' worth of average data available for BSM (2004–2005).

Investment deposits/total deposit (R10)

This ratio measures the extent to which the Islamic bank contributes its investment to the real sector. Hence, over 90% of BSM's total deposit is for investment purposes. IIAB, BIB and IBB have over 80% of their deposits for investments. However, BMMB's investment deposit represents almost 70% of its total, compared to SIB, where it is only 14%. Whereas the liability side of these banks is represented by a large proportion of investment deposit one expects their contribution to the real sector on the asset side to be enormous. Unfortunately, this is not the case. Most of these investment deposits are used to finance debt-related activities such as the purchase of assets and investment in securities. Accordingly, debt financing using *al-bay' bithamanin ajil, al-murabahah, al-salam* and *al-istisna* modes represent, on average, over 80% of their investment activities; equity-based modes represent only 4%, on average. Similarly, investment in sectors such as agriculture, mining, and fishing represent an average of 10% of the total assets. As far as this *shari'ah* objective is concerned, more needs to be done.

Ranking the six IB based on their performance indicators (PI)

Table 5.7 Performance indicators (PI) for 1st and 3rd *shari'ah* objectives

Banks	PI for 1st objective					PI for 3rd objective			
	PI11	PI21	PI31	PI41	Total1	PII3	PI23	PI33	Total3
SIB	**0.0074**	0.0003	0.0004	0.0004	**0.0085**	0.0013	**0.0055**	0.0155	0.0223
IIAB	0.0011	**0.0016**	0.0002	0.0014	0.0043	0.0008	0	**0.8826**	**0.8834**
BIB	0.0008	0	0.0001	0.0020	0.0029	**0.0015**	0.0036	0.0923	0.0974
BSM	0	0.0004	0.0018	**0.0063**	**0.0085**	0.0013	0.0003	0.0980	0.0996
IBB	0.0004	0.0007	0.0004	0.0005	0.002	0.0007	0.0006	0.0941	0.0954
BMMB	0	0	**0.0055**	0.0016	0.0071	0.0002	0.0035	0.0743	0.078

(The figures are rounded up to the nearest 4 digits.)

1st shari'ah objective

As mentioned above, the Performance Indicators (PIs) are the products of the weighted objective times the weighted elements times the ratios. The total of the four PIs for the 1st objective constitute the total performance indicator for that objective.

Accordingly, SIB is in the forefront in terms of providing education grant to the public (PI1). IIAB, BMMB and BSM are leaders regarding research (PI2), training (PI3) and publicity (PI4) respectively.

3rd Shari'ah objective

Based on the figures for the 3rd objective, *maslaha*, BIB has performed better in relation to profitability (PI1). SIB has outperformed other banks in *zakah* while IIAB has achieved the highest in investment deposits.

With regard to the total performance indicators (Total 1) for the first objective – education, SIB and BSM have a leading role in achieving that objective. This is partly due to the high weighted performance of SIB in providing education grants or scholarships and BSM's weighted achievement in publicity. For the total performance indicator (Total 3) of the third objective – *maslaha*, IIAB has taken the lead. This is attributed partly to the high weighted score it has attained in its contribution in attracting investment deposits.

2.2 Ranking the IB based on the *Maqasid* indexes (MI)

Table 5.8 Maqasid indexes (MI)

No.	Names of Banks	PI (O1)	PI (O3)	MI [PI (O1) + PI (O3)]	Ranking
1	Sudanese Islamic Bank, Sudan	0.0085	0.0223	0.0308	6
2	Islamic Int'l Arab Bank, Jordan	0.0043	0.8834	0.8877	1
3	Bahrain Islamic Bank	0.0029	0.0974	0.1003	3
4	Bank Syariah Mandiri, Indonesia	0.0085	0.0996	0.1081	2
5	Islami Bank Bangladesh	0.002	0.0954	0.0974	4
6	Bank Muamalat Malaysia	0.0071	0.078	0.0851	5

The *Maqasid* Index measures the overall performance for the two *shari'ah* objectives, namely the 1st and 3rd. Accordingly, overall, IIAB has outperformed all the other banks in the 1st rank, followed in the sequence in a descending order by BSM, BIB, IBB, BMMB and SIB respectively.

Conclusion

The greatest significance of this study is that it proposes the objectives of IB from the *maqasid as-shari'ah* perspective. It has also suggested a methodology that could be used to develop IB performance measurement based on the *shari'ah* framework. The result of the study has shown variations in the performances of the selected Islamic banks. No one bank is able to achieve high performance in all the seven performance ratios, alternatives and performance indicators. Such variations show an inconsistent focus on the part of the individual Islamic banks on achieving overall *shari'ah* objectives. This study has come at an opportune time for Islamic banks, allowing them to revisit their objectives after nearly four decades in operation. Since this is an exploratory study, hopefully future research will take it as a point of departure for developing further the objectives and performance measurement of IB based on the *shari'ah* framework.

Editor's Comments

This well-written chapter considers the measurement of the *shari'ah* basis of Islamic banking. This pointer to the importance of measuring the impact of *maqasid as-shari'ah* in terms of the *maslaha* function is an important academic issue. However, the method used based on linearized weighted aggregation of various objective contributions to the *maslaha* is subject to substantive criticism. The editorial dialogue here is to generate critical debate and discourse. The implications of the author's usage or its alternative can have far-reaching implications in the empirical evaluation of the wellbeing function, *maslaha*, arising from the meaning of *maqasid as-shari'ah*.

Let us examine this issue critically. The weighted average measure used is a combination of perceptions of respondents to a questionnaire; annual reporting of Islamic banks, and certain prioritizing of the objectives of *al-shari'ah*. There are flaws that arise when using such perceptual ordinal measurements. Objectivity is lost in the measurement exercise as a result.

Besides, in the measurement of different categories of shari'ah objectives no complementary (participative, interlinked, networked) approach is used to study the interactive relationships between the economic and social factors. It is, therefore, not possible to pursue the intercausal study of the various *al-shari'ah* variables that would otherwise show complex and nonlinear interaction and reveal the complementarities between the variables as *maqasid as-shari'ah* choices.

A better approach with its deep methodological link to the foundational precept of the *maqasid as-shari'ah*, namely, *Tawhid*, understood as organic unity of knowledge between the inter-causal variables, present the following method of evaluation of Islamic banking in reference to *maslaha*.

The *maslaha* $W(.)$ is defined here as the functional measure for reading and establishing intercausal complementarities between the *maqasid as-shar'ah* choices $(\mathbf{x}(\theta))$. The elasticity coefficients of the variables in respect of $W(.)$ now reads the contributions of the Islamic bank variables to maslaha.

Evaluate $W = W(\mathbf{x}(\theta))$ (A5.1)

Subject to, $x_i(\theta) = f_i(\mathbf{x}_j(\theta), \theta)$, $(i \neq j) = 1,2,3,\ldots,n$ (A5.2)

$\theta = F(\mathbf{x}(\theta))$ (A5.3)

Expressions (A5.1) and (A5.2) are equivalently the conceptual and empirical versions of *maslaha*, respectively. θ denotes the average of the variable-specific levels of complementarities assigned as ordinal ranks. Indeed, the complementarities (participation, linkages, and networking out of interaction, integration, and evolutionary learning) between the *maqasid as-shari'ah* variables of choices signify the sure sign of *Tawhid* as epistemology represented in θ-variable according to *maqasid as-shari'ah* choices of the represented variables.

Notes

1 This chapter was presented at the IIUM International Accounting Conference (INTAC IV) held at Putra Jaya Marroitt, June 25, 2008. The chapter won the best paper award for the Conference. Some updates have been made in the present chapter in terms of the figures and literature review.
2 Assistant Professor, Department of Economics and Center for Islamic Economics, Kulliyyah of Economics and Management Sciences at the International Islamic University Malaysia (IIUM). He can be contacted at mustafa@iium.edu.my.
3 Professor and Dean of the School of Management, Universiti Sains Malaysia. She can be reached at mfauziah@usm.my.
4 *Time Europe Magazine*, December 16, 2002.
5 Available at: www.msu.edu/course/aee/806/snapshot.afs/syllabus/notes7.htm
6 AAOIFI stands for Accounting and Auditing Organization for Islamic Financial Institutions.
7 Rosylin Mohd. Yusof, Mejda Bahlous (2013). "Islamic banking and economic growth in GCC and East Asia countries: a panel cointegration analysis", *Journal of Islamic Accounting and Business Research*, 4:2.
8 Al-Rum, 30:39.
9 The author would like to acknowledge the help of Assoc. Prof. Dr. Moussa Larbani of the Department of Business Administration, Kulliyyah of Economics and Management Sciences, International Islamic University Malaysia for introducing to him the SAW mathematical model and giving valuable inputs for improving the chapter.

References

Abu Zaharah, M. (1997). *Usul al-Fiqh*, Dar al-Fikr al-'Arabi, Cairo.

Akkas, Ali S.M. (1996). *Relative Efficiency of Conventional and Islamic Banking Systems in Financing Investments*, Dhaka University, PhD Thesis.

Al-Osaimy, H. M. and Bamakhramah, S. A. (2004). "An early warning system for Islamic banks' performance", *Islamic Economics*, 17:1, pp. 3–14.

Al-Raysuni, A. (1992). *Nazariyat al-Maqasid 'Inda al-Imam al-Shatibi*, International Institute of Islamic Thought, Herndon.

Ariff, Moha.med (1988). "Islamic banking", *Asian Pacific Economic Literature*, 2:2, September 1988, pp. 46–62.

Brignall, S. (1993). "Performance measurement and change in local government: A general case and childcare application", *Public Money and Management*, Oct–Dec, pp. 23–9.

Chapra, M. Umer (1985). *Towards a Just Monetary System*, The Islamic Foundation, Leicester, UK.

Dusuki, A. W. (2005). *Corporate Social Responsibility of Islamic Banks in Malaysia: A Synthesis of Islamic and Stakeholders' Perspectives*, UK, Loughborough University, PhD Thesis.

Hasan, Z. (2004). "Measuring the efficiency of Islamic banks: criteria, methods and social priorities", *Review of Islamic Economics*, 8:2, pp. 5–30.

Ibn 'Ashur, M. al-Tahir (1998). *Maqasid as-shari'ah al-Islamiyyah*, ed. al-Misawi, Muhammad al-Tahir, al-Basa'ir, Kuala Lumpur.

Kamel, S. (1997). "Development of Islamic banking activity: problems and prospects", Jeddah, IDB Prize Winners' Lecture Series No.12, Available at: www.irtipms.org/PubAllE.asp, downloaded June 8 2006.

Lynch, R. (1997). *Corporate Strategy*, Pitman Publishing, London, UK.

Mustafa O.M. (2007a). "The objectives of Islamic banking". *Islamic Finance Today: The Pulse of Ethical Business*, March–May, pp. 35–43.

Mustafa O.M. (2007b). "The performance of Islamic banking: A *maqasid* approach. IIUM International Conference on Islamic Banking and Finance 2007". Crowne Plaza Mutiara Hotel, Kuala Lumpur, April 23–25.

Mustafa, O.M. (2006). "Objectives of Islamic banking: *maqasid* approach". International Conference on Jurisprudence. IIUM, August 8–10.

Rouse, P. and Putterill, M. (2003). "An integral framework for performance measurement", *Management Decision*, 41:8, pp. 791–805.

Sekaran, U. (2000). *Research Methods for Business: a Skill Building Approach*, John Wiley and Sons New York, NY.

Shahul Hameed, Sigit Pramano, Bakhtiar Alrazi and Nazli Bahrom (2004). "Alternative performance measures for Islamic banks", 2nd International Conference on Administrative Sciences, King Fahd University of Petroleum and Minerals, Saudi Arabia.

Siddiqi, M. Nejatullah (2000). "Islamic banks: concept, precept and prospects", *Review of Islamic Economics*, 9, pp. 21–35.

Valiris, G., Chytas, P., and Glykas, M. (2005). "Making Decisions Using the Balanced Scorecard and the Simple Multi-attribute Rating Technique", *Performance Measurement and Metrics*, 6:3, pp. 159–71, available at: www.emeraldinsight.com/researchregister, downloaded on June 6, 2006.

Chapter 6

The Global Implications for the *Shari'ah* Market

Abstract

The market system is defined as a domain of conscious interplay between embedded moral and ethical values in variables representing economics, finance, science, and society. The nature of market exchange thus governed by the endogenous learning nature of preferences and exchange of goods and services in the *Tawhidi* epistemological context is examined. The theoretical and behavioural implications of the emergent market concept as a system of exchanges are formalized.

Background

According to economic theory (Henderson and Quandt, 1971) the market system is a conglomerate of inter-related markets in the exchange of goods and services among many buyers and sellers and many possible varieties of goods and services. Such multi-markets of goods and services individually and collectively pursue the axioms and objectives of economic theory. These comprise the axioms of economic rationality, resources in production, consumption, and distribution, also termed in mainstream economics as resource allocation, and the objective of maximizing gains and minimizing costs.

The consequence of such a delineation of market in the midst of a system of exchange and exchangeable is price determination and an equilibrium state of market clearance between buyers and sellers. Such a state of market clearance is theoretically called market equilibrium in states of perfectly competitive or imperfectly competitive market order. The value of exchange is reflected in the price system, so much so that the absolute prices of goods and services in classical economic thought, and the relative prices of goods and services and of productive inputs in neoclassical economic thought frame concepts of efficiency and productivity.

When the pursuit of efficiency is invoked, then the organization of consumer preferences on the demand side and the production menu commonly responds to clear the market exchange in the co-terminous states of market equilibrium in the general equilibrium state of allocation of resources for optimizing consumer utility and producer output. The result, then, is a joint attainment of optimum utility by way of given fixed preferences and maximum production with minimum cost. This state of resource allocation between buyers and sellers is maintained both in perfect and imperfect market exchanges.

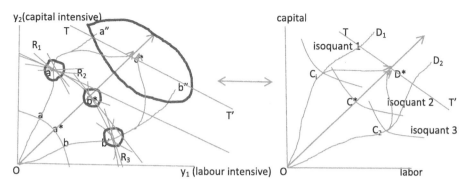

Figure 6.1 Resource allocation in mainstream economic theory and its criticism by *Tawhidi* evolutionary learning methodology

The following simple formalism supported by Figure 6.1 points out that there is no place for ethical and moral considerations in optimal resource allocation in the general economic equilibrium model in either the goods and services markets or in the markets of productive inputs. The inference, then, is that both economic reasoning and theory, and the history of economic thought, are all bereft of a methodology to endogenously understand the conscious forces of ethics and morality in individual and social choices.

The general equilibrium system of goods/services and factor markets can be explained in the following way:

y_i denotes quantities goods and services; i = 1,2.
p_i denotes prices for x_i, respectively.
x_j denotes productive factors; j = 1,2.
r_j denotes prices of productive factors.
R denotes financial resources commonly for consumers and producers.

Using the theory of inter-temporal general equilibrium theory (Walras, 1954) and that of the production of commodities by means of commodities (Dorfman et al., 1958; Sraffa, 1960) we explain Figure 6.1 and its concomitant mathematical content.

Points like a, a', a" etc.; b, b', b" etc. denote mutually exclusive optimal choices where the same amount of resources R in the form R_1, R_2, R_3, etc. are allocated to optimize the same consumer utility function with various marginal rates of commodity substitution shown by dy_1/dy_2; and to optimize the same output level of production with respective to marginal rates of substitutions.

Corresponding to Diagram 1 on the general equilibrium between consumers and producers joint market equilibrium there is the allocation of the same R-resources of consumers and producers to factors of production. This is shown in Diagram 2. The same kind of explanation applies to Diagram 2 as to Diagram 1 in respect of the determination of resource allocation points like C's and D's in Diagram 2 as with a's, b's in Diagram 1. According to optimal choice conditions based on the marginal rate of substitution, neoclassical economic rational agents could choose uniquely the resource allocation trajectory Oc* in Diagram 1 and OD* in the corresponding (double arrows) Diagram 2 so that across the exogenous technological effect of outwards shifting optimal production surfaces, the progress of commodity production and the corresponding exogenous technological augmentation of factor inputs, produces the convergence of the resource allocation choice to point c* in Diagram 1 and point D* in Diagram 2.

Resources are uniformly determined by TT'. Only the marginal rates of substitution, in respect of relative prices, change by choice of goods and services. The time continuity of resource allocation along changing and shifting TT', and therefore of optimal production surface and iso-cost line, is explained by expression (6.1):

Let $R = R(\mathbf{x}, \mathbf{y}; T)$; T as technological effect is exogenous in such neoclassical analysis. $\mathbf{x} = (x_1, x_2)$, $\mathbf{y} = (y_1, y_2)$.

$$dR/dt = \Sigma_i(\partial R/\partial x_i).(dx_i/dt) + \Sigma_j(\partial R/\partial x_j).(dx_j/dt) + dT/dt$$
$$\succ 0 \qquad <0 \qquad >0 \qquad >0 \qquad <0 \qquad >0 \qquad >0$$
$$= \Sigma_i(\partial R/\partial x_i).(dx_i/dx_j)(dx_j/dt) + \Sigma_j(\partial R/\partial x_j).(dx_j/dx_i)(dx_i/dt) + dT/dt < 0 \text{ identically.}$$

Marginal Rate of Substitution (MRS)	MRS	exogenous technology	resource scarcity as caused by MRS denying complementarity between goods and services in consumption and production.

$$(6.1)$$

Expression (6.1) remains true for both commodities (Diagram 1) and inputs of production (Diagram 2). The only way that the result of expression can be reversed is by allowing for $(\mathbf{x}, \mathbf{y})$ complementarities.

Exogenously enforced ethical and moral considerations or forms of externally induced behavior are governed by a levy of policies and externally supplied resources that are not continuously changing over time. Exogenous ethical actions and responses are externally enforced by regulation, policy, and regimentation. These are not spontaneously actualized. Hence, such incidence of ethical action is not only socially costly to realize, implement, and maintain, but it also involves conflicts in the enforcement stage. Examples here are the enforcement of interest-free resources and saving policies as opposed to interest-bearing banking and financial transactions. The result of such conflict has been the inability to establish an interest-free monetary system and monetary policy nationally and uniformly in the Muslim World. Likewise, price controls could not be continued in any country establishing non-inflationary economic growth. Many argue (see Bodo, 1989 on the views of Friedman and Schwartz) that contractionary monetary policy was the cause of the Great Depression. The market-determined complementary use of money and spending in relation to the advancement of the real economy would have been the proper way to avoid it.

The Islamic epistemological contrasts to mainstream resource allocation and axiomatic rules

In the light of *Tawhidi* epistemology governing the Islamic methodological world-view, all traces of exogeneity are replaced by the continuous existence of endogeneity. Continuous endogeneity results from the continuity and pervasiveness of unity of knowledge derived from the *Tawhidi* epistemological premise. This is cast in terms of pervasive complementarity as an organic relationship of continuous unity between the good things of life and the rejection of those which cause harm, as embodied in Islamic law (*shari'ah vis-à-vis maqasid as-shari'ah*). The continuity of such endogenous acquisition proceeds through the experiential world-system in its generality and details (as with the study of *shari'ah* markets) until its closure by the Great Event (the Hereafter).

The results of the attenuating property of systemic interaction, integration, and evolutionary learning in stages of unity of knowledge and its induction of ethical and conscious reconstruction of the experiential world-system are shown in Figure 6.1. Each of the resource allocation points like a's, b's, c's; C's and D's is a learning point according to the *Tawhidi* epistemic property of organic relationships of unity of knowledge (θ) and the θ-induction of the $(x,y,R,T)(\theta)$-vectors. The parameter of θ-values is derived from the permanent ontology of (Ω,S) as was explained earlier. Its induction of the organic relationship between the variables is explained by the obviated signs of pervasive and continuous complementarities between such variables in conformity with and in extension of *maqasid as-shari'ah*.

Thus, every resource allocation point has a horizontal learning intra-system and forward evolutionary learning inter-systemic region around it. Consequently, the endogenous technological effect by virtue of θ-induction is complemented by and is discursively inter-related with $(x,y,R)(\theta)$. Thereby the vector of $(x,y,R,T)(\theta)$-vectors and their elements are organically complementary.

Instead of given resource lines like TT' in both Diagram 1 and Diagram of Figure 6.1, we now have the continuous distribution of a plethora of resource distribution lines around a's, b's, c'c, C's and D's. Any one of these lines is equally selectable. The probability law to reduce these choices to an expected value does not work. The impact of knowledge flows (θ-values) continuously induces the variables. The knowledge-induced preferences underlying choices as consciousness, cause subjective probability. The inter-causality of the plethora of knowledge-flows with the preferences and the variables over processes of evolutionary learning of the same type in continuums altogether deny the probabilistic determination of the resource allocation points in their neighborhoods of θ-induced perturbations (Choudhury, 2014).

The result of such epistemological effects in respect of mainstream economic theory is damaging to it. For now, there are no smooth convex and concave to the origin surfaces as in Figure 6.1. Consequently, there are no observable relative prices of commodities and factors. Thereby, the marginalist doctrine does not exist. The opportunity cost concept is rejected and replaced by pervasive complementarities between the *maqasid as-shariah* choices.

As for other forms of choices, the same kind of dynamics exist due to a combination of truth and falsehood (Choudhury, Hossain and Suriadi, 2014). The neoclassical marginalist results following optimality, steady-state equilibrium, and the axioms of economic rationality, especially the axiom of resource scarcity, can be derived from the condition of knowledge, $\{\theta\}$ as truth; and $\{\theta'\}$ de-knowledge as falsehood, being individually equal to null spaces, ϕ. Hence, considerations of both truth and falsehood remain independent from mainstream economics. They are exogenous effects. No form of consciousness exists in mainstream economics.

Furthermore, as in Kantian *problematique* of heteronomy involving the dichotomy between truth (a priori = *noumena*) and its disjointed relationship with the world-system (a posteriori = phenomenon), θ is not functionally related with $f(\mathbf{x,y,R,T})$ (θ). Likewise, for any $\{\theta'\} \in$ a priori domain, there is no functional relationship like $f(\mathbf{x,y,R,T})(\theta')$. Truth and falsehood are thereby left out as sheer conditions of the mind. This frames the postulate of rationalism.

Thus, while the *Tawhidi* epistemic approach to socio-scientific reasoning explains by its own epistemic reasoning how it negates the marginalist assumptions of economics and the episteme of rationalism, neither marginalist reasoning nor rationalism is capable of explaining the ethically induced market system. The three opposite cases of the market system are now defined. The price vectors are included with $(\mathbf{x,y})$ with or without the ethical induction by knowledge flows.

(1) Mainstream economics (Debreu, 1954):

$$\{\mathbf{z}(\theta \cup \theta' = \phi) = (\mathbf{x,y,R,T})(\theta = \phi; \theta' = \phi)|\,\wp\,(\theta \cup \theta') = \phi\} \tag{6.2}$$

and any functional transformation of this topological expression.

(2) Rationalism (*Erasmus Journal* interviews T. Lawson, 2009):

$$\{\mathbf{z}(\theta \cup \theta') = (\mathbf{x,y,R,T})(\theta, \theta')|\,\wp\,(\theta \cup \theta'); \text{ but } (\theta \cup \theta' \leftrightarrow / \; f(\mathbf{z}(\theta \cup \theta'))\} \Rightarrow (\theta \cup \theta') \in \mathfrak{R} \tag{6.3}$$

episteme of rationalism.

(3) *Tawhidi* epistemology:

$$\{\mathbf{z}(\theta \cup \theta') = (\mathbf{x,y,R,T})(\theta, \theta')|\,\wp\,(\theta \cup \theta'); \text{ and } (\theta \cup \theta' \leftrightarrow f(\mathbf{z}(\theta \cup \theta')). \tag{6.4}$$

The limiting case of market choice is defined by evolutionary learning as:

$$\text{plim}\{\theta \cup \theta'\} = \text{plim}\{\theta\} \cup \text{plim}\{\theta'\}; \text{plim}\{\theta \cap \theta'\} = \text{plim}\{\theta\} \cap \text{plim}\{\theta'\} = \phi. \tag{6.5}$$

$$(\theta \cup \theta') \in (\Omega, S) \supset \mathfrak{R}(\theta \cup \theta') \supset \text{mainstream economics with } \theta = \phi; \theta' = \phi. \tag{6.6}$$

In the *Tawhidi* epistemological case, all events are consciously determined endogenously by organic inter-relationships between the *maqasid as-shari'ah* variables and learning to reject the contrary goods as evolutionary learning proceeds out of discursive interaction and integration. In the pure *Tawhidi* transformation of unity of knowledge we would write a market event, $E(\theta, \mathbf{z}(\theta))$ and its positive transformation, as between simple markets transforming to unified perspectives of multi-markets.

Expression (6.1) is now written down as follows in the case of *Tawhidi* epistemology (expression (6.7)). The observation is over time. Yet 't' is not the cause of change. Time is simply the recorder of change.

$$\left[dR / d\theta \ = \ \Sigma_i (\partial R / \partial x_i).(dx_i / d\theta) + \Sigma_j (\partial R / \partial x_j).(dx_j / d\theta) + dT / d\theta \right]_t$$

$$\succ 0 \qquad > 0 \quad > 0 \qquad > 0 \qquad > 0 \quad > 0 \qquad > 0$$

$$= \left[\Sigma_i (\partial R / \partial x_i).(dx_i / dx_j)(dx_j / d\theta) + \Sigma_j (\partial R / \partial x_j).(dx_j / dx_i)(dx_i / d\theta) + dT / d\theta > 0 \right]_t \text{ identically.}$$

$$\downarrow \qquad\qquad \downarrow \qquad\quad \downarrow \quad \downarrow$$

| | complementarities | complementarities | endogenous technology | No resource scarcity affirming complementarity by relational unity of knowledge and denial of opposite |

(6.7)

The needs basket of the *shari'ah* market

It is well known in reference to Imam Shatibi's idea on moderation in consumption (the same idea can be applied to all other economic and social activities) that the Islamic basket comprises needs (*dhururiyath, Du*), comforts (*hajiyath, Ha*), and refinements (*tahsaniyath, Th*). This is a cursory overview of the Islamic basket. Yet it has an extended meaning in the case of implicating the *Tawhidi* epistemological context in consumption, production, and distribution as market economy activities differently from a state activity. The market economy in the Islamic case with *Tawhidi* methodological connotations has been defined above. The state-run economy is one with government intervention and the command economy to regulate the activities of the market economy upwards or downwards.

Imam Shatibi was an inductive thinker in spite of invoking the divine will in his explanation of *maqasid as-shari'ah* and the wellbeing function, *maslaha*. Being an inductive thinker, Shatibi could examine the positive effects of things as they are in the perspective of *maqasid as-shari'ah*. To Shatibi, the greater expanse of what could be the potential of *maqasid as-shari'ah* beyond the limits of world affairs (*muamalat*, as in the case of markets) did not draw particular attention. As an example, production diversification causing continuous conversion between (Du,Ha,Th) can be seen in the case of 'an apple a day keeps the doctor away' across (Du,Ha,Th). Yet, at the same time, large businesses once thought to be essential for the economy can be turned into smaller enterprises for better sustainability. Such is the present-day idea of Blue Ocean Strategy (Kim and Mauborgne, 2005). In another example, waste as outputs of Du is recycled into Ha and Th. Likewise, new and subtle ideas of the universe and worldly affairs can be generated by deep reflection on the ontology of human purpose: as Coase (1994) states, 'the most powerful of all markets is the market of ideas'. Imam Ghazali said that the movement of prices in Madinah markets was by any law of demand and supply. It was due to the will of God. This is a sharp implication of the role of 'θ' in $z(θ)$ characterized above. To form an event, $E(θ,z(θ))$.

In brief, therefore, the inductive reasoning in the Shatibi-kind Islamic basket is simply one dichotomous side of the complete *Tawhidi* meaning of market exchange as event $E(θ,z(θ))$. The complete picture on the market events would be to combine Imam Ghazali, the deductive thinker, with Imam Shatibi, the inductive thinker on the occurrence of multi-dimensional event $E(θ,z(θ))$ in the continuum of knowledge, space, and time. A similar idea in terms of energy, space, and time is presented by Turney-High (1968).

Neither Ghazali nor Shatibi's reasoning regarding the economic implication of *maqasid as-shari'ah* looks at the holistic worldview of unity between deductive and inductive reasoning. More acutely, such holism, according to the *Tawhidi* meaning of Signs of God (i.e. His monotheistic law explained by the *Qur'anic ayath Allah*), implicates events in the continuity of knowledge, space, and time by virtue of the discrete observations of man of the otherwise continuous organic unity of being and becoming in the order of things. The latter organic phenomenon is referred to in the *Qur'an* in various ways.[1] In other words, the *Tawhidi* methodological worldview gives an organically unified multi-dimensional evolutionary learning precept of holism between the deductive and inductive reasoning underlying events in the continuum of creation.

Our holistic understanding in organic unity of knowledge for a market event is like the following:

$$\text{Event} = E(θ,p,x,y,R; \wp(θ);t)(θ) \tag{6.8}$$

The multi-market relationsips between the price vector of goods, services and productive inputs are given by,

$$p(θ) = f_1(θ,p',x,y,R; \wp(θ);t)(θ), \tag{6.9}$$

depending upon demand and supply price corresponding to the demand and supply treatment of $(θ,x,y,R; \wp(θ);t)(θ)$, respectively. $p'(θ)$ symbolizes the vector $p(θ)$ without the regressed element $p(θ)$, and so on over the whole vector.

Furthermore, expression (6.9) is studied conjointly with the following:

$$x(θ) = f_2(θ,x',p,y,R; \wp(θ);t)(θ) \tag{6.10}$$

formed recursively over all the variables. The meaning of the vector $x'(θ)$ is similar to $p'(θ)$.

In the same way we have the following recursive equations:

$$y(\theta) = f_3(\theta,\mathbf{x},\mathbf{p},\mathbf{y}',\mathbf{R};\wp(\theta);t)(\theta) \qquad (6.11)$$

$$R(\theta) = f_3(\theta,\mathbf{x},\mathbf{p},\mathbf{y},\mathbf{R}';\wp(\theta);t)(\theta). \qquad (6.12)$$

If $\mathbf{x}(\theta)$ is n_1 dimensional vector; $\mathbf{y}(\theta)$ is n_2 dimensional vector; $\mathbf{p}(\theta)$ is n_3-dimensional vector; and $\mathbf{R}(\theta)$ is n_4-dimensional vector, then the number of equations in the system (6.9–6.12) in the vector completeness is $(n_1+n_2+n_3+n_4)$. Besides these equations, the wellbeing function replacing the utility function, the welfare function, production function, profit function and similar optimal objective function of mainstream economics, is the wellbeing function,

$$\theta_{new} = F(\mathbf{p}^\wedge,\mathbf{x}^\wedge,\mathbf{y}^\wedge,\mathbf{R}^\wedge;\wp(\theta);t)(\theta) \qquad (6.13)$$

The hatted-variables are estimators of the variables in the complete system (6.9–6.12).

Since all of the variables in Event = $E(\theta,\mathbf{p},\mathbf{x},\mathbf{y},\mathbf{R};\wp(\theta);t)(\theta)$ are suitably complementary as organically evolutionary learning variables, the concept and nature of the equilibrium are changed. There cannot be steady-state equilibrium because of the evolutionary learning dynamics. There are now only evolutionary learning equilibriums. Besides, because of the nature of simulacra generated by the system of equations (6.9–6.13) over the continual occurrence of sets of inter-related events no objective form of optimization is logical.

The nature of simulacra of changing coefficients in expressions (6.9–6.13) contra steady-state optimal states implies that the coefficients are dynamic by virtue of continuous simulation. Hence the simulated forms of expressions (6.9–6.13) over continuous processes form complex and non-linear forms (Bertuglia and Vaio, 2005).

It is sufficient to interpret the (price, goods), and (labour, capital) relationships in equations (6.9–6.12). Milk and cheese are obviously complements. Their state of complementarity remains intact when combined with, say, bread and tea. How does this happen? What is the result on the demand and supply of milk, cheese, bread, and tea? The cooperative mechanism as a way of establishing complementarities suggests that the revenue and profit sharing between these activities on the supply side would support their interactive activities. On the demand side, the complementary production in the joint output, revenue, cost, and profit-sharing enterprise between the activities will make each of these goods affordable as *maqasid*-goods.

On the side of labour and capital relationships in production, the financing instruments of *musharakah* (equity-participation) and *mudarabah* (profit-sharing) and their diversities, such as revolving Islamic bonds (*sukuk*) around these principal instruments of Islamic financing, can solve the labour-capital conflicts. Yet in all such contracts of choices of technology, payments, and strategic participation, the wellbeing (expression (6.13)) must be evaluated by suitable complementarities between the variables in the perspective of *maqasid as-shari'ah*.

Take the example of placing Islamic funds in the capital and financial market. This activity, although permitted in conventional Islamic economic and *shari'ah* rulings (*fatwa*), remains untenable in the *Tawhidi* context of unity of knowledge reflected in participation and complementarities as signs of induced unity of knowledge in *maqasid*-activities. The reason for this rejection of capital and financial markets is the impossibility of complementing the plethora of financial instruments, many of which are interest bearing. Capital cannot inter-flow between these financing instruments. Instead, a fully segregated capital and financial market of Islamic financing instruments ought to be developed with evident relationship between money, spending, and real economy interconnections. The result, then, in a global sense across segmented markets will be,

$$(r_i/r_j)(\theta) = f_{ij}(M_{ij}, Sp_{ij}, y_{ij})(\theta) \tag{6.14}$$

(r_i, r_j) are rates of return on i-instruments and j-instruments that are organically paired by relationship, $i = 1,2,3,..,m_1, j = 1,2,...m_2$. M_{ij} denotes micro-money (Yaeger, 1997) flowing into assets and projects financed jointly by (i,j). Sp_{ij} denotes spending like investment in participatory ventures (i,j). y_{ij} denotes the value added generated by the joint venture (i,j). The induction by 'θ' signifies the participatory (unity) effect of consciousness in our particular study of world-system problems.

The participative nature of all choices in the *Tawhidi* meaning of organic relationships by unity of knowledge implies that preferences are constructed out of integration following interaction in a discursive environment between conscious participants. We write this as follows:

$$\cup_{i=interaction} \cap_{i=integration} E(\theta, p, x, y, R; \wp(\theta) = \wp_{ij}(\theta); t)(\theta) \tag{6.15}$$

$$\text{Here, } \wp_{ij}(\theta) = \cup_{i=interaction} \cap_{i=integration} \{\wp_{ij}(\theta)\}_{ij}, i = 1,2,..m_1; j = 1,2,..m_2. \tag{6.16}$$

The intertemporal valuation of market assets in respect of expressions (6.15–6.16) is done in the following way (see Figure 6.2). The evaluation formula points out the importance of including ethical and moral issues of discourse in the light of the *Tawhidi* epistemology. For example, social and ethical issues as interest-free financing of projects, poverty alleviation, microenterprises, capital ownership, environmental factors, sustainability, and moral issues of project selection and the like, all play an important role in discursive project evaluation, and thereby, the evaluation of rates of return like $r_{ij}^t(\theta_t)$. $r_{ij}(\theta) = (r_i/r_j)(\theta)$ and are functions of event variables as shown in expressions (6.15) and (6.16). In the simplified, but unrealistic, case when each of time-specific r_{ij}^t remains unchanged, then it is necessary only to complete a first-process evaluation by expression (6.14).

Formalism of market event and the ethical objectivity

Let an Event, $E(\theta, z(\theta))_t$ in knowledge (θ), space $(z(\theta))$, and time ('t') be treated as a function according to the tenets of *maqasid as-shari'ah*. An event as so defined is one complete occurrence of all the estimators and the wellbeing valuation done by the equations (6.9)–(6.13). Every such complete evaluation of an event comprises a process of the history of interaction, integration, and evolutionary learning experience, as in time-periods $t = 1, 2, ... n$ in Figure 6.2. The totality of such IIE processes over time comprises the definition of history.

Asset value   as function of discoursed values

By Time   between market and institution and compounded r_{ij} as 'nearest' rates of return

-period

| 0 | 1 | 2 | | n | time periods |

A_0

$A_1 = A_0(1+r_{ij}^1)(\theta_1)$ $A_0 + A_1(1+r_{ij}^2)(\theta_2)$ $A_0[1 + (1+r_{ij})(\theta_1) + \ldots \Pi_{t=1}^n (1+r_{ij}^t)(\theta_t)]$

$$= A_0 + A_0(1+r_{ij}^1)(\theta_1) + A_1(1+r_{ij}^2)(\theta_2)$$

$$= A_0 + A_0(1+r_{ij}^1)(\theta_1) + A_0(1+r_{ij}^1)(\theta_1).(1+r_{ij}^2)(\theta_2)$$

$$= A_0[1 + (1+r_{ij}^1)(\theta_1) + (1+r_{ij}^1)(\theta_1).(1+r_{ij}^2)(\theta_2)]$$

Figure 6.2 Asset valuation in knowledge-induced cash-flows and rates of return

Note: 'nearest' rates of return are those apprised nearest to the events at given time periods subject to the expected contingencies of markets, economy, and preferences to occur at given points of time.

When Douglas North (1981) studied the evolution of western economic history it was such a delineation of the western cultural, institutional, and market system that characterized his study. Likewise, the totality of the *Tawhidi* way of explaining the evolution of the world-system over knowledge, space, and time marks the continuum of the Islamic historical and civilizational change. In the context of market history, this is inscribed by the organically unified totality of Shatibi's inductive *maqasid* basket and Ghazali's deductive knowledge brought together in the *Tawhidi* recursive cycles of inter-causality between wellbeing and sustainability across continuum.

Such dynamics of history and civilization particularized for market relationships, but generalized for all world-systems offers a universal picture. Neither the Muslim World nor the other world markets, and their behavioural financial economics represent the *Tawhidi* universal worldview. Yet such a worldview provides an endogenous moral, ethical, and conscious design of behavioural economics and finance for all historical systems of the *longue dure'e*.

Examples of market characterization in special cases in the Muslim world

After presenting the formal characteristics of a theory of markets in the presence of conscious choices and productive sustainability, we would like to examine the degree to which the underlying trends hold true in terms of the component of household consumption per capita in GDP per capital. We have selected Indonesia and Bangladesh as two massively populated countries to reveal the relative cost of household consumption per capita in the GDP per capita.

Our analysis proceeds along the following lines:

(GDP per capita)/(consumption per capita):

(i) Increasing implies improving productivity and declining social cost of household consumption.

(ii) Decreasing implies declining productivity and increasing social cost of household consumption.

(iii) Constant implies unchanging behavioural attitude to consumption and productivity.

In the three countries examined below, approximately have more than three features of productivity versus social cost. We find that, of the three countries in their varied stages of development, the richest (UAE) has increasing household consumption cost per capita in the GDP per capita. However, the poorest (Bangladesh) is not without its problems.

Using the indicator (GDP per capita = $\alpha(\theta)$)/(consumption per capita = $\beta(\theta)$)) has the following analytical benefits. We note that, in line with the Shatibi market basket of life-fulfilment needs of development, the role of heightened consciousness (θ) in such a choice and in the choice of a regime of sustainable development, the following results would hold:

$$(d/d\theta)(\alpha(\theta)/\beta(\theta)) = (g_\alpha - g_\beta) > 0 \text{ implies, } \theta\text{-induced rate of change in } \alpha(\theta)$$
$$\text{(productivity] exceeds the social cost of}$$
$$\text{consumption per capita, } \beta(\theta); \qquad (6.17)$$

$$(d/d\theta)(\alpha(\theta)/\beta(\theta)) = (g_\alpha - g_\beta) < 0 \text{ reverse of above; a de-knowledge}$$
$$\text{effect ensues.} \qquad (6.18)$$

$$(d/d\theta)(\alpha(\theta)/\beta(\theta)) = (g_\alpha - g_\beta) = 0 \text{ no effect either ways. That is the}$$
$$\theta\text{-effect is neutralized.} \qquad (6.19)$$

Table 6.1 Computing (GDP per capita)/(consumption per capita) to study productivity versus social cost of household consumption per capita, Indonesia

Years	Population Size	Household consumption (2005 prices)	Household consumption Per capita	GDP per capita (USD)	(5)/(4) ↑: improving productivity decreasing social cost of household consumption per capita
1	2	3	4	5	6
1995	194112556	128706000000	6.63	1114.09	168.04
2000	208938698	151028000000	7.23	789.81	109.24
2012	246864191	254216000000	10.29	3566.79	346.62

Source: Statistical Economic and Social Research and Training Center for Islamic Countries (SESRIC)

Table 6.2 Computing (GDP per capita)/(consumption per capita) to study productivity versus social cost of household consumption per capita, Bangladesh

Years	Population Size	Household consumption (2005 prices)	Household consumption Per capita	GDP per capita (USD)	(5)/(4) unstable ↑ improving productivity and social cost of household consumption per capita
1	2	3	4	5	6
1995	119869585	35486274258	29.60	356.24	12.03
2000	132383265	39559760279	29.88	387.34	12.96
2012	154695368	68534117472	44.30	822.23	18.56

Source: Statistical Economic and Social Research and Training Center for Islamic Countries (SESRIC)

Table 6.3 Computing (GDP per capita)/(consumption per capita) to study productivity versus social cost of household consumption per capita, United Arab Emirates

Years	Population Size	Household consumption (2005 prices)	Household consumption Per capita	GDP per capita (USD)	(5)/(4) ↓ average decreasing productivity increasing social cost of household consumption per capita
1	2	3	4	5	6
1995	2346305	55514106180	2366.02	28020.06	11.84
2000	3026352	80551961089	2661.69	34476.32	12.95
2012	9205651	133777000000	14532.05	41691.68	2.87

Source: Source: Statistical Economic and Social Research and Training Center for Islamic Countries (SESRIC)

From the analytical arguments and the empirical examination of facts it is clear that the Islamic socio-scientific thought, specific to the study of Islamic financial economy, and as developed on the basis of *Tawhidi* epistemology, is a mixed scenario. Though the trends observed are not altogether off track from the fairly balanced direction of GDP per capita per unit of household consumption per capita. A further empirical observation in respect of Saudi Arabia also points out the following trend in respect of expression (6.17): The average annual rate for the period 1995–2010, $g_\alpha = 38.53\%$> the average annual rate $g_\beta = 23.66\%$ for the same time period. Nonetheless, these kinds of Islamic behavioural results of financial economics in endogenously, ethicality induced, cases are applicable to all cultures and regions of the world at all times as far as consciousness (θ) in behaviour and choice remains paramount.

The emergence of *shari'ah* market in the Islamic global environment

The understanding of *shari'ah* on specific economic and financial issues is not uniform across regions and groupings and methods of derivation of rules in the Muslim World. The meaning of *shari'ah*, as opposed to the purpose and objective of the *shari'ah* (*maqasid as-shari'ah*) can be stated as follows (Figure 6.1):

$(\Omega,S; \ \theta^*) \rightarrow (\theta) \rightarrow \{\theta,z(\theta)\}$: differently induced world-system by meanings of *shari'ah*

$\quad$ Continuous discourse and interpretation in reference to (Ω,S) $\qquad$ (6.20)
$\quad$ Continuous jurisprudential interpretation (*fiqh*) in reference to (θ^*). (6.21)

The process shown by (6.20) is that of *maqasid as-shari'ah*. The order of discursive derivation of rules and its application in the generality and specifics of issues always refers back to the *Qur'an* and the *sunnah* and then processes knowledge through the guidance of the learned participants of the consultative experts. This direction is shown by knowledge by way of guidance 'θ^*', not discourse, which is towards formation of 'θ'. The *Tawhidi* epistemological process upholds the foundation process (6.20) without discarding (6.21) as a follow-up of (6.20).

The process shown by (6.21) is a secondary process. It relies fundamentally on the traditions of the Islamic learned minds in the jurisprudential interpretation of derived Islamic law from (Ω,S); traditionally, these are the reference points. The *fiqh* and *fatawa* clergy pronouncements have traditionally emanated from 'θ^*'. The derivation and practice of the idea called '*shari'ah* compliance' is linked to understanding the meaning of *shari'ah* in (20). This does not necessarily refer to the practice of (6.20). The practice of '*fiqh al-muamalat*' in (6.21) does not necessarily invoke *maqasid as-shari'ah*. Such a disjointed result has become one of the major problems of the man-made *shari'ah* ('*shari'ah*-compliance') at present. It takes the understanding of *shari'ah* as a juridical practice away from reference to *maqasid as-shari'ah*. The result has been an unhappy one in the development of *Tawhidi* epistemological thought and its induction of the world-system, such as financial economics (Attia, trans Roberts, 2010; Mydin and Larbani, 2006).

Yet another glaring drawback is found in the failed extension of *shari'ah* to issues in much wider fields of social valuation (e.g. the harnessing of energy by techno-logical methods, extra-terrestrial discoveries, and mathematical and engineering modeling to increase terrestrial resources for human wellbeing). Cosmology and the analytical study of consciousness as opposed to simply the behavioural implications of these attributes in worldly affairs have remained outside the domain of *maqasid as-shari'ah*. Yet, this broader outlook is capable of including the higher dimensions of intellectual inquiry.

A wonderful piece in this regard can be found can be found below:

> We use 'the horizon of hope' to mean traveling beyond the visible dimension of existence, and considering existence as an interrelated whole in the absence of which things and events cannot be perceived as they really are. Nor can its essence and relationship with the Creator as well as the relationship between them and humanity be grasped. Scientific disciplines that conduct their own discourse largely in isolation from one another and the prevailing materialistic nature of science that has compartmentalized existence and life cannot discover the reality of things, existence, or life.

I now extract from Choudhury (2011) to present the above viewpoint:

> The idea of '*shari'ah*-compliance' is not that of *maqasid as-shari'ah*. Most often it is found that *shari'ah*-compliance' as an idea has fallen victim to an overly legal-religious interpretation of the *shari'ah* to specifics taken separately from the overarching general system worldview of Islam. Besides, the tenets of Islamic law became increasingly surrendered to such piecemeal interpretations and appli-cations. The result was a differentiated interpretation (*fiqh*) on the Islamic law by different Islamic schools. Some of these interpretations have lost legitimacy across changes of events and their complexity in time. Above all, in none of these piecemeal approaches to the *shari'ah*-compliance concepts the epistemic idea of unity of knowledge and the world-system, the participatory worldview of this conscious oneness and the human future, in place. These greatest precepts are merely expressed in utterance without delivering the functional ontological understanding of the being and becoming of a dynamic sustainable moral devel-opment future.

The role of trust as social lubricant excited by moral consciousness

Trust is most often an informal contract between buyers and sellers in the marketplace that may not be enforced by edicts of law. Yet consumer protection law can incorporate this as a social contract that is agreed between the systems of market exchange in goods and services. Goodwill is an informal attribute of the first kind. Consumer protection is a social obligatory implement of the second kind. Indeed, the small and micro-enterprises survive on the basis of the first kind of goodwill, honesty, and trust. Corporate bodies build on the demand and supply preferences for good corporate governance and corporate social responsibility to establish the second kind of institutions of all forms of protection of both buyers and sellers.

In this regard, our formalization of dynamic preferences under the impact of ethicality and knowledge-forming consciousness takes us back to expressions (6.15–6.16). The origin of conscious actions, Amartya Sen's (1992) deontological consequences in human dealings in the world-system, as of buying and selling as human transactions for the common good, depends upon ever-increasing interactions and consensus (integration) of knowledge-induced collective preferences towards forming rules of behaviour and the social contract.

The *sunnah* of the Prophet is evident in regard to this conduct of human mutuality of goodness. The Prophet saw a man selling golden fresh wheat in the market of Madinah. When He slipped his hand inside the wheat heap, he found wet wheat under the golden dry and fresh wheat. The Prophet disdained the action as dishonesty of transaction, which creates mistrust between buyers and sellers. It has its implications in society at large, just as markets overarch social domain. The *Qur'an* (2:42) declares in this regard: "And cover not Truth with falsehood, nor conceal the Truth when you know (what it is)."

We can formalize in the following way to lay down an approach towards measuring the social impact of social trust:

The Social Contract is described by,

$$SC(E(\theta,p,x,y,R;\wp(\theta);t)(\theta)) \tag{6.22}$$

$$\text{With, } \cup_{i=\text{interaction}}\cap_{i=\text{integration}} E(\theta,p,x,y,R;\wp(\theta) = \wp_{ii}(\theta);t)(\theta)$$

$$\wp_{ii}(\theta) = \cup_{i=\text{interaction}}\cap_{i=\text{integration}}\{\wp_{ii}(\theta)\}_{ij}, i = 1,2,..m_1; j = 1,2,..m_2.$$

In the case of a firm (producer, seller), survey results can generate various types of responses to $\{\wp_{ii}(\theta)\}_{ij}$, i = 1,2,..$m_1$; j = 1,2,..$m_2$. These occur by interaction and integration (learnt consensus) in a knowledge-inducing experience of evolutionary learning by virtue of corporate social responsibility and good corporate governance or voluntarily by goodwill in the workplace environment. This is also the practice of industrial democracy whose learning effects on employees can be measured by an ordinal response on the degree of ethical learning intensity and choices. The result is encapsulated in $\{\wp_{ii}(\theta)\}_{ij}$. These responses are ranked by ordinal values achieved using questionnaire surveys of workers and administrators.

By collecting non-parametric ordinal values as ranks with $\{\wp_{ii}(\theta)\}_{ij}\in\aleph$, the natural number system, we can then assimilate these survey values with the rest of the socio-economic statistics. Thereby, the circular causation equations now comprise expressions (6.9–6.13) with the data now being represented by the Event,

$E(\theta,\mathbf{p},\mathbf{x},\mathbf{y},\mathbf{R},\aleph;t)(\theta)$, with $\{\wp_{ij}(\theta)\}_{ij} \in \aleph$. We now have a combination of parametric and non-parametric variables in the circular causation evaluation model.

The meaning of the expression, $\aleph = G(\theta,\mathbf{p},\mathbf{x},\mathbf{y},\mathbf{R};t)(\theta)$, in the sense of counts associated with specific questionnaire items of ethical value related to signals of consciousness $\{\wp_{ij}(\theta)\}_{ij}$, comprising consciousness based on trust, honesty, consumer satisfaction, producer stability, and a host of CSR and GCG values. The sampling is done using many questions, firms, workers, and consumers as the need arises.

Social trust as a social lubricant is now tantamount to a systemic way of understanding the market system, not simply as a multi-market. Rather, the emergence of the organically inter-related multi-markets are sustained by interactive, integrative, and evolutionary learning by inter-causal relationships between its various parts that are ethically and morally induced by $\{\theta \in (\Omega,S)\}$. Consciousness borne out of the *Tawhidi*

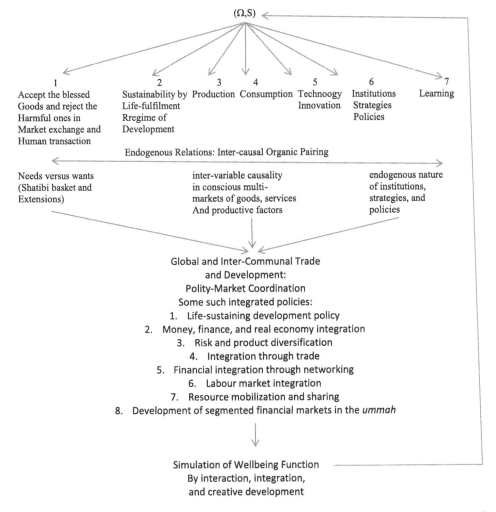

Figure 6.3 Development of interactive, integrated, and evolutionary learning market system with moral consciousness

episteme exclusively thus plays a central role in establishing the moral standing of the marketplace. In this regard there is the declaration of the *Qur'an*.[2] On the felicity of the marketplace is the saying of the Prophet regarding markets of heaven where the blessed ones will enjoy the blessings of markets. Indeed, the whole of the *Qur'an* is a declaration of blessings for the good actions on human transactions concerning him and the other in the light of righteousness that emanates from *Tawhid* as law.

The result of solidarity and relationship through human transaction in the good things of life, as through market activity of buying (consumption) and selling (production) and benefits (rewards from market transaction), yields bounty with increasing returns to scale. The *Qur'an* (2:261)[3] declares the abundant rewards of blessings in this regard.

The multi-marketplace of righteous choices and the blessings harvested therefrom can be formalized as a particular system adapting the general system of *Tawhidi* methodological worldview. The *shari'ah* market as a system centered on *Tawhidi* consciousness by its design and functions can be depicted in the following nexus of organic relationships (Figure 6.3).

Conclusion

The central characteristic, indeed the differentiating philosophy of the *shari'ah* market is its endogenous and conscious element of moral epistemology and reconstruction derived and executed by the *Tawhidi* law of unity of knowledge and the knowledge-induced world-system. Centered in this kind of moral reconstruction is a complete negation of the Smithian postulate of the 'invisible hand' principle and the

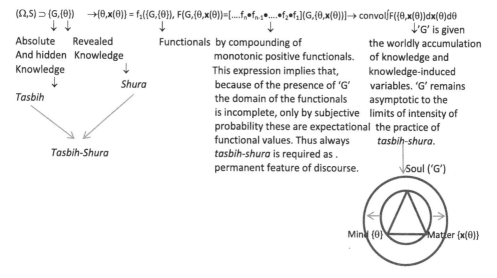

$$(\Omega,S) \supset \{G,\{\theta\}\} \quad \rightarrow\{\theta,x(\theta)\} = f_1(\{G,\{\theta\}\}, F(G,\{\theta,x(\theta)\})=[....f_n \bullet f_{n-1}\bullet....\bullet f_2\bullet f_1](G,\{\theta,x(\theta)\})]\rightarrow \text{convol}\!\int\! F(\{\theta,x(\theta))dx(\theta)d\theta$$

				'G' is given
Absolute	Revealed	Functionals	by compounding of	the worldly accumulation
And hidden	Knowledge		monotonic positive functionals.	of knowledge and
Knowledge			This expression implies that,	knowledge-induced
	Shura		because of the presence of 'G'	variables. 'G' remains
Tasbih			the domain of the functionals	asymptotic to the
			is incomplete, only by subjective	limits of intensity of
			probability these are expectational	the practice of
			functional values. Thus always	*tasbih-shura.*
Tasbih-Shura			*tasbih-shura* is required as .	
			permanent feature of discourse.	Soul ('G')

Mind {θ} Matter {x(θ)}

Figure 6.4 Soul, mind, matter circular causation relationships in *tasbih-shura* phenomenology

Note: On the inaccessibility of the hidden knowledge in reality the *Qur'an* (72:26,27) declares: "He (alone) knows the Unseen, nor does He make any one acquainted with his Mysteries, -- :except an apostle whom He has chosen: and then He makes a band of watchers march before him and behind him."

ethical insensitivity of the market process, as such properties are evinced in mainstream economic theory. Instead, we have argued in various formal ways that interaction, integration, and evolutionary learning as dynamics being at the center of the *Tawhidi* methodological worldview that induces the conscious world-system, market systems being a particular case of the multidimensional nature of markets forms a polity-market organic relationship.

In its endogenous, consciously invoked self-actualized form, the learning process excites the informal and the formal institution of learning by discourse. Such a polity is known as the *shura* in Islam. Consciousness being combined with *shura* as a consultative and discursive experience in Islam invokes both discourses with the analytical knowledge of the state of reality (e.g. the market reality). The reality as an organic inter-causal unity of being is called *tasbih* in the *Qur'an*. *Tasbih* recognizes the universal worshipping of *Tawhidi* unity of knowledge in the order and scheme of all things. We refer to this true Islamic intellection in the light of *Tawhidi* epistemology of unity of knowledge as *tasbih-shura*. The meaning conveys that Islamic discourse is regarding understanding the *tasbih* (moral consciousness) in the generality and particularity of issues. This concept brings out the meaning of the conscious role of polity-market interaction in diverse issues under investigation.

A modern implication of the *tasbih-shura* form of interactive, integrative, and evolutionary learning dynamics is the neural representation of learning systems, artificial intelligence, and social neuroscience (Choudhury, 2009). The underlying man-machine relationships on analytical matters are the reality of the post-modern age that premises its future on such formalism (Russell, 1954, 1970).

It is useful here to place a *tasbih-shura* figure (Figure 6.4) for subtle socio-scientific communication.

Notes

1 *Qur'an* (59:24) on *tasbh* and the universal totality; *Qur'an* (36:36) on universal organic pairing; *Qur'an* (1:2), on *Alhamdulillah*: 'Praises be to God, the Cherisher and Sustainer of the Worlds; *Qur'an* (30:19), the reorigination process in earth and evidences: "It is He Who brings out the living from the dead, and brings out the dead from the living, and Who gives life to the earth after it is dead: and thus shall you be brought out (from the dead).".

2 *Qur'an* (62:9): "O ye who believe! When the call is proclaimed to prayer on Friday (the Day of Assembly) hasten earnestly to the Remembrance of God, and leave off business (and traffic): That is best for you if ye but knew!" *Qur'an* (62:10): "And when the Prayer is finished, then may ye disperse through the land, and seek of the Bounty of God: and celebrate the Praises of God often (and without stint) that ye may prosper."

   Qur'an (62:11): "But when they see some bargain or some amusement, they disperse headlong to it, and leave these standing. Say: "The (blessing) from the Presence of God is better than any amusement or bargain! And God is the Best to provide (for all needs)."

3 *Qur'an* (2:261): "The parables of those who spend their substance in the way of God is that of a grain of corn: It grows seven ears, and each ear has hundred grains. God gives manifold increases to whom He pleases: And God cares for all and He knows all things."

References

Attia, G.E. trans. Roberts, N. (2010). "A new conceptualization of maqasid", in his *Towards Realization of the Higher Intents of Islamic Law, Maqasid al-Shari'ah a Functional Approach*, pp. 77–149, Islamic Book Trust, Kuala Lumpur, Malaysia.

Bertuglia, C.S. and Vaio, F. (2005). "Dynamical systems and the phase space", in *Nonlinearity, Chaos and Complexity, the Dynamics of Natural and Social Systems*, pp. 49–70, Oxford University Press, Oxford, UK.

Bordo, M.D. (1989). "The contribution of a monetary history of the United States, 1867–1960", in M.D. Bordo (ed.), *Money, History, and International Finance: Essays in Honour of Anna J. Schwartz*, pp. 15–70, The University of Chicago Press, Chicago, IL.

Choudhury, M.A. (2009). "A neurocybernetic theory of social management systems", in Guneshkaran, A. Sandhu, M. (eds), *Handbook of Business Information Systems*, Chapter 9, World Scientific Publications, Singapore.

Choudhury, M.A. (2011). *Islamic Economics and Finance: an Epistemological Inquiry*, Emerald Publishing, Derby, UK.

Choudhury, M.A. (2014). "Subjective probability and financial valuation: contrasting paradigms", *Journal of Financial Reporting and Accounting*, 13:1, pp. 20–38.

Choudhury, M.A. and Hossain, M.M. (2013). "A probabilistic evolutionary learning model with epistemological meaning in Islamic economics and finance", *Journal of Financial Research and Accounting*, 11:1, pp. 64–79.

Choudhury, M.A. Hossain, M.S. and Suriadi, J. (2014). "Quantitative issues to the tawhidi epistemology in circular causation, in Choudhury, M.A. *Tawhidi Epistemology and Its Applications*, Chapter 13. Cambridge Scholars' Publishing, Cambridge, UK.

Choudhury, M.A. Zaman, S.I. and Harahap, S.S. (2007). "An evolutionary topological theory of participatory socio-economic development", *World Futures*, 63:1, pp. 1–15.

Coase, R.H. (1994). *Essays on Economics and Economists*, The University of Chicago Press, Chicago, IL.

Dorfman, R. Samuelson, P.A. and Solow, R. (1958). "Efficient programs of capital accumulation", in *Linear Programming and Economic Analysis*, McGraw-Hill, New York, NY.

Erasmus Journal for Philosophy and Economics (2009). "Cambridge social ontology: an interview with Tony Lawson", 2:1, pp. 100–22.

Henderson, J.M. and Quandt, R.E. (1958). *Microeconomic Theory, A Mathematical Approach*, McGraw-Hill Book Co., New York, NY.

Kim, W.C. and Mauborgne, R. (2005). "Creating blue oceans", in their *Blue Ocean Strategy*, pp. 3–22, Harvard Business School Press, Boston, MA.

Meera, A.K.M. and Larbani, M. (2006). "Part I: Seigniorage of fiat money and the *maqasid al-shari'ah*: the unattainableness of the *maqasid*", *Humanomics, International Journal of Systems and Ethics*, 22:1, pp. 17–33.

North, D. C. (1981). "A theory of institutional change and the economic history of the Western World", in his *Structure and Change in Economic History*, Chapter 15, New York: W.W. Norton.

Russell, B. (1954). *The Analysis of Matter*, Dover Publications, Inc., New York, NY.

Russell, B. (1970). "Descriptions" in *Introduction to Mathematical Philosophy*, George Allen and Unwin, London, UK.

Sen, A. (1992). "Conduct, ethics and economics", in his, *On Ethics and Economics*, pp. 88–9, Basil Blackwell, Oxford, UK.

Sraffa, P. (1960). *Production of Commodities by Means of Commodities, Prelude to a Critique of Economic Theory*, Cambridge University Press, Cambridge, UK.

Turney-High, H.H. (1968). "System and change", in his *Man and System*, pp. 52–76 Appleton-Century-Crofts, New York, NY.

Walras, L. trans. W. Jaffe. (1954). *Elements of Pure Economics*, Richard D. Irwin, Homewood, IL.

Yaeger, L.B. (1997 reprint). *The Fluttering Veil, Essays on Monetary Disequilibrium*, The Liberty Press, Indianapolis, IN.

Chapter 7

A Generalized Islamic Development-Financing Instrument

Abstract

Tawhid, meaning oneness of God and of the divine law (monotheism), is the worldview of 'everything' in Islam. This epistemic precept is extended by the meaning and application of the epistemology of unity of knowledge. The episteme forms the true foundational praxis of Islamic thought and world-system.

The episteme of divine oneness as law and its application is introduced in the contrasting development of the participatory nature of development-financing portfolio against the prevailing idea of *shari'ah-* compliance in so-called financial product choice. The prevailing Islamic development financing instruments have no organic meaning of interrelationship between them. They individually form distinct legal contractual instruments. On the contrary, the generalized development-financing instrument is grounded in the participatory portfolio theory. It ties up development-financing in accordance with the precept of unity of knowledge conceptualized and applied across interacting and integrating systems. This is done first, by integrating the various financing instruments into a diversified wholeness. This allows financial resources to flow freely between the diversified instruments without legal restrictions. Second, the generalized diversified development-financial portfolio also overarches across economic, social, and ethical values as derived from the law of *Tawhid* in the epistemological sense of systemic unity of knowledge. The wellbeing criterion, as opposed to the maximizing objective, becomes the governing focus of the ethico-economic type portfolio.

As an important application in the field of Islamic economics and finance, the episteme of oneness and rationalist methodology are used to understand two distinct development-financing sets of instruments. The Islamic development-financing instrument derived here is unique; it has not been perceived either in Islamic scholarship or by Islamic financial institutions. The proposed instrument is different from the usual profit-sharing (*mudarabah*), equity-participation (*musharakah*) and cost-plus pricing (*murabaha*) and *mudarabah* bonds, and the so-called Islamic bonds (*sukuk*) as financing instruments now being theorized and practised in Islamic economics, finance, and banking within the rationalist lens. The contrast is due to the gap in knowledge of the monotheistic law in action within the general-system approach. This chapter fills this gap.

Background

The history of Islamic banking is about 30 years old. The history of Islamic economics is about 70 years old. The emergence of the field of Islamic finance dates back only a few years. In comparison, the history of banking and economic thought in the western world as a whole is about 200 years old. Yet, if one were to extend the history of Islamic thinking on science and society to include all its elements, we would mark the eleventh and twelfth centuries as the pinnacle of such Islamic thinking. This was well over 400 years before Adam Smith and the school of Physiocracy who claim to have given the occidental world the study of political economy (George, [1897]).

In recent years, Muslims and their financial institutions have again raised their heads to emulate something being referred to as 'Islamic economics and finance'. Yet, like the Occidental worldview, the empiricist fervor devoid of substantive meaning and contrary to their moral foundations (Husserl, trans. Lauer, 1965), Islamic economists and financial experts do not understand the substantive foundations of the truly *Qur'anic* worldview and its methodology for the world-system.

What is the distinction between these two contrasting epochs of thought and which one can shine a light in the direction of human wellbeing and sustainability for a stable, just, and progressive world-system? The answer can be delivered on two levels.

First, the new worldview, which has been much awaited in socio-scientific thinking, must be delivered. This is an academic issue of significant import. Second, the application of this worldview to the practical world must be disseminated to establish its high watermark. The phenomenological concept of 'pairing' in the worldview with practical aspects of human betterment, therefore comes about by using the medium of application and scientific proof.

The 'pairing' of entities of good things in the form of unity of being is referred to in several verses the *Qur'an*. Verse (36:36): "Glory to Allah, Who created in pairs all things that the earth produces, as well as their own kind and other things of which they have no knowledge." Thus, the realm of 'pairing' is extensive. It conveys the idea of pervasive complementarities, which we will use in this chapter to propose our development-financing instrument and the generalized methodological formalism.

The application and verification of the 'pairing' principle is referred to in the *Qur'an* as *burhan* (evidence = *ayath Allah*) (10:6): "Verily, in the alternation of the Night and the Day, and in *all* that *Allah* has created, in the heavens and the earth, are *Signs* for those who fear Him."

These *Qur'anic* verses and many others similar to them signal the unification between the worldview and its proof using a methodological formalism. This chapter will first delineate the methodology of such a unified phenomenological principle. Our generalized formalism will be applied to propose a unique development-financing instrument. The financing instrument claims to be unique because a similar one does not exist in the literature on Islamic economics and finance. Besides, the construct of this development-financing instrument reflects the worldview of unity of knowledge and systems in terms of the *Qur'anic* precept of *Tawhid*. *Tawhid* means oneness of *Allah* (monotheism). However, the precept is extended to the worldview of unity of the divine law and of the world-systems (*a'lameen*) that are spanned by the evidence (*ayath Allah*) of the divine law of oneness.

What has been omitted in today's culture of Islamic economics and finance and in occidental thought? The answer is *Tawhid*: a methodological explication of the divine unitary worldview and its application. This is a huge oversight. The absence of the *Tawhidi* worldview as a methodological praxis in Islamic economics and finance fails to qualify these fields as being authentically Islamic. Consequently, like any other science in the hands of the Islamic modernists, the enterprise has become a sheer imitation of Occidentalism and an engine for the spread of occidental institutionalism and culture in the Muslim world (Murden, 2002; Choudhury, 1997).

Objective

This chapter has three essential objectives. First, the differences between the *Qur'anic* worldview and the mimicry of Occidentalism in Islamic economics, finance, and banking are discussed in a methodological way. We point out that the prevalent imitation has sounded the death knell for Islamic economics. Second, the methodology derived from the essential *Qur'anic* worldview of *Tawhid*, the oneness of *Allah*, and thereby the unity of the divine law, which is the praxis of unity of knowledge and systems, is contrasted with the occidental worldview of rationalism. The methodology of Islamic economics and finance premised on such rationalism is then critiqued. Third, the evidence of the *Tawhidi* worldview methodology is represented in the derivation and application of the principle of pervasive complementarities derived from the principle of paired universes of the *Qur'an*. This principle is used to propose a unique Islamic development-financing instrument.

This chapter studies the *Qur'anic* verses (2: 164–167) to establish the nature of the contrast between the *Tawhidi* episteme and rationalism. The *Tawhidi* episteme is then singled out in proposing a unique Islamic development-financing instrument. Such a development-financing instrument, one which would help the common shareholder, does not exist in Islamic finance today. This is remiss because of the absence of the systemic understanding of *Tawhid* as the law of unity of knowledge and the world-systems. However, the practical issue of deriving a pervasively complementary development-financing instrument from the *Tawhidi* implications of the verses (2:164–167) results in a novel application in Islamic economics and finance. A unique development-financing instrument not yet understood nor practiced in Islamic economics and finance is then proposed.

Substantive concepts

The precept of *Tawhid* as unity of knowledge in 'everything' is referred to in this chapter as the unique and universal episteme in and between matter and mind. The scientific overarching idea of 'everything' is invoked as a philosophy of scientific thought by Barrow (1991. The complementarities encompassing matter, mind, and the spiritual realm arising from the divine law of monotheism in the domain of 'everything' become the ontological and epistemological force of systemic unification between artifacts, entities, and socio-scientific variables. The medium of knowledge-flows emanating from the *Tawhidi* unity of knowledge thus predominates in the synergetic dynamics of systemic unity. This chapter derives such methodological orientation from the verses (2:164–167).

Contrary to the *Tawhidi* precept and its configuration of the world-system is the premise of falsehood. Falsehood is represented here by rationalism. The character of rationalism is pervasive methodological individualism (Sullivan, 1989; Taylor, 1967).

See Kant (trans. Paton, 1964) for a philosophical meaning of rationalism involving the partitioned dualism between a priori knowledge and a posteriori knowledge

The verses (2:164–167) selected here, but complemented by many other similar verses of the *Qur'an*, bring out the distinctiveness between the two well-defined but opposite epistemological praxes. In the end, the *Qur'anic* argumentation points to the utter disgrace and defeat of Falsehood *vis-à-vis* Rationalism along with its character and institutions of methodological individualism. From the distinct but well-defined epistemic premises of *Tawhid* and rationalism emerge the opposite world-systems. The two have nothing in common.

Tawhid and the unified world-system

Formalizing Tawhid and the world-system

How can the lessons of verses (2:164–167) be formalized into a world-system modelling? The *Qur'an* is not detached from the delineation of its world-systems. *Qur'anic* truth is not of the nature of metaphysical speculation. Rather, every guidance of the *Qur'an* (*Sunnat Allah*) carried through by the guidance of the Prophet Muhammad (*sunnah*) is as much a worldly explanation. They have their final determination in the context of *Tawhid* and the Hereafter as terminal Events. However, organic systemic learning never ends between these Eventual Ends in the evolutionary learning world-system.

The elimination of metaphysical speculation from the *Qur'anic* precept of knowledge as totality between *Tawhid* and the world-systems alters much of the logical formalism of the philosophy of science. Ontology is not, now, the domain of the metaphysical that is separate from reality (Maxwell, 1962). As we will show below, ontology, in terms of *Qur'anic* meaning, is better taken up using the concept of engineering ontology (Gruber, 1993; Hossain, 2007). I prefer to refer to it as functional ontology, such as that used in the concept of large cardinalities by Rucker (1983).

Likewise, the concept of epistemology stands for the episteme, which is the totality of the formalism of knowledge and the world-system. Our idea of episteme is similar to that articulated by Foucault (trans. Sheridan, 1972, p. 191): "By *episteme* we mean ... the total set of relations that unite, at a given period, the discursive practices that give rise to epistemological figures, sciences, and possibly formalized systems ... The episteme is not a form of knowledge (*connaissance*) or type of rationality which, crossing the boundaries of the most varied sciences, manifests the sovereign unity of a subject, a spirit, or a period; it is the totality of relations that can be discovered, for a given period, between the sciences when one analyses them at the level of discursive regularities."

Logical formalism

In reference to verse (2:164), let an inter-system(s) matrix of interactive, integrative, and co-evolutionary interrelationships between variables (*ayath Allah*, x_{ij}) be denoted by, $[x_{ij}^{s}(\theta_s)]$.

Here, the knowledge-flow induced in the matrix is denoted by θ_s. Due to its intrinsic unifying nature across system(s) 's', the knowledge-flows are bound to be derived from the epistemic core of *Tawhid* as the universal law of unity of knowledge. The totality of the divine law is denoted by the abstract 'open' super-space (denumerable) denoted by Ω (Maddox, 1971). Ω is the explanatory premise of both truth and falsehood by the essential character of uniqueness and universality of oneness of knowledge. For more on the precept of uniqueness and universality of the symbiotic relational world-view of *Tawhid* and the world-systems the reader can refer to Choudhury (2007a).

Formalism step 1

Thus, $(\theta_s \in \Omega) \rightarrow$ world-system, $\{[x_{ij}{}^s(\theta)], \theta_s\}$. $\qquad(7.1)$

$\{.\}$ denotes spanning the matrix $[.]$ by the Signs of *Allah* (*ayath Allah*) across world-systems (*a'lameen*) and thus (s,i,j);
    s = 1,2, .., N; i =1,2,..,m; j=1,2,..,n. Thus $([x_{ij}{}^s(\theta)], \theta_s)$ is [m x (n+1)] dimensional matrix.

In order to avoid the influence of rationalism, and thereby, strictly induce *Tawhid* into relationship (1), the mapping $\rightarrow$ must be well-defined (unique). We must first determine the θ_s-value. This is followed by the knowledge-induction of the world-system. We signify this unique mapping by $\rightarrow_s$. S denotes the Guidance of the Prophet Muhammad (*sunnah*). Ω and S are taken together within the *Tawhidi* episteme and denote this total premise by (Ω, S). The *Qur'anic* verses (53:1–5) declare this inseparability between the *Qur'an* and the *sunnah*.

Formalism step 2

Relationship (7.1) is now deconstructed as follows:

$(\theta_s \in \Omega) \rightarrow_S \lim\{\theta_s\} = \theta_s \rightarrow \{[x_{ij}{}^s(\theta)], \theta_s\} = \text{World-System}. \qquad(7.2)$

$\{.\}$ denotes the spanning Signs of *Allah* (*ayath Allah*) across world-systems (*a'lameen*), (s,i,j). Say that s = 1,2, .., N; i =1,2,..,m; j =1,2,..,n

Expression (7.2) means that the *sunnah* is the functional carrier of the divine laws into the explanatory knowledge-induced world-systems. S initiates social discourse in determining the knowledge-flows pertaining to specific issues under investigation. The *Qur'an* affirms this function of the *sunnah* (4:58–59). The limiting value of θ is determined out of discourse (interaction) followed by consensus (integration) over several $\{\theta\}$-values. Such social discourse is referred to in the *Qur'an* as the consultation (*shura*) (42:38). Knowledge of unity of the divine laws gained through the experience of the *shura* explains the first reflection of unity of knowledge $\{\theta_s\}$ obtained by virtue of the diversity of Signs (*ayath Allah*) at the realm of knowledge formation (*Qur'an*, 2:164).

Formalism step 3

We re-write (2) as follows:

$(\Omega, S) \rightarrow \theta_s \rightarrow \{[x_{ij}{}^s(\theta s)]\}, \qquad(7.3)$

$\downarrow$

$\{\{[x_{ij}{}^s(\theta_s)], \theta_s\}\} = $ World-System induced by the
Tawhidi episteme of unity of knowledge

Because $[x_{ij}^s(\theta_s)]$ is multivariate with each variable interrelating with the rest through the induction of θ_s-values that are premised on the episteme of unity of knowledge (Ω,S), we can further disaggregate for a specific system 's' in two multivariate components, such as, $[x_{ij}^s(\theta_s)]$ now disaggregated as $[x_{12}^s(\theta_s)]$, and $[x_{21}^s(\theta_s)]$. Relation (7.3) is re-written as follows:

Formalizing step 4

$(\Omega,S) \to \theta_s$ (7.4)

$([x_{12}^s(\theta)],\theta_s) \leftrightarrow ([x_{21}^s(\theta)],\theta_s)$ =World-System induced by the *Tawhidi* episteme of unity of knowledge

More closely, (7.4) is shown as follows. Note the subscript 's' is dropped from θ_s henceforth.

(7.5)

Explaining the systemic dynamics of formal relationships

We note in (7.5) that only (Ω,S) and its primal mappings to the world-system, denoted by F_1, F_2 and F_3, remain exogenous in the total system of relationships. However, the mappings from θ to the multivariates, and the mappings between the multivariates, are endogenous in the system of interrelationships as shown by the f-mappings. This is indicated by the reflexive relationships indicated by two-way arrows: these denote functional maps. However, the endogenous relationships cannot stand by themselves, unless they are first generated by the primal relationship F arising from the *Tawhidi* episteme (Ω,S).

These kinds of endogenous relationships that are induced by the exogenous episteme of unity of knowledge, (Ω,S), are said to exhibit moral and ethical endogeneity. Ethical endogeneity is carried by the F and f-relationship from (Ω,S) through θ-values across the multivariate interactive and integrative world-system. The world-system is thereby fully induced and endogenized by interrelationships between the $([x_{ij}^s(\theta)],\theta_s)$-values. Such two-way *inter*-relationships involving the $([x_{ij}^s(\theta)],\theta_s)$-values are called circular causation (see Choudhury (2006)).

According to verse (2:164), the Signs of *Allah* (*ayath Allah*) generate such endogenous relationships across multivariates spanning diverse intra- and inter-systems. For instance, the creation of the heavens is one system; the creation of the earth is another *inter*-related system. The evidence for these Signs of *Allah* that learn by 'pairing' both between them and continuously across space, time and knowledge dimensons, are shown diversely across intra- and inter-systems. The phenomenology of consciousness for actions and responses (circular causation) by way of reflection is summarized in verse (2:164): "Behold!" and "(Here) indeed are Signs for a people that are wise."

(7.5) shows the interactive and integrative processes of intra-systems, where the two multivariates are shown by the matrixes. Take the example from verse (2:164) – rain (i = 1) causes vegetation (life, j = 2); in turn, vegetation causes rain for sustenance, etc. Other circular causation can be identified from the verses. We take the circular causation between $([\mathbf{x}_{ij}^{s}(\theta)],\theta_{s})$-values within the same ecological system 's'. Estimation of θ by ordinal values in terms of the learning parameters of the circular causation relating to $[\mathbf{x}_{ij}^{s}(\theta)]$-values in any one system is done by weightings applied to average θ-values (Choudhury, Zaman and Nasar, 2007).

Next, the knowledge-induced processes evolve into extended learning involving unified systems. In verse (2:164), the examples are 'the heavens and the earth'. In the sub-system of the total cosmic system are the 'heavens' with their multivariates such as the paired realities of 'Night' and 'Day'. In the sub-system 'earth' are paired realities of 'rain' and 'life'. These two sub-systems are *inter*-related in terms of their jointly 'paired' entities. Others can be treated similarly.

When evolution takes place from one system to extended and unified systems, we have an extension of the complex set of relationships across systems, as shown in (7.5). Nonetheless, (Ω,S) permanently remains the exogenous episteme of reference. The f-kinds of relationships now emanate from newly derived rules of unity of knowledge for 'pairing' extended $([\mathbf{x}_{ij}^{s}(\theta)],\theta_{s})$-values inter-systems. This marks the evolutionary stage of learning from the interactive and integrative experience of any one process in a system to linked systems. Thereby, new processes 's' take values from s = 1,2,...,N. In verse (2:164), sub-systems of the two major systems, the 'heavens' and 'earth', can be enumerated, such as, 'ecology', 'life-sustenance', 'agriculture', 'economy', 'transportation', and 'science and society'. Such specifics can be extended widely as embedded sub-systems in the universal system.

We have now delineated the multisystem evolutionary learning processes that together carry forward new θ-values derived continuously from the *Tawhidi* episteme of (Ω,S) and through the learning processes. Such continuous processes of learning across knowledge, space, and time permanently exhibit the formalism of interaction leading to integration. Interaction and Integration together co-Evolve across systemic learning processes (IIE-processes). *Tawhid*, as the systemic unity of knowledge emanating from the episteme and instruments of the divine law, has thus been induced in 'everything'. The synergy of unity of knowledge between systemic artifacts and their entities defines the symbiotic dynamics. The character of such evolutionary learning in unity of knowledge is represented by the IIE-processes.

Moral valuation in the *Tawhidi* methodology of the world-system

We now represent the intersystemic learning experience in the *Tawhidi* unity of knowledge by a two-stage extension of (7.5). The relational diagram is now collapsed into a chain-relational system, as shown in (7.6).

Wellbeing criterion

The first stage to note in our formalization is the important evaluative criterion function known as the Wellbeing Function. This is according to the *Qur'anic* meaning of blessings gained through pairing by knowledge premised on the *Tawhidi* worldview (2:164; also see 36:36). This $W([\mathbf{x}_{ij}^{s}(\theta)])$, as shown (7.6), makes possible the evolutionary transition and continuous learning by unity of knowledge across IIE-processes of Islamic transformation. This dynamic and synergetic experience is referred to as the Islamicization of knowledge in the world-system.

The Wellbeing Function is simulated at the end of a process. This takes place by changes in parameter values in terms of targeted degrees of complementarities ('pairing') that are desired between the multivariates to reflect the unity of the system 's' in terms of these estimated predictors. The circular causation between the $([\mathbf{x}_{ij}^{s}(\theta)], \theta_{s})$-values yield the simulated θ-value and the multivariates. Thereby, the degree of complementarities between $([\mathbf{x}_{ij}^{s}(\theta)], \theta_{s})$-values can be suitably targeted to attain simulated estimates in the system under study, given the dynamics of a discursive Islamic society at work. Policy implications on politico-economic, financial, socio-scientific and institutional, organizational and strategic changes are implied by such targeted simulated results.

Systemic extension of the wellbeing criterion: Tawhidi phenomenology

In the second stage, extensions appear across system 's'. Such extended processes of learning in the unity of knowledge experience evolve from the interactive and integrative character of a prevalent process. The complete phenomenology of the *Tawhidi* worldview is thus characterized by interactive, integrative, and evolutionary (IIE) dynamics in organic learning-type symbiosis. Such dynamics repeat across the coevolution of the IIE-processes intersystems, as in intrasystemic cases. Verse (2:164) yields the extended microsystems that remain embedded and continuously evolving in the realm of belief and practice of the *Tawhidi* Law: "But those of faith are overwhelming in their love of *Allah*." (2:165).

$$
\begin{array}{l}
\underline{\text{endogenous learning process } 1 \rightarrow \text{ process } 2 \rightarrow} \\
(\Omega,S) \rightarrow_{F} \theta = \lim\{\theta\} \rightarrow_{f} [x_{ij}^{s}(\theta)] \hspace{4cm} \text{continuity} \\
\quad | \quad \text{episteme} \\
\quad | \quad \text{exogenous} \hspace{2cm} \downarrow ([\mathbf{x}_{ij}^{s}(\theta)], \theta_{s}) \rightarrow \text{Simulate } W([\mathbf{x}_{ij}^{s}(\theta)]) \\
\quad | \hspace{4cm} \text{Subject to circular causation} \hspace{2.5cm} (7.6)\\
\quad | \hspace{4cm} \text{Between } (\theta, [x_{ij}^{s}(\theta)])\text{-values} \\
\quad | \hspace{6cm} \downarrow \quad \text{continuity of} \\
\quad | \hspace{2.5cm} \text{Exogenous recalling} \quad ([\mathbf{x}_{ij}^{s}(\theta)], \theta s)_{new} \rightarrow \text{IIE-processes} \\
\quad \downarrow
\end{array}
$$

Occidental contrast: formalizing rationalism, methodological individualism, and their world-system

The complete phenomenological formalism of (7.6) uniquely explains both Truth (*Tawhidi* worldview) and falsehood as rationalism. Verses (2:165–167) bring out the self-defeated nature of falsehood. Rationalism is equated with falsehood by its character of methodological individualism and denial of oneness, replacing it with self and ego (von Mises, 1976). Methodological individualism is the core postulate of mainstream economics (Buchanan, 1954, 1999). It has been thoroughly imitated in Islamic economics and finance for using the maximization methods of analysis.

In the case of rationalism, we note that the continuity of (7.6) eventually (as in social Darwinism; see Dawkins (1976)) or primordially (as in neoclassical economic theory) breaks apart after some processes. Continuing in this way, by a recursive process of deconstruction of methodological individualism and plurality of knowledge, we obtain a plethora of atomistic discontinuities. This could be shown in (7.6). Thus, the character of IIE-processes according to unity of knowledge is replaced by competition, marginalism and individualism between the multivariates. These are induced by their 'de-knowledge'-flows (signified here by ~). We denote the 'de-knowledge' entities by their tuple, $([\mathbf{x}\sim_{ij}{}^{s}(\theta\sim)],\theta_{s}\sim)$-values.

Fragmentation of the IIE-processes of unity of knowledge signifies permanent loss of systemic oneness. Hence, the relational symbiosis that characterizes complexity by richness is replaced by linearity of the optimal and competing processes of methodological individualism. In such optimal and steady-state equilibrium states, learning ends and novelty is lost (Shackle, 1972). Such beliefs have become the permanent mark of all scientific episteme that emulate rationalism; although unity of the sciences remains the desired, yet a floundering scientific research programme can lead to a scientific muddle (Neurath, 1970). In Marxist political economy, for example, the assertion of a plethora of episteme between competing sources bedevils any epistemic uniqueness, purpose and predictive power. The multiplicity of competing episteme in Marxist political economy gives rise to the problem of 'overdetermination' (Resnick and Wolff, 1987).

Expression (7.7) is an overdetermined formalism of (7.6). It shows the impossible project of unification of the sciences despite this intended scientific end-goal (Hawking, 1980). All that is endogenous in this system of epistemic fragmentation is the continuity of states of competition and individualism converging to atomism over space, time and 'de-knowledge-flows'. That is, $([\mathbf{x}\sim_{ij}{}^{s}(\theta\sim)],\theta_{s}\sim)$-values span the entire rationalism domain with the epistemic overdetermination condition: $\theta_{s}\sim \in \Omega_{s}\sim$, with $\cap_{s}\Omega_{s}\sim = \phi$ almost everywhere $\Rightarrow \cap_{s}\theta_{s} = \phi$ almost everywhere $\Rightarrow \cap_{s}[\mathbf{x}\sim_{ij}{}^{s}(\theta_{s}\sim)]) = \phi$, almost everywhere, for every 's'.

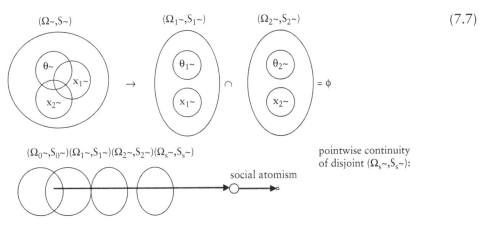

$$(\Omega\sim,S\sim) \qquad (\Omega_{1}\sim,S_{1}\sim) \qquad (\Omega_{2}\sim,S_{2}\sim) \qquad\qquad (7.7)$$

The mainstream 'economic welfare function' corresponding to (7.7) is,

$$\text{Max } W\sim(\theta\sim) = W\sim([\mathbf{x}\sim_{ij}(\theta\sim)]), \qquad (7.8)$$

subject to the relationships between the variables under the conditions manifest in (7.7). That is, $\theta_s \sim \in \Omega_s \sim$, with $\cap_s \Omega_s \sim = \phi$ almost everywhere $\Rightarrow \cap_s \theta_s = \phi$ almost everywhere $\Rightarrow \cap_s [x \sim_{ij}{}^s(\theta_s \sim)]) = \phi$, almost everywhere, for every 's'.

Circular causation now fails to exist when some of the variables become exogenous in nature. An example here is the targeting of interest rates in a contractionary money supply regime. In the Islamic case, interest rates are replaced by rates of return on productive *shari'ah*-compliant investments as an endogenous variable. Another example is the maintaining of fiscal balance by targeting price levels. However, in the Islamic case, price levels automatically adjust under dynamic, basic-needs, regimes of development. This causes sustainable fiscal balance by the endogenous relationship between knowledge-flow (a dynamic basic-needs regime of development), price level, and the resulting fiscal balance over time. We then have endogenously sustainable *inter*-relationships over knowledge, space, and time dimensions. Indeed, dynamic basic needs comprise the *Shatibi*-basket of goods and services (Biraima, 1998/99).

Because of the above-mentioned conditions of rationalism, some elements of the matrix $[\mathbf{x} \sim_{ij}(\theta \sim)]$ will reduce to zero. Substitution between variables in (7.8), the marginal rate of substitution between the $[\mathbf{x} \sim_{ij}{}^s(\theta_s \sim)]$-values will yield negative coefficients. That is, if $[\mathbf{x} \sim_{ij}{}^s(\theta_s \sim)]$-values are interpreted as output elasticity coefficients, then these will be negative, given the neoclassical postulate of marginal rates of substitution that follow from the optimization and steady-state equilibrium, competition and economic rationality conditions of (7.8). These link up with the character of rationalism in world-systems (Choudhury, 2000a; Etzioni, 1988).

Consequently, the complementary forms of $[\mathbf{x}_{ij}{}^s(\theta_s)]$-variables implied by $(d/d\theta)$ $(\mathbf{W}([\mathbf{x}_{ij}{}^s(\theta_s)])) > 0$ in the Islamic case is never attainable in the case of induction of $\mathbf{W}(.)$ by $\theta \sim$-values. The latter case cannot be evolutionary by learning. The properties of sharing, participation, resource augmentation and endogenous growth and development are therefore denied in the case of (7.8).

Verses (2:166–167) point out this self-defeating and deceptive nature of rationalism, equated with falsehood. Also, the premise of uniqueness, as in the *Tawhidi* episteme, is lost. It is now replaced by an epistemic overdetermination property that remains embedded and universal in competition and methodological individualism. Verse (2:166) implies that, not only individual entities but also the entire episteme, mindset, and artifacts of methodological individualism, are afflicted by the same character of moral non-sustainability. These characteristics form the constitutional core of liberalism, which derives from the episteme of Rationalism (Buchanan, 1999).

A theorem on uniqueness and universality of the *Tawhidi* worldview methodology

We also note from verse (2:167) that the model of rationalism (falsehood) cannot revert to truth. There is no such methodology in 'de-knowledge' to enable such a reversion. Truth and falsehood are incontrovertible, disjointed realities. The completeness of this state of opposed reality is fully realized in the Hereafter as the Great Event of feat for Truth – *Tawhid* (*Qur'an*, 78:1–5) and complete destruction of falsehood (*Qur'an*, chapter 88).

Likewise, the rationalism model of extensive individualism and denial of unity of the divine law does not have a methodology to explain and return to the unified world-systems. In other words, there is no episteme which this model can use to bring about the unification of knowledge between systemic artifacts, variables and their entities. There is absolute methodological void in rationalism for such an enterprise. The human ego prevails over all (Russell, 1991, 2001), though there is an earnest search by science for a formalism of unity of 'everything' (Barrow, 1992).

On the contrary, the *Tawhidi* phenomenological model explains both the unity of knowledge as truth and the rationalism model as falsehood. Consequently, the *Tawhidi* worldview is both unique and universal as an episteme to explain 'everything'.

The above-mentioned statements can be stated in the form of a theorem:

> The Tawhidi unity of knowledge is the necessary and sufficient episteme for uniquely and universally explaining both the nature of truth and falsehood as distinct and opposed realities. Any episteme that cannot explain these unique and universal conditions of opposed realities, cannot be a worldview.

A particular derivation from the generalized model: a development-finance instrument

The generalized formal model established above can now be particularized to a specific application: the development of an innovative Islamic financing instrument. It is the first of its kind in Islamic economics and finance literature that rests solely on the *maqasid as-shari'ah*, the objectivity and purpose of the Islamic Law.

Some problems of Islamic economics and finance

The principal Islamic project financing instruments are profit-sharing (*mudarabah*) and equity-participation (*musharakah*). Nowhere in the conventional literature in Islamic economics and finance are these instruments treated in the *economy-wide and society-wide* context of learning linkages – systemic synergy. Hence, the fundamental essence of cooperation and participation across sectors has not been treated in the literature and practice. Consequently, the above-mentioned MM-instruments turn out to be focused merely on the profitability goal of a project. Short-term financing is emphasized. Long- and medium-term financing are treated residually in Islamic finance.

Consequently, the socio-economic development issues that rest on the *maqasid as-shari'ah* are, by and large, ignored on the pretext of 'priority'; the *one* focus of all other *shari'ah* injunctions is the maintenance of shareholders' property rights. This translates into maximization of shareholders' wealth, and thus the maximization of the value of the financial firm. Islamic financing institutions have remained ambivalent about the social application of project-financing by sectoral links and institutional networking. As an example, no MM-project with a component goal of poverty alleviation is complemented by a profitability goal.

Consequently, the comprehensive objectivity and purpose of the *shari'ah* (*maqasid as-shari'ah*) has been sacrificed in this property-rights based, one-dimensional economic and financing focus. See Jabsheh et al. (2007) for a comprehensive coverage of the short- versus the long-term issues of Islamic economics and financing institutions who ignore the importance of the *maqasid as-shari'ah*.

The cost-plus pricing method (*murabaha*) is another instrument that is extensively practised in trade-financing and asset sales. Yet, to be *shari'ah* friendly, *murabaha* must revolve around *mudarabah* and *musharakah* taken up *conjointly* in reference to the market valuation of assets. Such complementary development-financing instruments (MMM) would then possess the essential characteristics of economy- and society-wide diversity and holistic linkages by the synergy of *inter*-relationships according to the comprehensive objectives of the *maqasid as-shari'ah* (Choudhury, 2000b).

As the above-mentioned MMM-financing instruments are devoid of the essential need for economy-wide participatory extensions, both in theory and practice, any secondary financing instrument revolving around MMM-financing, seen as sleeping partnerships, cannot qualify for the truly Islamic instrument of development-financing (e.g. unit trusts (*amana saham*) and *sukuk* (bonds)). Likewise, even shareholdings in Islamic bank PLS and similar instruments must be refined by accommodating the extensive meaning of the *maqasid as-shari'ah* (Mydin and Larbani, 2006).

The substantive issues here are more than just an asset-backed as opposed to liquidity-backed instrument. *Mere* asset-backed financing can fail to meet the *maqasid as-shari'ah*, if the social and economic sustainability is not conceptualized and applied on the basis of the *Tawhidi* implication of learning intra- and intersystems through complementarities ('pairing'). Thus, the argument made by some in support of *sukuk* (Kahf, 2007) remains untenable in the absence of such embedded linkages *vis-à-vis* the *maqasid as-shari'ah*. Along with this grand oversight, both in Islamic economic and finance scholarship and in banking practice, the sustainability of these fields for the uplift of the *ummah*, the conscious world-nation of Islam, remains in serious question. The absence of the *Tawhidi* worldview of unified linkages by evolutionary learning drives the Muslim mind and institutions into this kind of isolationism; the Islamic methodological worldview is absent.

Asset-backing in both the economy-wide and society-wide sense with a mix of short-term, medium-term, and long-term complementary goals, can be attained by linking the monetary sector with the real sector using new financing instruments. Unless the resulting circular causation as an endogenous learning relationship is attained between money, real economy and financing instruments in the comprehensive sense of *maqasid as-shari'ah*, the goal of the Islamic economy to attain wellbeing (*falah* and *tazkiyah*) through the medium of a *riba*-free economy and a just society, cannot be achieved. In the absence of such an economy- and society-wide participatory transformation, neither an Islamic change is possible nor can the large liquidity of Islamic banks can be mobilized into true *maqasid as-shari'ah* outlets.

The extension in such a transformation process invokes important possibilities for the coterminous attainment of both production- and risk-diversification. These conditions are essential to attain both cost-effective sustainable growth, and the development and creative evolution of economy and society. A joint production function is now made the engine of resource mobilization in the complementary domain of total economic-diversification. The financing instruments in the money-real economy linkage must both be based on and be capable of mobilizing resources to achieve this extensive intersectoral picture (Choudhury and Hoque, 2004). Such an extensively paired meaning of socio-economic structure can be derived from verse (2:164). It is guidance, premised on the organic unity of the divine law, working throughout all world-systems.

We will now use the *Tawhidi* episteme to enact a rule (*ahkam*) of organic participation for the attainment of social wellbeing in the extensive sense of the *maqasid as-shari'ah*. Ours is a matrix, $[\mathbf{x}_{ij}^{s}(\theta_s), \theta_s]$, of participatory interrelationships. The *maqasid as-shari'ah* will be reflected in and by the Social Wellbeing Index (SWI). We will create a financing instrument that will simulate the SWI under conditions of circular causation in $[\mathbf{x}_{ij}^{s}(\theta_s), \theta_s]$, in reference to the *maqasid as-shari'ah*, while interconnecting money, real economy, and the proposed financing instrument.

A financing instrument for attaining Islamic transformation by the *maqasid as-shari'ah*

In the expression for $[\mathbf{x}_{ij}^{s}(\theta_s), \theta_s]$, let i,j = Money (1), Real Economy (2), Finance (3). In any given process of learning according to the *Tawhidi* Law of systemic oneness, denoted by s = socio-economic system, let the weighting on the degree of acceptability of $\mathbf{x}_{ij}^{s}(\theta_s)$-variables be set by θ_s.

We now exhibit the following matrix:

$$
\begin{array}{lll}
\text{Inter} - \text{sectoral} & \text{weighting of } \theta - \text{values} & \text{Circular causation} \\
& \text{From the ranking of} & \\
\text{variables} & \text{Performance of the} & \\
& \text{Respective x} - \text{values}^* & \\
\end{array}
$$

$$
\begin{array}{lll}
x_{11} \quad x_{12} \quad x_{13} & \theta^1 & x_{11} = f_1(x_{12}, x_{13}, \theta_s), \text{ money with other} \qquad (7.9) \\
x_{21} \quad x_{22} \quad x_{23} & \theta^2 & x_{22} = f_2(x_{21}, x_{23}, \theta_s), \text{ real economy with other} \\
x_{31} \quad x_{32} \quad x_{33} & \theta^3 & x_{33} = f_3(x_{31}, x_{32}, \theta_s), \text{ finance with other} \\
\text{Average } \theta_s = \Sigma_k \theta^k & &
\end{array}
$$

* θ^k = Average of $[(x_{ij}/x_{ij}^*).10]$, where the observations for x_{ij} record a best value x_{ij}^* for which the ranking is 10 out of 1–10; i,j=1,2,3.

The SWI is defined by,

$$\text{SWI} = A(\theta_s).\prod_{i=1}^{3} x_{ii}^{a_{ii}} \qquad (7.10)$$

SWI is simulated over θ_s-values, subject to the circular causation relationships,

$$x_{ii} = f_i(\mathbf{x}_{ij}, \theta_s) \qquad (7.11)$$
$$\theta_s = f_{\theta s}(\mathbf{x}_{ij})$$

i,j = 1,2,3 for a given 's' as socio-economic system. $a_{ii} > 0$, i =1,2,3 are simulated parameters of the estimated and simulated versions of (10)-(11). Hence these parameters are θ_s-induced elasticity coefficients of SWI in terms of the x_{ii}-variables.

Simulation of the estimated values by assigning new parameter values proceed in light of levels of complementarities that can be attained in the system 's'. These signify strategic and policy targeting in the reformed system 's'.

Finally, our financing instrument is a combination of MMM-instruments that satisfies the *maqasid as-shari'ah* by mobilizing all forms of resources economy- and society-wide to attain Social Wellbeing. At a pragmatic level, such a financing instrument is a pure shareholding. It swims across hybrid capital stocks in diverse sectors. Funds can freely diversify between MMM-instruments according to the SWI-criterion. Thus, while a legal ledger will be maintained for the respective M, M, M for the benefit of the shareholders and financiers, the economic and social meaning is an integrated one. Invested funds can flow freely between the MMM (Choudhury, 2000b).

The close management of such a fund necessitates cooperation between banking and non-banking institutions. Therefore, complementarities must be progressively extensive both between the sectors, and between institutional and policy simulations economy- and society-wide. Islamicization, in its true sense of synergetic learning in unity of knowledge referring to *ayath Allah*, becomes the goal of the *ummah*. Verse (2:164) implies such blessings that ensue from the evidence of *ayath Allah*.

We will call our proposed development-financing instrument of the Islamic *ummah* the SWI instrument. It has appeared in the Islamic economics and finance literature and practice to date. There are two reasons for this: first, the failure of Islamic economics and finance to understand the principle of pervasive complementarities and the consequential sectoral links that spring from the *Tawhidi* unified world-system dynamics. Second, the focus on short-term financing goals to maximize wealth and value for shareholders in Islamic financial firms has ignored the comprehensive meaning of *maqasid as-shari'ah*. Systemic pairing and the blessings derived from this is conveyed by verse (2:164) and many similar verses of the *Qur'an*.

A particular way to operate the SWI instrument

One particular way to operate the SWI instrument is to have MMM revolve around trade financing. The term 'trade' is taken here in its broadest sense of market-based transactions in *maqasid as-shari'ah* goods and services (i.e. the good things of life). Consequently, according to this concept, the MMM are not based on sheer contractual determination of profit-sharing and the cost of assets for hire and purchase. Any asset when evaluated for cost-plus pricing in resale by the buyer (*sahib al-mal*), such as a house or equipment, must be tallied against the market value of such assets. However, a mechanism of cost-plus pricing based on sharing excess rents can be exercised; such rents can be distributed over time between partners in trade so as to ease the repayment of financial liabilities. The costing mechanism is a similar to that of hire-purchase transactions (*ijara*).

Shareholders of such a trade-based SWI instrument sold by Islamic banks would be quoted a unit-value derived from a rate applied to the share capital. The total value would be distributed for recovery over time. Such share values will be derived from the ongoing (earnings/resource) ratios over time until the asset liabilities matured. The corresponding value on the ratios will be distributed over time for the mutual benefit of shareholders and the Islamic bank in such market-based trades. Therefore the (earnings/resource) ratio may be variable over time according to the market-values of the asset under circulation net of depreciation.

The total share capital will thus be circulated economy-wide in a diversified portfolio of MMM types of *shari'ah*-investment with no restrictions on financial interflow between the MMM categories. The result of product-diversification and risk-diversification in such trade flows and diversified financing outlets would help to sustain the value of the traded shares.

At presently, no Islamic bank has a trade-based instrument revolving around trade financing that can be held by the common public. Consequently, the economy- and society-wide benefits of Islamic development-financing cannot be attained by Islamic banks.

The system of equations (7.10)–(7.11) can be used to construct and evaluate the foreign trade development-financing instrument revolving around MMM as follows:

$$\text{Evaluate}^1 \ \text{SWI} = M_1^a M_2^b M_3^c, \tag{7.12}$$

a,b,c are coefficients, estimated as learning coefficients by means of the random-coefficients method.

Subject to,

$$M_1 = f_1(\mathbf{x}, M_2, M_3, \theta)$$
$$M_2 = f_2(\mathbf{x}, M_1, M_3, \theta)$$
$$M_3 = f_3(\mathbf{x}, M_2, M_2, \theta)$$
$$x_{ii} = f_i(\mathbf{x}_{ij}, \theta_s)$$
$$\theta = f_\theta(\mathbf{x}_{ij})$$

M1: Mudarabah; M2: Musharakah; M3: Murabaha, all of which are taken up in the market-driven sense of trade and complementarities. All other variables have already been defined.

The contrary scenario of financing instruments

In the interest-ridden economy and society in which we exist, it is almost impossible to think of extensively participatory financing instruments. Impediments to resource mobilization are created by the existence of methodological individualism. Its mark is self-interest and ownership: the ultimate man-made rights. In such an economic and social milieu, the animal spirit of competition and self-interest forms individualist behavior and social preferences according to the tenets of methodological individualism (Buchanan and Tullock, 1999). Since the prevalence of interest rates limits resource mobilization, any model of pervasive participation (e.g. the *Tawhidi* worldview and world-systems) remains fragmented. We have already explained these consequences.

As an example, the monetary sector, the real economy and the financial sector compete and marginalize each other because of individual preferences – those who choose between these sectors for the growth and market-share of private ownership. Sectoral linkages are disrupted, so organic learning remains absent. Hence, no concept and practice of systemic unity of knowledge is possible. No relational learning occurs at any level of the economy or society.

Interest-ridden economies must be perpetually volatile and unstable. Growth, development, social and ethical values remain unsustainable. Now the wider understanding of verses (2:165–167) is that social and economic systems based on rationalism remain deprived in life. Such deprivation will be complete and falsehood terminally punished in the Hereafter. Only the ultimate truth of *Tawhid* must prevail to remove every trace of moral entropy. In the *Tawhidi* worldview, it is impossible for the false-hood model to yield and receive any reward and fruitful recompense.

Many of the economic and social implications of the rationalism model can be worked out by referring to the 'de-knowledge' model of denial of unity of divine knowledge given in expression (7.8). The starting point here is to note that the following result must be permanent for this case:

$$dW\sim(\theta\sim)/d\theta\sim = \{dW\sim([\mathbf{x}\sim_{ij}(\theta\sim)])/dx\sim_{ji}(\theta\sim)\}.\{d\ x\sim_{ji}(\theta\sim)/d\theta\sim\} \qquad (7.13)$$

$$= \Sigma\{\partial W\sim([\mathbf{x}\sim_{ij}(\theta\sim)]/\partial x\sim_{ij}(\theta\sim)).(dx\sim_{ij}(\theta\sim)/dx\sim_{ji}(\theta\sim)\}.\{dx\sim_{ji}(\theta\sim)/d\theta\sim\}$$

By the postulates of neoclassical so-called welfare economics, $dW\sim(\theta\sim)/d\theta\sim = 0$, for optimal $W\sim(\theta\sim)$. However, by the postulates of 'welfare' economics, $dW\sim([\mathbf{x}\sim_{ij}(\theta\sim)])/dx\sim_{lk}(\theta\sim) > 0$; $dx\sim_{ij}(\theta\sim)/dx\sim_{ji}(\theta\sim) < 0$; and $dx\sim_{ji}(\theta\sim)/d\theta\sim > 0$; for each i,j.

Therefore, each of the terms of expression (7.13) reduces to zero.

That is,

$$\partial W\sim([\mathbf{x}\sim_{ij}(\theta\sim)]/\partial x\sim_{ij}(\theta\sim)).(dx\sim_{ij}(\theta\sim)/dx\sim_{ji}(\theta\sim)\}.\{dx\sim_{ji}(\theta\sim)/d\theta\sim\} = 0,$$

identically.

This implies that in the optimal state of $W\sim(\theta\sim)$, the following must be true identically:

$$\partial W\sim([\mathbf{x}\sim_{ij}(\theta\sim)]/\partial x\sim_{ij}(\theta\sim)) = 0; (dx\sim_{ij}(\theta\sim)/dx\sim_{ji}(\theta\sim) = 0;$$
$$dx\sim_{ji}(\theta\sim)/d\theta\sim = 0; \text{ for each i,j.}$$

The inference drawn is that the growth of rationalism in the system increases material and moral entropy. In this situation, each x_{ij} shuns its complementary partner x_{ji}. The growth of total entropy increases falsehood, until it is destroyed and terminal equilibrium is established. This is indeed the meaning conveyed by verses of the *Qur'an* (2:165–167).

Reverting to Islamic economics and finance today

The episteme of methodological individualism, and every different terminology and belief of rationalism including its model has entered Islamic economics and finance lock, stock and barrel. This field has therefore no worldview of its own. There are only shadows cast by the setting sun of Occidentalism. Postulates of marginal rate of substitution, scarcity, competition, and the postulates of optimization, economic rationality, steady-state equilibrium, self and ego have been borrowed from the occidental model in both scholarship and practice.

Using these foundations, the Islamic banking, financial and economic sectors are today moulding their architecture to fit into the capitalist globalization agenda (Ahmad, 2004). Traditional rules governing Islamic banking and government financing surrender to the institutional directives of global governance whose sole objective is to maximize shareholder wealth and the value of the Islamic financing firms. In these situations, the *Qur'an* and the *sunnah* are forgotten as the episteme of Islamic resurgence. The reign of *fiqh* (personal and institutional legal interpretations of the *shari'ah*) has taken over (Asad, 1987).

Such a prevalent state of affairs has caused divisions and isolationism in the rules that should bind, rather than separate, Islamic financing institutions. The result is the absence of Islamic networking in trade, development and finance. The corporate governance of Islamic institutions lacks the standardization of *shari'ah* rules. Effective regulation of Islamic financing institutions by and for the *ummah* does not exist (Choudhury and Hoque, 2006).

Muslim empiricists do not understand the meaning of reflective empiricism that springs from the *Qur'an* and the *sunnah*. Imitative financing indicators fill the pages of egoistic publications, without any Islamic meaning and reconstruction for the guidance and evaluation of Islamic financing institutions or projects for the comprehensive model of the *ummah* (Islamic world-system) via the *maqasid as-shari'ah*. These works remain areas of futile scholarship.

The *Tawhidi* episteme of the *maqasid as-shari'ah* is neither understood nor practised in the goals of Islamic financing institutions and their modes of financing that are carried out today. Inextricably hinged to the rationalism model, Islamic scholarship and its institutions have forgotten the *ummah* (Choudhury, 2007b).

The *Tawhidi* worldview methodology must be revived to put Islamic scholarship, Islamic development instrumentation and institutions into the *ummah* context. *Tawhid* is merely used as jargon today. Its deeper epistemic import is shunned.

Conclusion

This chapter has undertaken a worldly interpretation of verses (2:164–167) in view of *Tawhid* and the world-system. The verses point out the promised success of truth and the defeat of rationalism. Rationalism is shown to be defeated both by the overwhelming power of the divine law of unity of knowledge and by its own morally void self-contradictions.

We have argued in the spirit of the *Qur'an* and *sunnah vis-à-vis* the project of Islamicization of knowledge and the world-system that the verses (2:164–167) instil a wider field of understanding and application from the moral high ground. Every part of the *Qur'an* acts as a framework of consciousness (scientific phenomenology) for understanding the unity of the divine law as the precept of *Tawhid*. It points out the profound application of the *Tawhidi* worldview to worldly matters. Together, these will enable humankind to construct a morally aware, socio-scientific order.

In this spirit of the total phenomenology of the *Tawhidi* worldview, we proceeded to derive a comprehensive logical formalism from the verses (2:164–167). This answers both the questions of Truth and falsehood as signs of *Allah*. Truth points to those signs of *Allah* which establish the good society. Falsehood points to the negative signs of *Allah* and are self-annihilated. Rationalism is the model of falsehood by its thought and application based on methodological individualism and denial of the law of divine unity and the world-system.

This chapter has established the logical formalism of *Tawhid* and its world-system. In its treatment of both Truth and falsehood, it has yielded a generalized model that applies to both the sublime and mundane issues of life.

One such issue, using a limited matrix treatment, was the proposal of a new financial instrument. To date, this has eluded academics and practitioners in the field of Islamic economics and finance. The new financial instrument that we have presented here in the light of the generalized *Tawhidi* worldview methodology is shown to answer the comprehensive questions of the *maqasid as-shari'ah* for the benefit of the individual and the firm embedded in the *ummah*.

Note

1 Evaluation here means the two steps of empirical work. First, the model shown is statistically 'estimated' and the coefficients examined for inter-variable complementarities. Next, the changes in the coefficients to attain normative degrees of complementarities lead into 'simulation' of the model system and the estimators of the 'evaluated' model.

References

Ahmad, K. (2004). "The challenge of global capitalism – an Islamic perspective", in Dunning, J.H. (ed.), *Making Globalization Good*, pp. 181–209, Oxford University Press, Oxford, UK.

Asad, M. (1987), *This Law of Ours*, Dar al-Andalus, Gibraltar.

Barrow, J.D. (1991). *Theories of Everything*, Oxford University Press, Oxford, UK.

Biraima, A.H. (1998/99). "From rationalities to righteousness: a universal theory of action", *Humanomics, International Journal of Systems and Ethics*, 14:4 and 15:1, pp. 207–63.

Buchanan, J.M. (1954). "Social choice, democracy, and free markets", *Journal of Political Economy*, 62, pp. 114–23.

Buchanan, J.M. and Tullock, G. (1999). "Individual rationality in social choice", in *The Collected Works of James M. Buchanan*, 3. pp. 31–42, Liberty Fund, Indianapolis, IN.

Choudhury, M.A. (1997). *Reforming the Muslim World*, Kegan Paul International London, UK.

Choudhury, M.A. (2000a). "A social contractarian theory of markets: neoclassicism, Rawls, Gauthier and the alternative", *International Journal of Social Economics*, 27:3, pp. 194–213.

Choudhury, M.A. (2000b). "Venture capital in Islam: a critical examination", *Journal of Economic Studies*, 28:1, pp. 14–33.

Choudhury, M.A. (2006). *Circular Causation Model in the Koran*, Vol 3 of *Science and Epistemology in the Qur'an*, The Edwin Mellen Press, Lewiston, NY.

Choudhury, M.A. (2007a). *The Universal Paradigm and the Islamic World-System*, World Scientific Publication, Singapore.

Choudhury, M.A. (2007b). "Development of Islamic economic and social thought", in Hassan, M.K. and Lewis, M. (eds), *Handbook of Islamic Banking*, Edward Elgar Publishing Ltd., Cheltenham, UK, pp. 21–37.

Choudhury, M.A. and Hoque, M.Z. (2004). "A paradigm for Islamic banking", in their *An Advanced Exposition of Islamic Economics and Finance*, Lewiston, NY: The Edwin Mellen Press, pp. 159–83.

Choudhury, M.A. and Hoque, M.Z. (2006). "Corporate governance in Islamic perspective", *Corporate Governance, the International Journal of Business in Society*, 6:2, pp. 116–28.

Choudhury, M.A. Zaman, S.I and Nasar, Y. (2007). "A knowledge-induced operator model", *The Journal of Science*, 12:2.

Dawkins, R. (1976), *The Selfish Gene*, Oxford University Press, New York.

Etzioni, A. (1988). "What is rational?" in his *The Moral Dimension, Towards a New Economics*, The Free Press. New York, NY.

Foucault, M. trans. A.M. Sheridan (1972). *The Archeology of Knowledge and the Discourse on Language*, Harper Torchbooks, New York.

George, H. [1897]. *The Science of Political Economy*, Robert Schalkenbach Foundation, New York, NY.

Gruber, T.R. (1993). "A translation approach to portable ontologies", *Knowledge Acquisition*, 5:2, pp. 199–200.

Hawking, S.W. (1980). "*Is the End in Sight for Theoretical Physics?*" Cambridge University Press, Cambridge, UK.

Hossain, S. (2007). "Resolving geo-spatial semantics conflicts – an interoperability issue", *Humanomics, International Journal of Systems and Ethics*, 23:2, pp. 102–9.

Husserl, E. trans. Lauer, Q. (1965). *Phenomenology and the Crisis of Philosophy*, p. 155, Harper & Row Publishers, New York. Note his comment on the perceived absence of ethical roots in occidental scientific inquiry.

Jabsheh, F. Behbehani, W. Al-Shamali, S. and Dashti, B. (2007). *The Impact of Financial Liberalization on the Islamic Banking Industry*, mimeo. Kuwait Institute of Scientific Research, Kuwait.

Kahf, M. (2007). "Bridging the gap", *Business Islamica*, February, pp. 64–6.

Kant, I. trans. H.J. Paton (1964). *Groundwork of the Metaphysics of Morals*, Harper& Row Publishers, New York.

Maddox, I.J. (1971). *Functional Analysis*, Cambridge University Press, Cambridge, UK.

Maxwell, G. (1962). "The ontological status of theoretical entities", in H. Feigl and G. Maxwell (eds), *Minnesota Studies in the Philosophy of Science, II: Scientific Explanation, Space and Time*, pp. 3–27, University of Minnesota Press, Minneapolis, Minnesota.

von-Mises, L. (1976). "The human mind", in his *The Ultimate Foundation of Economic Science*, pp. 11–33 Sheed Andrews and McMeel, Inc., Kansas City, Kansas.

Murden, S.W. (2002). "Islam and the liberal idea", in his *Islam, the Middle East and the New Global Hegemony*, pp. 155–84, Lynne Rienner, London, UK.

Mydin, A.K. and Larbani, M. (2006). "Seigniorage of fiat money and the maqasid al-shari'ah: the unattainability of the *maqasid*", *Humanomics, International Journal of Systems and Ethics*, 22:1, pp. 17–33.

Neurath, O. Carnap, R. and Morris, C. (eds) (1970). *Foundations of the Unity of Science 2*, The University of Chicago Press, Chicago, IL.

Resnick, S.A. and Wolff, R.D. (1987). "A Marxian theory" in their *Knowledge and Class*, University of Chicago Press, Chicago, IL.

Rucker, R. (1983). "The universe of set theory" in his *Infinity and the Mind*, pp. 211–18, Bantam Books, New York, NY.

Russell, B. (1991). *A History of Western Philosophy*, Allen and Unwin, London, UK.

Russell, B. (2001). "Truth and falsehood" in his *The Problems of Philosophy*, pp. 69–75, Oxford University Press, Oxford, UK.

Shackle, G.L.S. (1972). *Epistemics and Economics*, Cambridge University Press, Cambridge, UK.

Sullivan, W.M. (1989). "The contemporary crisis of liberal society", in McCullough, H.B. (ed.), *Political Ideologies and Political Philosophies*, pp. 57–9, Wall and Thompson, Toronto, Ont.

Taylor, O.H. (1967). "The future of economic liberalism", in *Economics and Liberalism*, pp. 294–311, Harvard University Press, Cambridge, MA.

Chapter 8

The Role of *Zakah* in the Mainstream Economic Model

Masudul Alam Choudhury and Kabir Hassan[1]

Abstract

A contrasting approach to modeling the general equilibrium model of the Islamic financial economy is presented between the usual Islamic mainstream economic approach and the *Tawhidi* epistemological approach. The Keynesian model of general equilibrium is used to explore the contrasting views. The chapter establishes the fundamental critique that has been presented throughout this work: Islamic financial economics in its mainstream context has failed to contribute any fresh learning to the world. The mainstream approach of Islamic financial economics has led to opposing worldviews between the *Tawhidi* methodological worldview and the Islamic mainstream model.

Introduction

In this chapter we develop a Keynesian-style macroeconomic general equilibrium model that can be modified to be compatible with a mainstream Islamic economy. Interest rates play a key role in general equilibrium models. However, in Islamic economies in particular, the use of interest is forbidden. This poses a problem when applying traditional interest-based macroeconomic models to Islamic economics. Given the increased predominance and growth of interest-free financing and Islamic economics, it is vital to develop a macroeconomic model that is consistent with an interest-free framework. We, therefore, have modified a traditional Keynesian model to a more appropriate model of economic behavior in interest-free economics. This is achieved chiefly by replacing interest rates with the expected profit rate obtained from real investment opportunities. We also place particular emphasis on the role of *zakah* in an Islamic economy; this is another way in which Islamic economics significantly differs from its counterparts. We show that *zakah* can have a dramatic multiplier effect on the amount of investment in the economy.

Zakah is essentially a tax levied on wealth. It is not an income tax, rather a tax on accumulated wealth. The purpose of *zakah* is to improve social welfare by redistributing wealth from the wealthy to the needy. The result is that idle capital in the economy is reduced, resulting in greater levels of real investment. An increase in real investment increases the demand for labor and equilibrium wages. This results in increased demand, and drives overall higher economic output. In effect, *zakah* acts as a multiplier for real capital that can be linked to significant increases in employment, output, and profit. This effect may be so powerful that real investment occurs even if the profit rate is zero (Metwalli, n.d.).

The increased employment encouraged through the incorporation of *zakah* can also be seen to have a particularly pronounced impact on structural unemployment. Structural forms of unemployment typically arise in an economy due to problems of underdeveloped human and real capital, poverty, age, and disability. Increasing aggregate demand does not usually help to alleviate these problems. However, *zakah,* by its nature, can have a particular impact on reducing these social problems, because its goal is to increase investment in these areas of structural underdevelopment.

We continue by defining a modified Keynesian macroeconomic model that incorporates the qualities of interest-free investment as well as *zakah*. We incorporate the expected profit rate from real investment to function in a way that eliminates the need for interest rates. Additionally, we study the multiplier effect of *zakah*. Due to the importance of *zakah* in reducing structural problems, we separate government expenditure into two components: *zakah* expenditure and other government expenditure. Since *zakah* expenditure is focused on reducing structural unemployment, this expenditure can be seen as non-inflationary in our model. Once the macroeconomic model is defined, we examine several important relationships such as that between the profit rate and the investment–consumption plan as well as the multiplier effect of *zakah* on employment, investment and output.

The characteristics of the monetary sector in an Islamic economy

We first examine the monetary sector in an economy where there is no interest rate. The central bank is not able to generate a supply of liquidity based on the demand for cash balances by creditors. This means that there are no gaps between the *ex ante* demand for cash balances and the supply of liquidity that would otherwise result from a speculative demand for cash balances (Choudhury, 1986).

An interest-free monetary sector needs a mechanism to determine monetary equilibrium. In the context of Islamic finance, this is the system of *mudarabah*. This is essentially the system in which the banking sector provides investment capital not on the basis of charged interest, but via a profit-sharing scheme. In essence, banks under this system engage in joint ventures with business entrepreneurs. Thus, the mechanism through which the liquidity equilibrium is reached is the expected profit rate of real investment. This can be thought of as the average profit rate from a random sample of firms. The supply of liquidity under an Islamic economy is determined by this rate, as opposed to being provided by the central bank. This is a key departure from the traditional Keynesian model (Choudhury, 1986).

Siddiqui (1983) defines a similar model where the monetary sector equilibrium is determined through a profit-sharing mechanism. In this model, the money supply curve shifts to the right due to increases in the level of income, following increased prospects of profits. At the same time, the demand curve also shifts to the right as entrepreneurs channel funds into profitable ventures. It is unclear, however, whether the money demand and supply curves will experience their full shifts, due to the fact that some of the demand for liquidity may be satisfied by internal sources.

Money supply in the traditional Keynesian sense is often modeled as an exogenously (central bank) determined, inelastic supply. A major departure in the Islamic monetary sector under *mudarabah* is that the supply curve of liquidity is elastic and positively sloped. This is intuitive, as increasing profit rates will drive an increased demand for investment, thus, liquidity supplied will increase to meet this demand. Additionally, increasing profit rates reduce the risk for Islamic banks under *mudarabah*; they are therefore willing to supply more funds (Choudhury, 1986).

Similar to that of the traditional Keynesian model, the demand curve for liquidity under *mudarabah* is negatively sloped and elastic. However, the justification of this shape is somewhat different, and is as follows. As the intensity of capital invested into the real economy increases, the marginal efficiency of those capital flows decline. This is reflected in lower profit rates for investment projects as markets become saturated. Alternatively, as the profit rate for investment projects increases, entrepreneurs are able to generate relatively more internal capital, thus the demand for external capital declines. The demand for cash balances will therefore decrease with increasing rates of profit (Choudhury, 1986).

With positively sloped, elastic money supply and negatively sloped, elastic money demand, the equilibrium profit rate for real investment and the level of liquidity in the economy are determined by supply and demand at the equilibrium. This occurs at a feasible normal rate of profit, which can be defined as a weighted average of the profit rates for a random sample of diverse Islamic-funded projects. Due to the potential sample biases and changing economic conditions, this normal rate of profit can be seen to have a range of acceptable levels. Thus, a minimum acceptable profit rate remains. At such a rate, the demand for liquidity is likely to be very high. Investors will invest this liquidity into the real economy in search of higher returns (Choudhury, 1986).

The monetary sector equilibrium: the LM schedule

The relationship between the IS-LM curves has been used to explain equilibrium in the monetary and expenditure sectors of the economy under the Keynesian setup. In our model of the Islamic economy, we replace the interest rate with the rate of profit from real investment. Accordingly, we denote the Islamic IS-LM counterparts as the IIS-ILM relationship.

The model of Metwalli illustrates the departure of an Islamic model from that of the traditional Keynesian model. In this model, liquidity is defined by the *ISZ* (investment, savings, *zakah* rate) curve. First, in the Islamic model, the demand for liquidity is solely a function of income. This is due to the fact that the speculative motive does not exist in Islamic finance. Thus, the demand is defined purely from a precautionary perspective. Second, the *zakah* rate must also be incorporated into the model. Since total investment must equal savings in the Keynesian model, the monetary equilibrium in an Islamic economy is the locus of income and profit rates where investment, savings and *zakah* rates are simultaneously determined.

Our model builds on the motivation of Metwalli's model, but diverges somewhat in terms of the macroeconomic relationships presented. Similar to Metwalli, the demand function for cash balances is determined by the transaction and precautionary motives. The speculative motive is ignored. However, in Metwalli's formalization, the *zakah* rate is the principal instrument which determines monetary equilibrium. In our model, the primary instrument is the rate of profit on real investment.

We define the demand function for monetary balances as

$$M_d = l_1(Y,P) + l_2(Y,P) \tag{8.1}$$
$$= l(Y,P),$$

which can be rewritten in linear form as

$$M_d = a + a_1 Y + a_2 P, \tag{8.2}$$

Here, M_d denotes the total demand for cash balances. l_1 (Y, P) denotes transaction demand. l_2 (Y, P) denotes precautionary demand. l (Y, P) denotes the general function combining l_1 (Y, P); and l_2 (Y, P). Y denotes the level of nominal income. P denotes the rate of profit. a, a_1, a_2 are coefficients.

The following relationships also hold:

$$\frac{\partial M_D}{\partial Y} > 0, \frac{\partial M_D}{\partial P} < 0. \tag{8.3}$$

The supply function of liquidity is given by

$$M_s = M_s(Y,P), \tag{8.4}$$

which can be rewritten in linear form as

$$M_s = b + b_1 Y + b_2 P, \tag{8.5}$$

where M_s denotes the total supply of liquidity; b, b_1, b_2 are coefficients.

The following relationships also hold:

$$\frac{\partial M_s}{\partial Y} > 0, \frac{\partial M_s}{\partial P} > 0. \tag{8.6}$$

For monetary sector equilibrium to exist, we must have

$$M_d = M_s. \tag{8.7}$$

This is the monetary equilibrium defined by the traditional LM schedule in the Keynesian model. However, we have modified this model in several key ways, including the elimination of the exogenous, inelastic money supply function. In our model, the supply of liquidity is determined by the interaction between the quantities of liquidity demanded in response to changes in the profit rate on real investment. We now examine this relationship further.

The monetary sector equilibrium is then given by

$$M_d = M_s,$$

which can be rewritten in linear form as

$$a + a_1 Y + a_2 P = b + b_1 Y + b_2 P. \tag{8.8}$$

This yields

$$P = \frac{a_1 - b_1}{b_2 - a_2} \times Y + D. \tag{8.9}$$

D is a constant and may be a function of the monetary reserve, which can be considered an exogenous parameter. The reserve ratio can be manipulated by the Islamic Central Bank by suitable open market operations.

Equation (8.9) is the ILM-schedule. The sign of equation (8.9) is not determined. It may be positive or negative, depending on the response of the marginal efficiency of capital in response to changes in investment. For example, an increase in investment may lead to a reduction in the efficiency of capital. As a result, the profit rate decreases, even though levels of output will increase. In this example, the slope of (8.9) is negative. In other cases, it may be positive.

The traditional Keynesian equilibrium occurs at the intersection of the negatively sloped LM and positively sloped IS curves. This is consistent with the existence of a positive rate of interest; decreases in this rate bring about a greater demand for investment capital. However, due to the exogenous supply of liquidity, equilibrium may not occur until the Central Bank is able to restore the equilibrium.

In the Islamic system, there are no interest rates and the exogenous money supply is not assumed. Therefore, the disequilibrium (or lagged equilibrium described above) does not occur in the Islamic macroeconomic system, because the supply of money is always constrained by an *ex ante* demand for cash balances. Under this process, as output increases, the demand for investment capital, as well as the profit rate of return on that capital, also increases. The Islamic bank, in turn, due to increased profit rates, has the incentive to engage in profit-sharing ventures and provides a corresponding increase in the amount of liquidity supplied. Thus, under this framework the demand for the investment and supply of liquidity will remain steady. In addition, shifts in the monetary supply curve are caused by exogenous variations in the monetary reserve variable by the buying or selling of securities in an Islamic capital market in accordance with the requirements of an easier or tighter money supply.

The expenditure sector equilibrium: the IS-schedule

In the expenditure sector, the investment function I is defined as

$$I = I(Y, P, Z), \tag{8.10}$$

This can be rewritten in linear form as

$$I = c + c_1 Y + c_2 P + c_3 Z, \tag{8.11}$$

where Z denotes the *zakah* expenditure and c, c_1, c_2, c_3 are coefficients.

The following relationships also hold:

$$\frac{\partial I}{\partial Y} > 0, \frac{\partial I}{\partial P} < 0, \frac{\partial I}{\partial Z} > 0. \tag{8.12}$$

The negativity of $\partial I/\partial P$ can be interpreted as increasing costs of investment that are undertaken. Therefore, the profit rate declines as investment increases. This is consistent with declining marginal efficiency. As the amount of investment rises and markets become saturated, the marginal efficiency of capital declines and profit rates declines accordingly.

The expression $\partial I/\partial Z$ is positive, however. This means that as the amount of *zakah* spending increases, investment also increases. This is consistent with the multiplier effect of *zakah*. However, just as there are limits as to what can be considered a reasonable profit rate, there is also a reasonable *zakah* range. Traditionally, the *zakah* rate can only range marginally above the rate of 2.5%. There are differences of opinions on this issue. Some Islamic scholars do not believe the rate of *zakah* should be allowed to fluctuate, as the level is set at 2.5% by the Prophet Muhammad (SM) in the *Qur'an*. However, more progressive Islamic scholars believe that economic conditions may allow the rate to rise above 2.5%. It is agreed that the *Qur'an* forbids the rate from falling below 2.5% for either individuals or businesses.

Although the *Qur'an* stipulates a *zakah* rate of at least 2.5%, in macroeconomic models, the rate appears as a coefficient. Often, in estimations of macroeconomic models, the rate appears to diverge from 2.5% quite substantially. In a recent study, the *zakah* rate was estimated at a mere 0.04% paid by OIC funds under the management of Rayo Withanage Asset-management Company.

The consumption function for our model is given by C,

$$C = C(Y). \tag{8.13}$$

This can be rewritten in linear form as

$$c = d + d_1 Y, \tag{8.14}$$

where d and d_1 are coefficients.

The national accounting identity in the Islamic economy is given by

$$Y = C + I + Z + G, \tag{8.15}$$

where Z denotes *zakah* expenditure and G denotes other government expenditure. This is a departure from the traditional national accounting identity used in Keynesian models.

The *Zakah* expenditure can be further expressed as a function of savings:

$$Z = e + e_1 S, \tag{8.16}$$

where S denotes savings; e, e_1 are constants; e_1 can be interpreted as the *zakah* ratio.

Substituting the various national income accounting identities, we obtain

$$Y = \frac{c + d + G}{1 + C_1 - d_1} + \frac{C_2}{1 - C_1 - d_1} \times P + \frac{1 + C_3}{1 - C_1 - d_1} \times Z. \tag{8.17}$$

We take G to be exogenously determined, so $G = G_0$.

Furthermore, setting $S = I$ for expenditure/savings equilibrium, and from expression I of equation (8.11), we obtain,

$$Z = e + e_1 S$$
$$= e + e_1 I$$
$$= e + e_1 (c + C_1 Y + C_2 P + C_3 Z),$$

$$\text{i.e.} \, Z = \frac{e_1 c_1}{1 - e_1 c_3} + \frac{c_1 e_1}{1 - e_1 c_3} * Y + \frac{e_1 c_2}{1 - e_1 c_3} * P. \tag{8.18}$$

Substituting Z from expression (8.18) into expression (8.17), we obtain an expression for Y:

$$Y = A + BP, \tag{8.19}$$

where A is a function of the exogenous parameter G_0. B can be either positive or negative, depending on the sign of

$$\left(1 - \frac{1 + c_3}{1 - c_1 - d_1} \times \frac{e_1 c_1}{1 - e_1 c_3} \right)^{-1}. \tag{8.20}$$

Expression (8.19) is our formulation of the IIS-relationship, which incorporates *zakah* and the profit rate into the system. The IIS-curve can be either positively or negatively sloped. In the case of a negatively sloped IIS, we can say that the marginal efficiency of capital becomes lower as investment increases; this is reflected by lower average profit rates. This is also consistent with rising investment costs associated with a large amount of liquidity chasing fewer investment opportunities. Note, however, that a decline in the rate of profit would not necessarily imply a decline in output Y, because there is already an existing stock of capital expenditure in the economy sufficient enough to generate increasing levels of income.

As in the traditional Keynesian model, we can also have a positively sloped IIS. Here, we have the sum of the marginal propensities to consume and invest out of the national product that exceeds unity. This results in a situation where such an economy remains unsatisfied by the available savings, mainly due to excess demand for investment in the Islamic economy. This corresponds to disequilibrium in the expenditure sector in the Islamic system. Equilibrium can be restored in this case by distributing profits as dividends; this would allow most investment to be funded internally. Alternatively, the money supply would have to be increased in order to fulfill investment demand. The latter would come at the expense of demand-pull inflation. This would likely be a temporary situation, however, because economic agents in the Islamic economy will redistribute dividends to restore monetary equilibrium. Hence, the interpretation of the IIS is slightly different than that of the traditional Keynesian IS relation.

Another major difference in the Islamic system presented here is a mitigation of cost-push inflation. We assume that the speculative demand for cash is nonexistent due to the absence of interest rates in the economy. As a consequence, monetary authorities can much more easily reconcile the gap between the *ex ante* demand with the supply of liquidity, given the reserve of the central banks. The ability of the monetary authority to maintain monetary equilibrium through continuous monitoring therefore reduces the problem of cost-push inflation in an Islamic economy.

The properties of the Islamic economy described above show that there is a very low propensity for prolonged inflation in the Islamic economy under the model. The real values of macroeconomic equilibriums are only affected by sustained, long-term movements in the price level. Therefore, including macroeconomic values in their real form will not affect the stability of the macroeconomic equilibrium in an Islamic economy under this system.

The product and labor market equilibrium

We now describe the conditions of equilibrium in the Islamic product and labor markets. In our previous discussion, we submitted that inflationary pressures under this Islamic macroeconomic model are only temporary. Therefore, inflation should have little impact on the equilibriums defined under this system. Accordingly, we continue our discussion of the product and labor markets using nominal values.

A primary goal of our analysis is to study the impact of *zakah* programs on the Islamic macroeconomic system. *Zakah* expenditures are focused primarily on labor training and income subsidization programs for a targeted group of workers. The results of such programs, therefore, should be an increase in labor force participation from workers most affected by typical structural problems in the economy. As a result, we expect lower structural unemployment as well as an increase in economic output and real investment, due to both the direct and multiplier effects of *zakah* expenditure.

Zakah expenditure, the demand for labor, and the supply of labor in the Islamic economy are all a positive function of income and profit. Accordingly, we develop the following specification of the Islamic product and labor markets.

The production function for the Islamic economy is given by *f*,

$$Y = f(K, L),$$ (8.21)

where *K* denotes capital input. Capital stock in the Islamic economy cannot be seen as static, compared to the traditional Keynesian model, due to a higher propensity to invest in real assets. *L* denotes labor input.

Cooperative conditions in the Islamic economy require that the marginal rate of substitution of labor by capital remain constant. We take the constrained form:

$$-\frac{dK}{dL} = m$$ (8.22)

In equation (8.22), '*m*' takes strictly positive values, and its optimal value is determined by the equilibrium levels of wages and profit.

The rate of profit is related to the marginal efficiency of investment and is defined by

$$\frac{\partial Y}{\partial K} = P \tag{8.23}$$

Labor demand, L_D, is given by

$$L_D = L_D(W, Y, I, Z), \tag{8.24}$$

which is homogenous of degree zero.

Labor supply, L_S, is given by

$$L_S = L_S(W, Z) \tag{8.25}$$

Y and I are not expected to affect labor supply.

In labor market equilibrium we have

$$L_D = L_S. \tag{8.26}$$

Equation (8.26) determines the equilibrium wage rate W^0, given Y, Z, *and* I. It is significant that *zakah* plays an integral role in the determination of the wage rate. Also, marginal productivity theory is not used in the determination of equilibrium wages.

We have now defined the equilibrium characterizations of the monetary, expenditure, product, and employment markets in an Islamic economy using a modified Keynesian macroeconomic approach. We now use these relationships to define the Islamic economy as a system in a general equilibrium framework.

General equilibrium in an Islamic macroeconomic order in the light of mainstream theory

Figure 8.1 describes the relationships of the Islamic macroeconomic equilibrium discussed in the preceding sections. These results would be completely different in the contrary Islamic economic and finance theory with the epistemological condition of evolutionary learning premised in unity of knowledge affecting the general macroeconomic relationships. Thus, our results in this chapter outline the irreconcilable contrast between the mainstream approach to Islamic economic theory and the epistemological approach based on the methodological foundation of unity of knowledge. They also detail the permanently evolutionary learning conditions of the Islamic economy and finance (Choudhury, 2011).

Diagram I of Figure 8.1 shows the relationship between profit rate P and output level Y. The equilibrium shown includes a given level of *zakah* expenditure, which acts as a tax on accumulated wealth for high net worth Muslims. The curves shown in Diagram I represent the *IIS* and *ILM* curves of the Islamic economy and are based on the existence of marginal efficiency of capital and profitability replacing the traditional role of the interest rate.[2] The macroeconomic equilibrium *E1* of (Y, P) is shown.

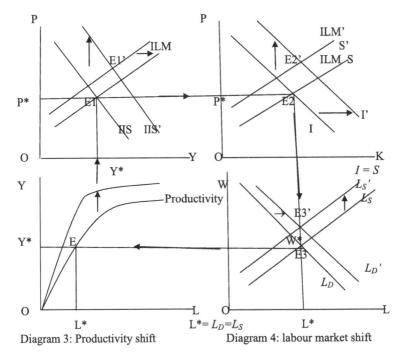

Figure 8.1 Macroeconomic general equilibrium system of the Islamic economy in mainstream economic perspectives

Diagram II shows the relationship between the profit rate P and the level of capital expenditure K, given the level of output and the existence of marginal efficiency of capital.[3] The equilibrium point for Diagram II holds for the same value of P as that of the equilibrium of Diagram I. The equilibrium $E2$, where $I = S$, and the profit rate are shown.

Diagram III shows the resulting equilibrium in the labor market with the labor supply and demand curves corresponding to a given level of *zakah* and the same conditions as that of Diagrams I-II. The equilibrium condition $E3$, where $L_D = L_S$, and the equilibrium wage rate W are shown.

Diagram IV shows the productivity curve in labor subject to diminishing marginal efficiency. The assumptions of marginal efficiency of investment and the marginal productivity curve are applicable under the assumptions of the Islamic economy. The optimal relationship under the constraints of marginal productivity is shown in terms of Y and L. The same condition will hold for the other factor inputs.

Additionally, the diagrams show that increases in the *zakah* expenditure portion of GDP correspond to upward shifts in the curves. This corresponds to the multiplicative effect of increasing *zakah* on income, expenditure, output, and wages. As the levels of these values increase, the resulting equilibria $E1$, $E2$, $E3$, and $E4$ shift upward. The level of the workforce may also increase, provided that there is no crowding-out effect caused by increasing wages.

The complete general equilibrium relationship of the Islamic economy in our modified Keynesian system is described by the following set of equations:

IIS schedule

$$Y = A_0 + A_1 P + A_2 G_0, \tag{8.27}$$

where, Y denotes national income or output,
　　　P denotes profit rate,
　　　G_0 denotes other autonomous government expenditure,
　　　A_0, A_1, A_2 are coefficients.

ILM schedule

$$P = B_0 + B_1 Y + B_2 R, \tag{8.28}$$

where R denotes exogenously set monetary reserves and B_0, B_1, B_2 are coefficients.
Product market:

$$Y = f(K, L), \tag{8.29}$$

where, K denotes the capital stock, L denotes labor input, and $f(K, L)$ denotes the production function.
Factor markets:
　　Labor demand is given by L_D:

$$L_D = L_D(W, Y, I, Z), \tag{8.30}$$

where W denotes the wage rate, I denotes investment, and Z denotes amount of *zakah*.
　　Labor supply is given by L_S:

$$L_S = L_S(W, Z) \tag{8.31}$$

Wage determination:
　　The equilibrium wage level is therefore determined where

$$L_D = L_S. \tag{8.32}$$

Equations (8.27)–(8.30) and (8.32) are the general equilibrium relationships of an Islamic macroeconomic system as construed in the garb of neoclassical and Keynesian economics. There are five equations with five unknowns, Y, P, L_D, K, W, so the system will have a unique solution.

Contrasting the *Tawhidi* methodology to mainstream Islamic economic treatment of general equilibrium: Towards a generalized system modeling in the *Tawhidi* methodological framework

The mainstream Islamic formalism of the general economic equilibrium remains disabled in incorporating and explaining the purposive foundation of the philosophy of Islamic law (*maqasid as-shari'ah*) as derived from the *Qur'an, sunnah*, and the juristic interpretations by learned Islamic scholars, particularly of the Islamic scholastic age. Thus, Islamic economics and finance, and their inspired disciplines today, are epistemologically benign to authentic foundations to explain their methodological worldview. The essential nature of Islamic economics and finance, and thus the idea of Islamic banking, cannot be ascertained by simply adapting the Islamic mainstream imitation to construct the genuinely Islamic nature of what can be critically referred to as the generalized system framework. Within that, the particular model of a general equilibrium model can be taken up, but with a substantive new meaning, methodology, and properties. We examine the substantive differences between the *Tawhidi* methodological approach and the formalism of the general equilibrium model within the broader framework of the generalized system. We also examine the *Tawhidi* methodological approach to the formulation of this kind of a model with a substantively critical outlook. The resulting arguments will point out the critical negation of the mainstream approach to the study of Islamic economics, finance, and banking among today's academics and practitioners. The mainstream approach, when contrasted with the *Tawhidi* methodological approach, points out the Islamic irrelevance in the mainstream formulation of Islamic economics, finance, and banking as a substantively new discipline with its epistemology. This result would remain as an academic warning to the conventional Islamic economic, finance, and banking field of the epistemological emptiness of this pursuit as exemplified in the foregoing mainstream model.

The *Tawhidi* methodology in socio-scientific study was explained earlier. We apply it here to the construction of the general equilibrium model within the generalized system methodology of *Tawhidi* epistemology.

At the outset, we point out that the understanding of the epistemolgical premise of *Tawhid* as unity of knowledge conveys the oneness of the monotheistic law. Such unity, as the oneness of *Allah* ingrained in the unity of knowledge of the monotheistic law, is explained by the organic evolutionary epistemology of systemic unity between the good things of life. In this way, the universe in general and in all its particulars are depicted and explained by the process-oriented continuity of interaction, integration, and the creative evolution of complementary relationships between all the good things of life. It also means the avoidance of the differentiated and conflicting things of the *Qur'anic* good and recommended things of life (*halal al-tayyabah*).

Once the above deduction is made respecting the knowledge-flow as systemic consciousness to derive the meaning of organic oneness and symbiosis of intervariable intercausal relationships every point in the *Tawhidi* dimensions of knowledge, space, and time embeds the events such as $E\{\theta, x(\theta), t(\theta)\}$, all along the continuous evolution of knowledge in the historical trajectory commencing from *Tawhid* in the beginning to *Tawhid* in the end as the closure of the ensuing evolutionary epistemology of unity of knowledge.

The inter-causal variables denoted by the vector (matrix, tensor etc.), $\{x(\theta); \theta \in (\Omega, S)\}$ are complementary in the *Tawhidi* perspectives, although the *Tawhidi* model of circular causation can reveal the differentiation and marginalist substitution intervariable that exist in the inductive examination of the 'as is' states of the problem under study. With the property of pervasive complementarities (participation, symbiosis) intervariables in the deductive state of 'as it ought to be'state of the issue under study. Consequently, the complementary events as described above charaterize every point continuously of the monetary regime in concert with the spending regime. The role of endogenous technology and monentary and spending (fiscal) policies and the ensuing production relationships include price stability and productive employment. Thereby, the condition of the quantity of money equals the spending, as in the classical equation of exchange but revised to its induction by the knowledge variable derived from the epistemology of *Tawhid*.

Consequently, $M(\theta) = y.P(\theta) + G(\theta) + T(\theta)$. Here $M(\theta)$ denotes the quantity of money; $y(\theta)$ denotes the real economic output; $P(\theta)$ denotes the price level; $G(\theta)$ denotes government expenditure; $T(\theta)$ denotes endogenous technology. Each of these variables is induced by $\theta \in (\Omega, S)$ to imply intercausality between these variables in the deductive sense of complementarities between them. Such relationships are also said to be endogenously inter-related by the epistemic premise of unity of knowledge.

The relationship, $M(\theta) = y.P(\theta) + G(\theta) + T(\theta)$ result in the following relationship:

$$dM(\theta)/d\theta = d(y.P(\theta))/d\theta + dG(\theta)/d\theta + dT(\theta)/d\theta > 0, \text{identically.} \quad (8.33)$$

Hence knowledge induction and endogenous intervariables relationships at every part of the event space cause the monetary stability relationship move in complementary fashion with the spending relationship and endogenous technology effect. The limitations of inflation, full employment output, underemployment, and sterility of monetary and spending aggregates do not exist in the Islamic case of the *Tawhidi* knowledge induction of all these variables. The IS-LM mainstream formalization does not exist.

Figure 8.2 shows how the *Tawhidi* knowledge-induced complementarities between monetary and spending relationships work in respect of the effects of endogenous productive returns, prices, and technology.

OL1 denotes the 45 degrees line from the origin in accordance with equation (8.33). For every technologically induced learning point like a_1 and a_2 there are codetermined

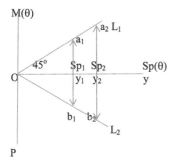

Figure 8.2 Explaining complementarities between money and spending

technoligically induced learning points like, $(y_1, Sp_1)(\theta)$ and $(y_2.Sp_2)(\theta)$, respectively. But the real output y = Y/P, with Y as nominal output and P as price level. Now, because y is increasing along with Sp, Y must be increasing at a rate higher than the rate of change in the price level, P. The latter category is the rate of inflation. Consequently, the nominal output is maintained at a sustainable level with non-inflationary real economic growth. The conclusion, then, is that there are codetermined movements between money and spending under the effect of knowledge-induced learning induced in all the variables that cause complementarities between the variables, $\{M, Sp, y, Y, P, T\}(\theta)$.

Summary and conclusion

In this chapter, we developed a model of an Islamic economy in the tradition of the classic Keynesian general equilibrium framework. However, the Islamic model diverges from the traditional model in several significant ways. Most importantly, the lack of interest rates in Islamic economies makes the traditional Keynesian model inapplicable. Instead, the interest rates typically used in IS-LM analysis are replaced by the profit rate on real investment assets. At the heart of this substitution is the important role that the profit-sharing, *mudarabah* framework of the Islamic financial system plays in the development and allocation of capital. It is this allocation process that allows the profit rate from investment projects to substitute for interest rates as the driving investment incentive in the Islamic Keynesian model.

Additionally, we also modify the traditional Keynesian model to focus on the impact of *zakah* spending in the Islamic economy. *Zakah* is a percentage tax on accumulated wealth that is redistributed from wealthy Muslims and directed towards social welfare programs. Thus, *zakah* fundamentally changes the national accounting identity, and therefore, has an impact on the resulting equilibrium. We show that the incorporation of *zakah* into the Keynesian model has a multiplicative effect on investment in real capital. As a result, the equilibrium levels of capital investment, output, employment and wages are all positively related to changes in *zakah* rates and expenditure. Additionally, due to the fact that *zakah* is aimed at alleviating structural social problems, its implementation leads to a reduction in structural unemployment and is therefore non-inflationary.

At the end, we critique the mainstream model of general equilibrium as a method based on methodology that remains foreign to the *Tawhidi* methodological worldview as the true Islamic epistemological manifestation. We have thus rejected the mainstream methodology and method of so-called 'Islamic' economics today as a borrowed idea from mainstream economics. Instead, we have explained that the existence of knowledge induction of all variables causes inter-variable complementarities between the good things of life. The emergent system of study attains the meaning of a generalized system study. Within this there is the computational evolutionary equilibrium of the complementary system of inter-variable causal relationships, $\{M, Sp, Y, y, P, L, K, T\}[\theta]$.

Notes

1 Professor of Finance, University of New Orleans, New Orleans, Louisiana, USA.
2 If the marginal efficiency of capital in terms of marginal conditions of the investment and production functions is dropped, then the IIS and ILM curves would both turn into positively sloped curves with almost same slopes.
3 The same result as in the above footnote will hold. The investment and savings curves will have almost identical slopes.

References

Ahmad, K. (1980). *Studies in Islamic Economics*, Islamic Foundation, Leicester, UK.

Ahmad, Z. (1983). *Fiscal and Resource Allocation in Islam*, Institute of Policy Studies, Lahore, Pakistan.

Ariff, M. (1982). *Monetary and Fiscal Economics in Islam*. International Center for Research in Islamic Economics, Jeddah, Saudi Arabia.

Choudhury, M.A. (2013). "Complementarities between monetary and spending regimes for socio-economic sustainability", *International Journal of Management Science*, 20:1, 1–39.

Choudhury, M.A. (1986). *Contributions to Economic Theory*, Macmillan, New York, NY.

Choudhury, M.A. (1983). "Principles of Islamic Economics", *Middle Eastern Studies*, 19:1, 93–103.

Choudhury, M.A. (1983). *An Islamic Social Welfare Function*, American Trust Publications, Indianapolis, IN.

Choudhury, M.A. (1981). "An analytical model of profit rate-ratio adjustment under the profit-sharing system in Islam and its implications on risk diversification", *Hacettepe University Bulletin of Administrative Sciences*, 1:4.

Choudhury, M.A. (1979). "The doctrine of *riba*", *Journal of Development Studies*, University of Peshawar, 2:1.

Friedman, M. (1983). "The Keynes centenary: a monetarist reflects", *The Economist*, 4 June.

Haveman, R.H. (1980). "Toward efficiency and equity through direct job creation", *Social Policy* (May/June).

Mannan, M.A. (1986). *Islamic Economics: Theory and Practice*, Hodder and Stoughton, Cambridge, UK Revised Edition.

Metwalli, M. (n.d.). *Macro-economic Models of Islamic Doctrine*, Department of Economics, University of Queensland, Australia.

O'Brien, J.C. (1981). "The economist's quandary: ethical values", *International Journal of Social Economics*, 8:3, 26–46.

Schumpeter, J. (1968). *History of Economic Analysis*, Oxford University Press, New York, NY.

Stigler, J. (1960). "The influence of events and policies on economic theory", *American Economic Review* 50 (May), 36–45.

Siddiqui, N. (1983). "Economics of profit sharing", in *Fiscal Policy and Resource Allocation in Islam* (eds), Z. Ahmed, M. Iqbal and M. Fahim Khan International Centre for Research in Islamic Economics, Jeddah, and Institute of Policy Studies, Islamabad, Pakistan.

Streeten, P. (1982). 'Approaches to a new international economic order', *World Development*, 10:1, 1–17.

Streeten, P. (1981). *Development Perspectives*, St Martin's Press, New York, NY.

Streeten, P. (1980). 'Basic needs in the year 2000', *Pakistan Development Review*, xix:2 (Summer).

Venieris, Y.P. and Sebold, F.D. (1977). *Macro-Economics Models and Policy*, pp. 167–69, Wiley and Sons, New York, NY.

Zarqa, M.A. (1983). "An Islamic perspective on the economics of discounting in project evaluation", in *Fiscal Policy and Resource Allocation in Islam* (eds), Z. Ahmed, M. Iqbal and M. Fahim Khan International Centre for Research in Islamic Economics, Jeddah, and Institute of Policy Studies, Islamabad, Pakistan.

Chapter 9

Human Potential, Wellbeing and Philanthropy

A Philosophical–Financial Economic Inquiry

Abstract

This methodological chapter addresses the formalism of the model of the evolutionary learning paradigm conceptualized within the framework of the sustainable development paradigm. The methodological substance of this chapter crosses interdisciplinary boundaries of epistemology, political economy, and mathematical modeling, formalizing a cogent model of sustainability and sustainable development. It uses synergistic circular causation relationships between human potential, philanthropy and the measurement of the wellbeing objective criterion. The conceptual and applied perspectives of this kind of evolutionary learning model are presented. The evolutionary learning model of circular causation between human potential, philanthropy and the objective of wellbeing of the interactive, integrative and evolutionary variables is shown to apply to the labor market adaptation issues of Canadian Natives. The principal contribution of the chapter is its epistemological groundwork of formalizing a moral–social reconstructive model of unity of knowledge. The positivistic and normative unified perspective of the model is presented.

Introduction

The study of the entitled theme in this chapter will be examined by the concept of endogenously interrelated variables and goals. The field of development is emphasized. Endogeneity in development issues, as mentioned in the title, will be done by way of the recursive and thus evolutionary complementarities between the selected variables representing what we will refer to as 'the good things of life'. The unity between such variables will project the meaning of the episteme of unity of knowledge relating to the specific problem and issue under investigation. This revolves around the methodology, formalism and application of the overall organic relationship between the three interrelated topics mentioned in the title.

This chapter will thus formalize what such organic relationships mean in reference to the episteme of unity of knowledge expressed as complementarities between the selected variables addressing wellbeing. The concept of wellbeing is thereby formalized within the episteme of unity of knowledge by looking at the specific problem of using and regenerating philanthropy by feedback in resource allocation and development between the donor and the recipient via a reproductive system of inputs and outputs.

The integrated approach described above constitutes the essential Islamic way of addressing any socio-scientific theme on the basis of its epistemology of divine oneness referred to as *Tawhid*. This is a *Qur'anic* term. We will invoke it in this chapter to imply the divine law of the oneness of God as a systemic precept. Such an epistemology of divine systemic oneness can be used for the socio-scientific study of 'everything' (Barrow, 1991) beyond only mainstream Islamic issues, for example the wellbeing issue of the Canadian Native People in light of their spirituality question in human resource development.

Objective

This chapter will formalize the following endogenous organic relationship and examine its application to the problem of uplifting the development of marginalized communities: A rigorous formalism is undertaken. A fairly extensive literature review in evolutionary economics is carried out to compare the contending methodologies with those on evolutionary learning that we use in this chapter to address the problem of wellbeing for the grass roots community.

On the applied front, we will examine the wellbeing of Canadian Natives. We do this by using the formalism of endogenous relationships between human potential as creativity, and feedback of resources (philanthropy in the productive sense) that are generated in the circular causation relationship between human potential, wellbeing and resource development to realize the goal of sustainability.

Such an organic relational formalism by endogenous feedback between the critical targets conveys the meaning of interactive, integrative and evolutionary learning in this chapter. Its empirical perspective is conveyed by the method of circular causation between the selected variables.

Human potential

The concept of human potential

The concept of human potential invoked in this chapter is that of human learning within and alongside the specifics of the world-system in which the human being participates and actualizes Mind and Matter interrelated dynamics. Thereby, human potential comprises the perpetual capability of the human becoming in the interactive realms of consciousness, actuality, and sustainability involving meaningful organic pairing between self and the other. This particular precept is a central note in the *Qur'an* towards conveying a systemic symbiosis in the framework of unity in diversity derived from the law of oneness, *Tawhid*. In this extended meaning lies the endless domain of learning with the microcosms of the world-system in which the human individual and totality interacts, integrates, and thereby rises to evolutionary learning processes enabled by the Mind-Matter dynamics.

By Mind we mean the domain of consciousness that is invoked by a well-defined relationship between the inner self (Heart) and the thoughtful mind. By Matter we mean the specific and the general domain of worldly relationships generated by participation. In this is invoked the objectivity of social actions and their responses. The realm of Matter thereby overarches the domain of cognition into sensate and abstract comprehension. These exist together as an organic unity; one cannot exist without the other.

Finally, there exist the critical interrelationships in evolutionary learning between the realms of Mind and Matter, within which are found the meaningful circular causation relationshipbetween consciousness, actuality, and human sustainability understood as extended social and scientific relationships – the socio-scientific order. The inner self as the seat of objectivity establishes a teleological relationship representing circular regeneration between Mind and Matter.

So what comprises human potential according to the evolutionary learning worldview? Human potential is centered on a unified worldview of relationships between Mind and Matter born out of consciousness. The Mind, in turn, is primordially affected by the heart. That is the soul. But consciousness in the soul and in connection with the material and cognitive order emanates from the episteme of unity of knowledge in relation to the unification of the world-system and its details. Within this overarching worldview of unity of knowledge in relation to the generality and particularity of issues under investigation, human potential comprises the integration of the seats of consciousness. The organization of consciousness in relation to the cognitive framework of a unified world-system stands on the episteme of unity of knowledge. The application of the Matter-Mind unity of being and becoming arises from the evolutionary learning process model of the conscious organization of the emergent social and moral reconstruction.

The participatory example of business for human potential

An example of human potential is found in the kind of Blue Ocean Strategy prescribed by Kim and Mauborgne (2005). They prescribe an inclusive model of Blue Ocean participatory and cooperative worldview in business. The Blue Ocean Strategy is contrary to the Red Ocean Strategy of mainstream economic theory and application, behavior and organization, pedagogical practice, and intellection. Consequently, the entrepreneurial spirit and human development reflected in the cognitive and real world constructs mark the ever-progressive learning processes of participation and complementarities between the micro, forming the aggregate (e.g. macro) entities of the macro scheme.

With the free entry of firms in an environment of participatory market exchange, sustainability of survival and growth can proceed. Survival is manifest along the learning path of complementary relationships between the good choices of life as determined by epistemic consciousness of goodness (Moore, 1962). Human potential is not the property of perfect and imperfect competition economic theory, based as these are on optimality and steady-state conditions of the marginalist world-system. In fact, all economic theory, both microeconomics and macroeconomics, is found to be premised on the postulate of marginalist hypothesis (Dasgupta, 1987).

Shackle (1972, p. 97) remarks on the fictive nature of optimality and steady-state equilibrium born out of the postulate of marginalism in mainstream economics: "Equilibrium is a solution, and there is, in the most general frame of thought, no guarantee that a problem which presents itself, unchosen and undersigned by us, will have any solution, or that it will not have an infinity of solutions. In either case, there is no prescription of conduct."

Human potential and its incorporation in human development and the design of sustainability must necessarily hold knowledge to remain incomplete, while learning perpetually in the framework of unity of being and becoming (Prigogine, 1980). Besides, since knowledge cannot be complete in the evolutionary learning universe, and because human potential in the midst of evolutionary learning embraces all of reality comprising mind and matter, therefore, knowledge regarding anything cannot be complete in the small and in the large separately. This is a *Tawhidi* property of the moral law in relationship to the learning universe in human intellection.

Only instantaneous knowledge formation is fictively possible. But such instantaneous knowledge-flow, as an equilibrium state in the core of economics is a fictive concept in the conscious universe. Such is the idea of the core of economics conceptualized by Debreu (1959). In reference to this knowledge-based interrelated cause and effect writes Shackle (1972, p. 26): "... we cannot claim Knowledge, so long as we acknowledge Novelty. Novelty is the transformation of existing knowledge, its reinterpretation; in some degree necessarily its denial and refutation."

Placing human potential in the evolutionary learning formalism

Figure 9.1 displays the above kind of regenerative relationships that explain the concept of evolutionary learning, and thereby establishes the extended version of the concept of sustainability. The regenerative elationship ensuing in this way is studied by means of what we call circular causation. It is the method representing the connected world-system of symbiosis and continuity by organically unifying relationships (pairing = complementarities) *vis-à-vis Tawhid* as unity of knowledge and its constructed world-system of unity of being. This empirical method is similar to a widely extended version of Myrdal's idea of cumulative causation. In this chapter, both the conceptual and empirical and applied version is endowed with the concept of circular causation in the light of unity of knowledge.

Figure 9.1 is a depiction of the circular causation concept of evolutionary learning model used in this chapter. Circular causation as the model of endogenous relationships implies that human potential is an evolutionary learning precept, which arises from and continues to sustain a given epistemic praxis (Sztompka, 1991; Resnick and Wolff, 1987). The emergent dynamics comprise the domain of Mind. They are organically connected with Matter in the sense of circular causation in the evolutionary learning worldview. The emergent nature of recursive evolution centered in the relationships that Mind-Matter interaction and integration harbors is like the Mobius String that remains intact in the space–time structure (Boslough, 1985). The world-system of human potential is thus continuously and perpetually re-originative. There is no terminal point as per optimum and steady-state resource allocation conditions.

Time, which is essential in defining the condition of the terminal points, as in optimum control theory, is not the essential element of learning. It is replaced by knowledge-flows as the substantive element of learning, change, reconstruction, and

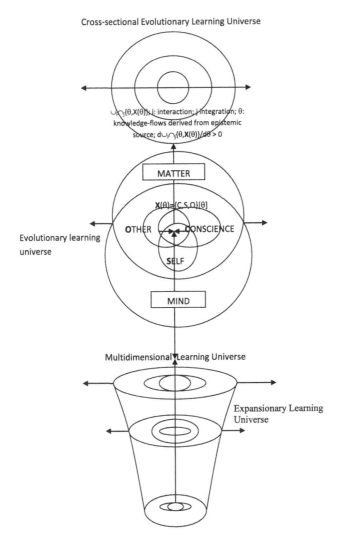

Cross-sectional Evolutionary Learning Universe

$\cup_\cap\{\theta,X(\theta)\}$; i: interaction; J: integration; θ: knowledge-flows derived from epistemic source; $d\cup_\cap\{\theta,X(\theta)\}/d\theta > 0$

MATTER

$X(\theta)=\{C,S,O\}[\theta]$

OTHER   CONSCIENCE

SELF

MIND

Evolutionary learning universe

Multidimensional Learning Universe

Expansionary Learning Universe

Figure 9.1 Evolutionary learning in Mind-Matter universe

continuity. Time simply records such coordinates. Knowledge causes them to occur. Events are happenings as coordinates defined by the tuplet of knowledge flow and its causation on social actions and responses that occur over time 't'. We define an event along the learning trajectory by $(\theta, x(\theta); t(\theta))$.

In the absence of steady-state equilibrium and the optimal states of events in the absence of the time factor, which is replaced by knowledge-flows occurring continuously and perpetually, the concept of human potential acquires its substantive meaning. It is different from the concept of human capital, a neoclassical resource. Consequently, many of the economic analyses and the social and public perceptions relating to human capital and economic growth and development are altered. These are replaced by altogether new concepts. We will note such substantive changes in concepts and application.

Formalizing human potential in the evolutionary learning universe governed by the episteme of unity of knowledge

The epistemic characterization of consciousness (Mind)

Let Ω denote the epistemological premise of unity of knowledge. It is treated as a topological super-space, that is, as the unbounded open cardinality measure (Rucker, 1983). Here is a *Tawhidi* formalism derived from the *Qur'an* as it applies to 'everything'.

Let $\theta \in \Omega$, such that there exists a mapping denoted by S that maps Ω on to knowledge-flows denoted by $\{\theta\}$. Thus, $S(\theta) \in \Omega$, for $\forall \theta \in \Omega$. Thereby, for different θ-values, $\{\theta_1\} \cup \{\theta_2\} \in \Omega$; $\{\theta_1\} \cap \{\theta_2\} \in \Omega$; $\{\theta_1\} \cup \{\theta_2\} \in \Omega$; $\{\phi\} \in \Omega$; $\Omega \equiv \Omega$ in the sense of closure of the very large-scale universe of Ω (*Tawhid* as the moral aw of divine oneness). Thereby, $\{\phi\} \cup \Omega' = \Omega$, where $\Omega' \subset \Omega$; $\{\phi\} \cap \Omega' = \{\phi\}$. Ω' has the topological properties mentioned here. Finally, any monotonic functional of the values as shown here has the same topological order-preserving properties.

$$\text{The expression, } \{\phi\} \cup \Omega' = \Omega, \text{ where } \Omega' \subset \Omega; \{\phi\} \cap \Omega' = \{\phi\}, \tag{9.1}$$

has a special significance. Expression (9.1) means that a set of false statements signified by $\{\phi\}$ represent disjointed or differentiated relationships. This is contrary to the organically unified relationships, which are treated as the set of truth statements denoted by Ω' in the normative sense of the episteme of unity of knowledge. Relationships in Ω' are established by pervasive complementarities or in a development model by participation between entities.

In summary, the fundamental epistemological characterization of unity of knowledge in terms of the super-topological relationship is as follows:

$$(\Omega,S) \equiv \Omega \rightarrow_S [\{\theta\} \subseteq \Omega' \cup \{\phi\}] \ldots\ldots\ldots \rightarrow_S [\Omega] \tag{9.2}$$

Expression (9.2) can be written as the disjoint composition of the following two independent chains:

$$(\Omega,S) \equiv \Omega \rightarrow_S [\{\theta\} \subseteq \Omega'] \ldots\ldots\ldots \rightarrow_S [\Omega] \tag{9.3}$$

$$\text{and } (\Omega,S) \equiv \Omega \rightarrow_S \{\phi\} = \{\phi\} \ldots\ldots\ldots \rightarrow_S \{\phi\} \subset [\Omega] \tag{9.4}$$

with the topological properties stated on $\{\theta\}$ and $\{\phi\}$.

Now if a measure-theoretic function, say $\mu(.)$, is applied to the functionals in expression (9.3) and (9.4), then the following result holds:

$$\mu(\{\phi\}) = 0; \text{ therefore, } \mu(\{\theta\} \subseteq \Omega') = 1 \tag{9.5}$$

$$\text{Therefore, } \Omega \rightarrow_S \{\theta\} \rightarrow_S \Omega, \text{ as } \mu(\Omega') = 1, \text{ with } \mu(\{\phi\}) = 0 \tag{9.6}$$

This summary relationship has significant implications on the existence of evolutionary learning equilibriums in open and unbounded subspaces that are contained with the closed and unbounded super-space of Ω (Choudhury, 2011). The mathematical results in such continuous and differentiable mappings of $\{\theta\}$ give rise to an extension of the Fixed Point Theorem to evolutionary ones that are not locally bounded and closed, and hence not locally compact (Nikaido, 1987). In the large-scale universe of $\Omega \rightarrow_S \Omega$, the evolutionary learning functions become compact once again.

The epistemic characterization of materiality (Matter)

By a further extension of the mappings on $\{\theta\}$ and $\{\theta^c\}$ the complement of $\{\theta\}$ on Ω, such that $\cup \cap \{\theta^c\} = \{\phi\}$, causes monotonic positive transformations to exist, such as $\{x(\theta)\}$. The $\{x(\theta)\}$ (likewise, $x^c(\theta^c)$) as vector, matrix, tensor and further relational extensions of the same, represent the material domain of the knowledge-induced (de-knowledge-induced $\{\theta^c\}$) variables of various systemic entities to which the Mind and Matter relate.

Consequently, all the topological properties of the $\{\theta\}$ and $\{\theta^c\}$ spaces apply to $\{x(\theta)\}$ and $\{x^c(\theta^c)\}$. It is to be noted that, x-type or x^c-type functionals cannot apply in (Ω,S). By the property of super-cardinality of this super-topology, any functional transformation on this limiting super-space will be of the super-cardinal or infinite dimension. That would be absurd for any cognitive artifact to assume.

The epistemic characterization of human potential

Human potential denoted by the functional $h(.)$ is the totality of monotonic positive transformations of the type $\{h(x(\theta))\}$. $h(.)$ denotes continuously and positively differentiable functional with respect to θ-values. Such functionals emerge along the paths of evolutionary learning processes.[1]

The functional $h(.)$ can be composed of different levels of micro-aggregation. We can distribute $h(.)$ by categories of target groups, sectors, regions, projects, etc. $h(.)$ can also be constructed as an index, such as a human potential index for targeted marginalized groups in the context of development, etc. With such aggregation, a development planning can be designed, centered on the concept of human potential rather than human capital. The latter is a neoclassical concept that does not fit into the phenomenology of our evolutionary learning model.

The characterization of human potential in the development model is as follows: Development $(D(..))$ may be defined as the following extensively participatory process along the evolutionary learning path, with many interacting, integrating, and evolving entities that remain complementary to each other in circular causation relationship. Such an experience in the normative perspective of moral–social reconstruction remains continuous and pervasive. Such a continuous learning experience conveys the meaning of sustainability and of participatory development as a process. Indeed, the South Commission (1990, p. 13) defines the meaning of socio-economic development in the broad sense, encompassing economic, social and human factors. Some of these factors are as follows. To sum up: development is a process of self-reliant growth, achieved through *participation* of the people acting in their own interests as they see them, and under their own control.

We can now define development as a process, $D(..)$, in terms of the relationship concerning human potential as a compounded functional relationship signifying complementarities between the critical variables denoted by $\{\theta,x(\theta)\}$. The epistemologically induced evolutionary learning path by $\{\theta\} \in (\Omega,S)$ signifies sustainability:

$$D(f(h(x(\theta))) = \{\theta\}o\{x(\theta)\}o\{h_i(x(\theta))\}o\{f_i(h_i(x(\theta))\} \tag{9.7}$$

The composite mapping in expression (9.7) means that the epistemic knowledge defines the parameters of development via its induction of the development variables. For example, financial and real resources, GDP, HDI, HPI, GEM, employment, price level, trade, capital/labor ratio, GINI coefficients, etc. are now induced by the normative condition of circular causation between the variables. Such θ-induction generates the endogenous relationship between the development variables. The variables then feed into the specific human potential indexes and their further monotonic transformations.

The latter kind of mapping is shown by f(..) in the complementary implication of the compound index. An example of the complementary index of specific categories ('i') of human potential functions is $h(.) = \prod_i h_i^{\alpha i}(..)$. Here α_i denote h_i-elasticity coefficients of the total h(.)-index.

A further disaggregation is also possible, given i=1,2,..,n. The implication of such a disaggregate composition of the human potential index is a new form of human development index that can be composed of the human poverty index, human empowerment index, corruption index, equality index and the like (Demarting, 1999; UNDP, 1997, 1998, 1999, 2000 issues; Millennium Development, May 25, 2012).

Wellbeing

The concept and measurement à la unity of knowledge as the functional ontology

Since the concept of human potential is a dynamic form of generating and mobilizing human resources within a complex of evolutionary learning processes, it upholds a permanently creative nature. Therefore, when we link the concept of human potential with the issues of philanthropy and wellbeing through circular connection between these goals, the concept of philanthropy must be understood as a productive resource that generates self-reliance and sustainability both among, and by, its participants.

Thereby, the circular causation endogenous relationship between human potential, philanthropy and wellbeing cannot result in idle charity. This precisely is the meaning underlying the *Qur'anic zakah*. *Zakah* is a mandatory 2.5% of liquid wealth for human resource uplift at the grassroots. Hence, such endogenous relationships between the three elements hold up both a dynamic and a sustainable perspective of human resource development.

Therefore, philanthropy as a morally embedded productive resource feeds into and regenerates human potential. Such a recursive relationship and its sustainability along the evolutionary learning processes is formalized and measured by the objective criterion of wellbeing. We therefore define wellbeing as the functional of the complementary and regenerated relationships between philanthropy and human potential. Such organic relationships evaluate and assign levels of unification between the variables in the light of the episteme of unity of knowledge. The normative reconstruction of the unifying relationships between the selected variables and their functions represent the ethical reconstructive possibilities using philanthropy and human potential as goals. Such organic relationships are explained in Figure 9.1.

The concept and empirical nature of the organically unifying relationships comprise the normative worldview. The evaluation takes its course from the positive stance of the issues as they are to what they ought to be. Thus, the positive and normative states together form the possibility for moral-social reconstruction in the applied and empirical sense. The empirical implication underlying the positive evaluation of the relationships between the variables representing philanthropy and human potential is to lead to simulation to realize the changes required for transforming a differentiated state of human wellbeing into a system of complementary relationships. Complementarities and participation represent the sure signs of unity of knowledge and its moral–social reconstruction of the specific issues under consideration. This is the consequence of the action of unity of knowledge in practical experience as *Qur'anic* pairs.

In this sense of a normative simulation of the positive state of differentiation or a reconstruction of a weak form of complementary relationship between philanthropy and human potential, the wellbeing objective criterion assumes both a concept as well as a measurement of unity of knowledge.

Wellbeing as concept in objective criterion explains the cognitive stage of understanding unity of knowledge as episteme at the *functional* ontological level. No metaphysical meaning of ontology is invoked here. *Functional* ontology presents the operational formalism derived from the episteme of unity of knowledge. The operational consequences of unity of knowledge are found in the reconstructed world-system of complementary (participatory) relationships between the selected variables of the specific problems under study.

The evaluative stage of the wellbeing index: from 'estimation' to 'simulation'

The evaluative stage of wellbeing comprises the conceptualization, measurement, and inferential and policy-theoretic implications of social reconstruction. This version of the functional ontology of unity of knowledge reflecting the episteme working itself in the framework of unity of the specified problems and issues at point reflects two stages of valuation of facts.

First, there is the 'estimation' stage. Here, the circular causation between the representative variables $\{\theta, \mathbf{x}(\theta)\}$, and the human potential index $h(\theta, \mathbf{x}(\theta))$, are 'estimated' by the facts as they are.

Second, the 'estimated' evaluation of results examined the relationships between the variables. That is, the degree of complementarities between the variables is evaluated. A lack of complementarities between the selected variables of the problem at hand indicates differentiation and marginalism.

Such a lack of complementary state is improved by simulating the 'estimated' results. This 'simulation' process improves the degree of unity of knowledge by normatively characterizing the problem and issue at point.

Such empirical evaluation between 'estimation' and 'simulation' can be further disaggregated into the component human potential indexes $h_i(..)$ and the multifarious systemic variables involved in such an exercise of disaggregation. In expression (9.7), such a disaggregation is explained by the non-linear processes that remain embedded in economic development. Further on, the positive monotonic transformation, $f(h(\theta, \mathbf{x}(\theta)))$, extends the disaggregation levels to various micro inter-systemic relationships.

The empirical and policy-theoretic, institutional, structural and discursive nature of participatory changes that are embedded in the development process by transition from the 'estimation' stage to the 'simulation' stage marks the being and becoming of stages of evolutionary learning in unity of knowledge. Empirically, the participatory change that ought to be induced in the development process is carried out by the 'simulation' stage.

In this chapter, the specific issue is that of attaining higher levels of the human potential index by means of inducing complementarities between the variables of the disaggregate human potential indexes. The empirical exercise of leading the 'estimation' stage to the 'simulation' stage is carried out by the system of circular causation relationships.

The phenomenological model of wellbeing in terms of human potential index

Stage 1: The conceptual formalization of wellbeing

Our selection of the wellbeing function is human potential index in the sense of the composition of the development process symbolized in expression (9.7). We re-write the problem of evaluation of wellbeing as follows, subject to its subsequent empirical 'estimation' followed by policy-theoretic 'simulation' of the 'estimated' results. We refer to the stages between 'estimation' and 'simulation' together as to 'evaluate'.

$$\text{Evaluate } h(\mathbf{x}(\theta)) = \prod_i [h_i(\mathbf{x}(\theta))]^{\alpha i}; \ i = 1, 2, .., N \tag{9.8}$$

Subject to the circular causation relationships:

$$x_j(\theta) = f_j(\mathbf{x'}(\theta)), \tag{9.9}$$

where, $x_j(\theta)$ is an element of the vector $\mathbf{x}(\theta)$;
      $\mathbf{x'}(\theta)$ is the vector $\mathbf{x}(\theta)$ without $x_j(\theta)$;
      $j = 1, 2, 3, \ldots n$

The 'estimated' values of the $x_j(\theta)$-variables in the system of relationships signified by (9.9) are theoretically fed into (9.8) to yield the measure of the human potential index as the wellbeing index. But this part of the theoretical exercise is not empirically possible, for values of the coefficients, while they are estimable in the system of equations of (9.9) are not estimable in (9.8): Data on $h(\mathbf{x}(\theta))$ are not available *ad hoc*. Thus stage 1 remains simply a theoretical construct of the Wellbeing Function with its evaluation stages of 'estimation' and 'simulation'.

Now Stage 2 of 'estimation' leading to 'simulation' begins. This is the main empirical exercise pertaining to wellbeing and the human potential index.

Stage 2: The empirical formalization of wellbeing

We note that (9.8) is simply a monotonic form of the relationship,[2]

$$\theta = F(\mathbf{x}(\theta)) \tag{9.10}$$

Expression (9.10) can be taken as the proxy for wellbeing or human potential index in the epistemic sense of 'estimation' followed by 'simulation' of knowledge-value in respect of unity of knowledge (i.e. complementarities, and organic participation).

The empirical system (9.9) and (9.10), together with their multifarious equations and variables, now represents the *functional* ontological nature of 'estimation' and 'simulation' as the formal model of circular causation. We write this complete circular causation system as follows:

'Estimation' stage: Positivistic state of examining complementary relationships between variables or otherwise

$$x_j(\theta) = f_j(x'(\theta)), \tag{9.11}$$

where, $x_j(\theta)$ is an element of the vector $x(\theta)$;
$\quad\quad x'(\theta)$ is the vector $x(\theta)$ without $x_j(\theta)$;
$\quad\quad j = 1,2,3,\dots n$

$$\theta = F(x(\theta)) \tag{9.12}$$

The estimation of the coefficients of these equations is done by (i) the data on $x(\theta)$-vector; and (ii) the ranks generated for θ-values by noting the observed degrees of complementarities between the selected $x(\theta)$-variables. Such a rank-assigning exercise examines the degree of complementarities of the $x(\theta)$-variables and determines their corresponding pair-specific θ-ranks using the variables selected. Then these pair-specific θ-values are averaged against the paired variables as they appear. Such rank-setting can also be carried out by institutional and group discourse in rank-selection. The θ-values can also be assigned algorithmically.

The 'estimated' coefficients present the positivistic state of the complementarities, and thereby their participative nature of development, by focusing on human potential, philanthropy and wellbeing as complementary goals. As in the neoclassical case of marginal substitution between variables, which signifies a non-learning state of resource generation and mobilization, the negative signs of the coefficients or their weakly positive signs in the estimated circular causation variables will contradict complementarities and participation. Such results would negate the development process in the human potential context with sustainability gained along the evolutionary learning path of unity of knowledge of Mind-Matter interrelationship.

'Simulation' stage: Normative state of examining complementary relationships

The 'simulated' normative corrections to the 'estimated' positivistic results now follow. The simulated coefficients are assigned by changing their values to positive or near positive ones by institutional and policy discourse to the extent of possibility in attaining such simulated coefficient values. Such a simulation exercise marks the potential for moral–social transformation required in realizing expression (9.7) of development and sustainability.

The results of simulated changes in the estimated coefficient values show up in the new 'predictor' $x(\theta)$-values; and thereby on the simulated θ-value in expression (9.12). The simulated relationships are thus obtained including the 'simulated' as well as the 'estimated' θ-value as the proxy of human potential. In this way, the human potential index is premised on knowledge-flows that are gained by discursive learning in a continuously participatory development scenario. Such a development scenario marks sustainability in the good things of life (e.g. *dynamic* basic-needs regime of development).[3]

Summary of the circular causation method applied to the methodology of unity of knowledge

The phenomenological model of unity of knowledge and its conceptualization and application to the issue of human potential comprises the totality of the expressions (9.8)–(9.12) along with the details of the 'estimation stage', the 'simulation stage', and the 'predictor stage', all as explained and encapsulated by the term 'evaluating' the wellbeing objective.

Through the combined method in such a case, the positive and the normative consequences are combined to establish the non-demarcation rule between these, and between the deductive and inductive reasoning in the development debate. Each of these ways of reasoning is the recursive product of the other in cycles of evolutionary learning. Hence there exists continuous and pervasive interaction, integration and evolutionary learning between the variables and the goals. Such a methodological result represents the unity of knowledge in the phenomenological model. It is applied, measured, and explained by the method of circular causation in the human potential index as wellbeing manifesting development sustainability.

Recently, such a method of scaling and interpreting survey data was done by Bloom and Reenen (2010). They measured the differences found in inter-firm and inter-country economic performances, and associated this with differences in management practices. Their empirical measurement technique is based on scaling of survey results to prove this fact. Scaling for rank-assignment of the relationship between population and economic growth by circular causation method was done by Choudhury, Hossain and Hossain (2011). Maurer (1999, p. 21) wrote on a similar notion of organizing order out of complexity and of the inevitability for causality in a heavily stochastic nature of organic system: "… regularities in biological systems arise through a statistical process of causality."

The moral-social embedding of the wellbeing criterion has been formalized by Sen (1990) in the deontological framework. Sen writes against the transitive axiom of rational choice and invokes moral judgment. The ethical deontological consideration in moral choice is preferred to the utilitarian instrumental rationality in Sen's (op cit p. 78) discussion of the wellbeing criterion in the following words: "I have tried to argue that the distancing of economics from ethics has impoverished welfare economics, and also weakened the basis of a good deal of descriptive and predictive economics."

The extension of the utilitarian postulate of economic rationality and its implication on optimal social choice is both over the set of goods/services and utilities. For if the welfare function comprises the map of individual utility functions, each and all of which are optimized by the agents and society at large, then in utilitarianism the welfare is independently established on individual utility functions. This is a logical result. But it remains devoid of any substantive meaning in collective choice and interaction that make up society.

This chapter has extended the arguments of the impressive writing in the direction of establishing wellbeing as an epistemological concept that combines the deductive and inductive reasoning, the normative and positive reasoning, and the a priori with the a posteriori, contra Kantian phenomenology (Seidel, 1986). The same is true of a methodological proof of Popper's idea of demarcation in his concept regarding the separation of the deductive from the inductive reasoning (Popper, 2004 reprint; Blaug, 1993). Instead, the unification between deductive and inductive combines the conceptual precept with the empirical inductive part. This is how the problem of demarcation is replaced by the non-demarcation nature of unified reasoning combining deductive with inductive, normative with positive. Such a unification of reasoning is conveyed by the system of relationships in (9.8)–(9.12).

Consequently, as a result of such methodological unification in the human potential-centered development paradigm (9.7) the inherent evolutionary learning processes arising out of the properties of interaction and integration between target variables and their relations (i.e. $(\theta,x(\theta))$, $f(h((\theta,x(\theta))))$), and which are continuously pervasive across continuums of development stages establish unbroken endogenous relations between state-variables and the ethical policy and institutional variables. Thereby, all variables in (9.7), further detailed in the remaining expressions, are endogenous in nature. The only exogenous premise in the entire system of circular causation relationshipsis the episteme of unity of knowledge at the formal ontological level denoted by the primal governing premise, (Ω,S).

Philanthropy

Philanthropy comprises charitable resource. In human relations it is considered as part of the organized relationship of human resource mobilization for attaining self-reliance and productivity gains in the development of human potential, as we have explained it in the context of human potential. Philanthropy thereby becomes a pooled financial and productive resource bundle that may be invoked at the level of the individual or group donor. Its social implications and effectiveness in the uplift of human potential are gained by the organization of such resources at the collective social level. The organizer may be the national government (e.g. development expenditure), the non-governmental level (e.g. non-governmental organizations), the integrated community level (e.g. pooled charity network), and the international organizations (e.g. international development finance for philanthropy).

Charity now assumes a productive and human resource development perspective. Its directions being productive and ethical development according to the development of human potential in target-group philanthropy, together with its relationship with the evolutionary learning process, becomes a target of sustainable development planning. This is true, particularly in the micro-entrepreneurship that aggregates complementary effects in a dynamic unified way to the social whole.

When philanthropy is included as an endogenous variable in the sense of organized charity that plays its catalytic role in human potential role in development (i.e. expression (9.7)), it becomes a variable in the vector $\{\mathbf{x}(\theta)\}$. The variable representing philanthropy is thereby subjected to circular causation in the system of relationships (9.8)–(9.12). Thereby, in the stages of 'estimation' followed by 'simulation' of the circular causation relationship with philanthropy, we infer that organized charity is represented by social aggregation realized by societal, institutional, and policy effects in developing human potential by way of the productive and conscious transformation of the labor force.

The concept of consciousness used here is that of realizing the unification – complementarities and participation between philanthropy as social obligations – and its productive use in regenerating the momentum of unification. Unification by sustainability is exhibited by the basic-needs regime of development. This signifies development along the path of the good things of life.

Examples of the productive use of philanthropy and its regeneration by the social system to sustain the philanthropy-human potential-wellbeing relationship are microenterprise (e.g. Grameen Bank) and micro-entrepreneurial development through strategic interaction with large corporations (Choudhury and Harahap, 2009). Grameen, a non-governmental development-oriented bank based in Bangladesh, has now become a social bank. It makes small loans to impoverished village-based recipients without requiring collateral, thereby promoting microenterprises based on cooperative ventures. These have a high recovery rate. A trust is thereby established using the circular regenerative flow of human resources that we refer to here as 'Philanthropy'.

The system of circular relationships based on the episteme of unity of knowledge (system (9.7)–(9.12)) is fully encapsulated in Figure 9.2. Loan recovery (i.e. voluntary loan payment by the borrower) is the start of the recursive relationship that regenerates the conscious process of evolutionary learning in sustaining Grameen-type, [philanthropy – human potential – wellbeing] circular causation relationships. Consciousness as the commencement and regeneration of the knowledge-induced process driven by the episteme of unity of knowledge is sustained by the endogenous evolutionary learning process of unity of organic relationships between [human potential – philanthropy – wellbeing]. Establishing and sustaining this kind of unified endogenous interrelationship requires *functional* ontology first to formalize the relationships and then to 'estimate' and 'simulate' the empirical results. This is signified by complementarities, participation, and continuity in the basic-needs regime of development [micro-entrepreneurial development denoted by $f(H(P(D(\theta))))$] as the good things of life (Streeten, 1981).

Philanthropy dynamics in Grameen Bank (P(D))

By reference to expression (9.7)

(*Consciousness* [unity of knowledge as episteme and development construct, D)

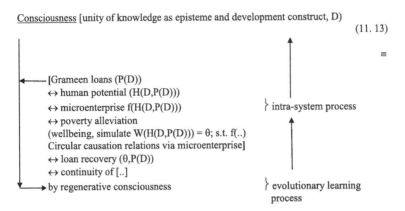

Figure 9.2 Circular causation by regenerative consciousness in the Grameen-type wellbeing model

Philanthropy dynamics in the cooperative arrangement between microenterprise and corporation

In many Muslim countries the emerging Islamic banks promote microenterprises by joint venture financing of small operations with corporations. An example of such a project is the Underprivileged Children Educational Program (UCEP) in Bangladesh. UCEP is funded by foreign donors, whereby panhandling children are taken off the street and put in fast-track vocational training programs combined with basic education. The trained students of UCEP are then employed, and further trained on-the-job by corporations in Bangladesh. The marginal labor force is not unionized. This allows the corporations to carry on their productive activity uninterrupted and at low cost.

Figure 9.3 explains that, similar to Grameen philanthropy in human potential and sustainable development, UCEP's foreign training donations can also be viewed as philanthropy as they develop human potential in the (otherwise ignored) destitute population. The resulting trust as human value in the workplace, the productivity gains, empowerment, entitlement, income generation, and human potential, together form the recursive forces for regenerating the conscious sustainability. The entire regenerative system is established by such recursively regenerative circular causation relationships.

Unifying philanthropy with human potential in the wellbeing human development index

In the definition of sustainable development by (9.7) the critical interactive, integrative, and evolutionary relationship of regenerative circular causation is identified between (i) the epistemic origin of unity of knowledge, functionally denoted by $\{\theta\} \in (\Omega,S)$; and (ii) its unifying influence on the world-system under study. This is human potential $h(.)$ in its complementary relationship to the state, policy, institutional, and behavioral variables $\{x(\theta)\}$. This includes philanthropy in terms of the other stated types of variables. The result of the circular causation denoted by $f\{\theta,x(\theta)\}$ and $h(\theta,x(\theta))$ is the consequence on evolutionary learning denoted by evolutionary values of wellbeing proxy

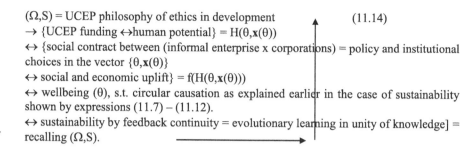

(Ω,S) = UCEP philosophy of ethics in development (11.14)
$\rightarrow$ {UCEP funding $\leftrightarrow$ human potential} = $H(\theta, \mathbf{x}(\theta))$
$\leftrightarrow$ {social contract between (informal enterprise x corporations) = policy and institutional choices in the vector $\{\theta, \mathbf{x}(\theta)\}$
$\leftrightarrow$ social and economic uplift} = $f(H(\theta, \mathbf{x}(\theta)))$
$\leftrightarrow$ wellbeing (θ), s.t. circular causation as explained earlier in the case of sustainability shown by expressions (11.7) – (11.12).
$\leftrightarrow$ sustainability by feedback continuity = evolutionary learning in unity of knowledge] = recalling (Ω,S).

Figure 9.3 Circular causation between 'estimation' and 'simulation' of UCEP

by $\{\theta\}_{evol}$-values along the evolutionary learning path. Such evolutionary values in new emergent paths are determined by recalling the epistemic core, $\{\theta\}_{evol} \in (\Omega,S)$, etc.

By the implicit function theorem applied to $h^* = h(\theta, \mathbf{x}(\theta))$ (.) we can write for the wellbeing index,

$$\{\theta\}_{evol} \in (\Omega,S) = H\{\mathbf{x}(\theta)\}_{evol} \qquad (9.15)$$

Subject to circular causation between the $\{\mathbf{x}(\theta)\}$-variables.

Expression (15) is subjected to 'estimation' and 'simulation' by means of predictor values, as explained earlier.

We now combine interactive, integrative, and evolutionary learning by embedding human potential with philanthropy and wellbeing in the sustainable development context. The result is a derivation of the following general-system model of epistemic unity of knowledge and evolutionary learning in the Mind-Matter relational context, with reference to the functional ontology (epistemologically endowed formalism) (Gruber, 1993):

In conclusion to this section we note that philanthropy in the development debate is not to be treated as a *hand-out* from a charity. For philanthropy, to enhance human potential and wellbeing, which is a participatory concept of learning and unity of knowledge, it must have both productive and social factors. The general-system model of unity of knowledge, now applied to the specific case of philanthropy-human potential-wellbeing synergy now becomes an application in sustainable development.

Review of the literature on evolutionary economic dynamics

Introducing the comparative and contrasting views

The evolutionary learning methodology used in this chapter is akin in explanation, but not in analytics, to the ideas of Myrdal (1958), and to Schumpeterian economic growth and development presented by Cantner,. Gaffard, J. and Nesta (2009). In sociology of knowledge, it is similar to the dialectical thesis presented by Sztompka, 1991 and the Marxist methodology reproduced by Resnick and Wolff 1987 We will review these works in the light of the evolutionary methodology presented in this chapter. Hegel's (Hegel trans. Sibree, 1956) theory of dialectical historicism of the rationalist

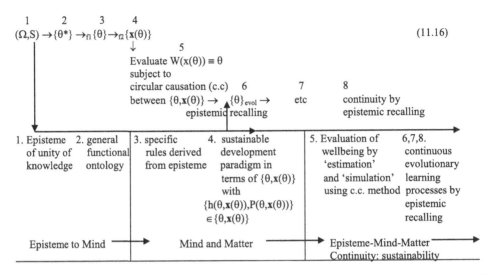

Figure 9.4 Sustainable development by circular causation in the human potential, philanthropy, and wellbeing relationship: the general-system approach

world is well known to be an occidental search for the ultimate truth of the world spirit. However, it was simply of rationalist origin, and was nothing to do with the nature of primal ontology and closure of the evolutionary universe of the law of unity of knowledge and the creative world-system.

The substantive difference between the methodology of this chapter and of the rest mentioned here is the great epistemic divide of unity of knowledge. To quote Hawking (1988) on this matter of unity of the scientific worldview, the essential nature of the unitary episteme in 'everything' (Barrow, 1991) remains the core of the new scientific episteme. Such assertion centering on unity of knowledge and its construction of the unitary knowledge-induced world-system projects the epistemological nature of scientific revolution. We need to appreciate this viewpoint, for although it arises from the natural sciences it is also relevant to social sciences, keeping in view the intra- and intersystemic unity made possible in the general system depicted in Figure 9.4.

Hawking (1988, pp. 10–11) writes in terms of the unitary scientific project:

> The eventual goal of science is to provide a single theory that describes the whole universe. However, the approach most scientists actually follow is to separate the problem into two parts. First, there are the laws that will tell us how the universe changes with time … Second, there is the question of the initial state of the universe. Some people feel that science should be concerned with only the first part; they regard the question of the initial situation as a matter for metaphysics or religion. They would say that God, being omnipotent, could have started the universe off any way he wanted. That may be so, but in that case he also could have made it develop in a completely arbitrary way. Yet it appears that he chose to make it evolve in a very regular way

according to certain laws. It therefore seems equally reasonable to suppose that there are also laws governing the initial state.

Barrow (1991, pp. 15–16) writes about the unitary law of 'everything' (slightly edited):

> The current breed of candidates of the title of a 'Theory of Everything' hopes to provide an encapsulation of all the laws of nature into a simple and single representation. The fact that such unification is even sought, tells us something important about our expectations regarding the Universe. These we must have derived from an amalgam of our previous experience of the world and our inherited religious beliefs about its ultimate Nature and significance. Our monotheistic traditions reinforce the assumption that the Universe is at root a unity that is not governed by different legislation in different places neither the residue of some clash of Titans wrestling to impose their arbitrary wills upon the Nature of things, nor the compromise of some cosmic committee.

Gunnar Myrdal and the evolutionary economic worldview

There are a number of similarities between Myrdal's (1968) idea of 'the wider field of valuation' in development theory and our formulation of the wellbeing criterion. The moral and social spectrum of valuation in the development worldview led Myrdal to become utterly dismayed with neoclassical economic theory. He attached the utilitarian foundation of welfare economics and suggested academic change in this regard. Myrdal (1987, p. 274) wrote in this regard:

> Hundreds of books and articles are produced every year on 'welfare economics', reasoning in terms of individual or social 'utility' or some substitute of that term. But if the approach is not entirely meaningless, it has a meaning only in terms of a forlorn hedonistic psychology, and a utilitarian moral philosophy built upon that psychology. I have always wondered why the psychologists and philosophers have left the economists alone and undisturbed in their futile exercise.

Likewise, there is the profound commonness in the concept of circular causation between our method and Myrdal's, further carried over by Streeten (1958), Kaldor (1975), Toner (1999) and others. On this point Toner (1999, p. 124) writes that it is important to emphasize the distinction between mainstream economic theory, principally neoclassical economics, and the theory of circular causation. The latter endogenously integrates economic and non-economic elements of a comprehensive understanding of economic theory for studying total wellbeing: "The notion of complementarity in production and consumption is central to CC (circular causation in the process of cumulative causation) theory. For Kaldor, given his concern with growth and dynamics as opposed to the allocation of fixed resources, complementarity in production and consumption is far more pervasive and significant than the neoclassical principle of substitution." The same kind of strong circular causation between economic and non-economic complementarities is vouched by Kaldor (op cit).

Joseph Schumpeter on evolutionary economics à la Austrian economic legacy

Schumpeter, like Myrdal and Boulding (1981) in the literature on evolutionary economics, modeled the development paradigm as a dialectical process in creative destruction. The states of economic change were not to be found in equilibrium. Rather, disequilibrium and its cumulative deepening were seen as the perpetual design of change. This can be seen in the Schumpeterian argument of technology in development. The most important factor is human potential. How can we treat this idea in the combined anticipated effects of Schumpeter and Myrdal's theories of evolutionary economic dynamics relating to development?

Gafford (2009) refers to Schumpeter's disequilibrium approach in such a case with technology-like effects, which we take as human potential: "As shown with the model used by means of numerical simulations, the introduction of the new technology generates an initial fluctuation, which brings about temporary unemployment as well as a temporary fall in productivity. However, this fluctuation very soon dampens down and the economy converges to a new steady-state corresponding to the superior technology, with a higher level of productivity – which allows lower prices and higher real wages – and full employment." But if such temporary disequilibrium effects remain in abeyance, Myrdal's circular causation will cause a multiplying and deepening of the temporary perturbations into large proportions. An example is the flare of inflation, which as Winston Churchill remarked, is like pregnancy; it runs its course. Myrdal's cumulative causation also has such 'butterfly effects' to multiply the small and temporary disturbance à la Schumpeter into large consequences.

The evolutionary learning approach, while dialectical, agrees with the dynamic process implied in the development approaches of both Schumpeter and Myrdal. Yet, it is not a normative disequilibrium model. Instead, the epistemic model of evolutionary learning in unity of knowledge at large is an evolutionary equilibrium model of creative evolution carrying the past into the ever-new future continuously and across systems. Here, then, is a critical difference, despite the methodical similarities in the approaches of all these general-system models of sustainable development. We have defined this in accordance with the continuous synergy between human potential, philanthropy, and wellbeing.

The dialectical and evolutionary learning models of unity of knowledge

Sztompka and Resnick and Wolff formalize their dialectical models of circular causation which agree, methodically, with our evolutionary learning model. Yet the two sets of models remain apart. The difference lies solely in the nature of the epistemic source of knowledge affecting the Mind-Matter interrelationship in respect of the development problem. In the dialectical reasoning of the rationalist authors, Mind-Matter both starts, and ends, in the rationalist premise.[4]

So, when this epistemological premise is brought into the development of economic theory, the issues of transitivity and economic rationality arise. As a consequence of such an old mainstream postulate, which Amartya Sen (1977) refers to as the domain of the 'rational fool', human potential becomes human capital. The neoclassical postulates of optimality, stead-state equilibrium, predictability, and permanence of economic rationality define individual, market, and social behaviors.

In such cases, human potential ceases to be a continuous and pervasive evolutionary learning over the dimensions of knowledge, space, and time in which our epistemic model abides. If this possibility was allowed, then two consequences will arise. First, the existence of utility, welfare, and production functions is denied. No convex to the origin or well-defined surfaces of resource allocation between competing agents can exist. Second, predictability in the midst of the simulacra of possible resource allocations is lost. The probability distribution of resource allocation is not acceptable as a way out of the unmeasured uncertainty that remains. See O'Donnell (1989) on Keynes' epistemology.

The evolutionary learning dialectical model of development in respect of expression (9.7) and Figure 9.4 overcomes the mainstream indeterminateness of development dynamics. This is realized by assigning 'near' spot-valuation of uncertain events by reading the probabilities of occurrence of given contingent states with a better-accumulated stock of knowledge-flows. Such 'near' spot-valuation points are the nodes of the overlapping generation model for simulating allocation resources in order to attain the objective of intertemporal wellbeing along the sustainable path of evolutionary learning. Prediction in such an overlapping generation model is thus attained by convergence under the evolutionary learning process. This is both an endogenous process of consciousness and is participative in nature in the model of participatory development. This is the epistemic consequence of unity of knowledge. Here human potential necessarily remains predominant.

Figure 9.5 shows the congruence in the domain of the Mind-Matter dialectical relationship between the rationalist doctrinaire and the episteme of unity of knowledge (Choudhury, 2009).

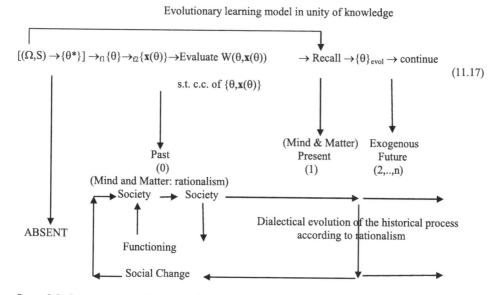

Figure 9.5 Contrasting the dialectics of the evolutionary learning system to rationalism

Note: Resnick & Wolfe referred to the continuous exogenous process as newly emergent dialectical processes from the previous ones or a plethora of such processes by competition between the entities. This is referred to as the Marxist problem of overdeterminsm.

Amartya Sen: an adaptation of the paradigm of commodities, capabilities, and wellbeing to circular causation organic relationships of epistemic oneness

Here is a straightforward adaptation of Amartya Sen's paradigm to the evolutionary learning worldview of unity of knowledge explained by expression (9.7).

Sen (2010) formalizes his paradigm as follows. We have dropped the specification to individual 'i' in Sen's actual formulation; and replaced this with the social choice equivalence.

What is the path toward reaching D(..) from either side of the spectrum in expression (9.18)? In the absence of the epistemic premise there are no binding grounds for the interrelationships to exist between the commodity variables and their various functional transformations. Consequently, Sen's paradigm can equally invoke the utilitarian-type aggregation of happiness, of the Benthamite form. Or, by Sen's arguments against utilitarianism, the aggregation may be a complex, but not ethical way, of unity of knowledge between the good things of life, that is, in the life-sustaining paradigm of development. Consequently, the mix of needs and wants as acceptable choices are permitted in the sustainable development regime. Yet the consequence of individualism and independence of preferences in such social aggregations is not recognized.

In brief, Sen claimed that an ethical–social aggregation of individual preferences in his development paradigm is not epistemologically viable. It is simply an exogenously enforced state of preferences of a sheer analytical nature. Sustainable development cannot be the endogenous achievement of such learning otherwise attained by the moral reconstruction towards unity of the development worldview by the episteme of unity of knowledge.[5]

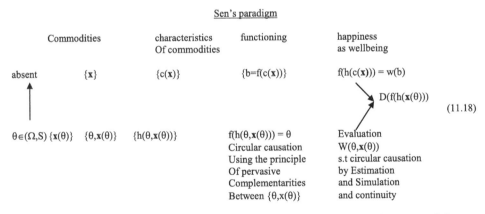

Figure 9.6 Comparing the epistemic evolutionary worldview of sustainable development with Amartya Sen's paradigm

Note: Sen (op cit, p. 8) defines wellbeing: "'Well-being', then, can plausibly be seen as an evaluation of this bi, indicating the kind of being he or she is achieving". Besides, Wellbeing in such a sense also represents an evaluation of capabilities.

Application of the evolutionary learning paradigm of endogenous development: Canadian Natives

Development paradigms centered on human potential with development expenditure as a case of philanthropy in the wellbeing function provides a fresh policy perspective for Canadian Natives. Thus far in Canadian Native history, the framework of economic development has focused on the model of catching-up of the Aboriginal Peoples to the non-Aboriginal levels of education and training, reducing the unemployment rate to non-Aboriginal levels, and raising tax revenue from a fast-growing population of Canadian Natives. The focus is on economic efficiency and productivity gains. This presents a neoclassical framework of development using the target of optimal human capital investment in economic growth.

Yet, the recent history of the Canadian Native labor force and population change reveals no significant gains. On this issue Mendelson (2004) writes:

"Whereas fewer than one-third (31.3%) of all Canadians have less than high school graduation, almost one-half (48.8%) of the Aboriginal identity population did not graduate from high school. Only 9.9% of the Aboriginal identity population graduated from high school, as opposed to 14.1% of the population overall. About 9.1% of the Aboriginal identity population had a trades certificate or diploma, and another 12% graduated from a college. A mere 4% of the Aboriginal identity population had a university degree, as opposed to 15.4% of all Canadians. Only in trades certificates and diplomas is the Aboriginal identity population achieving better than the rate of course-completion among the total population."

In 2006, the employment rate of First Nations people living on reserves was 51.9%. Those living off reserves recorded an employment rate of 66.3%. First Nations People living off reserve, but who were registered for Native Indian status recorded 71.4% employment rate. In 2006, on-reserve Native Indians had an employment rate of 51.9% compared with 50.0% in 2001. Thise living off reserve, but without registered status, had an employment rate of 64.0% (an increase from 58.2% in 2001).

The unemployment rate among First Nations people aged 25 to 54 living on reserve was 23.1%. By comparison, 12.3% of those living off reserve, and 5.2% of non-Aboriginal people were unemployed. Among First Nations people living off reserve, unemployment rates for people with Registered Indian status was 13.7% in 2006 compared to 9.4% of people without Registered Indian status.

Projections between the years 2006 and 2026 under the assumption of Aboriginal People catching up with the educational levels of non-Aboriginal People in 2006 show the following trends: Labor force participation rate of Aboriginal People will change by between 9.50% to -7.02% according to the best and lowest projection scenarios, respectively. This compares with a percentage change of -9.59 for non-Aboriginal People for the same time period. The percentage change in employment for Aboriginal People to those for non-Aboriginal People between 2006 and 2026 will stand at 347206/1225071 = 28.34%; or 155857/1225071 = 12.73% on the basis of best or worst scenario of projection, respectively. Contribution to productivity in the best scenario of projection by 2026 is expected to be between 0.007% and 0.014% in 2026.

Additional growth contribution to output is expected to be 0.015% of GDP. Additional employment growth would be between 0.008 and 0.016% by 2026. See Gionet (2009).

Inference from the Canadian Native statistics

The above projections point out that the model of human capital development relating to an expected positive correlation between education, employment, labor force participation, and income generation is an efficiency approach that overlooks the importance of labor market adjustment issue by way of adopting empowerment and cultural sensitivity to work. Canadian Natives would rarely gain even with massive expenditure, as philanthropy by the Canadian Government. On the other hand, human potential with national development expenditure to generate endogenously progressive labor force adaptation requires the involvement of Canadian Natives in their own culture of development, yet within the Canadian national perspective (Battiste, 2002).

Indeed, even though the unemployment rates of Canadian Natives remain very high, the increasing population size and the resulting increasing labor participation rate requires labor market adaptation. This can be realized by the cultural sensitivity of the Canadian Natives in the Canadian national perspective of Aboriginal development paradigm we have presented in this chapter. The objective is to integrate the goals of human potential, philanthropy, and wellbeing. This is a sign of the working of the episteme of unity of knowledge in development planning of the Canadian Aboriginal People.

An explanation of the efficacy of human resource development in Islamic financial economy

Throughout this work, and in the discussion on human potential and wellbeing, the point has been established that unity of knowledge as episteme works in favor of complementing the *maqasid*-variables. *Maqasid*-choices are shown to be prescriptive for all people in all levels of development, not just Muslims. Among such variables are financial economic benefits and human capital along with the incidence of technological change in the imminent complementary framework arising from the episteme of unity of knowledge. Here is a formal proof of this fact.

This comment shows that the Islamic methodical approach arising from the *Tawhidi* epistemic groundwork is universally applicable. It is thereby applicable to the study of development and human potential problems of Canadian Natives as for any other problems of deprived communities in need of moral, social, and economic uplift.

Let the simulated wellbeing (*maslaha*) objective function in the complementary variables, {output, $Y(\theta)$; finance, $F(\theta)$; human capital, $H(\theta)$; technology, $T(\theta)$} be,

$$\text{Sim}_\theta W(\theta) = W(Y,F,H,T)[\theta] = A(\theta).Y^a F^b H^c T^d.$$

All variables and coefficients are θ-induced by learning in the episteme of unity of knowledge.

The circular causation equations of complementarities between the variables can be readily written down, as is done throughout this book.

Next, we note that any and all coefficients can be interpreted as the wellbeing elasticity of the variables corresponding to the coefficients 'a', 'b', 'c':

Say, $c = dlogW(\theta)/dlogH = (H/W).(dW/dH)$

Likewise, $a = (Y/W).(dW/dY)$

$b = (F/W).(dW/dF)$

Now consider any ratio like, $c/a = (H/Y).(dY/dH)$. That is, $dH/dY = (H/Y).(c/a) > 0$

This result means that, human capital and the financial economy move together in terms of their complementarity. Likewise, H and F move in a complementary fashion. The common effect of technological change on each of the complementary variables proves its foundational role in integrating all the *maqasid*-variables. Thus knowledge-induced technological change, as in the Islamic financial economy with inter-variable complementarities, causes all variables to interact, integrate, and evolve together. This is the nature of *maqasid*-choices.

Conclusion

This chapter has contributed a new paradigm of participatory development in the context of a general-system model of evolutionary learning. This development worldview involves a specific phenomenological model of epistemic unity of knowledge. We constructed the model in the generalized case and particularized it to the case of human potential as a goal of participatory development. In the phenomenological model, philanthropy is treated as a productive resource. Wellbeing is the ultimate evaluative criterion. It conceptualizes and measures the epistemic criterion of organic unity between human potential, philanthropy and the gambit of other variables that either complement or show differentiation between them. The latter kind of relationship needs ethical reconstruction as the normative perspective in simulation.

Following the formalism of the general theory of sustainability in the context of the immanent evolutionary learning model that arises, the applied case of Canadian Native wellbeing in such a model was addressed. A wider range of data could extend the empirical exercise to a policy-theoretic study of Canadian Natives wellbeing using the circular causation method, which we treated in this chapter.

Notes

1 By Taylor's theorem of expansion of a continuously differentiable around a point, say θ^*, hence $\mathbf{x}^*(\theta^*)$, we obtain,

$$h(\mathbf{x}(\theta)) = h^*(\mathbf{x}^*(\theta^*)) + \Sigma_i\{(x_i - x_i^*)/1!\}*[(dh/x(\theta)).(dx_i(\theta)/d\theta)]_{|\theta}$$
$$+ \Sigma_i\{(x_i - x_i^*)^2/2!\}*[(d/d\theta)(dh/x_i(\theta)).(dx_i(\theta)/d\theta)]_{|\theta} + \text{higher terms}.$$
Here $\mathbf{x} = \{x_1, x_2, ..., x_n\}$

Writing the above expression in the following form yields the development meaning of change:

$[h(.)-h^*(.)]$ representing advancement in human potential is caused (on the right-hand side of the Taylor series) by factors of enhancement in resources and the many-faceted factors on which development as a process stands, while allowing the human potential to progress positively by the evolutionary knowledge value that reflects unity of being and becoming between the good things of life. Elsewhere, I have explained the primal characteristic of the good choice of life in development to be the *dynamic* basic-needs or life-sustaining choices that are aggregated from the micro-level to the complex nature of social aggregation (Choudhury, 2013).

2 The expression for θ is the implicit function derived from $h^* = h(\theta, x(\theta))$ in expressions (7) and (8). By the condition of continuously differentiable over continuums of knowledge, time and space dimensions, the Jacobian determinant of the inversion will exist. Hence, $\theta = F(x(\theta))$. This equation comprises expressions (11.10, 11.12).

3 *Qur'an* (14:24–27).

4 Sztompka writes (op cit, p. 115): "Therefore we cannot but seek the ultimate, primary mover of society in their traits and properties – in brief, in human nature." In this chapter we have equated the claim of human nature with rationalism as a dialectical philosophy.

5 Consider Sen's entitlement failure in his starvation set (1986). In order to restore optimal entitlement, Sen argues that the interior point can be moved on to the welfare surface by means of endogenous (consciousness) and exogenous (government development expenditure as policy). But because of this incongruent mix there can be two effects. First, the endogenous and exogenous preferences will break apart. The exogenous preferences will yield a utilitarian welfare function. The endogenous preferences will yield continuous perturbations of the welfare surface. In this case, Sen has nothing to impart in respect of control and predictability. The second effect is that an interior point cannot be moved on to the welfare surface because of the perturbations caused between the exogenous and endogenous mic of preferences. Thereby, no optimal welfare surface will ever exist. On this issue Sen's starvation and entitlement failure methodology will never reach an optimal and predictive state.

References

Barrow, J.D. (1991). *Theories of Everything, the Quest for Ultimate Explanation*, Oxford University Press, Oxford, UK.

Battiste, M. (Oct. 31, 2002). "Indigenous knowledge and pedagogy in First Nations Education, a Literature Review with recommendations", *Report*, Indian and Northern Affairs Canada, Ottawa, ON. p. 69.

Blaug, M. (1993). *The Methodology of Economics*, Cambridge University Press, Cambridge, UK.

Bloom, N. and Reenen, J.V. (2010). "Why do management practices differ across firms and countries?" *Journal of Economic Perspectives*, 24:1, pp. 203–24.

Boslough, J. (1985). *Stephen Hawking's Universe*, Avon Books, New York, NY.

Boulding, K.E. (1981). *Evolutionary Economics*, Russell Sage, New York, NY.

Cantner, U. Luc Gaffard, J. and Nesta, L. (eds) (2009). *Schumpeterian Perspectives on Innovation, Competition, and Growth*. Springer, New York, NY.

Choudhury, M.A. (2009). "Dialectics in socio-scientific inquiry:Islam contra Occident", *International Journal of Sociology and Social Policy*, 29:9/10, pp. 498–511.

Choudhury, M.A. (2011). "On the existence of evolutionary learning equilibriums", *Journal for Science*, 16:2, 68–81.

Choudhury, M.A. (2013). *Socio-Cybernetic Study of God and the World-System*, IGI-Global Publishers, Pennsylvania, PA.

Choudhury, M.A. and Harahap, S.S. (2009). "Complementing community, business and micro-enterprise by the Islamic epistemological methodology: a case of Indonesia", *Islamic and Middle Eastern Finance and Management*, 2:2, pp. 139–59.

Choudhury, M.A. Hossain, M.Z. and Hossain, M.S. (2011). "Estimating an ethical index of human wellbeing", *The Journal of Developing Areas*, 45:1, pp. 375–409.

Dasgupta, A.K. (1987). *Epochs of Economic Theory*, Basil Blackwell, Oxford, UK.

Debreu, G. (1959). *Theory of Value, an Axiomatic Analysis of Economic Equilibrium*, John Wiley, New York.

Demarting, G. (1999). "Human development index", in P.A. O'Hara (ed.), *Encyclopedia of Political Economy*, Routledge, London, UK.

Gafford, J. (2009). "Innovation, competition, and growth: Schumpeterian ideas within a Hicksian framework", in Cantner, U. Luc Gaffard, J. and Nesta, L. (eds), *Schumpeterian Perspectives on Innovation, Competition, and Growth*, pp. 7–24, Springer, New York, NY.

Gionet, L. (2009). *First Nations People: Selected Findings of the 2006 Census*, Statistics Canada, Ottawa, ON.

Gruber, T.R. (1993). "A translation approach to portable ontologies", *Knowledge Acquisition*, 5:2, pp. 199–200.

Hawking, S.W. (1988). *A Brief History of Time*, Bantam Books, New York, NY.

Hegel, G.W.F. trans. J. Sibree (1956). *The Philosophy of History*, Dover Books, New York, NY.

Kaldor, N. (1975). "What is wrong with economic theory?" *Quarterly Journal of Economics*, LXXXIX:3, 347–57.

Kim, W.C. and Mauborgne, R. (2005). *Blue Ocean Strategy*, Harvard Business Press, Boston, MA.

Maurer, B.A. (1999). "From micro to macro and back again", in *Untangling Ecological Complexity*, pp. 21–2, University of Chicago Press, Chicago, IL.

Mendelson, M. (2004). *Aboriginal People in Canada's Labor Market: Work and Employment Today and Tomorrow*, The Caledon Institute of Social Policy, Ottawa, ON.

Millennium Development Goals, Wikepedia. (May 25, 2012). http://en.wikipedia.org/wiki/Millennium_Development_Goals

Moore, G.E. (1962). *Principia Ethica, Chapter II: Naturalistic Ethics; Chapter IV: Metaphysical Ethics*, Cambridge University Press, Cambridge, UK.

Myrdal, G. (1958). "The principle of cumulation", in Streeten, P. (ed.), *Value in Social Theory, a Selection of Essays on Methodology by Gunnar Myrdal*, pp. 198–205, Harper and Brothers Publishers, New York, NY.

Myrdal, G. (1968). "The wider field of valuations", in *Asian Drama, an Inquiry into the Poverty of Nations, 1*, pp. 49–127, Pentheon, New York, NY.

Myrdal, G. (1987). "Utilitarianism and modern economics", in Feiwel, G.R. *Arrow and the Foundations of the Theory of Economic Policy*, pp. 273–97, Macmillan, London, UK.

Nikaido, H. (1987). "Fixed point theorems", in J. Eatwell, M. Milgate and P. Newman (eds), *The New Palgrave: General Equilibrium*, pp. 139–44, W.W. Norton, New York, NY.

O'Donnell, R.M. on J.M. Keynes epistemology (1989). "Types of probabilities and their measurement", pp. 50–66, also "Epistemology", in his *Keynes: Philosophy, Economics and Politics*, pp. 81–105, Macmillan Press Ltd, London, UK.

Popper, K. (2004, reprint). *The Logic of Scientific Discovery*, Routledge, London, UK.

Prigogine, I. (1980). *From Being to Becoming*, W.H. Freeman, San Francisco, CA.

Resnick, S.A. and Wolff. R.D. (1987). "A Marxian theory" in their *Knowledge and Class*, University of Chicago Press, Chicago, IL.

Rucker, R. (1983). *Infinity and the Mind, the Science and Philosophy of the Infinite*, Bantam Books, New York, NY.

Seidel, V.J. (1986). *Kant, Respect and Injustice, The Limits of Liberal Moral Theory*, Routledge and Kegan Paul, London, UK.

Sen, A. (1977). "Rational fools: a critique of the behavioural foundations of economic theory", *Philosophy and Public Affairs*, 6.

Sen, A. (1986). *Poverty and Famines, An Essay on Entitlement and Deprivation*, Clarendon Press, Oxford, UK.

Sen, A. (1990). "Freedom and consequences", in his *On Ethics and Economics*, pp. 58–89, Basil Blackwell, Oxford, UK.

Sen, A. (2010). *Commodities and Capabilities*, Oxford University Press, New Delhi, India.

Shackle, G.L.S. (1972). *Epistemics and Economics*, Cambridge University Press, Cambridge, UK.

South Commission (1990). *The Challenge to the South*, Oxford University Press, Oxford, UK.

Streeten, P.A. (1981). *Development Perspectives*, Macmillan, London, UK.

Sztompka, P. (1991). *Society in Action, The Theory of Social Becoming*, The University of Chicago Press, Chicago, IL.

Toner, P. (1999). "Conclusion", in *Main Currents in Cumulative Causation, the Dynamics of Growth and Development*, Chapter 7, Macmillan Press Ltd, Houndmills, UK.

United Nations Development Program (UNDP) (1997, 1998, 1999, 2000) issues. *Human Development Report*, Oxford University Press, New York, NY.

Chapter 10

The Islamic Panacea to the Global Financial Predicament

A New Financial Architecture[1]

Abstract

The roots of the 2008 global financial crisis that originated in the United States subprime mortgage market are firstly traced to the demand side of financing. Borrower preferences are based on excess ownership and spending. Such consumer preferences were matched by the suppliers' decisions to allow easy lending and the accumulation of multiple loans. The cost of such financial excess is shown to be the rate of interest. The relevance of interest rates in efficient financing and economic resource mobilization is here questioned from a theoretical point of view. Its rejection and replacement by participatory financing instruments in the good things of life is formalized. A new financial architectural is thus laid out in terms of the central issue of money, finance and real economy complementary relationships. These can be simulated by circular causation equations. The foundational conceptual premise is governed by the episteme of unity of knowledge. Thus, the Islamic worldview of unity of knowledge is invoked to address the theme of 100% Reserve Requirement Monetary System (100% RRMS). Its social and economic implications are discussed.

Causes of global financial predicament

The following is a summary of the causes of the global financial meltdown that brought about a mammoth injection of bailout funds by national world governments. The debts and assets of major banks in the West had to be guaranteed by government protection. This is tantamount to the nationalization of the banks: quite contrary to free market ideals.

1. The financial crisis arose in the mortgage market. Large debts had been accrued by borrowers in the housing market in the face of low subprime mortgage interest rates. Borrowers took advantage of such an easy borrowing situation to build up debt that they could not repay. Such is the case of over-investment in the housing market that was not in tandem with the capability of being paid out in the short run. Thus defaults in mortgage payments commenced from excess consumer spending. The financial institutions allowed consumers to spend to excess.
2. Mortgage funds are borrowed from banks and lending institutions to the mortgage markets. These are then returned to investors. The mammoth debt that arose

from default in mortgage payments naturally placed a crushing weight on the lending banks and corporations.

3. Real estate assets were foreclosed due to unwieldy loans which had accrued. These could not be serviced in the face of high mortgage payments, even at sub-prime mortgage rates.

4. For some time in 2006, the high price of real estate properties raised the volume of total mortgage payments. Together with this mortgage crunch, the illiquidity of expensive property assets led to a real estate market correction. This caused house prices to decline. During the period 2007–8, owners and investors experienced the adverse financial effect of losses in real estate properties. Lending banks and corporations lost heavily in the wake of low returns on the uncapitalized value of their financed assets.

5. Easy and ineffective global financial regulations compounded these problems. Monetary policy was influenced by fluctuating borrowing rates in response to the volatility of the real estate market fueled by speculative investors. This was a repeat of the financial crunch that burst the growth bubble of East Asian economies during the late 1990s. Fluctuating short-term rates of interest and speculative aggressiveness among investors entrenched the volatility fears in the financial markets. The worst affected were the equity and bond markets, as capital flowed freely between the bonds during high short-term interest rates and equities with higher but volatile yields with low interest rates.

6. While the domestic financial markets reacted to the financial volatility and corporate insolvency, the contagion was spread across the global financial markets by the adverse effects transmitted by the real economy and international trade in both merchandise and capital.

7. Economic and financial indicators that worsened the relationship between financial and real sectors were legion. Industrial production in the US slumped. The rate of growth of real GDP slowed down considerably in China. The International Labor Organization predicted 20 million people unemployed globally. Several sovereign nations, Iceland, Pakistan, Ukraine and Hungary came close to bankruptcy and had to be rescued with high levels of borrowed funds. Heightened debt-service charges fell upon the immense amount of borrowed funds needed to bail out large banks across the world. Taxpayers' resources were used to finance these large debt hangovers. A slowdown in consumer spending and investor confidence led to a subdued recovery of the stock markets globally despite the mammoth financial bailout packages for banks, financial corporations and nation states. These causes compounded to worsen the relationship between the financial sector, the real sector and foreign trade flows. Relations reached an all-time low in the stalled ideas and mechanisms of western capitalism with its political and institutional backing under neo-liberalism.

8. The long-term worry for the western capitalist and the neo-liberal system is the fear of instability. Within this climate of change, economic, financial and social relations cannot be maintained for the common good. The IMF has already predicted this long-term financial Armageddon (Claude-Strauss Kahn, 2008). There is structural problem in the neo-liberal western capitalist system that cannot be resolved by empty slogans like 'a new global financial architecture', 'new

international economic order', 'western democracy', 'new world order', and the faded ideas, mechanisms and applications of an unworkable free-market.

Summarizing the roots of the global financial crisis – the permanent human and economic malaise

The basis of the present financial crisis, which will continue to inflict its venom because of structural problems in society, the economy, finance and its institutions, are the households and investors that fuel the real estate market. Then there is the effect that this kind of preference has on the economy and the uncertain market expectations everywhere. Finally, the excessiveness is allowed to survive and proceed with unrelenting speed by weak government polices, an outmoded understanding of the economic and financial world-system, which is unable to simulate the otherwise complex system by using a spent-out methodology.

At the level of preference interactions is a complete lack of consciously responsible behavior in individuals, households, and institutions. These agents reinforce each other in their acquisitive passion to acquire. This is the permanent character of global capitalism under neo-liberalism (Dunning, 2004; Sklair, 2002).

Learning with consciousness remains absent in the face of gullible self-interest in the midst of the greed and passion that triggers the passion to acquire. The perennial financing instrument upon which the acquisitive animal spirit survives is the rates of interest of every kind – short, long, term-structure and shadow-rates. Interest rates as an instrument of volatility carry with them the permissiveness of the acquisitive spirit and silence the conscious elements from everyone's preference maps.

In this chapter we will examine the global financial crisis as a permanent case of large business cycles caused by multidimensional factors. This is different from the textbook explanation. They are quite apart from the narrow limits of the investment and spending scenario that marked the Great Depression of the 1930s due to the complexity caused by multidimensional factors, which cannot be simply analyzed by the existing straightforward economic and financial methods. The present business cycles move away from stability due to structural causes fueled by the capitalist passion to acquire. Such is the character of greed and disorder in which the high grounds of capitalism, born out of liberalism, survives and mutates.

Around the basis of individual and collective preferences organized into institutional forms, systemic chaos becomes a permanent character of global capitalism. To get out of this permanent environment of chaos and disturbances no quick fix will be adequate. While the need for an immediate halting of the financial crisis is called for, its long-term implications regarding substantial change ought to be the goal (Mankiw, December 28, 2008).

Substantial and revolutionary change will require bold negation of the neo-liberal premise. It will consequently entail great and bold questioning on economic, financial, institutional and social fronts. Julian Huxley wrote about the social engineering of planet earth in his *Brave New World*.

The entire concept of money and the real economy through the function of finance and institutional policies must be rethought. The concept of money itself will undergo a new definitive understanding. The resulting financial instruments will deny many of the underlying epistemological groundwork on which neo-liberalism and its model of global capitalism stands. We will argue that the central implement in all these is the rate of interest. Interest rates have been proven to be a financial instrument that is the cause and effect of vicious cycles of reinforcing individualism, acquisition, and institutional weakness arising from the under-mobilization of resources. In the end, we inherit a permanent lack of linkage and continuity that the monetary sector and real economy need to sustain in a stable and fulfilling economic, financial and social order. A thorough change of global capitalism and its epistemological roots in neo-liberalism is mandated.

A generalized schema of flows of funds

In Figure 10.1, problems of sustainability and stabilization arise when full or partial disconnect exists between the monetary, financial and real estate sectors. The depth of such differentiation is caused by the inability to mobilize financial and real resources in a complementary fashion to make the best use of money in the real economy. This requires appropriate financing instruments, supervision and learning in the system to transform or perpetuate consciousness through the interacting system with the labyrinth of their complex relationships. Interest rates are a barrier to such a possibility. The presence of interest rates diverts monetary and financial resources away from the real economy into financial savings to earn interest, without the turnover being linked to real productivity. Indeed Keynes, whose ideas of macroeconomics saved the western world from the Great Depression of the 1930s, encouraged spending in productive ways, opposing thus the propensity to save, to tax and cause unproductive leakages (Ventelou, 2005).

The arguments in respect of a new episteme for economic, financial and social sustainability

In this chapter, our objective is to point out the structural problems of that faded economic, financial and scientific rationalistic episteme of the neo-liberal genre that is unworkable in the face of social complexity. The socio-scientific system that humankind has inherited in this post-industrial age of production turning into high consumption, broadly defined, is complex due to its extensive relational and simulative nature. The idea of complexity is that of endless continuity of circular causation relationships, which delineate the nature of human problems. Myrdal (1968) wrote on this point in his explanation of the wider field of social causation in the context of socio-economic development. Fitzpatrick (2003, p. 128) writes on the endless simulative character of our learning and organic relationships within embedded socio-scientific problems: "Ours, then, is an age of simulations that endlessly refer only to other simulations. The infinite circularity of these self-references is what Braudrillard calls the *simulacra*: everything is a reproduction of other reproductions. Society explodes in on itself and we cannot liberate ourselves from the *simulacra*..."

In this chapter, the circular causality that we will study will point out how neo-liberal western socio-scientific episteme breaks away from the unity of the economic world-system. The particular case of such organic and learning understanding of systemic unity is the organic symbiosis between money, finance and the real

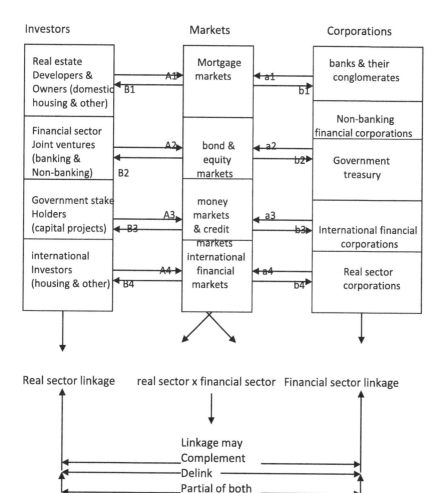

Figure 10.1 Nature of relationships between money and real economy in neo-liberal society

economy. Due to such a permanent entrenchment in a neo-liberal worldview, its episteme cannot address the structural problems and the social reconstruction towards attaining organic unity.

Our focus, then, is on the structural nature of organic and complex relationships that symbiotically embed the money, finance, real economy and exchange relationships within the framework of organic learning. Such learning occurs continuously in a complementary venue of market and institutional interaction. The idea is substantively defined to establish the episteme of unity of knowledge in such a pervasively unified, hence complementary, system of organic learning relationships.

Following this contrasting departure of the new structural reconstruction model as an epistemic novelty different from the socio-scientific oddity of the neo-liberal rationalist paradigm, we will present the new symbiotic worldview of unity of knowledge as the episteme of the new structural reconstruction. In the light of this episteme we will offer an alternative framework of reconstruction towards a participatory worldview involving money, finance, real economy, exchange and institutional circular causation relationships *qua* complexity caused by the systemic richness of learning.

Our search in the above directions of establishing the functional ontology (Gruber, 1993; Acikgenc, 1995) of unity of knowledge and its formalism and application to the case of money, finance, real economy, exchange and institutionally embedded symbiosis will take us to the Islamic foundations of oneness of God and the world-system. Divine Oneness here is a general, universal and unique epistemological precept. We will particularize its application to the case of money, finance, real economy, exchange and institutionally stimulated systemic symbiosis. Through our functional ontological formalism and its application and simulated inferences we will point out the strategic policies and programs that emanate from the epistemic worldview of symbiotic oneness in the context of organic learning systems that are complex by their relational complexity but unified by pervasive complementarities between the good choices of life.

Our objective is to alert the reader to the Islamic foundational worldview of divine oneness (*Tawhid*) at work in replacing and sustaining a new breed of thinking concerning economic, financial, institutional discursive theories and policy perspectives.

Where has neo-liberalism failed? The contrasting episteme of Islam and its world-system

What is the meaning of episteme? Foucault (see Sheridan, 1972 p. 191) defines the word *episteme* as follows:

By episteme we mean ... the total set of relations that unite, at a given period, the discursive practices that give rise to epistemological figures, sciences, and possibly formalized systems ... The episteme is not a form of knowledge (connaissance) or type of rationality which, crossing the boundaries of the most varied sciences, manifests the sovereign unity of a subject, a spirit, or a period; it is the totality of relations that can be discovered, for a given period, between the sciences when one analyses them at the level of discursive regularities.

Why is it essential to invoke an epistemic inquiry to lay down the altogether different and revolutionary original view of Islamic economic and financial architecture from its epistemic foundation of divine oneness in 'everything'? In answer to this question we point out that foundational axioms remain at the root of a conscious order. They do not simply operate mechanically, as by human desires and rationalism. Contrarily, morals, ethics, consciousness, logical formalism, based on such edicts of human values and the reason to decipher inferences premised on the epistemic axioms, play their organic roles in erecting the mind of civilization of the *longue dure* (Braudel, 1995).

Liberalism and economics (Taylor, 1967) and the emergent social, cultural, institutional and political order are examples of the epistemological entrenchment of a certain understanding of reality based on rationalism (Minogue, 1963). In rationalism, God and the moral order in organizing human experience remain isolated from the worldly function and model of the neo-liberalism worldview.[2]

Consequently, rationalism is a denial of oneness by the self-centered ego of competition and individualism, which exists in the agent and the social order. So when we apply this edict to 'everything', there then arises the corresponding form of civilization. This kind of rationalistic origin of self and methodological individualism promotes the differentiated system of economics, finance, society and institutions. Within this we find the partitioned views and functions of money and finance from the real economy.

The central premise of savings in capital accumulation rests on the perpetual withdrawal of a certain proportion of the potential output into interest-bearing idle capital. Such a continuous withdrawal of resources away from the formation of potential output causes the economy to under-perform. Business cycles now remain endemic in economic and financial flows. Thus, savings are never fully mobilized into spending in the good and conscious choices of life. Think of such goodly pursuits as the Rawlsian primary (Sen, 1989). The stability and sustainability of the economy, necessary to arrest these business cycles, are never attained in the presence of this failed mobilization of resources.

The monetary and financial sectors and the real economy have opposing goals and interests. Financial interest and savings promote the power of capital accumulation prevent potential resources from being fully mobilized into the real economy.[3] On the contrary, investments and spending in the good things of life promote the goals of productivity and creativity by the full mobilization of resources.

The economic problem of the financial sector in the neo-liberal heritage of economics is the maximization of expected utility function of a principal–agent contract subject to the present valuation of future cash-flows discounted at a rate of interest. The economic problem of the real economy in the differentiated economic and financial systems is construed as the maximization of output subject to the payments to factors of production and sources of economic profits according to prices set by a combination of market and institutional forces. A pervasively complementary relationship between financial and real economic activities is impossible. Otherwise, the relative interest-rate-to-output prices cannot be determined by the marginal productivity of commodity substitution the two kinds of goods and services (real economy and financial sector, respectively) are substitutes of each other (Henderson and Quandt, 1971). Pervasive complementarities between these sectors and their artefacts are thereby methodologically impossible in received economic and financial theory governing rational choices.

Contrary to the pervasive rule of marginal rate of substitution coming out of the kinds of competing opposites that are generated in a differentiated regime of money, finance and real economy, the principle of pervasive complementarities forms the sure and measured attainment of unity by participation and organic learning. In this case, relative prices cannot be determined by the first-order conditions of profit-maximization. Instead, prices are like those of classical markets. They are set by multimarket cause and effect between the endogenous variables that interrelate with their activities. These relationships generate the essential visage of learning by circular causation in the form of simulations between the endogenous variables. Learning causes all variables, including the policy variables and household and institutional preferences, to become endogenous. Only the precept of oneness remains the invariant, exogenously given, axiom that governs all other relationships as endogenous.

Circular causation across the domain of endogenous relationships is the sign of learning. Economic and financial systemic sustainability by such a participatory learning behavior establishes the ethics of the system. It is singularly derived from the moral law of oneness. We, therefore, have the money, finance and real economy, institutional and social relationships as a system of unified, complementary and participatory circular causation between endogenously learning variables on the basis of the precept of organic unity of knowledge in "everything."

There is no such epistemic methodology in the prevalent economic, financial, institutional and social world-systems to study the functional nature of the divine law of oneness by its various functional instrumentations. Contrarily, such instrumentations establish a sustainable economic, financial and social order by pervasively complementary learning relationships. Such a socio-scientific order rests primarily on the precept of unity of knowledge of a symbiotic, embedded and unified worldview. Unity of knowledge is thereby a systemic participatory and complementary reality. It invokes the moral law of conscious oneness as well as the functional ways of attaining that oneness by organic linkages between the good things of life.

In the financial world, interest rates are unacceptable for resource mobilization. They diminish the ability of resources to flow freely across complementing systems. Unfortunately, the neo-liberal financial system with all its theory, institutions and policies has not been able to liberate itself from the grip of the interest-rate mechanism, despite the realization that low rates of interest are necessary to step up spending on all fronts to evade a recession.

The Chairman of the Federal Reserve Board in the United States, Ben Bernanke (Oct. 7, 2008) in his speech on the present economic and financial conditions, repeated the economic argument of the opportunity cost of choices. He referred to the banking bailout with public funds as a trade-off between bailout and recession, despite the fact that the recession in America is expected to be prolonged. The concept of opportunity cost is static in a non-learning world. It cannot, therefore, be included within the organic learning of richly complex, but unifying, systems.

Contrarily, cooperative financing instruments replace interest rates and bring about cooperation, participation and complementarities in everything that revolves around accelerated resource mobilization. The consequential effects, such as employment, productivity and creativity in a conscious environment of learning within organic wholeness represent the systemic unity arising from the episteme of divine oneness. Such a systemic organism of oneness, derived from the episteme of divine oneness as the primal law, and around which everything revolves in the orbit of oneness and its continuity by learning, is the basis for the links that must exist between money, finance, the real economy and the social and institutional environment.

Why is the episteme of conscious oneness of symbiotic interaction between money, finance and real economy necessary?

Both the answer to the questions posed here and the status of the prevalent thinking in economics, finance and society shows that unity of knowledge between these mutually embedded systems and their representative variables is a long-forgotten ideal. Reintroducing the episteme of oneness and its functional ontology of unity of knowledge and the world-system into the issues of money, finance and the real economy with its social and ethical essence is a revolutionary project.

Ethics and human systems were deeply ingrained in Smith's theory of moral sentiments (Smith, eds Raphael, D.D. and Mackie, A.L., 1976). Ethics is deep in Keynes' economic epistemology of uncertainty, probability and the econometric method (O'Donnell, 1989). In the study of social dynamics and political economy, Hegel trailblazed thinking along the lines of the ethical concept of the World Spirit (Hegel, trans. J. Sibree, 1956; Hegel, trans. Dyke, S.W. 1996). Marx (Spechler, 1990) was not an ethicist. Yet the dynamics of social discourse and interaction colored his political economy. The Austrian School of Economics was deeply ethical by virtue of its epistemology of the learning model (Hayek, 1990; Kirzner, 1997).

In the age of Islamic scholasticism, almost every single idea was deeply epistemological and invoked the moral law of divine oneness to explain the central Islamic episteme of unity of knowledge in relation to the world-system (Choudhury, 2004). Worthy of particular mention are Imam Ibn Taimiyya (see Islahi, 1988) and his student Ibn Qayyim (see Islahi, 1988). They both wrote strongly in favor of gold and silver as the intrinsic bullion for the monetary standard. They opposed the policy of the Mamluk dynasty of Egypt during that time, which debased money by replacing gold and silver with copper. The result was a 400% increase in inflation in Egypt at the time. Imam Ghazali (trans. Rahman, undated) was strongly against the debasing of gold and silver coins, which were treated as currency during his time. A debased coin was valued less because it did not buy the same amount of goods as a non-debased coin in circulation. Ibn Khaldun (trans. Rozenthal, 1958) praised the artisans over merchants because of their productive contribution to the national output.

The most important sources of Islamic epistemology of divine oneness and unity of knowledge, namely the *Qur'an* and the *sunnah* (Prophetic guidance) present the architecture of symbiosis between 'everything'. The most powerful explanation of the underlying principle of pervasive complementarities is the principle of pairs in the *Qur'an*.[4] The model of development in the *Qur'an* is one of dynamic basic-needs comprising the good choices of life.[5] Upon this principle, Imam Fakhruddin Razi formalized his *ubudiyya* (worship theory) theory of life-sustaining goods (Noor, 1998). Imam Shatibi (Masud, 1995) established his wellbeing theory called *al-maslaha wal-istihsan* (wellbeing according to juristic preferences). The Prophet Muhammad had assigned values to smaller denominations of the Islamic Dinar (gold and silver currency) called *danaq* and *mithqal* in terms of basic foodstuffs (Allouche, 1994; Choudhury, 1997).

These developments in the history of Islamic economic thought amply establish the fact that currency as money was always thought of in terms of its required spending power in acquiring the basic needs of life. Financing of the dynamic basic-needs regime of development mobilizes real and financial resources in the direction of the Islamic Law governing money, finance and real economy inter-linked with the goal of attaining wellbeing.

The episteme of unity of knowledge: Is it a tall call?

So in the end, can it be expected that the economic and financial gurus will embrace the episteme of the unity of knowledge in Islam to reconstruct the fallen world into ethical and material sustainability? We hardly expect this to happen. That is not the intention of this chapter, which merely points out the logical formalism of this altogether different worldview of socio-scientific rethinking. After this, the essential elements of organic links involving the following circular causation relationships provide the way out and will put the economic and financial system on the path towards economic stabilization, growth and sustainability:

The extensive learning process as a functional phenomenological ontology will require continuous and vigorous discourse within western, Islamic and other cultures and across them on the groundwork of unity of knowledge in relation to the economic, financial and social world-system. This would invoke a combination of socio-scientific discourses in the problem areas through interfaith dialogues. There is much scientific and technological know-how in the West that can be used to promote the socio-scientific formalism of unity of knowledge according to the Islamic worldview. Conversely, there is always much that Islam can bestow by way of the methodology of unity of knowledge in relation to the world-system, from which the world can benefit. However, the essentials of the learning universe with its particular sub-systems as the global economy, finance and society cannot depart from the kind of schematic development of thought and application that we pointed out in Figure 10.2 or its diverse prototypes.

In summary, therefore, why is it necessary to study the epistemic origin of unity of knowledge in relation to the world-system, the reconstructive model, and the failed model of global capitalism in accordance with rationalism as the episteme of liberalism? It is to erect the new economic and social thought in the midst of complex processes that pervasively generate complementarities between the ethically induced choices. Such an extensively complementary and participatory view is expressed by the organic unity between money, finance and the real economy in accordance with the reconstruction of ethical preferences in individuals and social preferences in institutions.

Neither rationalism nor liberalism, and thereby global capitalism, can answer these questions and designs of pervasive complementarities in the light of symbiotic views. Ethics is always an exogenous element in these systems, not the endogenously embedded core of the learning, discursive and unitary worldview of moral consciousness. Buchanan (1999) writes emphatically on this point.[6]

In the Money-Commodity-Money (M-C-M) model, which was so much discussed by Marx, we also find the process whereby money increases in volume and circulation in the economy.[7] The idea is that the accumulation of capital which finances economic growth and sustainability is formed through the productive returns of commodity production. Such returns arise from trade and exchange in the good things of life. Contrarily, interest rates of all kinds and denominations impede resource mobilization by breaking down the complementarities between money, finance and the real economy. This is a reality that is not accessible to economics based on the opportunity cost of resource allocation under conditions of scarcity and competition in the economic world that does not learn and in which diminishing returns to scale as a condition of steady-state equilibrium and optimal resource allocation halts the learning process (Shackle, 1972). Technology and institutions remain exogenous or are endogenously hegemonic in imposing preferences (Becker, 1989).

The meaning of episteme that we have used throughout this work and which we have borrowed from Foucault agrees with our understanding of the totality of relationships between the ontology of unity of knowledge; its epistemological consequences on the derivation of knowledge; and formalizing and applying the emergent analytics to investigate the generality and the particulars of the world-system under study. Such a meaning of the totality in the phenomenology of knowledge is also what Foucault conveyed in his architecture of knowledge and the induced world-system.

The ineptness of Islamic economics to the crisis

In the financial and economic field, Islamic banks have mushroomed under an Islamicization agenda. Yet the foundation and principles of Islamic banks give no comprehensive vision of a background intellectual mass of ideas on how to transform the prevailing environment of interest-transactions into an interest-free system. How do the economic and financial sectors determine risk-diversification and prospective diversity of investment and production, thus *mobilizing* financial resources in the real economy along *shari'ah* (Islamic Law) determined opportunities?

The financial reports of Islamic banks show an inordinately large proportion of resources floating in foreign trade financing. These portfolios have only to do with sheer mercantilist business returns by charging a mark-up on merchandise in trade. This mark-up is called *murabaha*. This has nothing in common with real economic change arising from the use of trade financing. Consequently, the mobilization of resources through foreign trade financing alone has neither helped to increase inter-communal trade financing in Muslim countries nor to increase returns through development prospects in the real economic sectors undertaking foreign trade financing.

Islamic banks have not constructed a program of comprehensive development by re-thinking the nature of money in Islam in terms of the intrinsic relationship between money as a moral and social necessity linked endogenously to real economic activities. Here, endogenous money value is reflected only in the returns obtained from the mobilization of real sectoral resources that money serves to monetize according to the *shari'ah*.

Money does not have any intrinsic value of its own apart from the value of the precious metals that are to be found in real-sector production of the currency. The structural change leading to such transformation has not been possible for Islamic banks. Today, they are simply pursuing goals of efficiency and profitability within the globalization agenda as sponsored by the West and her international development finance organizations. Thus, Islamic banks have launched a neo-liberal model of economic competition in the midst of privatization, market openness, rent-seeking economic behavior and financial competition. This goes against promoting co-operation with other financial institutions and sectors.

A study carried out by Choudhury (1999) showed that although deposits have risen phenomenally in Islamic banks as a whole, the rate of profitability (distributed dividends/deposit) remained low at 1.66%. The investment portfolio of Islamic banks is overly biased toward foreign trade and equity financing. Yet, as we are aware, equity financing is destined to be highly risky when adequate sectoral diversification and progressive production and investments remain impossible for Islamic financial and non-banking institutions.

We therefore infer that the high level of deposits in Islamic banks comes from a sincere desire by Muslims to turn to meaningful modes of Islamic financing. The dynamics of Islamic transformation and an equitable and participatory framework of business operations as forms of Islamic relationships have received marginal attention at social and institutional levels and in reference to Islamic socio-economic transformation.

The Malaysian Islamic economic fiasco

Statistical interpretations for the distribution of investments by financing instruments are similar to those for sectoral allocation of investment. Besides, the pattern of such allocation was similar between Islamic and commercial banks in Malaysia during the period 2002–2006. The inference drawn goes strongly against the expected Islamic mode of financing in participatory development financing instruments and in favor of secondary financing instruments, which have doubtful legitimacy as Islamic investment modes in view of their management approach in Islamic banks. These have applications that are no different from the time-valuation methods, which commercial banks practice.

Paradoxically, commercial banks appear to enjoy the cost-plus pricing mode of financing more than Islamic banks. This has brought about a decline in Islamic financing instruments by Islamic banks, while the cost-plus pricing method of Islamic financing instruments are questionable as presently practised in the economy as a whole. The implication is damaging for Islamic banks from the perspective of the Islamic call for socio-economic development, provision of the good things of life and establishing a participatory economic, financial and social system along with pertinent policy measures embedded in this kind of systemic unification. The foundational principle arises from the true Islamic episteme of unity of knowledge, which reflects the ontology of the oneness of the divine law and its unification impact of the world-system.

A further implication is that neither Islamic nor commercial banks played an identifiable role in the productive transformation of the Malaysian economy. All the contributions to share-value and economic growth came from the secondary financial markets. In the end, a significant substitution of resources occurred in favor of both the financial sector and financing instruments and away from productive possibilities. These are unhealthy signs of a looming bubble in the economy, like that faced by Malaysia during 1994–1996, which caused the financial crisis (as foreseen by Jomo (1992) and Ali (1992)). Abdullah, Hassan and Mohamad (2007) pointed out that Malaysian Islamic unit trust funds did not perform any better than conventional unit trust funds in normal times. The funds were poorly diversified and did not reach the 50% level of diversification required for a strong portfolio.

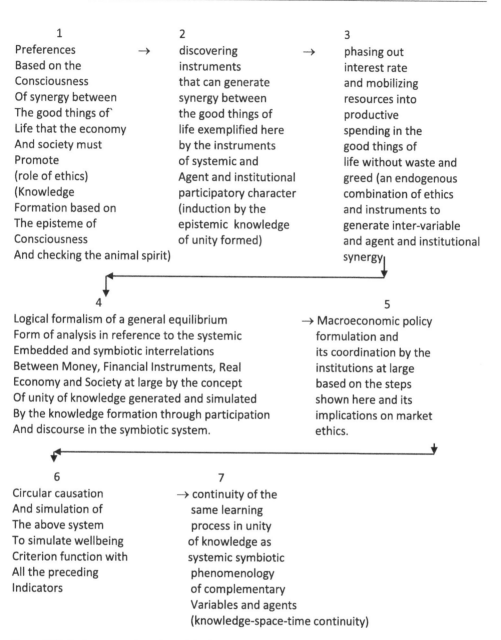

Figure 10.2 A phenomenological model of learning for a symbiotic system of relationships between economy, finance and society

The model of money, finance and real economy linkages in the light of unity of knowledge causing social wellbeing

The mathematical formalization of the schema of Figures 10.2 and 10.3 yields the general equilibrium model of circular causation relationships for simulating wellbeing.[8]

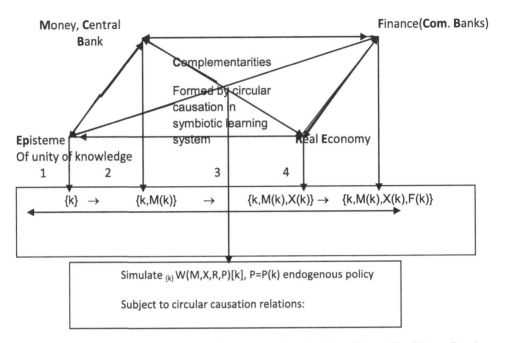

Figure 10.3 Complementary relationships of an epistemologically driven General Equilibrium Circular Causation System in money, finance, real economy with policy induction

The money, finance, and real economic system according to knowledge-induced dynamic preferences is schematized in Figure 10.3 and explained below.

The implications of complementary circular causation relationshipsbetween money, finance, real economy, policies and social and institutional variables

The relationship, $M = f_1(k^+,,F^+,X^+,P^{\pm})[k]$; [k] indicating induction of all the variables inside (...), means that the quantity of money has to be controlled ($P^{\pm}$) in the circular causation relationships such that financial instruments link up with the mobilization of quantity of money (M) to establish complementary relationships with the real economy vector (X) (e.g. real GDP, employment, price stability, growth, trade and distributive equity). Such policy variables (P) are cooperative within a climate of participation and complementarities between the variables shown. The sustainability of this complementary system, with price stability, requires that monetary transmission into the real economy must be proportionate to the requirements of the cooperative projects and outlets. Any excess of monetary transmission will be inflationary and harmful for the real productivity of the projects.

Examples of F are profit-sharing, equity-participation, joint ventures, cofinancing, mark-up cost-pricing and such secondary financing instruments as also revolve around profit-sharing and equity participation. The choice of projects must be in accordance with the sustainability of the **X**-vector in the real economy to generate the simulated levels of wellbeing.

The signs of the coefficients in the relationship, $F = f_2(k^+, M^+, X^+, P^\pm)[k]$ provides the same meanings in relation to complementarities between $(M, F, X)[k]$ with the use of the P-policy vector to help attain and sustain the complementarities.

A similar explanation can be attached to the circular causation relationship, $X = f_3(k^+, M^+, F^+, P^\pm)[k]$. This, in itself, is a multiple-equation system in respect of the vector **X**. Thus, an extensive system of circular causation relationships is opened up for study and estimation. Within this extended system there will be inter-**X** vector circular causation relationships along with $(M, F, X)[k]$, all based on the principle of inter-variable complementarities.

Finally, we note that the principle of pervasive complementarities is derived from the recursive learning and discursive processes that are enabled by the continuous induction of every learning process by consciousness of unity of knowledge in the systemic sense of 'pairing' or symbiosis between the variables representing the good things of life (e.g. the Rawlsian primary mentioned earlier). Such an ethical idea is also used by Hammond (1989) in his reconstruction of Harsanyi's fundamental utilitarian function as a welfare function.

In our case of social wellbeing function, we equate wellbeing with the degree of complementarities gained by estimation and reconstruction of the circular causation system by simulating the k-parameters across the (M, F, X, P) variables as explained earlier. The estimated and reconstructed social wellbeing function is given by the empirical version of $k = f_4(M^+, F^+, X^+, P^\pm)[k]$. The signs of the coefficients are explained, as before, in the sense of learning and consciousness by discourse emerging from and recursively leading to participatory unity. Thus unifying experience leads to systemic symbiosis.

From the above formalism it is obvious that money in the symbiotic sense with finance, real economy and society at large is a microeconomic entity. The theory of money and the real economy in this sense arises from a definition and analytical treatment of micro-money pursuing projects and spending through the relationship of commercial banks and the central bank. The quantity of money so pursing the demand of projects equals the value of spending in the project or groups of projects all linked to each other by circular causation relationships.

In such a case we interpret the quantity of micro-money (M_i) meeting the needs of a project (i) or other spending outlets as the total amount of spending $(P_i.Y_i)$ required for that project. That is, $M_i.V_i = P_i.Y_i$, with project-specific velocity of money circulation, $V_i \approx 1$. P_i denotes prices and Y_i denotes specific output, so that $P_i.Y_i$ is nominal output for project i = 1, 2,.., n number of projects. The total quantity of money in circulation across all projects and sources of output is $M = \Sigma_i M_i = \Sigma_i P_i.Y_i$; $V_i \approx 1$, for each i = 1, 2,,..., n.

The above project-specific (spending-specific) concept of micro-money increases the role of banks in mobilizing money into the real economy by the use of participatory financial instruments. A special kind of monetary transmission mechanism is now necessary to realize the productive mobilization of savings into the real economy, so that no savings are withheld to earn interest and savings = investment every time. It is important to note that in such a money and real economy circular causation, a relationship with the use of financial instruments and the productive mobilization of money through financing resources in the good things of life is necessary; the condition of savings = investment everywhere in the life of the economy narrows down the frequency of business cycles. Consequently, interest rates in savings, as holding idle financial resources, are redundant. They are replaced by participatory development-financing instruments.

A 100% reserve-requirement micro-monetary system (100% RRMS) is formed. However, we must understand the meaning of this concept, which is quite different from the idea of 100% reserve requirement monetary system in which the central bank has the authority to maintain the full reserve. Commercial banks cannot hold reserve. In our definition of the concept, the central bank receives the full deposit of the unmobilized funds through the commercial banks into the real economy. This residual reserve is 100% protected by a proportionate stock of gold and silver as bimetallic bullion. Arguments similar to those presented in this chapter appear in Currie's historic paper (1937 reprinted 2004).

Furthermore, the concept of 100% RRMS means, in our case that commercial banks are allowed to hold 100% of the deposits to mobilize them into productive investments and spending. When savings in the form of money in circulation are not fully mobilized, then the unmobilized savings can be deposited with the central bank. This is a residual case of the relationship between central and commercial banks protecting the value of money in reserve deposit and in circulation. The central bank safeguards the value of the unmobilized savings by a proportionate amount of bimetallic bullion (gold and silver).

It can be noted that only a small amount is required for this function in inverse proportion to the quantity of money mobilized. The higher the quantity of money mobilized through the commercial banks into the real economy, the smaller the residual savings transferred to the central bank. Hence, a smaller quantity of gold is needed to protect the value of the residual reserve with the central bank.

Besides, this small quantity of gold protects the overall currency value. This equals money in circulation, plus the residual reserve that is fully held in the central bank.[9]

The implication of 100% RRMS is wider. Since foreign trade is an important outlet of resource mobilization, the market catalytic effect of 100% RRMS still exists. Mydin and Larbani (2004) point out that a small amount of gold as the bimetallic bullion standard can support a large volume of trade. For this reason we refer to the 100% RRMS as being backed by the gold standard. Gold was a fairly stable asset until the end of the Bretton Woods Arrangement in the 1960's and has proved to be a stable monetary base. It was the self-interest of large banks and their national governments that ended the gold standard; central banks turned to paper money with a fractional reserve requirement monetary system. Multiple credit creation is the result of creating large sums of paper money without any asset backing. The study of the relationship between money, price, output and the real economy is a fascinating intellectual enterprise (Bordo, 1989).

Institutional implications: banking relationships in the 100% RRMs connecting money, finance and the real economy

Chart 1 explains the participatory relationships between the Central Bank and Commercial Banks to bring about money-finance-real economy symbiotic links.

Arrows 1 and 2 denote the flow of currency as money in circulation through the commercial banks and the central bank in response to real economic demand. Arrow 3 denotes the interbank and other needs of the real economy arising within a continuous need for quantities of currency to finance real economic activity. This amount belongs to the central bank whose currency stock it is. These deposits limit the excess production of additional currency stocks. However, suitable mechanisms can be developed between the central bank and the commercial banks to efficiently circulate the interbank borrowing and other deposits into real economic transactions as needed, under the supervision of the central bank through its networking with the commercial banks. Arrow 4 shows this possibility. Arrow 5 indicates other new currency flows needed for financing real economic activity.

The same mechanism exists in the case of an excess demand for a quantity of money to finance real economic transactions. The central bank can produce additional currency and also use its commercial bank residual reserve deposits. In this way, any excess demand is continually removed. There is therefore no price pressure, which otherwise would be caused by a shortage or excess of liquidity.

Since Arrows 3 and 4 (hence 7 and 8) represent the exact matching of demand with the quantity of money needed to finance such real economic activity, no excess demand or supply of money exists. Thereby, unstable consequences on prices and real output do not exist. In other words, the growth of currency = growth of demand for real economic transactions = growth of output = real rate of productive return. In an economy that moves according to the dynamic basic-need regimes of development there would be steady states for these various rates.

This, however, requires the active functioning of the two levels in the banking system: the discursive organization and the co-operative venture relationship. Such relationships are instrumental in the knowledge formation of the system. Knowledge formation is measured by active policies, performance of cooperative instruments, and discourse. All of these conditions are accounted for in terms of ordinal weights in the learning k-values.

Chart 1: Institution-market irelationships in the 100% RRMS: Central Bank, Commercial Bank (Islamic Bank) and the real economy

Central Bank: produces and manages stock of currency and oversees the money-economy relationship

Central bank produces currency stock = Dinar 100,000. Central bank maintains Dinar 100,000 level by producing residual stock of currency. The central bank can also produce stock in view of expected excess demand of the real economy.

Reserve ratio = 100%

Central bank oversees the money-real economy relationship in view of economic development and social perspectives for both the closed and open economy. Hence, domestic and external sector stabilization is part of the overall goals of the central bank to guide the allocation of funds. To stabilize the external sector, the central bank links exchange rate determination to productivity. Consequently, terms-of-trade and

1
↑Demand
for Dinar
Dinar 50,000

2
↑Deposits
all receipts
in central bank

→3
↓4

↓4

5
↓Quantity of
currency for transacting
real economic activity

↓5

6
↑Demand ≥
Dinar 100,000

↓7   ↓8

Co-operative Venture Relationship between Commercial Bank and Clientele in the Real Economy

Commercial Bank   Needs Dinar 50,000   Needs Dinar 100,000

1
↑Demand
for Dinar 50,000
for real economic
activity
Economy

2
↑

4
↓Quantity
of money
in real economy
= Dinar 50,000
Needs Dinar 50,000

5
↓

7
↓Quantity
of money
in real economy
≥Dinar 100,000
Needs Dinar ≥100,000

8
↓Quantity↓
of money
in real economy
≥Dinar 100,000
Needs Dinar ≥100,000

Figure 10.4 Discursive relationships according to the episteme of unity of knowledge

balance of payments in current and capital accounts are sustained. See below for formalization relating to these.

The 100% RRMS realizes the stability and sustainability of the economy in the midst of a dynamic life-fulfilling regime of development. The otherwise growth-oriented and lifetime cycle of capital accumulation through interest-based savings and economic growth are not the goals. These are replaced by the singular goal of simulating social wellbeing as the criterion for estimating the degree of systemic unity attained between the symbiotic relationships of money, finance, real economy and society explained earlier. The wellbeing function based on dynamic life-fulfilling goods and services becomes the criterion for reading sustainable stability and moral worth through the money-finance-real economy circular causation relationships. The interplay between stages of institutional organization and market transformation explains the circular causation model. That is, the interactive interface is explained by the underlying systemic participatory and institutional discursive relationship between institutions and markets denoted by the circular flows of arrows in Figure 10.4. It implies the principle of pervasive complementarities with diversity.

Economic productivity in 100% RRMS

We need to understand the productivity relation in the 100% RRMS. The usual definition of productivity is now understood in terms of the underlying knowledge-simulation in the 100% RRMS relating to discursive and organic relationships between the central bank, commercial banks (Islamic banks) and the variables of finance and the real economic economy.

Labor productivity is defined by, $\rho_L(k) = Y(k)/L(k)$, where L is a factor input (particularized to labor) in the production function that is now of the form, $Y(k) = F(L,K)$ [k], so that labor L is complementary with capital K through the knowledge variable 'k' that defines the interactive, integrative and dynamically evolutionary processes describing all relationships in the Islamic world-system. Total productivity is defined by $Y(k)$, this being distributed between labor and capital in a complementary way. There now comes about increasing returns to scale in the production function. On a simplified basis, we also note the following production relationships (Choudhury, 1998):

$$\text{Total productivity, } Y(k) = [\rho_L(k).L(k) + \rho_K(k).K(k)]/2.$$

The right-hand side of the above expression is a simulated parameter in terms of a combination of institutional and market forces. Thus, L(k) and K(k) are complementary to each other with respect to the simulation of k-values in the sense of the 100% RRMS.

In the end, we note that in the 100% RRMS the rate of growth currency money equals the rate of growth of output with prices and rates of return on assets remaining stable. The utilization of factors of production is also based on organic complementarities in terms of the unifying relationships between their factor productivities.

Macroeconomic policy implications of micro-money in 100% RRMS

All policies, financing instruments and institutional reformation matters are endogenous in nature by virtue of their learning and knowledge induction derived from the given epistemic premise of unity of knowledge. Thereby, money turns out to be a quantity of currencies that pursues projects. Contrary to the micro-level nature of money-finance-real economy circular causation relationships governed by the principle of complementarities, macroeconomic monetary and fiscal policy instruments remain unnecessary for a detailed understanding of the underlying dynamics of economic projects. Yet, to produce an economic forecast, it may be necessary to consider some macroeconomic models to estimate the general state of the economy.

A sample of projects representing diversified portfolios and the different levels of society could therefore be selected to enable an estimation of the state of the economy concerning money, finance, real economy and social wellbeing. In other words, such estimation is the result of establishing the appropriate kinds of complementary projects upon which the sample estimation can be based and the policy forecasts can be accomplished. The data for such estimation come from the relationship between microeconomic levels of money and real finance.

In our case, unlike the macroeconomic LM-curve of monetary equilibrium, and thereby the IS-curve of fiscal equilibrium, we have a system of circular causation between the variables. These help to generate pervasive and new levels of heightened complementarities together with the 100% RRMS attaining its heightened state of money-finance-real economy complementarities. The implications of the participatory policy variables and of the epistemic premise of unity of knowledge are implied.[10]

The income multiplier results in the two cases are quite different. According to the IS-LM General Macroeconomic Equilibrium, interest rates limit the output variables to attain the full-employment real GDP. In the case of 100% RRMS, the prototype of the monetary equilibrium and expenditure variables follow positive trends by the force of learning (k). The two trajectories are thereby simultaneously described by evolutionary learning equilibriums (Choudhury, 2008).

In conventional IS-LM shifts, a similar trajectory would be described by simultaneous shifts in the general equilibrium under the impact of productive spending and monetary expansion. This result is consistent with either a lower level of interest rate or a low level of liquidity traps where the interest rate remains low (Venieris and Sebold, 1977). Contrary to such shifts, the effects of real values of spending and GDP would be dampened by the increasing real rate of interest. The stabilizing effect of lower prime rates of interest is known to be effective for economic stimulation across the world during times of financial volatility and economic crisis.

Short- and long-term implications of policy simulation

The coterminous evolution of investment and quantity of money curves in the 100% RRMS, and thereby, the positive relationship between financing instruments and the real GDP are principally influenced by the impact of 'k'. Thereby, the question of short- and long-term adjustment in the investment-money relationships with respect to the real rate of return ('r') and real output (Y) is resolved by the simulation of these relationships in respect of 'r'-values.

Figure 10.5 shows that, in one case, the adjustment to evolutionary general equilibrium between money and investment (ee) in respect of (r, Y)[k] causes the investment curve to adjust towards the money curve with expanding levels of $(r,Y)[k]$. In another case, an equivalent adjustment is caused by the money curve adjusting towards the investment curve with expanding levels of $(r,Y)[k]$. Note the evolutionary learning equilibrium path is e'e'.

These adjustments mean, respectively, that the quantity of money in excess of investment first causes the central bank to hold the unmobilized funds (S) as the 100% reserve. Subsequently, as r increases in the real economy causing Y to increase by the complementary effect, then investment demand increases. This call for additional funds liquidates the withheld reserve in the central bank. Now the difference between the quantity of money and investment demand falls as $(r,Y)[k]$ increases by the money-investment, money, finance and real economy complementarities.[11]

The equilibrium towards E_1 from the region M_1 being in excess of I_1 is explained as follows: The excess of investment demand over the quantity of money available to finance it suppresses 'r'. Consequently, Y also decreases, until the complementary relationship between money and investment (i.e. between money, finance and the real economy) is established at the equilibrium point E_1.

Second, the way towards simulated evolutionary equilibriums by the force of learning (k) is for M to adjust towards I. This happens when an excess demand for investment either liquidates the quantity of money in reserve (S) with the central bank in 100% RRMS, or creates new money to finance it. Now $(r,Y)[k]$ increases along such adjustment, as in the first case. The equilibrium adjustment at E_1 from the region of I > M can be explained as in the first case.

The process continues until the equilibrium E_1 is established, only to evolve into subsequent levels of similar evolutionary E's (as shown), established by the shifting investment and money curves under the impact of evolution into higher learning processes under the greater effects of complementarities, institutional change and diversification of production (technologically induced production menus) and financial risk (new financial instruments).

The evolutionary processes (along the trajectories ee and e'e') are the consequences of continuous learning. Every such process is the result of short-term learning and adjustment. Therefore, there is no tenable concept of the long-term (across evolutionary processes) which remains independent of the short-term (intra-process) learning.

The evolutionary equilibrium path is now shown in Figure 10.5. It remains fairly coterminous between I and M curves under the monotonically positive impact of learning that causes unity of relationships (complementarities) between money, finance and real economy symbiotic interactions.

The equations of relationships between M, I in terms of $(k,r,Y)[k]$ are of the following form: I = b.M yields r = f(k,Y). Hence we have the $(r,Y)[k]$ coordinates. The curves connecting these coordinates yield the investment and money curves as shown. The evolutionary equilibrium adjustment between these (Δ) is equivalent to the money, finance and real economy complementarities as the sure conceptual and applied sign of unity of knowledge in this world-system. This can be obtained only in the presence of participatory financing instruments that replace interest rates. The reconstructive circular causation relationships between the organic variables indicate the transformation to be brought about by activating relevant institutional changes and adopting policy strategies towards attaining all of them.

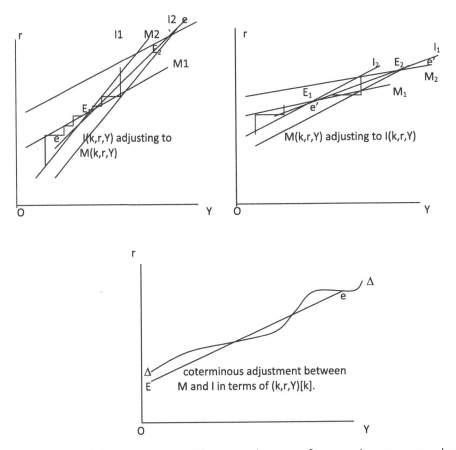

Figure 10.5 Evolutionary learning equilibriums in the money-finance-real economy complementary relationships

Conclusion

The economic and financial paradigms upon which the world had stood for quite sometime first lost its validity during the Great Depression. It then required the philosophical and insightful acumen of John Maynard Keynes to rescue economic theory from its inability to stabilize the fallen economy out of the desuetude of neoclassical economic and financial theory. Now the world has come to face another bitter reality. This is marked by the emptiness of all of economic theory towards addressing the sustainability issue of the global economy, which is teetering in financial and economic crisis. The very high cost of using tax-payers' money to rescue big banks, insurance companies and non-banking financial companies from bankruptcy has already proved that the high finance and macroeconomic ideas of so-called 'economic fundamentals' are flawed, even after Keynes and government protection by deficit financing and expansionary monetary and fiscal policies.

We have argued in this chapter that a thorough rethinking of both economic theory and its application must be undertaken to create a sustainable world-system of money, finance and real economy with the objective of attaining social wellbeing.

We have argued this theme and constructed alternative economic and financial argumentation in the light of the episteme of systemic unity of knowledge. We asked the question: Where is such an abiding episteme to be found, one that stands upon learning by pervasive complementarities between variables and agents and activates institutional changes to attain such systemic unity? We discovered that possibility of systemic unity in the Islamic worldview. It rests on the functional ontology of divine oneness in the order of 'everything'. Upon this epistemic background and its functional ontology a brave new world of economic and financial reconstruction was proposed for attaining social wellbeing as a criterion signifying the measure of systemic unity between the good choices of life.

The challenge of replacing interest rate instrument by participatory instruments of cooperation and organic complementarities and its various implications on money-finance-real economy relationships, and sustainability by discursive learning was formalized. This is the field of epistemological understanding and application of the paradigm of Islamic economics and finance in the light of its core episteme of divine oneness across learning domains of human experience.

Statistical appendix: Data on critical financial crisis indicators

The following information is gathered from Wikipedia (internet version) entitled 'Subprime mortgage crisis':

During the period 2007–2008

1.3 million properties were subject to foreclosure, up 79% since 2006. The value of US subprime mortgages amounted to USD1.3 trillion as of March 2007. Of this, 16% of the subprime loans were 90-days delinquent and declared for foreclosure. By January 2008, the delinquent rate had risen to 21% and by May 2008, it was 25%. By August 2008, this value also amounted to 9.2% delinquent and foreclosed loans out of USD12 trillion value of US mortgage market. During 2007, approx. 1.3 trillion US properties were up for foreclosure. This was an increase of 79% above the level for 2006. Taking advantage of low subprime rates and the foreign investments that were flowing into the US into the housing and mortgage market an average homeowner increased loans on housing property to 130% of household income in 2007. The 'greed'-driven preferences of the average American caused household spending to stand at USD 800 billion per year in excess of earned incomes. Household debt thus grew from USD680 billion in 1974 to USD14 trillion in 2008.

By March 2008, the value of mortgage payments by an average homeowner in 8.8 million homeowners exceeded the value of the housing property. This caused the incentive by owners to declare foreclosure. As a resulting, a record 4 million houses remained unsold and another 2.9 million remained vacant by January 2008. The excess supply of unsold and vacant houses caused an 18.4% drop in average house prices between November 2007 and May 2008. The securitized share of subprime mortgages among poor credit owners increased from 54% in 2001 to 75% in 2006.

The losses of banks and other financial institutions globally equaled USD435 billion as of July 2008. The US Housing Department and the banks issued low-interest loans to homebuyers in the face of expected loan default. Thus, many financial institutions borrowed enormous amounts of money and made enormous investments in mortgage-backed securities between 2004 and 2007. The top five US investment banks borrowed at low rates and loaned amounts at higher rates (financial leverage) to the amount of USD4.1 trillion (by borrowing) during 2007. This equaled 30% of the US economy.

On September 14, 2008 George Bush announced a banking bailout fund and subprime mortgage assistance amounting up to USD700 billion. On October 10, 2008, the Dow-Jones Index declined by a record 22% – the worst week in its 118-year history.

Between January 1, 2008 and October 10, 2008 owners of stocks in US corporations suffered a total loss of USD8 trillion, from USD20 trillion to USD12 trillion. In other countries, losses amounted to 40% of their stock value. On September 29, the Dow-Jones Index tumbled 7%, the worst in its history. NASDAQ tumbled 9.1% and S&P was down by 8.8%. These declining trends continued well beyond this date as sales reports and industrial production statistics, together with fears of a long and deep recession, continued.

Notes

1 Reproduced from the M.A. Choudhury's paper, "The Islamic panacea to global financial predicament: a new financial architecture", *Journal Hadhari, an International Journal*, 2:2, 2010.

2 Bakar (1999, p. 32) writes: "Rationalism is false not because it seeks to express reality in rational mode, so far as this is possible, but because it seeks to embrace the whole of reality in the realm of reason, as if the latter coincides with the very principle of things. ... the very rational faculty is placed at the disposal of faith or revelation in the sense that it is called upon to present and expound the contents of Revelation in a rational manner to the best degree possible, whereas in modern thought it has been used to rebel against truth claims which lie outside its cognitive competence."

3 Let Y_0 denote GDP at time t = 0,1,2,...; s_t denote saving ratio at time t = 0,1,2,...; g denote a constant growth rate of GDP at time t = 0,1,2,...

Disposable income after saving at time t = 0 is $Y_0(1-s)$, which increases to national income Y_1 at time t =1. $Y_1 = Y_0(1-s)(1+g)$. Likewise, $Y_t = Y_0 \cdot (1+g)^t (1-s)^t$.

Now consider, $\partial Y_t / \partial s = -t Y_0 \cdot (1+g)^t (1-s)^{t-1} < 0$

$$\partial Y_t / \partial g = t Y_0 \cdot (1-s)^t (1+g)^{t-1} > 0$$

only due to the positive effect of g but dampened by the negative effect of s.

The above results remain true irrespective of a moment of time and in the continuous sense. Besides, the argument that a higher volume of savings would grow into more resources for investment in the future contradicts the fact that at any moment of time that volume of savings is a resource withdrawal. That amount of potential resource could otherwise have been used to perpetuate economic growth and thereby development and social wellbeing.

4 *Qur'an* (36:36): "Glory is to Him, Who has created all in pairs of that which the earth produces, as well as of their (own) human kind, and of that which they know not."

5 The design of pervasively connected and diversely rich world-system is one that is morally induced by laws, reason and directions to create wellbeing and plenty. On this, the *Qur'an* (14:24–25) declares: "See you not how *Allah* sets forth a parable? A goodly word like a goodly tree, whose root is firmly fixed, and its branches (reach) to the sky, giving its fruit at all times, by the leave of its Lord, and Allah sets forth parables for mankind in order that they may remember."

6 Buchanan (1990) writes, "If we can disregard the revival of fundamentalism, notably in Islam, we can refer to this century as one "without God.""

7 Heilbroner (1985, p. 146) writes, "The structural logic of accumulation therefore begins from the powerful tendency of capital to develop its productive forces – a tendency we are familiar with as an integral aspect of the M-C-M' circuit."

8 A formal version of the above schema is this:

1	2	3	4	5	6
$\{\theta,Pr(\theta)\}=\{k\}$	$\rho\{k\}=\rho$	$\{k,x(k),\rho\}=\{k,z(k)\}$	repeat (3) for a three-sector model, {money M(k)), finance real economy, institutions} = x(k) Thus the relationships {k,z(k)}	simulate wellbeing W(k,z(k)) subject to circular causation between {k,z(k)}=vector by discourse and logical formalism.	policy and prescription on change in structure

9 Let total quantity of money (M^*) equal the money in circulation (M) and the amount not mobilized and remaining in savings with the central bank (S). Let G denote the quantity of gold as asset to support the value of currency in savings with the central bank.

We write, therefore, $M^* = M + S$. This is similar to the equation of total reserve = cash in vault + statutory reserve. But, in our case, S is a residual, not a policy requirement by the central bank.

With the gold standard, $S/G = a = (M^* - M)/G = (M^*/G) + (M/G)$.

The coefficient 'a' is a policy variable to set the quantity of gold required to shore the unmobilized funds that stays with the central bank, so that it does not create multiple credit creation if it were to stay with the commercial bank. The multiple credit creation is a subtle mechanism to create excess amount of money and unleash interbank lending interest rate.

As an assigned coefficient, 'a' gives $da = 0$. That is, $d(M/G) = d(M^*/G)$. This result implies that stability by gold-backing of the money in circulation equals the stability of total quantity of money. Hence the stock of gold used to stabilize the value of S also stabilizes the quantity of money in circulation.

10 At the background of simulating the complementarities between the variables of social wellbeing function are the two particular equations on money (M) and expenditure (I), respectively. These are namely,

$$M(k) = f_1(k^+,,F^+,I^+,P^\pm)[k],$$
$$I(k) = f_2(k^+,,F^+,M^+,P^\pm)[k].$$

All variables were defined earlier.

According to the banking relations of 100%RRMS, $I(k) = b.M(k)$, b being a coefficient. This relationship is true at each level of learning estimated by 'k'. Besides, the continuity of 'k' takes place over time. Hence, $I(k) = b.M(k)$ everywhere along 'k' and time, with $b \to 1$ as financial resources get fully mobilized by commercial banks. Note that, because of the microeconomic nature of spending relations, the idea of fiscal expansion is not limited to government expenditure. Hence we have subsumed all forms of spending in the good things of life in the variable 'I'. The LM and IS curves are elastically convergent in tandem to the extent that the policy variables and institutional transformation strategic variables (P) are activated to attain better states of the 100%RRMS. They revolve around the attainment of effective participatory development-financing variables.

11 Let $\Delta = |M-I|$, then $d\Delta/dk = (\partial\Delta/\partial Y).(dY/dk) + (\partial\Delta/\partial r).(dr/dk) < 0$ by the equilibrating effect of equilibrium. Since, k affects positively both Y and r, therefore, $dY/dk > 0$; $dr/dk > 0$. By the equilibrium effect, $(\partial\Delta/\partial Y)$ and $(\partial\Delta/\partial r)$ must be individually negative.

References

Abdullah, F. Hassan, T. and Mohamad, S. (2007). "Investigation of performance of Malaysian Islamic unit trust funds: comparison with conventional unit trust funds", *Managerial Finance*, 33:2, pp. 142–53.

Acikgenc, A. (1995). "The indefinability of being", in *Being and Existence in Sadra and Heidegger, a Comparative Ontology*, pp. 19–21, International Institute of Islamic Thought and Civilization, Kuala Lumpur, Malaysia.

Al-Ghazali, A.H. [Imam] trans. Karim, F. (n.d.). "Earnings, trade and commerce", in *Imam Ghazali's Ihya Ulum-Id-Din, Book. II*, pp. 53–96, Book Lovers Bureau, Lahore, Pakistan.

Ali, A. (1992). "Technology transfer in manufacturing industries via direct foreign investment", *Journal of Economic Cooperation among Islamic Countries*, 13:3–4, July/October, pp. 137–59

Allouche, A. (1994). *Mamluk Economics: A Study and Translation of Al-Maqrizi's Ighatah*, especially the chapter, "Currency", University of Utah Press, Salt Lake City, Utah.

Bakar, O. (1999). *The History and Philosophy of Islamic Science*, Islamic Text Society, Cambridge, UK.

Becker, G.S. (1989). "Family", in J. Eatwell, M. Milgate, M. and P. Newman (eds), *The New Palgrave: Social Economics*, pp. 64–76, W.W. Norton, New York, NY.

Bordo, M.D. (1989). "The contribution of *A Monetary History of the United States, 1867–1960* to Monetary History", in *Money, History, and International Finance: Essays in Honor of Anna J. Schwartz*, pp. 15–78, The University of Chicago Press, Chicago, IL.

Braudel, F. (1995). *A History of Civilizations*, Penguin Books, New York, NY.

Buchanan, J.M. (1990). "Socialism is dead but leviathan lives on", the *John Bonython Lecture*, CIS Occasional paper 30, pp. 1–9, Centre for Independent Studies, Sydney, Australia.

Buchanan, J.M. (1999). "The domain of constitutional economics", in *The Collected Works of James M. Buchanan, The Logical Foundations of Constitutional Liberty*, pp. 377–95, Liberty Press, Indianapolis, IN.

Choudhury, M.A. (1997). "The theory of endogenous money in comparative Islamic perspectives", in *Money in Islam*, pp. 38–70, Routledge, London, UK.

Choudhury, M.A. (1998). "The institutional basis of reformation: organizational theory of the firm", in *Reforming the Muslim World*, pp. 105–44, Kegan Paul International, London, UK.

Choudhury, M.A. (1999). "Resource Mobilization and development Goals for Islamic Banks", *Proceedings of the Second Harvard University Forum on Islamic Finance: "Islamic Finance into the 21st Century"*, Harvard Islamic Finance and Investment Program, Center for Middle Eastern Studies, Harvard University, Boston, MA.

Choudhury, M.A. (2004). *The Islamic World-System: a study in polity-market interaction*, Routledge Curzon, London, UK.

Choudhury, M.A. (2006). "Evolutionary equilibrium in learning spaces of unity of knowledge", *Middle East Business and Economic Review*, 18:2, pp. 39–53.

Choudhury, M.A. (2008). "Islamic dinar and 100 percent Reserve Requirement Monetary System", *International Journal of Management Studies*, 15:2, pp. 1–18.

CNNMoney.com "Bernanke's speech on economic conditions" (Oct. 7, 2008) (http://money.cnn.com/2008/10/07/news/economy,bernanke_remarks)

Dunning, J.H. (2004). "The moral imperatives of global capitalism: an overview", in Dunning, J.H. (ed.), *Making Globalization Good*, pp. 11–40, Oxford University Press, Oxford, UK.

Fitzpatrick, T. (2003). "Postmodernism and new directions", in Alcock, P. Erskine, A. and May, M. (eds), *Social Policy*, pp. 126–33, Blackwell, Oxford, UK.

Foucault, M. trans. A.M. Sheridan (1972). *The Archeology of Knowledge and the Discourse on Language*, Harper Torchbooks, New York, NY.

Gruber, T.R. (1993). "A translation approach to portable ontologies", *Knowledge Acquisition*, 5:2, 199–200.

Hammond, P.J. (1989). "On reconciling Arrow's theory of social choice with Harsanyi's Fundamental Utilitarianism", in G.R. Feiwel (ed.), *Arrow and the Foundation of the Theory of Economic Policy*, pp. 179–221, Macmillan, London, UK.

Hayek, F.A. (1990, reprint). "The use of knowledge in society", in M.C. Spechler (ed.) *Perspectives in Economic Thought*, pp. 183–200, McGraw-Hill, New York, NY.

Heilbroner, R.L. (1985). *The Nature and Logic of Capitalism*, W.W. Norton, New York, NY.

Henderson, J.M. and Quandt, R.E. (1971). "Pareto optimality in general", in *Microeconomic Theory, a Mathematical Approach*, pp. 259–62, McGraw-Hill, New York, NY.

Hegel, G.W.F. (1956). *The Philosophy of History*, J. Sibree (trans.), Dover Publications, New York, NY.

Hegel, G.W.F. trans. Dyke, S.W. (1996). "Conception of the philosophy of right", in *Philosophy of Right*, pp. 1–32, Prometheus Books, Amherst, NY.

Ibn Qayyim, see Islahi, A.A. on *Ibn Taimiyah*.

Islahi, A.A. (1988). "Ibn Taimiyah's concept of money and monetary policy", in his *Economic Concepts of Ibn Taimiyah*, pp. 139–43, The Islamic Foundation, Leicester, UK.

Jomo, K.S. (1992). "Manufacturing growth and employment", *Journal of Economic Cooperation among Islamic Countries*, 13:3–4.

Kahn, C-S, *World Economic Forum link 2* (1/27/2008).

Kirzner, I. (1997). "Entrepreneurial discovery and the competitive market process: an Austrian approach", *Journal of Economic Literature*, XXXV:1, 60–85.

Lauchlin, C. (2004). "The 100 percent reserve plan", *Journal of Economic Studies*, 31:3/4, pp. 355–65.

Mankiw, G. (Dec. 22, 2007). "How to avoid a recession", *Economist's View* (internet version).

Mankiw, G. (Oct. 8, 2008). "How to recapitalize the financial system", (http://cgi.stanford.edu/group/wais/cgi-bin/?p=21187) and Mankiw's blog: (http://gregmankiw.blogspot.com)

Masud, M.K. (1995). *Shatibi's Philosophy of Islamic Law*, Islamic Research Institute, Islamabad, Pakistan.

Minogue, K. (1963). "The moral character of liberalism", in his *The Liberal Mind*, pp. 166–74, Liberty Fund, Indianapolis, IN.

Myrdal, G. (1968). "The wider field of valuations", pp. 71–125 in his *The Asian Drama, an Inquiry into the Poverty of Nations*, Pantheon, New York, NY.

Mydin, A.K. and Larbani, M. (2004). "The gold dinar: the next component in Islamic economics, banking and finance", *Review of Islamic Economics*, 8:1, pp. 5–34.

Noor, H.M. (1998). "Razi's human needs theory and its relevance to ethics and economics", *Humanomics: International Journal of Systems and Ethics*, 14, 1, pp. 59–96.

O'Donnell, R.M. (1989). *Keynes: Philosophy, Economics and Politics*, Macmillan, London, UK.

Rozenthal, F. (1958). *Ibn Khaldun's the Muqaddimah: An Introduction to History*, 3 vols. Routledge and Kegan Paul, London, UK.

Sen, A. (1989). "Justice", in Eatwell, J. Milgate, M. and Newman, P. (eds), *New Palgrave: Social Economics*, pp. 181–89, W.W. Norton, New York, NY.

Shackle, G.L.S. (1972). *Epistemics and Economics*, Cambridge University Press, Cambridge, UK.

Sklair, L. (2002). *Globalization, Capitalism and Its Alternatives*, Oxford University Press, Oxford, UK.

Smith, A. [1790] (eds), Raphael, D.D. and Mackie, A.L. (reprint 1976). *The Theory of Moral Sentiments*, Clarendon Press, Oxford, UK.

Spechler, M. (1990). "Marxism and neo-Marxism", in *Perspectives in Economic Thought*, pp. 111–65, McGraw-Hill, Inc., New York, NY.

Taylor, O.H. (1967). "The future of economic liberalism", in *Economics and Liberalism*, pp. 294–311, Harvard University Press, Cambridge, MA.

Venieris, Y.P. and Sebold, F.D. (1977). "Liquidity trap", pp. 274–79 in *Macroeconomics, Models and Policy*, John Wiley and Sons, New York, NY.

Ventelou, B. (2005). "Economic thought on the eve of the General Theory", in *Millennial Keynes*, Chapter 2, Armonk, M.E. Sharpe, New York, NY.

Wikipedia (Oct. 2008). http://en.wikipedia.org/wiki/Financial_crisis

Chapter 11

The Possibility of Islamic Financial Economics and Islamic Banking

A Post-Orthodoxy Criticism

Abstract

This chapter investigates the current status of intellection in Islamic economics and finance and current practice by Islamic banks to discover whether this field as it has developed in contemporary times has any epistemological basis that can provide a revolutionary contribution to academia. An extensive review of the field of economic orthodoxy and, within that, Islamic financial economics, reveals that the latter is still contained within mainstream reasoning. Islamic financial economics has thereby failed to project its distinctively new methodology. Mainstream economics comprising neoclassical, Keynesian, monetarist, Austrian, and evolutionary institutional paradigms are examined against the backdrop of a freshly new heterodox economic structure that Islamic financial economics has the potential to provide if premised on its true epistemological foundations. However, this is not what has happened. Yet the predicament of Islamic financial economics is true only as it presently stands without an explained episteme. If Islamic financial economics were to be studied on the basis of its foundational epistemology of the monotheistic worldview and the methodical formalism that arises from it, then it has tremendous potential in the field of a truly socio-scientific revolution. Islamic financial economics then becomes a fresh socio-scientific thinking with profound applications. It can then find its place in the intellectual annals by its universality and uniqueness.

Objective

The chapter will critically examine the present state of Islamic financial economics within mainstream economics. It argues that, while the intellectual discipline of economics has been investigating the possibility of a heterodox school, Islamic financial economics, as it stands today, has failed to contribute any such challenging dimension. It has simply remained a minor addition within financial economic orthodoxy. This also extends to the associated discipline of so-called Islamic finance and Islamic banking.

This chapter points out that this intellectual gap in Islamic financial economics has occured because of the absence of any epistemological scholarship arising from a methodological understanding and its application of the principles laid down in the cardinal Islamic worldview. This worldview is of the monotheistic law in which most religions and people believe. It is the methodological derivation and the imminent methodical formalism arising from this, which remains absent. The chapter takes a critical look at present-day Islamic financial economics as a mainstream field searching for its identity; it then looks at the construct of the true monotheistic epistemological worldview, its methodical formal derivation, and the selected economic applications resting on such epistemological foundation. It is argued that, on the basis of such an authentic academic approach, Islamic financial economics can indeed become a distinctive scientific revolution.

I will start by referring to an important quote from Tony Lawson and Hashem Pesaran (1989, p. 1) which questions the scholarship of orthodox economic reasoning in the context of economic and social reality. They write:

> When a field of study becomes marked by dissatisfaction and disillusionment, methodological analyses and debates tend to become prominent and often provide pointers to faithful directions for the subject to move in. Economics is currently undergoing just such a period of crisis.

The questioning invokes epistemological and ontological arguments under the guise of critical realism to search for newer grounds of economic and social worldviews

A massive exclusion from economics has been the holistic worldview of embedding economics within the ethical and social perspective. Thus, ethics and morality have been divorced from economics and financial science. The greater the relationship of money, finance, real economy, and evolutionary learning by multi-causality between these variables and their diversities, has remained foreign to economic science until very recently. On the other hand, such a holistic embedded study of the financial economy forms the essential nature of Islamic financial economy.

A central keynote of post-orthodoxy debates and criticisms rests on the need for the moral, ethical, and social embedding of economic reasoning. This element in traditional economic reasoning was abandoned as economics took as its focus analytical specialization without social embedding. Holton (1992), borrowing the social embedding praxis from Polanyi (1957), sees the need for the economic worldview to be a study of social embeddedness. The differentiated perspective of economic reasoning is abandoned as it has been carried out in the name of specialization and a claim for distinction as science (Blaug, 1968). So, the rumbling debate claiming economics as a distinct specialized scientific discipline is not new.

The question that remains to be investigated is the new epistemological praxis that heterodox economic reasoning raises. The question is a wide one; for even the inception of economic theory over the ages has not remained independent of the value judgment of the proponents of the different schools of economic thought. Schumpeter writes (1968): "Economic analysis has not been shaped at any time by the philosophical opinions that economists happen to have." But this opinion was not sustained in the course of Schumpeter's bible of economic thought. Likewise, the argument for the moral and social embedding of economics in the present age of globalization raises serious voices. On this issue are the subtle words of Hazel Henderson (1999, p. 56): "... The good news is that this is forcing us to 'go inside ourselves' and ask some pretty basic questions. What do I want to pay attention to? Who am I and what do I want written on my tombstone? Such basic defensive reactions will define the growing sectors of our Attention Economies and their inexorable shift from material goods (measured by traditional GNP/GDP per capita), to services and more tangible factors in living standards, measured by the new Quality of Life scorecards."

The project of heterodox economic reasoning now rests on the new epistemological derivation, formalism, and application of a new body of thought which addresses economic issues and problems as moral and social embedding. Sen refers to such an approach of economics in the wider issues of social valuation as "deontological economics". The issues of preferences, choices, and objective criteria of economic theory within its social embedding are now examined accordingly. When such fundamental axioms are raised to oppose the postulates of rational choice, then the very foundation of economic reasoning is questioned. Such a fundamental reconstruction of the epistemological praxis moves into a new foundation for economic choices and human behavior. Even the methodology of microeconomics and macroeconomics as two distinct branches of economic theory is called into question. This is also taking place in the heterodox area of economic theory as it shapes the new epistemic approaches in theoretical physics between relativity physics and quantum mechanics. A path towards unification and harmonization is sought (Lee and Lavoie, 2013, p. 109; Hawking, 1988)

The possibility of heterodox economics needs to be answered on the basis of an epistemological argument, formalism, analytics, and applications, given the heterodox worldview (Laclau, 1996). Taken together, these do not escape the domain of scientific inquiry. Subjectivity must be replaced by objective criterion, without sacrificing the scope for the moral and social embedding of the new economic science. Feiwel (1987, pp. 1–115) remarked on why mainstream economic theory, despite its many failures in explaining reality from the institutional and policy realism, was still successful, while traditional economic historicism remained unsuccessful.

A similar kind of heterodox offshoot was Marxist political economy. It wanted to address the theme of social justice by the process of social collectivization. The procedural part of Marxist theory in explaining an epistemological prognosis of capitalism and asserting the economics of socialism (Marxism) was a fine work that was later expounded in terms of evolutionary social beliefs (Resnick and Wolff 1987; Sztompka, 1991). Yet, as Hayek points out, it is such ebullient ideas in sociological theory that made it dysfunctional while denying even alternative constructs replacing rational choice. In the same way, the grandiose moral treatise of Adam Smith in his *Theory of Moral Sentiments* faded away in his *Wealth of Nations* (Coase, 1994).

The emergence of Islamic financial economic reasoning: post-orthodoxy heterodox thought

Among the kinds of heterodox developments in the field of economics, markedly Marxism, post-Keynesianism, deontological economics, and the ontological project of economics by Lawson and his group (EJPE, 2009), there has arisen the field of Islamic financial economics. One starts by critically examining this new field of economic reasoning in terms of its possibility. As mentioned above, without the substantive groundwork of establishing the components of possibility, any such heterodox discussion remains an unsustainable exercise. The essential theme of social embedding explained in this chapter is unfit to explain realism, if it is not properly understood in the current heterodox discussion.

First, therefore, we define the scope of Islamic financial economics, as it has endeavored to survive during the last 100 years, if we are to look back at the resilient beginnings of Islamic economic thought among its scholastic past (Ghazanfar, 1991; Islahi, 1988). Islamic financial economics, conceived as a social science, is aimed at the broader field of moral valuation which must be embedded in economic and social domains. This wider field of valuation comprises the moral domain of 'good' choices found to arise from the verdicts of the *Qur'an* and the *sunnah* (prophetic guidance). A discursive process over the rules so derived in the context of the generality and particulars of issues and problems employs the rational process of human involvement in discoursing the rules derived from the *Qur'an* and the *sunnah* on diverse matters of choices in the 'good things of life'. This forms the groundwork of Islamic law, the *shari'ah*. The field of *shari'ah* is thus established by the objective and purpose of the moral choices to enhance the wellbeing of all in a codetermined way (*maqasid as-shari'ah*).

The above definition is a broad one by way of the vision of Islamic financial economics as a body of thought that extends the embedded moral and social inquiry of economic issues and problems in the wider field of the monotheistic law (*Tawhid*). Monotheism derived from the *Qur'an* and the *sunnah* becomes the ontological framework of all intellection and application in Islamic thought. Yet, by itself, this ontological premise is not fully functional without transmission via the edicts of discourse, formalism, analytics, and application in the wider context of the law of monotheism, bereft of metaphysical speculation, and aimed at the morally and socially embedded economic world-system.

While the vision of Islamic financial economics is generally described by the above-mentioned perspectives, this has not happened in reality. As it exists today, the *possibility* as opposed to the *vision* of Islamic financial economics is only known to be epistemologically premised in, but not formalized by, the explication of the monotheistic ontology. To address the *possibility of Islamic financial economics* as a field of heterodox economics we use the schema shown in Figure 11.1. We then disintegrate this schema to bring out the various unified components that can establish Islamic financial economics in its distinctive form of a truly heterodox domain of socio-scientific reasoning. This will ultimately be followed by a cursory explanation as to why the underlying epistemic methodology of Islamic financial economics as heterodox socio-scientific inquiry forms a universal and unique logical formalism premised on the *functional*[1] ontology of the monotheistic law.

The advent of the Islamic economic project in its contemporary form premised its reasoning in the nature of Step 1.

Step I:

Monotheism $\rightarrow$ *shari'ah* $\rightarrow$ application to world affairs $\rightarrow$ continuity   (11.1)

The scholarly developments that took place under Step 1 can be sensed in its almost random borrowing from mainstream or traditional thought in both Muslim and other schools. The writings represent the expressions of individuals on the basis of their own understanding of the themes without relying on a premise of epistemic argumentation and construction of challenging scholarly thought. Popular writings without the epistemological challenge can be found in the works of Chapra (1992),

Step 1:

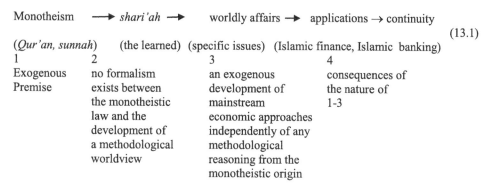

Figure 11.1 Phenomenological continuity of the monotheistic law

Siddiqi's works (online, 2013); and present day articles published in the *Review of Islamic Economics*. My own earlier works, excluding those of the last twenty years, were also of the hardcore neoclassical origin (Choudhury, 1986). Yet my current contributions have increasingly expressed dismay with these other approaches. I have now adopted the essentially epistemological content, with applications for the foundations of Islamic financial economics and world-system within the socio-scientific argumentation (Choudhury, 2013a). Much of the writing in Islamic economics today was critically examined by Mahomedy (2013).

The failure of Islamic financial economics as a socio-scientific inquiry has been due to the decline of the universal methodological formulation and the rise of a unique thinking arising from the universality roots of functional ontology. We mean here to show the possibility of Islamic financial economics by using the monotheistic law and the cardinal principle of Islamic world-system studies. It is in this light that a most credible foundation for scientific revolution can be laid down. The emergence of the methodological understanding and application of the monotheistic law in the *Qur'an*, known as *Tawhid*, would be of the nature of non-cumulative knowledge. Yet it would present a scientific revolution beyond being simply a paradigm. Thomas Kuhn (1970, p. 154) wrote on this point: "scientific revolutions are here taken to be those non-cumulative development episodes in which an older paradigm is replaced in whole or in part by an incompatible new one." Kuhn (p. 68) continues: "Such changes, together with the controversies that almost always accompany them, are the defining characteristics of scientific revolution."

The epistemological divide is projected in Figure 11.1 by the discontinuous nature of transmission and recursion between parts (1), (2), and (3). Thereby, the whole Figure 11.1 in light of the existing pursuit of Islamic financial economic thinking crumbles into pieces of discontinuous reasoning, formalism, analytics, and application. The Islamic financial economic project has moved forward using this kind of dissociative thinking. Consequently, no actualization of Islamic financial economics took place in the world of learning. Its applications to Islamic finance and banking remained mere expressions of avoidance of interest rates and their replacement with participatory financing instruments. Yet the inter-causality between participatory financing instruments, interest rates, and the greater moral, social, and development design was never understood, never formalized, and never applied.

It is a common complaint today that there are no higher educational institutions that would adopt a recognized field of Islamic financial economics and socio-scientific study beyond adapting to mainstream medium (Faruqi, 1982) with an Islamic palliative, not an originality (Rahman, 1988). The drawing boards of all major Islamic activities today fail to consciously recognize the great monotheistic understanding beyond simply a religious sanctimony. Among such leading platforms are the following: The learned conferences (International Conference in Islamic financial economics, ICIEs), the failed development outlook of the Islamic Development Bank (IDB) beyond mere financing of country projects, and the mainstream economic researche of the Islamic Research and Training Center of the IDB. The pedagogy and research programs of institutions of higher learning worldwide have all contributed to a stalemate in Islamic financial economics as a universal and unique heterodox discipline. This will have severe consequences for the world of learning beyond religious stricture. This epistemic challenge and its appropriate understanding, application, and sustainable continuity was not embraced by the traditional or the contemporary fields of Islamic financial economics, once they used rationalist groundwork to explain reality.

Some examples can be examined here in respect of the failure of Islamic financial economics and socio-scientific inquiry into the world of learning and applications. The time-trend of the rates of return (turn-over rates) and commercial interest rates and central bank rates (= prime rates) points to the absence of inter-causal relationships between Islamic participatory rates and interest rates. Yet the study of inter-causal relationships between these critical variables is essential to understand the organic evolutionary learning design of processes of social transformation into an Islamic economic community by an effective inverse relationship between Islamic participatory financing instruments and the rate of interest.

Even the global Islamic banking portfolio remains poorly diversified and non-complementary. Choudhury has argued that the concentration of Islamic funds has long been in *murabaha* and *musharakah*. There is now a growing increase of risky ventures in Islamic bonds called *sukuk*. All of these instruments defy the principle of inter-instrument links, which is otherwise so much needed to establish sustainability out of the organic unification of inter-causal relationships between financial instruments and real activities. The implication, then, is of a deepening failure of interaction and integration between the various parts of Figure 11.1, even as Islamic financial economics has evolved.

Islamic erudition and Islamic finance and banking are proving to be highly popular. Even the Vatican has commented on this issue (Bloomberg, Marc 4, 2009): "The ethical principles on which Islamic finance is based may bring banks closer to their clients and to the true spirit which should mark every financial service." The problem arises in the worldview, mobilization, and management of the Islamic way of using finance for the common good. This rests on the proper intellection in the Islamic methodological worldview of the monotheistic law and in explaining its formal and applied functioning in the world-system. Pope Benedict XVI, in a speech on 7 October 2015, reflected on the crashing financial markets saying that "money vanishes, it is nothing" and concluded that "the only solid reality is the word of God". The study of the circular relationship between money, the real economy, and the common good comprises a theme that is close to the epistemic community of true Islamic economic thought under *Tawhid*.

Step 2

Imam Ghazali as microeconomist

Looking back at the history of economic thought, we find original thinking among Muslims of the scholastic period. Some of these arose from the epistemic roots of the *Qur'an* and the *sunnah*; others from the rationalist roots of Greek thought, mixed up with the *Qur'anic* episteme and rationalist thinking (Qadri, 1988).

Ghazali (see Karim, n.d.) wrote incisively against the Muslim school of rationalist thought concerning monotheism and the world-system (Ghazali trans. Marmura, 1997, p. 217).[2] Indeed, Islam and rationalism are opposed to each other in the monotheistic worldview. The challenge for Islamic socio-scientific reasoning, specifically Islamic financial economics, is to formulate a methodological worldview which, on the one hand denies the rationalist approach to epistemology and formalism, but on the other hand, leads to the use of the monotheistic law on morally embedded perspectives of the economy driven by the good things of life. These comprise the goods and services belonging to *shari'ah* referred to as *maqasid as-shari'ah*, as mentioned earlier. The contributions of the Islamic scholastic thinkers were deeply epistemological in nature. Imam Ghazali needs a special mention in this area of intellection relating to God, self, and the world-system.

On the matter of money and its productive and just function, Ghazali considered financial interest as a form of counterfeiting or defacing the true value of money. The usual meaning of counterfeiting was shown to be a grave sin in Islamic financial arrangements. In respect of these two viewpoints, Ghazali wrote that the first man who uses counterfeit coins will receive the sins of every person who transfers it to others. Counterfeiting is seen to be worse than the theft of coins, as counterfeit coins circulate over long periods of time, thereby devaluing the currency. Consequently, it is unlawful to exchange even a large number of counterfeit coins for a small quantity of pure coins in economic exchange of any kind – consumption, production, investment and earnings.

Financial transactions based on interest rates were considered by Ghazali to be equivalent to a devaluation of pure currency. Ghazali followed the Prophet's saying: "A counterfeit coin is one which has nothing of gold and silver. The coin in which there is something of gold or silver cannot be called counterfeit." Now, referring to the circulation of pure currencies according to the gold standard, the stable value of the currency and its mobilization in good and productive activities equates to the use of currency in financing good spending and shuns bank savings. Saving (of the type that we will refer to as bank saving) was equivalent to hoarding in Ghazali's time.

Ghazali is of the utilitarian type in latter-days mainstream social choice theory. For the kind of lateral aggregation of morally framed preferences by consciousness to form social preferences, Ghazali appealed to personal psychology to establish goodness and moderation in the good things of life as ordained by the *maqasid as-shari'ah*. The institutional nature of moral and ethical preferences was reflected by their lateral aggregation. The implication of such an early version of utilitarian welfare function is Ghazali's wish for a good society formed by the aggregation of the conscious preferences of all morally transformed individuals. We find a similar implication of welfare function and social choice in Arrow (1951), Harsanyi (1955). and Hammond (1987). The latter-day Islamic scholars did not critically examine social welfare implications such as Ghazali's utilitarian, linearly additive concept of consciousness and a good society. This led them to study Ghazali's welfare implications as if they were in tune with the theory of consumer behaviour of mainstream economics (Islahi, 1988).

Ghazali's reflections on the theory of consumer behaviour predating utilitarianism find three states of acceptance of goods and services. Ghazali quotes the Prophet Muhammad (Karim, n.d., p. 86): "Lawful and unlawful things are clear in their own given states. In between these categories are the doubtful ones." Ghazali quoted the Prophet Muhammad as saying that he who saves himself from the doubtful things, upholds religious belief.

Ghazali points out four origins of doubtful things that ought to be avoided in the light of the *shari'ah*: (1) a thing that was determined as unlawful before is now considered to be possibly lawful. Such a thing should be declared as doubtful and hence unlawful. (2) A thing is known to be lawful; but if the situation changes, its legality comes into question. Such a thing should be avoided as unlawful. (3) A thing is known to be unlawful. But in a certain situation the thing becomes lawful, yet t doubts remain as to matters of legality. Such a thing remains lawful unless proven to be unlawful. (4) A thing is lawful, but is later declared to be unlawful by an interpretive ruling (*fiqh*). Doubt is created. Prevalence of doubt makes the thing unlawful. Ghazali pointed out that those lawful and unlawful things, if mixed together, cause doubt as to their lawful and unlawful nature and become unlawful. However, if the mixture cannot be proportioned exactly between lawful and unlawful, the whole is considered to be lawful. Thus, if the unlawfulness of a thing cannot be proven by strong proof and conclusively, that thing remains lawful in the *shari'ah*. Thus, if the lawful and unlawful proportions of mixed goods are known to the owner, he is required to separate the two kinds of goods; he must know the modes of spending in the lawful things.

Ibn Taimiyyah as macroeconomist

In contrast to Ghazali, who looked into the moral reconstruction of individual preferences leading to social preferences and choices, Ibn Taimiyyah was a macro-moralist. Ibn Taimiyyah's theory of the social regulation of market order called the *hisbah fil-Islam* (Ibn Taimiyyah, trans. Holland, 1982) placed a duty on all public authorities to perform ethical supervision in the light of the *shari'ah*. This was the opposite of moral preference formation for social choice. A criticism of *al-hisbah fil-Islam* can thus be raised from the unwanted hegemony of the state in a free, but conscious, market-based economy.

Indeed, the social welfare function is not a lateral utilitarian linear aggregation of perfectly formed indexes by ethical individual preferences as was Ghazali's form of moral utilitarianism. Likewise, it was not a state-formed concept of a good society regulated by the state. The theme of a discursive society towards injecting moral consciousness in socially embedded choices was found neither in Ghazali nor in Ibn Taimiyyah.

Rousseau (trans. Cranston, 1968) wrote on the impossibility of such kinds of aggregation in his *Social Contract*:

> It is said that Japanese mountebanks can cut a child under the eyes of spectators, throw the different parts in the air, and then make the child come down, alive and all of a piece. This is more or less the trick that our political theorists perform – after dismembering the social body with a sleight of the hand worthy of the foreground, they put the pieces together again anyhow.

Contemporary Islamic scholars: the absence of intellectual emergence

Contemporary Islamic scholars have found no challenge in critically investigating the theory of welfare and social choice in neoclassical economics on the one hand, and on the other, the non-optimal and non-Pareto states of an evolutionary Islamic society that can be raised by degrees of consciousness into a good society. Even at the level of semantics, but with substantive difference in meaning and formalism, Islamic scholars have not tried to find the true meaning of "wellbeing" (*maslaha*) as opposed to "welfare".

Wellbeing is a deontological objective criterion in the Islamic epistemological context of the integrated functioning of the law of monotheism in the world-system. Welfare is a neoclassical and utilitarian objective criterion based on the postulates of non-learning and non-evolution – that is optimality based on rational behaviour having full information and transitive alternatives with preferences as datum. Emanating from these two disparate premises of social contracts are different economic, institutional and social policy implications for moral transformation. At the level of intellection, these variant approaches lead to abiding differences in the distinct methodologies and methods that they use. Such meticulous research has not been launched on the theme of episteme and the explanation of the methodological inquiry of social contract of the Islamic social political economy.

Step 3

Step 3 comprises two important undertakings. First, we derive the methodological origin of the Islamic worldview from the *Qur'an* and the *sunnah* in reference to the cardinal postulates of Islamic financial economics. This is the monotheistic law expressed as the unity of knowledge of the good things of life. It is termed in the *Qur'an* as *Tawhid*. *Tawhid*, as monotheism, is understood as the total functioning of the monotheistic law.

Second, despite the disparate views between the methodology and the imminent methodical model of the epistemological foundation of unity of knowledge and the non-foundational perspective of Islamic financial economics and Muslim intellection in this area, there is scope for reforming the rationalist (*kalam*) ideas of the *kalam* school by the methodology of organic unity and relational symbiosis between the *maqasid* choices. The idea underlying such an authentic moral and social reconstruction of Islamic intellection was voiced by Imam Ghazali and Ibn Taimiyyah.

We proceed now by first formulating the epistemological methodology of Islamic financial economics. The epistemological origin of revolutionary thought must be

	Classical and Neoclassical Orthodoxy	Dialectical School	Evolutionary School
Praxis	liberalism neo-liberalism Economic Rationality	Rationalism human	Rationalism ego
Domain Of Ethics	ethically benign: exogenous endogenous as an economic theory of ethics and values	ethically benign: exogenous	
Agency	institutionalism defined by utilitarianism of welfare economics or political economy defined by conflict and power in the acquisition and distribution of of wealth		
Objective	Optimal and steady-state Equilibrium allocation of resources For self-interest and property rights	no precise objective function and equilibrium state is defined leading to openness and Dialectical randomness of Human behaviour.	

Figure 11.2 The universal rationalist basis of Occidentalism

based on foundational axioms that do not change in any scientific pursuit, be this mathematics or economics, social sciences or pure science. The world-system is then explained thoroughly by such a foundational and much-reduced methodological worldview. There are two premises for such an approach. First, there is the school of rationalism upon which all of occidental world-system is premised. This is true of the classical and neoclassical non-process orientation of optimal science (Shackle, 1971). It is also true of all of dialectical thought as in Hegel, Marx, Popper, Hayek, Spechler (1990); Adorno (2007); Resnick and Wolff (1987); Popper (2004). Second, there is the school of bounded rationality with such latter-day exponents as Herbert Simon (1957), Ronald Coase (1994), and the evolutionary school of Schumpeter (1968), Boulding (1967), Georgescu Roegen (1981), Piero Sraffa (1960), and the Austrian School of Economics (Nelson and Winter, 1982). More recent papers on economics and ethics *qua* rationalism and epistemic approach are by Encinar, Luis, and Munoz (2006); Tencati and Parrini (2011).

A perspective of all the different forms of intellection based on rationalism and economic rationality is summarized by Figure 11.2.

Epistemological basis of Occidentalism: rationalism

The most critical basis of rationalism is its Kantian heteronomy – separation between the a priori and the a posteriori praxes and their agential and institutional consequences based on such a disintegrated worldview. The problem of Kantian heteronomy is best explained in his own words (trans. Friedrich, 1949, p. 25):

The most critical basis of rationalism is its Kantian heteronomy – separation between the *a priori* and the *a posteriori* outlook of praxis and its agential and institutional consequences based on a differentiated worldview. Kant had written: 'This, then, is a question which at least calls for closer examination, and does not permit any off-hand answer: whether there is any knowledge that is thus independent of experience and even of all impressions of the senses. Such knowledge is entitled *a priori*, and is distinguished from the empirical, which has its sources *a posteriori*, that is, in experience.'

The a priori domain of reasoning may be identified in many ways. It can be the domain of the divine law; the deductive premise of reasoning; and the moral imperative formed out of pure rationalism. The a posteriori domain can be identified in many ways. It can be the domain of the material world; the inductive premise of reasoning; and the corporeal world-system of sensate phenomena. Heteronomy, then, is defined by the disjointed phenomenon of {a priori}∩{a posteriori} = φ. Such a relationship, being a universal fact in rationalism, induces all of Occidentalism. Thereby, individual and social ethics remain independent of each other. Such a social epiphenomenon is carried by institutionalism into culture, society, institutions, and the consequential concept of knowledge in science. Thereby, the field of mainstream economics remains independent of morality and ethics.

This is particularly true when morality and ethics are capable of discovering their roots in the divine law. Their meaning now takes up a methodological nature, being derived in formal ways from the monotheistic (*Tawhidi*) methodology. This is subsequently endowed by its methodical formal model as invoked by the *Qur'an* and the *sunnah*, the guidance of the Prophet Muhammad.

However, invoking scientific ways of understanding the meaning and ontological functions of morality and ethics is not new in the literature of mainstream thought. Edel (1970) and Albert Einstein (n.d.) wrote on such issues of ethics and science in the form of their endogenous interrelationships.

Where did these important conceptions of morality, ethics, and scientific thought go wrong? The problem arises from Kantian heteronomy. As a result, there is no well-defined correspondence (relational mappings) of the type of circular causation between the moral domain of the a priori and the sensate domain of the a posteriori. This dissociation of the (otherwise much needed) organic unity of circular causation relationships between the two premises is the most severe failure of heteronomy in respect of the episteme of unity of knowledge and its continuity over the dimensions of knowledge, space, and time.

This unity is the principal characteristic of the divine law. It comprises the law and function of monotheism in reality. In the two perspectives, namely, the unity of knowledge as episteme and its depiction of the world as it normatively 'ought to be' away from the morally fallen world 'as is' there stands the law of *maqasid as-shari'ah*. Methodology and its methodical formalism form the *functional* ontology of the endogenously moral and ethical world-system. Such a critical aspect of the monotheistic law and its functional working in the world-system is not to be found in all mainstream doctrines and in the mainstream pursuit of Islamic financial economics in contemporary times.

Taking this to the economic level as a particular sub-system of the world-system *res cogitans* and *res extensa*, we note the following fundamental flaws in economic reasoning:

(i) **The axiom of transitivity of choice under full or bounded information is inadmissible in reality.**

Let A, B, and C etc. be various alternatives, which in the mainstream axiom of rational choice under full information yields the transitivity axiom of (A $\wp$ B $\wp$ C $\wp$ ....). '$\wp$' means 'preferred to'. We now prove that this is rational foolishness as Sen (1977) remarks.

Consider that instead of the full-information condition, there exists evolutionary knowledge denoted by $\{\theta\}$. This set of knowledge variables is simulated to new levels of experiences, as any one choice continuously changes towards other continuous choices. In this sense, as 'θ' changes continuously, so also the alternative choices change continuously. This scenario is found with continuous technologically induced innovative human resource development in the growth function (Romer, 1986). We denote this case as a *possibility*,

$$\{A \; \wp \; (\theta_1) \; B \leftrightarrow B \; \wp \; (\theta_2) \; A \leftrightarrow \text{etc.}\}$$
as θ-values remain in evolutionary state. $\qquad\qquad$ (11.2)

Likewise, $\{B \; \wp(\theta_1) \; C \leftrightarrow C \; \wp(\theta_2) \; B \leftrightarrow \text{etc.}\}$. This implies, $\qquad$ (11.3)

$$\{A \; \wp(\theta_1) \; B \leftrightarrow B \; \wp(\theta_2) \; A \leftrightarrow \text{etc.}\} \leftrightarrow \{B \; \wp(\theta_1) \; C \leftrightarrow C \; \wp(\theta_2) \; B \leftrightarrow \text{etc.}\} \qquad (11.4)$$

$$\Rightarrow \text{convex indifference functions } do \; not \text{ exist between (A,B,C,....)} \qquad (11.5)$$

That is, we cannot define transitivity such as

$$(A \; \wp(\theta^*) \; B \; \wp(\theta^*) \; C \; \wp(\theta^*) \; .....) \text{ as under full-information}$$
with optimal θ^*. $\qquad\qquad$ (11.6)

Next, expressions (2)–(4) can be expanded by continuously differentiable mappings (fs, and f's) in respect of the continuity and differentiability of evolutionary θ-values, as,

$$f_1(A) \leftrightarrow f_1'(B); f_2(B) \leftrightarrow f_2'(C), \text{ etc.} \qquad (11.7)$$

$$\Rightarrow f_1(A) \leftrightarrow f_2'(C) \text{ etc.} \qquad (11.8)$$

Given the choices (A,B,C...) over evolutionary knowledge domain, transitivity axiom and convex indifference maps, utility functions and the like cannot exist. Consequently, the θ-evolutionary knowledge-induced bundle, (A,B,C,...)[θ] forms a non-optimal and non-steady state of equilibrium fields of continuously evolutionary learning. Such evolutionary learning equilibrium points are parameterized around their proximity by the expandable analytic function (Dadkhah, 2007).[3]

The above results can be further disaggregated to the components by inner variables. For example, if the vectors $\{x(A), x(B), x(C), \text{etc.}\}[\theta]$ denote such variable-specific disaggregation (e.g. work, leisure, work-leisure, etc.) then a greater degree of complexity is generated by the inter-variable organic causality. Examples are product-diversification, changes in preferences, cultural impact, social policies, ethical induction (e.g. the case of the Islamic basket of life-fulfilment needs) etc. We can now denote a complex field of evolutionary learning possibilities, whose interactions with unity of knowledge are represented by the expandable property of the f-functions around evolutionary learning equilibriums, as follows (Choudhury and Korvin, 2002):

$$\{f_1(x(A)) \leftrightarrow f_2(x(B)) \leftrightarrow f_3(x(B)) \leftrightarrow \text{etc}\}[\theta] \qquad (11.9)$$

When the above results on knowledge-induced dynamic effects are injected in preference maps, the mainstream economic theory of consumer behavior ceases to exist. Thereby, the entire field comprising utility function, its objective criterion of utility maximization, consumer indifference curves, concepts of opportunity cost, and the consequential entire gamut of demand curves, elasticity coefficients and their related predictions and policy implications, all fail to be accepted in the Islamic epistemological context. There is no linear way of aggregating the consumer demand curves to yield straightforward market demand curves for goods and services. The existence of complex evolutionary equilibriums denies the existence of steady-state or time-dynamic states of market equilibrium and Pareto-optimality. The axiom of rational choice in consumer theory is thus fully abandoned. Still, we find that such misleading perceptions are being followed in the outmoded precincts of Islamic financial economics today.

In the methodological explication of the monotheistic law of unity of knowledge in the unified world-system, the existence of evolutionary equilibriums extendable by analytic functions of complex interactive variables gravitates to inter-variable causal relationships. The inter-variable causality defines the objective criterion of wellbeing. The wellbeing function is the observed and reconstructed measure of the balance of unification relationships between critical selected variables, subject to the system of complex organic relationships under evolutionary learning impact.

Such a methodological feature of the monotheistic law in its extended *functional* ontology is unique to the Islamic methodological worldview of unity of knowledge. The monotheistic methodological approach, along with its imminent methodical formal model of wellbeing as balance, and simulated by circular causation in the complex field of interaction between the critical variables, is of significant import. First, it arises from and endogenously responds to unity of knowledge by the continuity of inter-causal relationships. Second, the selected vector of variables is of the good things of life. We have identified such bundles with life-fulfilment goods (*maqasid as-shari'ah*). Third, it establishes sustainability by continuity of evolutionary learning in the above features in every field of social action and response. These are the properties of the methodology of unity of knowledge and its methodical model formalism that make the Islamic monotheistic methodology uniquely universal.

Due to the unique properties of the above-mentioned methodological and methodical orientation of Islamic financial economics, premised indispensably in the episteme of unity of knowledge, important consequences arise in economic reasoning. The deductive and the inductive, as for the a priori and the a posteriori, are no longer disjointed areas of reasoning. They complement each other in the continuity and sustainability of the complementary (participative) field of inter-variable causality. This kind of methodological derivation of the methodical formalism invokes the circular causation between complementary variables that explains the simulation of the wellbeing criterion function.

Pricing theory of the firm in contrasting worldviews

Here, we investigate the opposing treatment of the pricing theory of the firm in mainstream economics; the Islamic economic approach that leans on mainstream economics; and then differently in the Islamic epistemological worldview. Islamic economists of the mainstream genre continue with the mainstream objective function of profit maximization. Yet in Step 3 of our reconstruction of economic methodology, we note that the optimal-equilibrium points of classical and neoclassical economic methodology are untenable in the evolutionary context.[4] Consequently, no relative price can logically exist in the latter case. The production possibility surfaces, like the consumer indifference curves, remain in complex perturbations. As a result, the postulates of marginal factor productivities, marginal cost of production, factor payments, prices, output and economic expansion path are all subject to non-steady, non-optimal fields of evolutionary equilibrium points. Such fuzzy points are extendable only by analytic functions around convergent points whichremain evolutionary in character (Choudhury, 2011).

Combining the knowledge-induced dynamic forms of consumer indifference and the production possibility curves, there cannot logically be any steady-state equilibrium. No optimal value of the objective criterion, such as utility maximization and profit-maximization, can exist. The intensity of such consequences deepens with the growing endogenous nature of knowledge-induced interaction and evolution in the midst of the unity of inter-causal systems. In such complex fields, the study of economics intersects with those of morality, ethics, institutions, society, and science. Likewise, none of these sub-systems remain independent of the others. The result is the socially endogenous embedding of systems. Economics now turns into a socio-scientific study of political economy from the combined positivist and normative states of the embedded world-systems.

The combination of the theory of consumer behavior with the pricing theory of the firm is now translated into the complex perturbations, but temporarily convergent, points of evolutionary fields. The result is shown in Figure 11.4, which summarizes the explanation on perturbations and interactive evolution of embedded systems in unity of knowledge of the monotheistic law. In Figure 11.4, all curves shown are in the three-dimensional (hence n-dimensional) space of $(\theta, X_1(\theta), X_2(\theta))$. It is best to define such spaces and their monotonic transformations, by the f'-functions, as topological spaces generated by the knowledge-flows. Knowledge-parameters are now expressed as ranks, though they are as yet derived from the monotheistic law of divine oneness in terms of unity of knowledge.

The uniqueness of the imminent methodical formalism arising from the methodology of monotheistic unity of knowledge is further established as the universal theory. To prove this, we note the permanence of heteronomy in every field other than the Islamic monotheistic methodological worldview. Consequently, reasoning in the heteronomy system remains divided in all of intellection other than Islam. This dichotomy happens between the deductive and inductive reasoning; between a priori and a posteriori domains of reality; and thus between God and the world-system taken in generality and specifics (Carnap, 1966). The consequence of the imminent knowledge-induced reality is the evolutionary learning, reasoning, and induction of the world-system by dynamic convergences to unity of knowledge. Yet the reality of the opposite kind of any world-system is contrasted with the unified world-system phenomena by the same methodical formalism, which is derived methodologically from the monotheistic unity of knowledge in 'everything' (Barrow, 1991).

In the topology of the continuously evolutionary learning world-system and its epistemic intellection, the points like 'A', 'A*' are θ-induced analytic 'neighbourhoods'.

These points are expandable by the continuity of θ-values, as by the Taylor series. Likewise, there is the similar resulting effect of continuity and sustainability on the incident world-system. For this reason, the annulment of the postulates of mainstream economics leads to the prevalence of the principle of pervasive complementarities (participation) in the monotheistic orientation of Islamic financial economics.

We therefore write: In the finite convergence points like 'A' to 'A*', $x_i(\theta) \rightarrow x_i(\theta^*)$, even though $|\theta-\theta^*|$ is not 'absolutely' less than an indefinitely small value (say, $\varepsilon > 0$). Continuity exists, but no optimal state from process-to-process of evolutionary learning exists. Hence A* is never attained. It is bypassed into sequential levels of evolutionary learning $\{\theta\}$-values, and thereby, the corresponding $\{x(\theta)\}$-values. The property of continuity and sustainability of the evolutionary learning topological space is critical in this deduction. In the discontinuous case too, the attained neighborhoods and their temporary non-evolutionary learning states can be contained in a mathematical set of finite measure. Consequently, the continuity and sustainable nature of the finitely and temporarily non-evolutionary learning points is said to be enclosed in a set of 'finite measure'. The entire evolutionary learning space is then said to be measurable 'almost everywhere' (ae) by dissecting the temporary non-evolutionary learning exceptions 'ae' (Halmos, 1974).

Hence, the property of evolutionary learning in the organically relational topological space governed by the positive aspect of unity of knowledge, remains universal (Maddox, 1970; Rucker, 1982). The principle of pervasive complementarities (participation) in unity of knowledge is universally valid. Marginal substitutions and the postulates of rational choice and of rationalism can form only temporary and finite incidents in the event space of (knowledge, space, and time)-dimensions.

The universality of the Islamic monotheistic law influencing the unification of the world-system in reasoning, concrescence, and participatory (complementarities) forms of evolutionary learning across processes, also establishes the finiteness of the non-evolutionary learning phenomenon 'ae' (language of mathematical measure theory stating 'almost everywhere'). The latter is exemplified by mainstream economic postulation and by the postulation of rationalist forms of evolutionary reasoning. This comprehensive explanatory worldview is uniquely universal in respect of the most extended domain of the monotheistic law. It explains 'everything' (Barrow, op cit). The monotheistic law now overarches the widening evolutionary learning of the intersected God and Universe embedded domains in terms of the episteme of unity of knowledge.

The end result of these arguments is this. As in the case of Keynes (O'Donnell, 1989), and recently of Lawson (1988) who explain why probability as we know it cannot help in the estimation of simulacra of functions for evaluations that ensue around points like 'A', there are sequential evolutionary convergent points in all inherent evolutionary learning processes. Frequency-related probability distribution functions relegate domains into measurable contexts to evaluate contexts out of simplification. Such a bounded nature of the probabilistic domains may not reflect reality. The exclusion of the 'butterfly' effects (Gleick, 1988) and the appearance of several 'Black Swans' (Taleb, 2007) reduces the space of reality into one of convenience. Yet within this bravado of thought, extreme forms of randomness that are rare are untenable (Choudhury, 2013b). Following this argument, the methods of frequency probability, stochastic surface studies, and data enveloping analysis cannot be acceptable methods for studying the simulacra systems for evaluation.

Critical realism and Islamic socio-scientific reasoning in the episteme of monotheistic unity of knowledge

The failure of mainstream economics, its dialectical and evolutionary outgrowth premised in rationalism and the Islamic imitation of these postulates point to yet another deeply rooted problem of studying critical realism of the socio-scientific methodological worldview. Furthermore, we will now argue that, in the absence of the foundational epistemology of uniqueness and universality, which stands for scientific self-referencing (Smullyan, 1992) and ontological arguments that can be also explained by the systemic closure based on circular causation as the methodical formalism of unity of knowledge, the perceived idea of critical realism runs into problems.

Roy Bhashkar (1978) explains his idea of critical realism by underlying the scientific enterprise in a purely reductionist way premised on rationalism. Bhashkar leaves out the substantive realm of knowledge emanating from and returning to the divine premise through actions and responses in the experiential and discursive world-system. He writes (p. 195): "Knowledge does not exist in a third world. Rather, it exists in our world, embedded in the scientific community. Without men there would be no knowledge, only its traces. In this sense it depends upon men." Yet Bhashkar does not fully reject the a priori existence of knowledge. Such a reductive character of knowledge is not of the integrative nature as was the problem with Kantian heteronomy.

In such a dichotomy of Bhashkar's formulation of reasoning we find the absence of the integrative function of reasoning as shown in Figure 11.3. Using his logic of scientific discovery, Bhashkar explains as follows (but note that I have reorientated Figure 11.3). The connection between a priori and a posteriori; transcendental 'idealism' and transcendental 'realism', are purely of an empirical nature that can be modeled using a human approach. This kind of methodical relationship is continued indefinitely. Thus inductive, as opposed to deductive, reasoning is emphasized by the force of empiricism and human modeling of events.

As opposed to the above explanation biased on empiricism and induction of the critical basis of realism, the organic relational embedding by unity of knowledge causes endogenous (learning) causality between empiricism, induction and abstraction, and deduction by means of the methodical construction of the epistemic methodology of monotheistic law of unity in being and becoming. This approach unifies the a priori and the a posteriori, which are now taken up together. Heteronomy is then rent asunder and replaced by unified and comprehensive reasoning.

In the Islamic monotheistic methodological worldview, with its methodical formal model of unity of knowledge, namely simulation of the knowledge-induced wellbeing (balance), objective criterion subject to the system of circular causation representing pervasive complementary, participation, and moral embedding, the dichotomy of heteronomy is replaced. Transcendental idealism is replaced by $T = \Omega$ with its mathematical continuous, derived function as S (*functional* ontology) mapping into methodological abstraction by the continuous generation of knowledge-flows, $\{\theta\}$.

These characteristics together comprise the deductive domain, $D(\Omega \cap S \cap \theta)$. 'D' next characterizes the world-system, $WS(\theta, x(\theta))$. 'D' is thus embedded in WS(.) by a methodical formalism representing the *functional* ontology of unity of knowledge in the world-system. Thus, abstraction and empiricism are cogently unified. Finally, the circular causality is continued across evolutionary learning in the emergent episteme of unity of knowledge. Deduction and induction of scientific logic are unified by abstraction and formalism (methodical modeling and testing) in evolutionary learning rounds of circular causation.

The epistemological foundation of Islamic financial economics and world-system study

No intellection, explicit or implicit, can be accepted as an Islamic act without the active invocation and utilization of the monotheistic epistemology of *Tawhid* to realize scientific universality, analytics, reasoning and evidence. Such an intellection would at best remain a rationalist endeavour with an exogenous invoking of *Tawhid*. But the rationalist approach here would mean the same thing as the exogenous treatment of morality and ethics – as in all of economics and finance theories today – indeed, in all of science. Choudhury (2006a) has pointed out that nowhere among the contemporary Islamic gurus has *Tawhid* been used as the epistemology to develop the socio-scientific order with the divine law and the world-system in the light of endogenous influence of morality and ethics. Islamic economists hold on to the mainstream economic axiom of resource scarcity and accept its central idea of marginal rate of substitution. Yet this is a most untenable axiom in the *Tawhidi* epistemological worldview.

Unacceptability of the postulate of marginal substitution in mainstream economics and Islamic financial economics by *Tawhidi* epistemology

How does Islamic argumentation bring into effect the phenomenon of dispensing with the mainstream postulates, principally of rational choice, scarcity and full-information leading to the optimization and steady-state conditions of marginal rate of substitution between competing ends? The facts are that a continuously learning world-system in the *Tawhidi* perspective of unity of knowledge, participation and complementarities between the 'good things of life' as ordained by *maqasid as-shari'ah* extends diversity in unity over ever-spanning domains of possibilities. The result is a continuous reproduction of output and resources, cooperation and empowerment, distribution and simultaneity of knowledge-induced events by virtue of links between the possibilities as created by knowledge production in the direction of the *maqasid as-shari'ah*. Consequently, this dynamic principle of pervasive complementarities rejects the postulate of marginal rate of substitution, which is a static idea, even if taken across time.

Together, the continuous learning in unity of knowledge liberates resources, resulting in the end of scarcity. These conditions cause wellbeing (*maslaha*) embedded in the *maqasid as-shari'ah* to continuously evolve. Optimization of the criterion function is then logically abandoned.

Yet there are those among Islamic economists who argue that optimization and steady-state equilibrium are constrained by the budgetary resources. This is an untenable argument. The presence of knowledge in continuum and the continuous learning in the *Tawhidi* unity of knowledge cause the budget to shift continuously and permanently. This causes the coefficients of the variables in the wellbeing function to vary along with the learning shifts in the variables. The resource equation then evolves

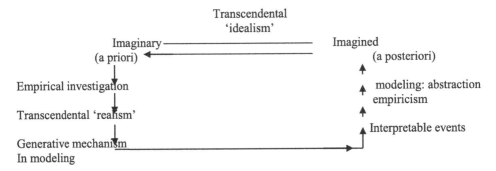

Figure 11.3 The logic of scientific discovery according to the theory of critical realism

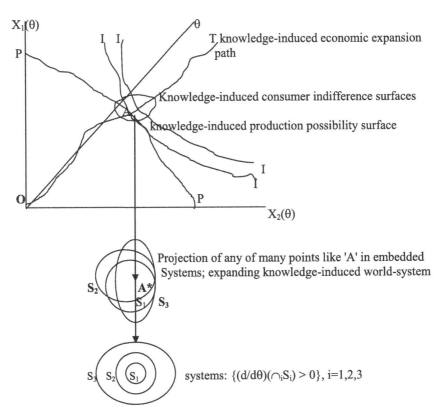

Figure 11.4 Perturbations everywhere in non-optimal and non-steady state conditions of knowledge-induced evolutionary economic surfaces

under the force of continuous knowledge reproduction and its effect on the variables. Consequently, no steady-state equilibrium can exist, as the budget line cannot be fixed on any optimal surface at a particular point. This is the message of Figure 11.4.

What about the household budget allocation to purchase say tea and coffee as substitutes? What about a firm's allocation of its costs between the production of tea and coffee as substitutes?

Tea and coffee appear as substitutes because the commercial world has not allowed for the possibility of blending these beverages and their economic and technological activities, as it has done with, say, carrot and orange juice and the like. Consequently, tastes have not been developed to overcome the scarcity problem driven by the assumed static nature of tastes and preferences. Yet, in a dynamic preference environment of decision-making and choices, it is possible for households to choose complementary goods, such as rice, wheat and fertilizers by technological fusion, conservation and recycling of waste on reproductive resources. The development of complementary technological change can expand the fertility of land for the complementary production of tea and coffee. It is the static preferences and menus linked with the assumptions of scarcity and competition of the western commercial world-system that has perpetuated the scarcity axiom of economics. The result is a marginal rate of substitution between competing ends.

Islamic economists have accepted mainstream assumptions without question. They fail to understand the episteme of *Tawhid* underlying the pervasively complementary, hence diversely unified world-system, under the continuous reproduction of knowledge and learning processes. This is in light of the epistemology of unity of knowledge and its induced unified possibilities in the choices of the world-system, specifically of economic 'possibilities' rather than competing 'alternatives'.

Thus, so-called Islamic financial economics has not understood the dynamic of *Tawhidi* epistemological methodology in constructing the Islamic economic, financial, social and socio-scientific methodological worldview. The *Qur'anic* rule of pairing, which results in abundance,[5] as the understanding and pursuit of learning experience progresses, has not moved the Muslim mind to build the learning universe in the framework of the monotheistic (*Tawhidi*) unity of knowledge and its methodological construction of the world-system.

Towards the construction of the *Tawhidi* methodology in Islamic financial economics, and the socio-scientific order

From our previous discussions, it is clear that the dynamics of knowledge are essential in understanding and constructing the *Tawhidi* epistemic worldview of the Islamic world-system. The failure to comprehend this essential and indispensable foundation of the *Qur'anic* epistemology has been at the root cause of the predicaments of anything that can be proudly called the theory and practice of Islamic financial economics and Islamic finance. Consequently, no fresh demands have been made by these disciplines. They staggered into disuse and fell prey to the sheer mechanical application of some superficial colouring by the customary term 'shari'ah-compliance' as opposed to the principles of *maqasid as-shari'ah*. The only beneficiaries have been the rich. Principal shareholders' interests have been well served by Islamic banks, Islamic financing, and the clamour surrounding interest-free financing. Despite all the claims, we still find that the participatory real-economy linked with development financing instruments have been increasingly abandoned by Islamic banks and financing houses. The focus has shifted to secondary financing instruments and *sukuk* (participatory bonds). These have many *shari'ah* financing weaknesses (Khnifer. n.d.; Gassner, 2008).

The emergence of the *Tawhidi* worldview with the epistemology of unity of knowledge and the world-system induced by such knowledge-flows is the way to substantially understand the logical negation of many of the postulates of mainstream economics and finance theory and practice. Some of these were mentioned above. To understand the substantively endogenous and applied worldview of *Tawhid*, the methodology underlying the *Tawhidi* epistemology must be understood.

The general system theory in light of monotheistic methodology

In this work we have presented the formalism to standardize a general system theory of 'everything' premised on the monotheistic methodology. Barrow (1991) used the term 'everything' to develop a unification theory in theoretical physics.

The coverage of the monotheistic (*Tawhidi*) methodological formalism was central. The reader can refer to many of the author's works (e.g. Choudhury, 2006b; Choudhury and Hoque, 2004).

The phenomenology of the circular causation and continuity model of unified reality in the Islamic world-system is explained by the string relation in (11.13). This is a version of the formal *Tawhidi* knowledge model and is referred to as the *Tawhidi* String Relation (**TSR**). TSR is summarized in (11.10):

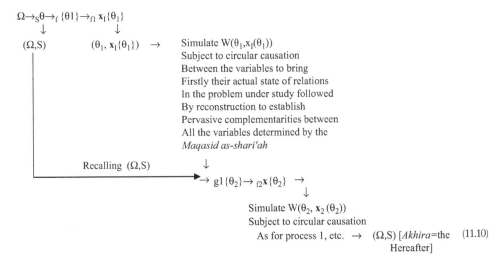

$$\Omega \to_S \theta \to_f \{\theta 1\} \to_{f1} x_1\{\theta_1\}$$

$$(\Omega,S) \qquad (\theta_1, x_1\{\theta_1\}) \quad \to \quad \text{Simulate } W(\theta_1, x_1(\theta_1))$$

Subject to circular causation
Between the variables to bring
Firstly their actual state of relations
In the problem under study followed
By reconstruction to establish
Pervasive complementarities between
All the variables determined by the
Maqasid as-shari'ah

Recalling (Ω,S)

$$\to g1\{\theta_2\} \to_{f2} x\{\theta_2\} \quad \to$$

Simulate $W(\theta_2, x_2(\theta_2))$
Subject to circular causation
As for process 1, etc. $\to (\Omega,S)$ [*Akhira*=the   (11.10)
Hereafter]

In (11.10), Ω denotes the super-cardinal topology (Maddox, 1970; Dewitt, 1992) of the *Tawhidi* stock of knowledge, which is the totality of the divine law (*Qur'an* refers to it as *Lauh Mahfuz*[6], *umm al-kitab*). Alternatively, it is the complete stock of knowledge of the *Qur'an* and uses the term 'super-cardinality'. Rucker (1982) refers to such incommensurately large topological phenomenon as having large cardinalities.

S denotes the mapping by the guidance of the Prophet Muhammad called the *sunnah*. S maps parts of Ω 'onto' conceptual and experiential worlds. The result is the discursive formation of rules and an understanding of the nature and functions of the derived knowledge-flows denoted by $\{\theta\}$. The discursive mechanism for deriving $\{\theta\}$ on the basis of the *Qur'an* and the *sunnah* (i.e. (Ω,S)), is called the consultative institution of the *shura*. The abstraction and analysis carried out in respect of the problem under discourse in the *shura* reveals the abstraction of the normative world-system for the problem. The emergent relationships are constructed by rules derived from the epistemology of (Ω,S).[7]

The embedded consciousness of the world-system premised on the problems studied is referred to as *tasbih*.[8] *Tasbih* also means consciousness of the world in its hidden worshipping of *Tawhid*.[9] This marks the intrinsic learning of the world-system in unity of knowledge. The rules derived from the *shura-tasbih* processes of interactive investigation manifest the rules of unity of knowledge in dealing with the unity of the world-system.

The *shura-tasbih* experience, being first interactive in terms of the diversity of being and approaches to human intellection of the *Tawhidi* implications of rules, derives consensus through learned discourse. This leads to integration. In the string relationship (11.13), the interaction taking place to form the *primal* $\{\theta\}$-denoted derived-rules leads to a consensual knowledge value denoted by $\{\theta_1\}$ through the discursive medium (here denoted by 'f' as the *functional* ontology). Advances in interactive learning in the *shura-tasbih* experience mark the emergence of the *shari'ah*. The *functional* ontology of the *shari'ah* denoted by 'f' is the enabling medium: this is called the *maqasid as-shari'ah*.[10]

'f1' denotes the mapping of the *maqasid as-shari'ah* f$\{\theta\}$ 'onto' specific sets of variables and their relationships.

The first set of interaction leading to integration is indicated by '1'. This set comprises many rounds of interaction leading to consensus or integration in the understanding of rules and guidance derived from (Ω,S), specific to the issues and problems that are subjected to the *shura-tasbih* discursive experience.

Subsequently, at the point of consensus (or majority rule), post-evaluation is carried out to reveal the reconstructed (normative) versus the prevalent (actual) state of the problem. Now the wellbeing function (*maslaha*) arising from the *maqasid-as-skari'ah* is simulated in reference to the circular (i.e. complementary relationships between the variables). Due to the need to restore or improve the participatory (complementary) nature of the *maqasid as-shari'ah* variables, the system of such relationships assumes the form of circular causation. The wellbeing function is thus simulated subject to the system of circular causation between the variables.

Following this stage, a new phase of learning process arises at the end of the first process and continues thereafter. Now (Ω,S) is recalled to restart the second process with fresh knowledge-flows denoted by $\{\theta_2\}$. The emergence of a new process following post-evaluation by the wellbeing function marks a creative evolution in the learning process. Each learning process is an experience of the derivation of knowledge-flows premised on the *Tawhidi* unity of knowledge and its induction of the problems at hand. The interrelated knowledge-flows and the knowledge-induced variables are shown by the *functional* ontologies (the f'-mappings). The domain of the problem under analysis is thus characterized by the wellbeing (*maqasid as-shari'ah*) function and the relationships between the circular causations.

Learning in unity of knowledge and its induction of the problem under investigation continues until the Hereafter. The Hereafter marks the Great Event mentioned in the *Qur'an*.[11] It is denoted by the ultimate completion of the knowledge stock in the closure of the very large universe. Thus (Ω,S) is once again attained, after proceeding through the continuums of Interactive, Integrative and Evolutionary (IIE) learning processes in the world-system. Each learning process is an advancement in unity of knowledge-flows$\{\theta\}$ derived from (Ω,S), and as evaluated by the *functional* ontology of the *maqasid as-shari'ah*. This establishes the learning world-system corresponding to such derived and reconstructed $\{\theta\}$-values across learning processes. The reconstructed variables entering the evaluative *maslaha* function comprise the $\{\theta,\mathbf{x}(\theta)\}$-tuples in continuums of the dimensions of knowledge, space and time.

Let the totality, $E = \{\Omega,S,\theta\}$ denote the extended Islamic epistemology (E-episteme) at the outset of any round of Interaction followed by Integration and then creative Evolution. IIE is written down in terms of Ω to signify the super-cardinal topological ontology of *Tawhid* in terms of the divine laws, which are embedded in the *Qur'an*. S denotes the *functional* ontological explication (mapping) of the *Qur'an* by the *sunnah*.[12] The *primal* knowledge derivation out of the ontological experience denoted by $\{\theta\}$ signifies the *shura-tasbih* essence of the *maqasid as-shari'ah*. This becomes the functional ontology to unravel the fundamental epistemology (Ω,S) through knowledge derivation in $\{\theta\}$. For the idea of functional ontology, see Gruber (1993).

Thereafter, $\{\theta_1\}$-knowledge-flows within Process 1 signify the guidance and rule derivation from the basis of the divine laws. $\{\theta_1\}$ thus carries its *functional* ontological impact on the relationships arising from the problem under study. The attributes that generate the functional ontology as derived from the epistemic premise of (Ω,S) are A = {Justice, Purpose, Certainty, Wellbeing, Creative Evolution[13] and the beatific attributes of *Allah*, the *Asma*}. Therefore, we can write, $\{\theta_1\} = \{\theta_1(A)\}$ in Process 1 followed by its recall in every subsequent emergent processes of deriving knowledge through the IIE-properties of the *shura-tasbih* experience. The primordial reference to the beatific names of *Allah* (*Asma*) signifies the importance of emulating the attributes of *Allah* in the functions of the world-system. Thus the *functional* ontology carries it towards consciously understanding and applying the *Asma* to their complex combinations of the specific issues and problems under investigation.

The essence of unity of knowledge derived from the epistemic origin of (Ω,S) is simultaneously induced into the *maqasid as-shari'ah* variables, $\{\mathbf{x}_1(\theta_1)\}$, using the *functional* ontology of *shura-tasbih* denoted by 'f' and 'f$_1$'.

The evaluation of the prevalent positivistic relationships of the world-system are then normatively reconstructed or improved by estimating the wellbeing criterion (*maslaha*) defined by the $\{\theta_1, \mathbf{x}_1(\theta_1)\}[A]$-tuple.

The wellbeing function

The *wellbeing function* is represented by $W = W(\theta_1,\mathbf{x}_1(\theta_1))$. The estimated value of $W(.)$ is equivalently represented by the estimated θ-relationship that appears as one of the circular causation relationships with ranked θ-values in general without subscripts. θ-values are ranked in reference to the performance of the $\mathbf{x}(\theta)$. Such calculated ranks for θ-values are then averaged across the x(θ)-values. *Rank-values of θ are not the same as the primal θ-value in any emergent learning process*. The *primal* θ-values are formed by the *shura-tasbih* discourse, yielding guidance and rules of the *maqasid as-shari'ah* on the problems and issues under study. W(.) or the estimated θ-relationship is thus the result of post-evaluation of a normatively reconstructed system with unity of knowledge represented in the reformation of an existing positivistic scenario. The wellbeing function is thus the representation caused by *functional* ontology. Its form, estimated value, and dynamics in the midst of circular causation on extensive complementarities signify the degree to which the system has been unified according to the *Tawhidi* worldview. Appropriate institutional and ethical market transformations, strategies, policies and the like are derived at the normative ('as it ought to be') evaluation stage of the *maslaha*.

Thus, following post-evaluation of W(.) in terms of $\{\theta, x(\theta_1)\}$, the creative evolution of similar 'processual' orders arise. Interaction leading to Integration through a set of *shura-tasbih* discourses within Process 1 finally leads to Evolution by recalling the epistemological beginning in subsequent learning processes. Such learning processes perpetuate in the midst of the epistemology of unity of knowledge with induction into the unified world-system. The emergent *Tawhidi* String Relations (**TSR**) describes how the *impact* of the divine law of oneness is learnt by simulation in the learning universe of unity of knowledge and the unified world-system.

Since all the inputs and outputs of this learning system are knowledge-induced, systemic 'universal complementarities' are established by means of organic unification between knowledge and the knowledge-induced variables. The principle of pervasive complementarities signifying the continuously participatory nature of the *Tawhidi* worldview and world-system is the surest sign of *Tawhidi* unity of knowledge which can be measured.

The f's and g's denote mappings signifying the *functional* ontological derivations of rules and guidance from the E-episteme. They are ontological forms of ethical endogeneity. The sequences, $P_i = (\{\theta_i\} \to_{f_i} \{x_i\} \to_{g_{i+1}} \{\theta_{j+1}\})$, i =1,2,..., comprise the chain of *shura-tasbih* experiences of unity of knowledge. The IIE-properties are thus realized both within and across these sequences as across similar sequences in extensively participatory types of multidimensional systems.[14]

Some economic issues from the *Tawhidi* methodological worldview

Markets in Tawhidi

The market system is influenced by exogenous preferences in prevalent Islamic financial economics and finance. The market is thus a consequentialist venue of ethics and values determined by exogenous individual behaviour. This is unlike the endogenous knowledge induction of preferences in ethicizing the markets. Islamic behavior in the ideal markets of Islamic financial economics is a pre-determined prescription. Its forces are not the result of a discursive learning process.

Chapra (1992) for instance, used the concept of a moral filter in the pricing and resource allocation mechanism of Islamic financial economics. According to this concept, market prices are assumed to be governed by the perfect Islamic baskets of goods and services to the exclusion of imperfect ones. The filtered output is the ideal Islamic one; prices are thereby ideal with respect to such a filtered market. The market order is thus segmented into a *shari'ah*-recommended part (*halal*) and a *shari'ah*-impermissible part (*haram*). The moral filter guides preferences towards the prescribed segmented market within such an assumed differentiation.

In all of the above studies on consumer behavior, the role of learning that progressively breaks down the market duality by moral induction is replaced by consciously ethicized behavior. Hence, a price-discriminating model is implied between the segmented markets. No analytical explanation is made clear regarding the gradual transition from one market sub-system to another by the force of inter-systemic learning and unification.

Instead, in the *Tawhidi* methodological worldview markets are progressively ethicized by the selections and choices of goods according to the *maqasid as-shari'ah*. The inherent learning process in such selections and choices, as induced by unity of knowledge, causes preferences to learn and evolve. Dynamic preferences thereby codetermine the *maqasid as-shari'ah* goods, and the progress of the Islamic political economy along the dynamic basic needs regime of life-fulfilling goods and services. This was the social market trajectory of Imam Fahruddin Razi (see Noor, 1998), Imam Ghazali (trans. Karim, n.d.), and Imam Shatibi (see Masud, 1997).

The dynamic learning transformation of embedded markets as multimarkets (**M**) into ethicized ones is defined by the following market topology: $\mathbf{M}(\theta, \mathbf{x}(\theta),$ $\mathbf{p}(\theta), \mathbf{R}(\theta); \wp(\theta))$ comprises the system of circular causation symbolized by $\otimes$ underlying the **IIE**-learning processes. These are denoted by $\{\mathbf{x}(\theta) \otimes \mathbf{p}(\theta) \otimes \mathbf{R}(\theta) \otimes \wp(\theta)\}$. All the properties of simulating the wellbeing criterion and the resource allocation complementarities in **TSR** remain intact. Such circular causation underlying $\otimes$ can be represented by,

$$[(\Omega, S) \Leftrightarrow \theta \Leftrightarrow \wp(\theta)] \Leftrightarrow [\mathbf{x}(\theta) \otimes \mathbf{p}(\theta) \otimes \mathbf{R}(\theta)] \Leftrightarrow [(\Omega, S) \Leftrightarrow \theta \Leftrightarrow \wp(\theta)]$$
in continuity

(11.11)

Resource allocation in Islamic financial economics

We have explained that the resource allocation of neoclassical economics that has penetrated deep into Islamic economic methodology, assumes the existence of opportunity cost of 'alternatives'. Behind this form of resource allocation is the prevalence of competing rather than co-operating market behavior. This is the cause and effect of the principle of economic rationality, scarcity, and marginal substitution that characterizes both microeconomic and macroeconomic theories of production and economic growth. Thus, although no aggregation is possible from the level of microeconomic decision-making to the macroeconomic level where decision-making and behavioral aspects of economic agents are absent, nonetheless Islamic economists emulate neoclassical economics to treat the microeconomic and macroeconomic as segmented fields, with their separate corresponding perspectives according to mainstream methodologies entrenched in Islamic financial economics. Such a perspective leaves void the epistemological foundation of morals and values that otherwise makes all of Islamic social experience a continuous learning behavior premised on the induction by the *Tawhidi* episteme of unity of knowledge. In this case, any aggregation to the economy-wide level is done by means of non-linear compound knowledge-induced variables and preferences in light of the IIE-processes of complex evolutionary learning in unity of knowledge.

We denote the complex aggregation underlying the economy-wide aggregation of knowledge-induced preferences, acting through the market-system as a world-system, by the following topology applying to economy:

Let 'i' denote interactions, thus $i \in I$ as the set of interactions. Likewise, 'j' denotes integration to come to consensus in choices over learning processes, $j \in J$; 'k' denotes number of multi-market systems, $k \in K$. Consequently, the complex interaction and integration dynamics across multimarkets, which defines the economy (E), is explained by,

$$E(M(\theta, x(\theta), p(\theta), R(\theta); \wp(\theta))) = \cup_i \cap_j \cap_k \{M_{ijk} \{x(\theta) \otimes p(\theta) \otimes R(\theta) \otimes \wp(\theta)\}_{ijk} \quad (11.12)$$

Similar definitions of the economy have been advanced by Debreu (1959) and Choudhury (1999).

The evolutionary property in IIE-learning processes in this case is explained by,

$$(d/d\theta)[\cup_i \cap_j \cap_k \{M_{ijk} \{x(\theta) \otimes p(\theta) \otimes R(\theta) \otimes \wp(\theta)\}_{ijk}] > 0; \theta \in (\Omega, S);$$
$$\text{for each } (i,j,k). \quad (11.13)$$

The evolutionary ethicized multimarkets and socially embedded political economy in complex aggregation via dynamic preferences are generalized in domains such as S_q, $q = 1,2,\dots$ in Figure 11.2 for the multidimensional case.

Money and the real economy

Yet again, a so-called macroeconomic topic of money and economy emerges. In the language of a 100% reserve requirement monetary system (especially with the gold standard) (Choudhury, 2012), Y (real economy output and prices) prevails over the savings environment. Interest rate, i, prevails in the savings function having a positive relationship. That is, $S = S(i^+)$. In the Islamic case the function of money is to finance Y. S is then treated as 'mobilized funds' from savings continuously converted to generate and sustain Y. The implication is that the function of money (MN) is understood simply in terms of its relationship with Y in the expression, MN = MN(Y). S is a connector which brings the monetary sector and the real economy into a complementary relationship. This is an example of money and real economy unification via the medium of financial instruments.

Thereby, this money-expression (MN) can be extended by replacing the rate of interest by a rate of return, r(p) on Y as a function of its price, p. Now, M = M(Y,r(p)). The way that r(p) arises is important. By extending to vector variables (Y,r(p)) (e.g. including real economic activity (Y) and respective rates of return) we write,

$$MN = MN(Y, r(p)) \quad (11.14)$$

In this form of the money equation, resembling the quantity theory of money and prices, money denotes the total value of spending in *maqasid as-shari'ah* goods and services. Thus, the flow of money equals the value of mobilized resources in the directions guided by *maqasid as-shari'ah* and the *maslaha*.

Furthermore, spending in *shari'ah*-recommended market activities is found to be the source of economic stabilization, economic growth, and social wellbeing. The last concept was explained in terms of the principle of universal complementarities between knowledge-induced goods and services. In the case of expression (11.13), such complementarities are seen between money, output and real rates of returns (S now becomes resource mobilization) in terms of exchange prices.

As one example of the form of expression (11.14), the total spending variable S can be related to real output by the equation,

$$S = A.(Y/p)^a, \tag{11.15}$$

where, Y denotes nominal GDP; p denotes the price level;
    A is a constant;
    a and b are elasticity coefficients of spending to output and price level, respectively.

Expression (11.15) is written in terms of growth rates as,

$$g_s = a_1.g_Y + c. g_u \tag{11.16}$$

where, g_s denotes the growth rate of spending;
    g_Y denotes the growth rate of output;
    g_u denotes the growth rate of the random variable.

It is known that the real aggregate demand (spending) function would be flatter than the supply curve of real output. Hence, $g_s < g_Y$. Therefore, the rate of growth of real output growth is expected to be higher than the real spending rate. Consequently, price-stabilization is realized.

The continuity of circular causation will depend on the formation of preferences for productive spending in accordance with the *maqasid as-shari'ah* (i.e. in accordance with the usage of *shari'ah* financial instruments that generate complementary relationships between money and the real economy). These bring about linkages to the general equilibrium system by the IIE-processes involving money, real economy and spending variables in the direction of *maqasid as-shari'ah* possibilities. The dynamic preferences so formed produce knowledge formation in the large-scale general equilibrium system of learning relationships. The analytical implications of circular causation between MN, Y, r(p) and S all induced by $(\theta, \wp(\theta))$ as explained above, can be explained.

Conclusion

This chapter has shown that the discipline of mainstream economics has serious problems in understanding a world-system which deals with economic problems in the midst of complex embedded moral and social systems. Indeed, this is how the study of economic issues and problems was pursued traditionally. For the Greeks, economics was considered as the study of family needs. It could not isolate ethical preferences and discourse from holistic decision making. The classical school treated the study of economics as political economy. It was the study of questions of conflict and social resolution in the production, distribution, and ownership of wealth and power.

Boulding (1971) explained economics as a moral science that was governed by three kinds of preferences: malevolent, benevolent, and integrative. Yet, in all such studies of economics, the field of interactive and dynamic preferences and object-ives were not studied by a socially embedded methodology. The field of economics thus remained a specialized, but differentiated, discipline bereft of moral, ethical, and social phenomena. Specialization at the cost of realism has driven economic doc-trines in recent times, although that was not the intention at the start of this age-old discipline.

Heterodox economic thinking recognizes this failure of economics. Yet we have noted that the methodological development of heterodox economics is still bounded by the domain of materialism. This excludes the critical understanding of the greater reality of the monotheistic methodology of unity of knowledge and its determination of the good things of life. A precise analytical methodology of heterodox economics has not yet been developed. The budding field of heterodox economics and its critics (Lee and Lavoie, 2013) has both failed to establish a realist and analytical field of inquiry within which economic issues, problems, and reasoning can be placed. This is the evolutionary learning epistemology of interaction and convergence of knowledge between monotheism as the broadest field of intellection and the material world with its generality in science and society and its particularity in economics.

The challenge to show the new and uniquely universal way in heterodox socio-sci-entific reasoning could not be taken up by the contemporary pursuit of a concocted term called Islamic financial economics. Islamic financial economics has remained but a whimper in the world of academia and realism. What we find is an Islamic thinking that is wrapped up in mainstream economic postulation. No epistemo-logical challenge is born in Islamic financial economics and socio-scientific thought. This is despite this field being apt for the study of discursive interaction leading to integration and evolution in light of its monotheistic methodology and materiality. The Islamic economic failure goes beyond one simply observing the flourishing of Islamic banks, and yet the dying of the the the *ummah*, the world-nation and community of Islam.

Is Islamic financial economics possible?

Is Islamic financial economics possible as it stands today? The answer is No. The impossibility of Islamic financial economics is due to its failure to render a univer-sal and permanently entrenched revolutionary worldview. This must emanate from and comprehend the episteme of monotheism within the phenomenology of the world-system. The methodology that so emerges is both *functionally* ontological as well as methodical by its unique formalism.

The possibility of Islamic financial economics as a particular sub-system embed-ded within the generality of the world-system lies in the much-needed refilling of the missing epistemic gap. Indeed, this was alive in the original formalism of the great

Islamic scholastic thinkers. The epistemology of oneness of the divine law in its form of the monotheistic methodology (*Tawhid*) together with the emergent scientific and methodical formalism pertaining of generality, particularized to economic issues, is the sure way out. This is a message for the entire world of academia and practitioners, not just Muslims alone.

Notes

1 Alfred North Whitehead defines ontology as follows and which serves our purposes ultimately to see how the Islamic socio-scientific reasoning in general and Islamic economics in particular converges into an organically unified evolutionary learning process theory of unity of knowledge. Whitehead writes (eds. Griffin and Sherburne, 1978, p. 43): "The ontological principle asserts the relativity of decision; whereby every decision expresses the relation of the actual thing, for which a decision is made, to an actual thing by *which* that decision is made. But 'decision' cannot be construed as a casual adjunct of an actual entity. It constitutes the very meaning of actuality."

Gruber (1993) defines *functional* ontology as follows: "In the context of knowledge sharing, I use the term ontology to mean a *specification of a conceptualization*. That is, ontology is a description (like a formal specification of a program) of the concepts and relationships that can exist for an agent or a community of agents. This definition is consistent with the usage of ontology as set-of-concept-definitions, but is more general. It is certainly a different sense of the word than its use in philosophy."

2 There is no way to cultivate morals except through observing in works the canon of the religious law so that man would not follow his whim, such that 'he makes his caprice his god' (*Qur'an* 25:45, 45:22). Rather, he must imitate the law, advancing on holding back [action] not as he chooses, [but] according to what [the law] directs, his moral dispositions becoming educated thereby. Whoever is deprived of this virtue in both moral disposition and knowledge is the one who perishes. For this reason: "Whoever purifies it has achieved success and whoever corrupts it fails" (*Qur'an* 91:9–10). "Whoever combines both virtues, the epistemological and the practical, is the worshipping 'knower', the absolutely blissful one ... "

3 Taylor series in cubic form approximation to account for inflexions of functions in complex domains:

$$W(\theta,x(\theta)) = W(\theta^*,x^*(\theta^*)) + [(d/d\theta).(W(\theta^*,x^*(\theta^*)))/1!].(\theta-\theta^*) + [(d/dx(\theta)).$$
$$(W(\theta^*,x^*(\theta^*)))/1!].(x(\theta)-x^*(\theta^*))] + [(d^2/d\theta^2).(W(\theta^*,x^*(\theta^*)))/2!].$$
$$(\theta-\theta^*)^2 + [(d^2/dx(\theta)^2).(W(\theta^*,x^*(\theta^*)))/2!].(x(\theta)-x^*(\theta^*))]^2 + [(d^3/d\theta^3).$$
$$(W(\theta^*,x^*(\theta^*)))/3!].(\theta-\theta^*)^2 + [(d^3/dx(\theta)^3).(W(\theta^*,x^*(\theta^*)))/3!].$$
$$(x(\theta)-x^*(\theta^*))]^3 + \text{Higher order terms.}$$

4 On this point others have prevailed. Hodgson (1989, p. 18) writes: " ... Behavioural theorists such as Cyert and March ... reject the very idea that the firm is maximizing at all: it is 'satisficing' instead."

5 *Qur'an* (15:21).
6 *Qur'an* (85:21,22).
7 *Qur'an* (42:38) (42:49–53).
8 *Qur'an* (59:24).
9 *Qur'an* (42:49–53).
10 *Qur'an* (30:8).
11 *Qur'an* (78:1–5).
12 *Qur'an* (53:1–7).
13 *Qur'an* (27:64).
14 *Qur'an* (13:1–5) brings out the nature of the pairing universe across and between diversities of multidimensional systems. Thus, unity in diversity is conveyed in the light of the universality of the divine law.

References

Adorno, T.W. (2007). *Negative Dialectics*, trans. E.B. Ashton, Continuum, New York, NY.

Arrow, K.J. (1951). *Social Choice and Individual Values*. John Wiley and Sons, New York, NY.

Barrow, J.D. (1991). "Laws", in his *Theories of Everything, the Quest for Ultimate Explanation*, pp. 12–30, Oxford University Press, Oxford, UK.

Bhashkar, R. (1978). "The logic of scientific discovery", in his *A Realist Theory of Science*, Harvester Wheatsheaf, Hertfordshire, UK.

Blaug, M. (1968). "Introduction: has economic theory progressed?", in *Economic Theory in Retrospect*, Richard D. Irwin, Inc., Homewood, IL.

Bloomberg (March 4, 2009). "Vatican Says Islamic Finance May Help Western Banks in Crisis".

Boulding, K.E. (1967). "Evolution and revolution in the developmental process", in *Social Change and Economic Growth*. Development Centre of the Organization for Economic Co-operation and Development, Paris, France.

Boulding, K.E. (1971). "Economics as a moral science", in Glabe, F.R. (ed.), Boulding: *Collected Chapters*, 2, Association of University Press, Boulder, CO.

Carnap, R. (1966). "Kant's synthetic *a priori*", in his *Philosophical Foundations of Physics* (ed.) M. Gardner, Basic Books, Inc., New York, NY.

Chapra, U. (1992). *Islam and the Economic Challenge*, The International Institute of Islamic Thought, Chapter 5, Leicester, Leicestershire, UK; The Islamic Foundation and Herndon, VA.

Choudhury, M.A. (1986). *Contributions to Islamic Economic Theory: A Study in Social Economics*. Macmillan, London, UK.

Choudhury, M.A. (1999). *Comparative Economic Theory, Occidental and Islamic Perspectives*, Chapter 3, Kluwer Academic, Norwell, MA.

Choudhury, M.A. (2006a). *Science and Epistemology in the Qur'an*, 5 volumes (different volume titles), The Edwin Mellen Press, Lewiston, NY. See by 'author': www.mellenpress.com.

Choudhury, M.A. (2006b). "Islamic macroeconomics?" *International Journal of Social Economics*, 33:2.

Choudhury, M.A. (2011). "On the existence of evolutionary learning equilibriums", *Journal for Science*, 16:1, pp. 49–61.

Choudhury, M.A. (2012). "The future of monetary reform and the real economy: a problem of trade versus interest", *International Journal of Management Science*, 19:1, June.

Choudhury, M.A. (2013a). *Handbook of Tawhidi Methodology*, University of Trisakti Press, Jakarta, Indonesia.

Choudhury, M.A. (2013b). "Perturbation theory in cognitive socio-scientific research: towards sociological economic analysis", *Mind and Society*, 11.

Choudhury, M.A. and G. Korvin (2002). "Simulation versus optimization", *Kybernetes: International Journal of Systems and Cybernetics*, 31:1, pp. 44–60.

Choudhury, M.A. and Hoque, M.Z.. (2004). *An Advanced Exposition in Islamic Economics and Finance*, Edwin Mellen Press, Lewiston, MA.

Coase, R.H. (1994). "Adam Smith's view of man", in *Essays on Economics and Economists*, The University of Chicago Press, Chicago, IL.

Dadkhah, K. (2007). *Foundations of Mathematical and Computational Economics*, pp. 288–91, Thomson, Mason, OH, USA.

Debreu, G. (1959). *Theory of Value, an Axiomatic Analysis of Economic Equilibrium*, John Wiley, New York, NY.

Dewitt, B. (1992). *Supermanifolds*, Cambridge University Press, Cambridge, UK.

Edel, A. (1970). "Science and the structure of ethics", in Neurath, O. Carnap, R. and Morris, C. (eds), *Foundations of the Unity of Science*, University of Chicago Press, Chicago, IL.

Einstein, A. (n.d.). "The laws of science and the laws of ethics", in his *Lectures in Physics*, Philosophical Library, n.d., New York, NY.

Encinar, M.I. Cendejas, J.L. and Fernando, F. (2006). "On the relationship between ethics and economics", *Cuadrnos de Economia*, 29: 3–28.

Erasmus Journal for Philosophy and Economics (EJPE) (2009). "Cambridge social ontology: an interview with Tony Lawson", 2:1, pp. 100–22.

Faruqi, F.R. (1982). *Islamization of Knowledge: General Principles and Workplan* International Institute of Islamic Thought, Herndon, VA.

Feiwel, G.R. (1987). "The many dimensions of Kenneth J. Arrow", in Feiwel, G.R. (ed.), *Arrow and the Foundations of the Theory of Economic Policy*, pp. 1–115, Macmillan, London, UK.

Gassner, M.S. (2008). "Revisiting Islamic bonds, are 85% of sukuk halal?", *Business Islamica*, March, pp. 22–3.

Georgescu-Roegen, N. (1981). *The Entropy Law and the Economic Process*, Harvard University Press, Cambridge, MA.

Ghazanfar, S.M. (1991). "Scholastic economics and Arab scholars: the 'Great Gap' thesis reconsidered", *Diogenes: International Review of Human Sciences*, 154 (April–June).

Gleick, J. (1988). *Chaos, Making A New Science*, PUKuin Books, New York, NY.

Gruber, T.R. (1993). "A translation approach to portable ontologies", *Knowledge Acquisition*, 5:2, pp. 199–200.

Halmos, P.R. (1974). *Measure Theory*, Springer-Verlag, New York, NY.

Hammond, P.J. (1987). "On reconciling Arrow's theory of social choice with Harsanyi's fundamental utilitarianism", G.R. Feiwel (ed.), *Arrow and the Foundations of the Theory of Economic Policy*, Macmillan Press, London, UK.

Harsanyi, J.C. (1955). "Cardinal welfare, individualistic ethics, and interpersonal comparisons of utility", *Journal of Political Economy*, 63:4, pp. 309–21.

Hawking, S.W. (1988), *A Brief History of Time, From the Big Bang to Black Holes*, Bantam Books, Inc., New York, NY.

Henderson, H. (1999), *Beyond Globalization, Shaping a Sustainable Global Economy*, Kumarian Press, West Hartcourt, CT.

Hodgson, G. (1989). "Persuasion, expectations and the limits to Keynes", in Lawson, T. and Pesaran, H. (eds), *Keynes' Economics, Methodological Issues*, Routledge, London, UK.

Holton, R.L. (1992). *Economy and Society*, Routledge, London, UK.

Ibn Taimiyyah trans. by Holland, M. (1982). *Public Duties in Islam (Al-Hisbah Fil-Islam)*, The Islamic Foundation, Leicester, UK.

[Imam] Shatibi trans. Abdallah Draz (n.d.). *Al-Muwafaqat Fi-Usul Al-Shari'ah*, Al-Maktabah Al-Tijariyah Al-Kubra, Cairo, Egypt.

Islahi, A.A. (1988). "Ibn Taimiyah's concept of money and monetary policy", in his *Economic Concepts of Ibn Taimiyah*, pp. 139–43, The Islamic Foundation, Leicester, UK.

Imam Ghazali, trans. M.F. Karim. (n.d.). *Ihya Ulum-Id-Din* in five volumes. See vol. 4 explaining the various stages of attaining belief on *tawhid*. Sh. Muhammad Ashraf, Lahore, Pakistan.

Imam Ghazali trans. by Marmura, M.E. (1997). *Al- The Incoherence of the Philosophers*, Brigham Young University Press, Provo, Utah.

Kant, I. (ed.) C.J. Friedrich. (1949). "Critique of pure reason", in *The Philosophy of Kant*, in C.J. Friedrich (ed.) *The Philosophy of Kant*. Modern Library, New York, NY.

Khnifer, M. (n.d.). "Shocking 21 defaulted sukuk cases in the last 20 months", *Business Islamica*, 4:6, pp. 24–26.

Kuhn, T.S. (1970). *The Structure of Scientific Revolution*, University of Chicago Press, Chicago, IL.

Laclau, E. (1996). "Universalism, particularism, and the question of identity", in E.N. Wilmsen and P. McAllister (eds), *Politics of Difference*, pp. 45–58, The University of Chicago Press, Chicago, IL.

Lee, F.S. and Lavoie, M. (eds) (2013). *In Defense of Post-Keynesian and Heterodox Economics*, Routledge, Oxford, UK.

Lawson, T. (1988). "Probability and uncertainty in economic analysis", *Journal of Post-Keynesian Economics*, XI:1, pp. 35–65.

Lawson, T. and Pesaran, H. (1989). "Methodological issues in Keynes' economics: an introduction", in their *Keynes' Economics, Methodological Issues*, Routledge, London, UK.

Maddox, I.J. (1970). *Elements of Functional Analysis*, Cambridge University Press, Cambridge, UK.

Mahomedy, A.C. (2013). "Islamic economics: still in search of an identity", *International Journal of Social Economics*, 40:6, 556–78.

Nelson, R.R. and Winter, S.G. (1982). *An Evolutionary Theory of Economic Change*, The Belknap Press of Harvard University Press, Cambridge, MA.

Noor, H.M. (1998). "Razi's human needs theory and its relevance to ethics and economics", *Humanomics*, 14:1, pp. 59–96.

O'Donnell, R.M. (1989). *Keynes: Philosophy, Economics and Politics*, pp. 93–100, Macmillan, London, UK.

Polanyi, K. 1957. *The Great Transformation, The Political and Economic Origins of Our Time*, Beacon Press, Boston, MA.

Popper, K. (2004). *The Logic of Scientific Discovery*, Routledge, London, UK.

Qadri, C.A. (1988). *Philosophy and Science in the Islamic World*, Routledge, London, UK.

Rahman, R. (1988). "Islamization of knowledge: a response", *American Journal of Islamic Social Sciences*, 5:1, pp. 3–11.

Resnick, S.A. and Wolff, R.D. (1987). *Knowledge and Class, A Marxian Critique of Political Economy*, The University of Chicago Press, Chicago, IL.

Romer, P.M. (1986). "Increasing returns and long-run growth", *Journal of Political Economy*, 94, pp. 1002–37.

Rousseau, J.-J. trans. Cranston, M. (1968). *The Social Contract*, Penguin Books, London, UK.

Rucker, R. (1982). "Large cardinals", in his *Infinity and the Mind*, pp. 273–86, Bantam Books, New York, NY.

Schumpeter, J.S. (1968). "The scholastic doctors and the philosophers of natural law", in his *History of Economic Analysis*, Oxford University Press, New York, NY.

Sen, A. (1977). "Rational fools: a critique of the behavioural foundations of economic theory", *Philosophy and Public Affairs*, 6, pp. 317–44.

Shackle, G.L.S. (1971). *Epistemics and Economics*, Cambridge University Press, Cambridge, UK.

Siddiqi, M.N. (2013). "Reflections on Islamic Economics", http://siddiqi.com/mns/Future_of_Islamic_Economics_2012.htm, Online.

Spechler, M.C. (ed.) (1990). *Perspectives in Economic Thought*, McGraw-Hill, New York, NY.

Siddiqi, M.N. (2013). "Reflections on Islamic economics", http://siddiqi.com/mns/Future_of_Islamic_Economics_2012.htm, Online.

Simon, H. (1957). *Models of Man*, John Wiley and Sons, New York, NY.

Smullyan, R.M. (1992). *Godel's Incompleteness Theorems*, Oxford University Press, New York.

Sraffa, P. (1960). *Production of Commoditis by Means of Commodities*, Cambridge University Press, Cambridge, UK.

Sztompka, P. (1991). *Society in Action, The Theory of Social Becoming*, The University of Chicago Press, Chicago, IL.

Taleb N.N. (2007). *The Black Swan: The Impact Of The Highly Improbable*, Random House, New York, NY.

Tencati, A. Perrini, F. (2011). *Business Ethics and Corporate Sustainability*, Edward Elgar Publishing Ltd., Cheltenham, UK.

Whitehead, A.N. (1978). *Process and Reality*, D.R. Griffin and D.W. Sherburne (eds), The Free Press, New York, NY.

Chapter 12

Conclusion

The Islamization of Knowledge and its Implication in Islamic Financial Economics

Isharaf Hossain and Masudul Alam Choudhury

The field of Islamic economics, finance, and banking gained momentum alongside the academic project of the Islamicization of knowledge and education. It is, therefore, briefly relevant to note whether or not the scholarship was synergized between these two areas of erudition and practice: ideas rule the world. The conclusive observation in this regard is that there have been multiple gaps between the two realms. They ought to be unified by a distinctive methodology of unity of knowledge as the foundational episteme. Such an episteme that has been developed and made functional in applications in this book is the monotheistic law of unity of knowledge and its consequential induction and interpretation of the unified world of matter and mind. The same kind of intellection has not been experienced in the presently held theory and practice of Islamic economics, finance, and banking.

The first gap that remains between the theory and practice of Islamic financial economics and banking is that the principle on which the Islamic intellection and the applications ought to stand, namely the methodology of the monotheistic law of unity of knowledge, never emerged at the level of scholarship and its applications. *Tawhid*, which is the *Qur'anic* terminology for monotheism, was simply considered as an exogenously implied cornerstone of Islamic intellection. Yet this had no formative role in the construction and reformation of the Islamic world-system and the Islamic worldview with a distinctive and extensively applied methodology of unity of systems. Examples of such dissociative studies on *Tawhid* and the Islamicization of knowledge and education separated from applications are those by Al-Attas (1997), Hassan (2009), Naqvi (1994) and Nasr (1987).

Consequently, the transmission of applied ideas and directions from the theoretical intellectual levels regarding *Tawhid* could not permeate the world-system of Islamic economics, finance, banking, and the Islamic socio-scientific field. The second problem that arose within the Islamic intellectual field was the absence of a scientific way of incorporating and explaining the dynamics of the monotheistic law in the development of a functional meaning of Islamicization. The project never rose beyond its heavily introverted field into anything of the stature of a global contribution to learning. There was no analytical and scientific depth to it.

There was also the utter indifference among scholars, practitioners, and Islamic institutions to promoting the *Tawhidi* methodological worldview. As a result, Islamic economics, finance, and banking, and the entire Islamic socio-scientific field remained rudderless, without a definitive foundational epistemology. Islamicization could not take up a consistent methodological worldview. No constructive forum was allowed for such intellectual growth. Many Islamic scholarship practitioners and institutions declined to participate in the project of foundational epistemology; to build a science out of it rather than be subjugated by mainstream thinking in general, and economics and finance in particular.

Today, there is no intellectual field that can be identified in the world of learning as truly representative of both Islamic economics, finance, and banking, and Islamic socio-scientific thought. The present work has brought these problems to the fore. The scholarly and practitioner problems in this field can be traced back to the project of Islamicization. However, this book has developed the distinctively different method of monotheistic law upon which Islamic financial economics and banking can be premised.

Muslim Scholars question:

> The Society is clamoring for intellectual diversity to solve the economic problems of mankind following the blatant failure of the neoclassical economic thinking framework. Idle action in the realm of academic would mean a bleak future ahead while the crisis would be prolonged by the inability of future economics and finance graduates to think and behave differently from their seniors (AbuSulayman, 2013, p, xiii).

Islamicization of knowledge and education

The concept of Islamicization of knowledge has many definitions and interpretations. Yet its central aim and objective is the same. It is to save, purify, preserve, and cultivate knowledge from faithless secularism, corrupt influences and neutrality to ethics, otherwise connecting human or modern knowledge with *Tawhid*, thereby strengthening its practical implications under the framework of the Islamic worldview. This comprises the methodology of Oneness of God (*Tawhid*), Prophethood (*Risalah*), and the belief in the Hereafter (*Akhira*). *Tawhid* refers to an advanced intellectual reform and construction of knowledge. It promises and ensures the dynamic process of treating and developing all kinds of human activities that are effectively good for humanity; generating wellbeing for both worlds.

In the light of *Tawhid* as worldview, Ashraf (2005, pp. 187–8) notes: 'Human being is the central figure for whom education is planned', with the conceptual belief of the relationship between God–Man; God–Nature; and finally, God–Man–Nature, as the educational classifications in three categories:

1. Religious Science (God–Man)
2. Human Science (Man–Man)
3. Natural Science (Man–Nature).

The concept of the Islamicization of education was based on this understanding with the acceptance of four fundamental beliefs (Aslam, 2009). These are:

1. Belief in One Unique Transcendental reality (God, Allah) who alone is worthy of worship.

2. Belief in the existence of divine spirit in every human being, which provides ability to human beings to acquire intuitive cognition of the True Reality and the establishment of goodness in the world.
3. Belief in the endowment of that divine spirit with inner and latent consciousness of the eternal qualities of God that alone are the sources of values for man.
4. Belief in the need for divine guidance from this source that transcends self. Thus, 'a real creative synthesis is the Islamicization approach to all branches of knowledge and fulfills the real aim of Islamic education as enunciated in the First World Conference on Muslim Education ...' (Ashraf, 2005, p. 39).

In this context, Choudhury (2005, pp. 247–80) emphasized a fundamental change of praxis in place under the epistemological understanding of the principle of unity of divine knowledge. This precept in the *Qur'an* is referred to as *Tawhid*, Oneness of *Allah* (God). He firmly asserted that Islamic economics and finance, Islamic banking and Islamic development organization, methods and thought, have forever been trapped in a fringed kind of neoliberal and neoclassical doctrine, from which they cannot liberate themselves without a fundamental change. He believes that real wellbeing and uplift for the *ummah* is impossible in these extant mechanisms that link the capitalist globalization systems of economics, finance and neoclassical socioeconomic thinking. Conversely, he proposed 'the systemic concept of pervasive learning' by completeness and participation in and across the grand relational world-system. This approach is the universal world-system or *Tawhidi* world-system governed by the domain of *Tawhidi* methodological worldview.

In the meantime, the IOKE[1] project has played a significant role in developing Islamic economics, banking and finance. Despite this, scepticism has festered over the last three decades due to the inability to produce any original contribution to knowledge in the practical field. Critics have pointed out that Islamic economics and finance is merely a duplication of conventional instruments.

Therefore, to study, develop, and implement a total programme of Islamic economics and finance by theory and practice in both fields (academic and society) certain areas ought to be studied as follows:

1. Concept, theory, philosophy, and methodological framework: Research Area.
2. Teaching – learning, training and academic development.
3. Practice, implementation, and establishment.
4. Promoting market research, programmes and publications.
5. The area of observation, evaluation by the Islamic Law (*shari'ah*), expertise, criticism and recommendations.
6. The area of comparative perspective with support, opposition, obstacles, and challenges from within and without (conventional system and non-Islamic world).
7. Areas of human resource development and management.
8. Areas of national co-ordination, international co-ordination, communication and networking with states, individuals, private sectors, and other organizations.
9. Islamic welfare and charitable activities: Islamic charity.
10. Social responsibility, wellbeing, education and culture, moral development for the universal community.

11. Islamic development for Muslim communities in all aspects as *deen*: Islamic Development for Muslim *ummah*.
12. Areas of professional research and activities with association, discourse, and exchanges of ideas and views: Organizational activism and academic discourse.
13. Producing, publishing, marketing and preserving text, literature, and research works: Text and literature.
14. Producing an Encyclopaedia of Islamic Economics and its Development covering all component areas such as economics, finance, banking, insurance, human development research, social development including teaching, research and professional activities.
15. To produce and publish annually or bi-annually an *Islamic World Economic Report* or *Islamic World Economic Indexes* using study, surveys, updates, data-mining, information dissemination, and comparative analysis.
16. To maintain worldwide networking and to strengthen dynamic activities by arranging and conducting significant events and programmes, such as COMCEC of OIC, IDB, ICCI, ICDT, World Islamic Economic Forum Foundation etc.[2]
17. To work towards reviving the original proposal to establish an Islamic Common Market in the Muslim world and to support and strengthen the proposals for forming some regional and sub-regional socioeconomic co-operation among the Muslim countries under the OIC banner such as SEACO: South-East Asian Co-Operation.[3]

This book is the first of its kind to formally present a methodological construct of the theory of Islamic financial economics and banking that is quite distinct from the received theory and practice in this field of study and in mainstream thought, theory, and practice. This book has presented an original intellectual body of thought on the functional nature of the monotheistic law of unity of knowledge (*Tawhid*) and its operational application in the world-system of Islamic financial economics and banking, and with a much greater perspective in the Islamic socio-scientific field.

Notes

1 Although several terms on the same concept are prevalent such as Islamicization of Knowledge (IOK of IIIT), Islamicization of Human Knowledge (IOHK of IIUM), Islamicization of Education (IOE of Islamic Academy Cambridge, UK, Nigeria, Pakistan and Bangladesh); it would be batter to use the term 'Islamicization of Knowledge and Education' (IOKE) as the 'comprehensive and combined manner' which has already been used by some renowned scholars and researchers.
2 The Standing Committee for Economic and Commercial Cooperation of the Organization of the Islamic Cooperation (COMCEC) is the main multilateral economic and commercial co-operation platform of the Islamic world. COMCEC serves as a central forum to address the common development problems of the Islamic *ummah* and provide solutions for them: Islamic Development Bank (IDB), Islamic Chamber of Commerce and Industry (ICCI), Islamic Center for Development and Trade (ICDT), World Islamic Economic Forum Foundation (WIFE), International Council for Finance Education (ICIFE).
3 SEACO is a proposal to form such kind of regional cooperation organization like ASEAN, GCC, among five Muslim countries in South and South East Asia with Indonesia, Malaysia, Bangladesh, Brunei and Maldives; this proposal has been approved by the OIC. It is an ongoing proposal only.

References

Ashraf, S.A. (2005). A Follow-up of the Sixth World Conference on Muslim Education, in Hossain, I. (ed.) (2005). *UNA Magazine: Participation to World Islamic Economic Forum'05*, Universal News Agency, UNA, Dhaka, Bangladesh.

Al-Attas, S.M.N. (1997). *The Concept of Education in Islam: A Framework for an Islamic Philosophy of Education*, Library of Islom Ltd, USA.

Al-Faruqi, I.R. (1982). *Islamization of Knowledge: General Principles and Workplan*, The International Institute of Islamic Thought, Herndon, VA.

Aslam, H.M. (2009). *A Critical Survey of Islamization of Knowledge*, IIUM Press, Kuala Lumpur, Malaysia.

Choudhury, M.A. (2005). "Islamic economics and finance: where do they stand?", *The Islamic Quarterly*, 49:4, 247–80.

Hassan, K. (2009). "*Islamization against the implementation of Islamization of knowledge Human Knowledge: Why and What?*", Presented at KIRKHS Islamization of Human Knowledge Discourse Series, No. 1, Port Dickinson, Malaysia.

Hossian, I. (2011). *Philosophical Foundation and Conceptual Framework of Syed Ali Ashraf: A Special Reference to Islamicisation of Education*, Proceedings of 2nd ISTAC International Conference on Islamic Science in the Contemporary World, ed. Ahmed, B. ISTAC, IIUM, Kuala Lumpur.

Naqvi, S.N.H. (1994). *Islam, Economics, and Society*, Kegan Paul International, Chapter 3, London, UK.

Nasr, S.H. (1987). "Science education, the Islamic perspective", *Muslim Education Quarterly*, 5:1, 4–14.

Sulayman, A.H.A. (2013). "Foreword-IIIT", in Mohd Nizaam Barom, Mohd Mahyudi Mohd Yusop, Mohammd Aslam Haneef and Mustafa Omar Mohammd (eds), *Islamic Economic Education In Southeast Asian Universities*, Center for Islamic Economics, IIUM, International Institute of Islamic Thought, Kuala Lumpur, Malaysia.

Index

For Product Safety Concerns and Information please contact our EU
representative GPSR@taylorandfrancis.com Taylor & Francis Verlag GmbH,
Kaufingerstraße 24, 80331 München, Germany

Printed and bound by CPI Group (UK) Ltd, Croydon, CR0 4YY
01/05/2025
01858409-0004